BOSTON

Contributing Authors:

Nancy Zerbey, Gerald Peary, John F. Persinos, Alexandra Todd,
Lisa M. Poniatowski, Jeffrey O. Krasner

Corporate Profiles by Nancy Walser

Produced in Cooperation with
the Greater Boston Chamber of Commerce

Windsor Publications, Inc.
Northridge, California

A new day dawns for the city of Boston.
Photo © Martha Everson

BOSTON

In a Class by Itself

Windsor Publications, Inc.—Book Division
Managing Editor: Karen Story
Design Director: Alexander D'Anca

Staff for *Boston: In a Class By Itself*
Senior Editor: Pamela Schroeder
Photo Editor: Loren Prostano
Manuscript Editor: Teri Davis Greenberg
Assistant Manuscript Editor: Suzanne Kelley
Production Editor: Amy Adelstein
Senior Editor, Corporate Profiles: Judith Hunter
Senior Production Editor, Corporate Profiles: Phyllis Gray
Senior Proofreader: Susan J. Muhler
Editorial Assistants: Didier Beauvoir, Thelma Fleischer, Kim
    Kievman, Rebecca Kropp, Michael Nugwynne, Kathy B. Peyser,
    Pat Pittman, Theresa J. Solis
Sales Manager, Corporate Profiles: Steve Hung
Sales Representatives: Marcia Cohen, Mary Whelan
Layout Artist: Tanya Maiboroda
Layout Artist, Corporate Profiles: Angela Ortiz
Designer: Brad Boston

Boston: in a class by itself/contributing authors, Nancy
    Zerbey [et al.]; corporate profiles by Nancy Walser: pro-
    duced in cooperation with the Greater Boston Chamber
    of Commerce. 1st ed.   p.   cm.
Bibliography: p. 441
Includes index.
ISBN: 0-89781-281-6
1. Boston (Mass.)—Economic conditions. 2. Boston
    (Mass.)—Economic conditions—Pictorial works.
    I. Zerbey. Nancy. II. Greater Boston Chamber of
    Commerce.
HC108.B65B67 1988
330.9744'61—dc19

Windsor Publications, Inc.
Elliot Martin, Chairman of the Board
James L. Fish III, Chief Operating Officer

Front Cover:
Though the Custom House was constructed be-
tween the years 1837-1847, the Clock Tower was
not added until 1914. Photo © Kathy Tarantola

Back Cover:
The John Hancock Tower and the Prudential
Center rise above scenic Back Bay and the Long-
fellow Bridge. Photo © Gene Peach

A full moon rises over Boston at dusk
Photo © Paul Corkum

Contents

Peabody

OFFICE FURNITURE CORPORATION

JOHN B. HALLORAN, JR.
President & General Manager

February 2, 1989

Ms. Joan Gregor
612 Harwood Lane
Thousand Oaks, CA   91360

Dear Joan:

Once again your elegant style shows through! As the instigator
of Peabody's participation in "Boston: In a Class by Itself", I
wanted you to be one of the first recipients of the book. It is
truly a great piece. Please accept this copy with my gratitude
and admiration. Your marketing expertise has left a strong
impression on us and you will not be forgotten. Like Boston, you
are also in a class by yourself.

I hope your new home and career are keeping you happy. Please
write when you get a chance.

Sincerely,

Jack

Jack Halloran

P.S. SAY hello to Chuck — he'd
better treat you well..!!

234 Congress Street
Boston, Massachusetts 02110
617-542-1902

"Since 1899"

This panoramic view across the Charles River includes Beacon Hill, downtown Boston and the Back Bay area. Photo © Stanley Rowin

PART II: BOSTON'S ENTERPRISES

This Boston skyline, which includes the Charles River, was photographed from the Boston University Bridge. Photo © Gene Peach

From Revolution To Rebirth

PART I

The sun rises, silhouetting the buildings of Boston's Back Bay. Photo © Kathy Tarantola

The Massachusetts State House is the location of
this stained glass reproduction of the State Seal.
Ense petit placidam sub libertate quietem
means: By the sword we seek peace, but peace
only under liberty. Photo © Ulkrike Welsch

PURITAN FOUNDING

In 1630 there came to Boston a resolute band of English Puritans whom King Charles I was soon to regret ever having permitted to leave his royal sight. The king had encouraged them to go—indeed, he had hounded them out—for John Winthrop's company were a stiff-necked and argumentative lot whose clacking calls for church reform had grown tiresome. Though nominally loyal to the Church of England, the Puritans quarreled with the Protestantism founded a hundred years earlier by the much-divorced Henry the Eighth. Incense, bells, and embroidered surplices offended them; so did bossy bishops brandishing catechisms and nosy kings with over-high opinions of their stations. The king and the Puritan divines were on a collision course and, "seeing the Church hath no place left to fly into but the wilderness," Winthrop boarded his band on the good ship *Arbella* and set sail for Massachusetts with Charles' blessing.

The king should have had the ship searched. For among their baggage of Bibles and teacups and plain worsted stockings, the Puritans had stashed away the original copy of their New World charter. In this single bold move the Puritans proved themselves as wily as they were pious, for to seventeenth-century thinking a charter was an efficacious instrument. Only in its presence, with the very letter of the law in hand, could stockholders meet to make decisions concerning the governance of the new colony. The Puritans wanted nothing to do with absentee landlords and speculating stockholders bent on profiting from their New World labors, so even before leaving England, Winthrop had rewritten the charter to provide that no one could hold stock in the Massachusetts Bay Company who did not also emigrate into that strange land. By taking the charter with them, the settlers guaranteed that no interfering Londoners could stay their determined course of self-determination in the New World. It was the first declaration of American independence, and its home port was Boston.

But Boston was not the Puritans' first choice for their bold New World experiment. After 26 days at sea, the *Arbella* landed in Salem, then made her way south 15 miles to Charlestown where an advance party had laid out a tiny hamlet on the headland at the mouth of the Charles River. Here the Puritans disembarked and immediately began forming a church, building a council house, and erecting palisades and flankers against alien attack. In this they miscalculated, for the danger to the young colony was to come not from without, but from within, for Charlestown had no fresh water. The settlers, coming now by the hundreds in a dozen ships from London, soon fell ill. Many died. After five months, the survivors packed up their few belongings, nailed together a small fleet of flat-bottomed ferries, and poled their godly colony across the river to the Shawmut Peninsula. They named their new hope Boston, and here they determined to stay.

Boston in 1630 was a small and watery place—home to gulls and clams and huckleberries and errant wolves. Encompassing no more than two square miles of solid ground, its hills and fields were hemmed in on all sides by mudflats, marshes, inlets, and coves. Only the narrowest neck of land connected the peninsula to Roxbury on the south, just barely saving Boston from being counted the greatest of the Harbor Islands in Massachusetts Bay.

The settlers soon set about taming this wilderness to which they had so gladly flown. From the rude thatched huts and borrowed wigwams of that first cold winter there grew, already by mid-century, a settlement of decidedly urban and seaside design. Docks and wharves marched out over the mudflats; creeks were dammed and mills set turning on their banks; the Common was laid out for cows to graze and citizens to stroll; America's first public schoolhouse, where Ben Franklin was later to fail arithmetic, was dedicated on School Street; batteries and artillery mounts appeared on the high ground, and a lamp was set high above Beacon Hill, ready to announce any danger to the town's now-prosperous good order.

CHAPTER 1

Puritans, Patriots, and Profiteers

BY NANCY ZERBEY

By 1663, when John Josselyn arrived from England to write one of the few surviving chronicles of New England in the seventeenth century, Boston had become a town to be reckoned with, "the Metropolis of this Colony, or rather of the whole Country."

Here the houses are for the most part raised on the Sea-banks and wharfed out with great industry and cost, many of them standing upon piles, close together on each side of the streets as in London, *and furnished with many fair shops, their materials are Brick, Stone, Lime, handsomely contrived, with three meeting Houses or Churches, and a Town-house built upon pillars where the Merchants may confer, in the Chambers above they keep their monethly Courts. Their streets are many and large, paved with pebble stone, and the South-side adorned with Gardens and Orchards. The town is rich and very populous, much frequented by strangers, here is the dwelling of their Governour. On the North-west and North-east two constant Fairs market-* *places are kept for daily Traffick thereunto. On the South there is a small, but pleasant Common where the Gallants a little before Sun-set walk with their Marmalet-Madams, as we do in Morfields . . . till the nine a clock Bell rings them home to their respective habitations, when presently the Constables walk their rounds to see good orders kept, and to take up loose people.*

Looseness of any sort alarmed the Puritan fathers, and Boston was ever a town absorbed with the power of ernance.

Little was left to chance or to choice. Solemn instructions were issued to the selectmen to be on the look-out for cracked chimneys and loose stones in the street, to inspect the cannon regularly, to keep stray pigs from wreaking havoc in the town, to see that every household had a fire ladder, and to punish sausage-makers who would cheat in packing pork barrels. Robert Nash, the butcher, was ordered to "remove the Stinking garbage out of his yard, nere the street, and provide some other remote place for slaughter of Beasts, that such loathsome smells might be avoyded, which are of great annoyance unto the neighbors, and to strangers." And, lest the town be overrun with loose-moralled damsels and dandies, constables were empowered to confiscate all lacy gowns and beaver hats, and eight watchmen were dispatched each night to round up any trysting couples discovered abroad after ten o'clock.

The town stocks had plenty of customers in this era of diligent town-keeping. Bigamists, drunken sailors, liars, and thieves took their turns shackled by the ankles within egg-throwing reach of the crowd on the Common. Even the carpenter Edward

Above: A replica of the boat on which the first Pilgrims arrived in Plymouth, Massachusetts, may be visited by the public in Plymouth. Photo © Stanley Rowin

Below: The site of Plymouth Rock is a popular tourist attraction. Photo © Stanley Rowin

rules. Making its own rules and breaking the kings' were Boston's chief political occupations from founding to revolution. Having hied themselves into the wilderness, their legitimating charter safe in their pockets, the Puritan fathers next enacted their own laws of town gov-

Palmer, who built the first stocks in 1639, had occasion to try out his handiwork. His lumber bill, the elders said, was much too high. To the stocks also was sent Captain Kemble, who spent two hours there contemplating his "Lewd and Vicious" crime of kissing a woman in public. The lady was his wife, and he had not seen her in three years. But it was the Sabbath, and this was Puritan Bos-

ton, where the Sabbath was taken very seriously indeed. So much so that the diarist Nathaniel Mather confessed in anguish this heaviest of his boyhood sins ("A great *reproach* of God! a specimen of that *atheism* I brought into the world with me!"): that he snuck away from prayers one Sunday, shut the door against the prying eyes of his righteous elders, and whittled.

There is a certain naive charm to these episodes of Puritan care for the tidy and chaste and devout. But Boston's early civic virtue was bought at a stiff price. Trusting the town's security to none but themselves, the Puritans by 1640 had entered one of those wrenching periods of xenophobia and intolerance that were to plague Boston throughout its 350-year history.

In the 10 years following the settlement of Boston, 20,000 people followed Winthrop's band to New England. While content to feed and clothe the newcomers for a modest

profit and to arrange their spiritual lives for the good of their souls, the Puritans harbored the deepest distrust of the "straungers." By the mid-1640s the General Court had passed the first of the "alien laws," limiting immigrants to a three-week stay in Boston unless an honest citizen could be brought forward to vouch for their integrity. By the 1650s all strangers 16 years and older were required to present themselves to the magistrates

Left: John Winthrop, a Puritan and a gentleman, was the first governor of the "City on a Hill," the New World Puritan Commonwealth. Courtesy, The Bostonian Society

Above: In 1730, Boston Harbor was bustling with activity.

Facing page: Boston Common was purchased by the town in 1634 from the Reverend William Blaxton. Residents used the Common to pasture cattle, train the militia, as a place for children to play and adults to stroll, and for occasional hangings. Courtesy, First National Bank Blotter Series, Boston Public Library Print Department

first decade was out, found there to be 82 heretical opinions alive among the populace, to say nothing of the 9 "unwholesome" ones. Anglican devotions they dismissed as "leeks, garlick, and trash," but the remedy for more serious religious error was eradication. Carnal sins were flogged out at the pillory in front of the Town House; blasphemers had their swearing tongues seared through with red-hot irons; in 1636, Roger Williams, a clergyman himself, was banished to Rhode Island for his Baptist opinions and for denouncing his brethren in print; a year later Anne Hutchinson, pregnant and prophesying doom from the dock, was expelled from the colony for the antinomian crime of stirring up women against their ministers. The spirit of this intolerant era was caught by Nathaniel Ward, who proudly announced to the world "in the name of our Colony, that all Familists, Antinomians, Anabaptists, and other enthusiasts, shall have free Liberty to keep away from us, and such as will come to be gone as fast as they can, the sooner the better." Four Quakers, three men and a woman, were hanged on the Common for their stubborn refusal to leave.

Zealous hearts alone could not sustain such public bigotry, for even contemporary voices were raised against the persecutions. It "makes us stinke every wheare," warned George Downing in a letter to Governor Winthrop's son in 1645. But zealotry

Above: Puritan settlers wanted their community to be a beacon to others, thus the name "Beacon Hill," which symbolized their special relationship with God. This monument replaces the original beacon which was constructed as a lookout on Boston's highest point of land. J.H. Bufford produced this lithograph in 1858, based on a watercolor by J.R. Smith, 1811-1812. Courtesy, The Bostonian Society

Facing page: Threatened with death twice for preaching the "inner light" faith of the Quakers, Mary Dyer returned to Boston a third time and was hanged. Photo © Kathy Tarantola.

for inspection immediately upon arrival in the town, and to make a written oath of loyalty to the court if their stay was to exceed two months. Strangers were to be queried closely on their intentions, their lodgings, their sponsors, their trade, and prospects of employment. Idle strangers would be thrown in jail; poor strangers would have their children taken from them and apprenticed out to useful service where they might earn their keep and learn sober citizenship. All this "for the good of the town, the glory of God, and establishing truth and love among us."

Most particularly the Puritans did

not want among them religious dissenters of any description. From King Charles the Puritans had learned the necessity of tight fellowship in the face of opposition to their Church. From him, too, they learned the expedient of religious persecution. "The Bostonians," remarked a London bookseller visiting the town in 1686, "though their forefathers fled hither to enjoy liberty of conscience, are very unwilling any should enjoy it but themselves."

It was a just indictment. Counting intolerance a virtue, the Puritan fathers kept careful watch on unorthodox thinking and, even before the

ERECTED BY THE ART COMMISSION OF
THE COMMONWEALTH OF MASSACHUSETTS
FROM THE LEGACY OF ZENAS ELLIS
OF FAIR HAVEN, VERMONT

DEDICATED 9 JULY, 1959

MARY DYER

QUAKER

WITNESS FOR RELIGIOUS FREEDOM

HANGED ON BOSTON COMMON 1660

"MY LIFE NOT AVAILETH ME
IN COMPARISON TO THE
LIBERTY OF THE TRUTH"

SYLVIA SHAW JUDSON — SCULPTOR

had the force of law in the early colony because the franchise was strictly limited to upright men of the Congregationalist persuasion. By 1676 this religious restriction on citizenship meant that fewer than 20 percent of the men had a vote in civic affairs. The women had no vote at all. Boston in the seventeenth century was governed by a willful theocracy bent on worldly isolation and otherworldly purity. It was not to last.

Boston had spelled trouble for the king of England from the moment the Puritans boarded the *Arbella*, but Charles' querulous demands for the return of the charter were silenced by Cromwell's chopping block in 1649. Cromwell himself was disposed to give

Above: Anne Hutchinson was banished from Boston in 1637 because of her heretical beliefs. This statue of Hutchinson, by Cyrus Dallin, stands before the Massachusetts State House, commemorating her fight for religious freedom. Courtesy, Massachusetts State Archives

Right: Martha Mary Chapel in Sudbury, Massachusetts is one of many Puritan-like chapels in New England. Photo © B. & J. McGrath

his fellow Puritans full rein in Massachusetts, so it wasn't until the monarchy was restored to Charles II in 1660 that the increasingly independent goings-on in New England were given much royal scrutiny. The second King Charles got as cold a reception in Boston as the first. The royal commission he dispatched to Boston in 1665 to investigate charges of insubordination and restrictive franchise was sent packing by the colonial magistrates, who hauled out their charter to the blast of trumpets and waved it in the commissioners' faces as evidence of royal permission to do whatever they damn well pleased.

And this they did with stubborn defiance as the charges mounted against them. The colonists minted their own illegal currency and used it openly. The magistrates refused to extradict the regicides Goffe and Whalley when they sought asylum in New England. A royal edict to extend the ballot to all landowners regardless of church affiliation was ignored. Boston merchant ships were found carrying tobacco from Carolina to Europe, while smugglers freely unloaded onto Boston docks French brandy, Irish wools, fruit from the Canary Islands, and furs from Nova Scotia—all in violation of imperial navigation laws.

By 1676, a full hundred years before independence was officially declared, king and colony had squared off. In that year the king's inspector and customs agent in Boston, Edward Randolph, reported unfavorably on the ministers and magistrates in charge of the town, finding them "generally inclined to Sedition being Proud Ignorant and Imperious," and recommended that the king "reduce Massachusetts to obedience" by force if necessary, for "that government would make the world believe they are a free state and doe act in all matters accordingly." To this charge

Captain John Bonner rendered this map of Boston in 1722. Courtesy, New York Public Library

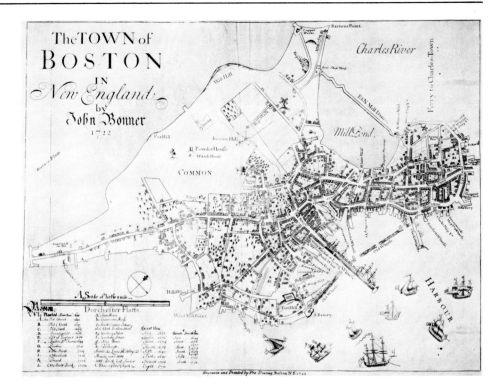

the Massachusetts Court replied with terse and stunning coolness that Parliamentary enactments "are bounded within the fower seas, and doe not reach America."

Charles II recognized treason when he heard it and, having more talent for direct action than his namesake, dealt swiftly with the intractable colony by the simple expedient of revoking its long-disputed charter. In December 1686 the frigate *Kingfisher* arrived in Boston harbor bearing 100 soldiers and Sir Edmund Andros, newly appointed governor general of the newly demoted Dominion of New England, a man intent on getting Boston under control at last. He didn't. By April 1689 rumors reached Boston that the new king, James II, had surrendered his throne to William and Mary. Rumor was sufficient. A victory flag was flown from Beacon Hill, as armed posses marching to drummers converged on the center of town from the north and south ends, seizing the jail, rounding up royalists, and demanding Andros' surrender. The restless colony that began with a godly congregation absconding with its charter into a huckleberry wilderness ended its first 59 years with a mutinous mob throwing the king's governor into the clink.

MERCHANTS AND PATRIOTS

Given the recalcitrant disposition of Boston, what is surprising is that it took nearly another hundred years to achieve independence. But in the first half of the eighteenth century Boston was otherwise occupied. A new insurrection was afoot in the town (a domestic adjustment this time) as the Puritan fathers were faced with a challenge to make some room for Mammon in their godly town. The merchants had come into their own.

The Puritan townskeepers had been suspicious of merchants from the start. Trade was a dangerous calling, they thought. It was dangerous to the soul and dangerous to the community because it invited entangling alliances with strangers. Greedy strangers, mean-spirited strangers; strangers hawking temptation and strangers shrugging off authority. Watch out for these traffickers with the Devil, warned Edward Johnson early on:

Let not any Merchants, Innkeepers, Taverners and men of Trade in hope of gaine, fling open the gates so wide, as that by letting in all sorts you mar the worke of Christ intended.

Much of the impetus for Boston's alien laws had been to keep such

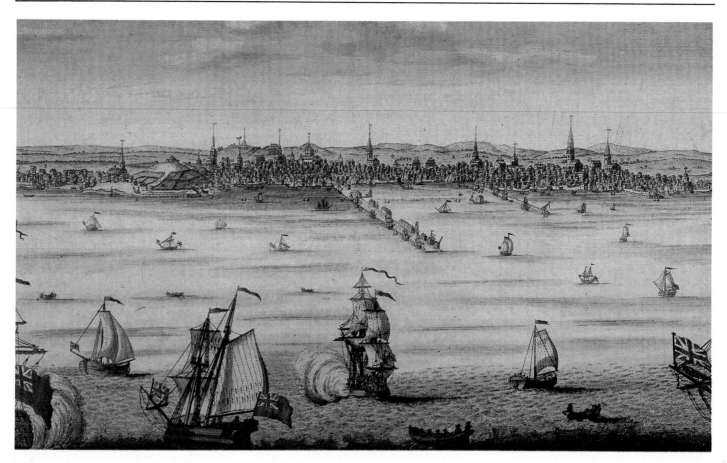

strangers out. But this was not possible. Indeed, had it not been for merchants, Boston would not have survived its first decade. As the 20,000 colonists in New England soon discovered, even saints need shoes.

When their shipboard provisions ran out, and the capital from liquidating their English landholdings was spent, the colonists had to face some hard facts. They were penniless, they needed supplies, and New England held no riches to interest London brokers. There were no lustrous beaver pelts to be found in Boston's tidal streams; no heady tobacco; no gold in the Berkshire hills. In such unfavorable circumstances the colony was kept alive purely on credit, and that credit was arranged by a small corps of urban tradesmen, artisans, and laborers who had come to Boston in the first wave of Puritan migration. Through their contacts in London, this humble group of tailors, drapers,

This engraving of "A Southeast View of the Great Town of Boston" depicts the New England town between 1731-1736, although it was not issued until after 1764. Courtesy, The Bostonian Society

ironmongers, skinners, and shop-keepers was able to import a steady supply of the homely necessities that the colony needed to see it through the first hardscabble years: buttons, shoes, and spools of thread; anvils, plows, anchors, and cordage; guns and powder; stools and spoons and cooking pots.

Great fortunes have been made on less in frontier towns, but this upstart group of provisioners would not be rich until they launched themselves on the sea. This was a matter of necessity, not choice, for though Winthrop had boasted that only the women had been seasick on the crossing to America, it cannot be said that this colony of gentlemen farmers, petty tradesmen, and men of the cloth had any particular talent for seafaring. But sail they would have to. Boston was surrounded by water; there were fish to catch; and the high cost of freightage was driving merchandisers out of business. Boston needed her own fleet of boats. So, with the determination that has ever been the mark of Boston commerce, the town set sail.

In 1643 Boston launched her first ship, aptly named the *Trial.* She was a success. Already by 1698, Boston and neighboring Charlestown were home to 129 overseas merchant ships weighing in at a total of 6,577 tons. It was the third largest fleet in Britain's merchant marine, trailing only Bristol and London itself. In the next 16 years the shipping industry exploded. Another 952 vessels were sailing from Boston and Charlestown, and their shipyards were turning out 30 ships a year, a third of them for export abroad. Wharves and ropewalks and sail lofts were thrown up all along the sea banks; Boston boys learned caulking, carpentry, chandlery, and warehousing; sailors overran the town. Shipping built Boston in the early eighteenth century, and provided her livelihood. It also attracted investment. By 1714 one of every three Boston men—tradesman and merchant prince alike—owned shares in the Massachusetts fleet.

Investors prospered in this risky trade, where fortunes could be made if only the ships did not sink. A good many did, of course, but many more

dashed madly port to port in further-
ance of the famous triangle trade. By
1740 Boston had already become
"The Hub," the moniker she still
proudly wears today. Hub of New
England, hub of the Atlantic basin
trade, Boston was "the very Mart of
the land." Carts trundled into Boston
from the countryside heavy with
produce; fishermen dumped their
catches on her docks; livestock lum-
bered down the cowpaths to the
wharves; barges brought timber from
New Hampshire—all to be loaded
onto Boston ships. London didn't
want these peas and cod and pigs and
boards, but canny Boston merchants
had discovered that other markets
did, and the everyday necessities Boston needed from England could be
bought with exotic merchandise
loaded onto Boston ships in foreign
climes. There were wine and tropical
fruits from Madeira and the Azores;
tobacco from the Carolinas; cotton,
sugar, and molasses from Barbados
and Jamaica. The sugar and molasses
were shipped back home where Boston distilleries turned them into rum
(an odd commodity, one might think,
for the once-saintly town). But the
good citizens of Boston did not drink
it all (though rum punches did become popular at fancy tables). Nor
did they virtuously ship it off to sotted
Englishmen to exchange for hardware
and haberdashery. No, Boston shipped
its rum to Africa and used it to buy
slaves.

Rum runners and slave traders,
Boston merchants in the eighteenth
century were also consummate smugglers. British navigation laws were
strict, but they were also easily
avoided. Bribe some customs agents,
fiddle some bills of lading, sneak into
some unwatched port or offload con-
traband in the dead of night—by
these and other measures Boston merchants moved fully half of their profitable cargoes illegally past the greedy
hands of the Crown. War was good
business, too, and England's endless
scraps with her colonial rivals pro-

vided ample opportunities for profi-
teers and privateers in Boston. Boston
ships supplied the Royal Navy with
masts and tar; Boston ships carried
ham and boots to British troops;
Boston ships captured enemy
merchantmen and divided up the
spoils. And Boston ships carried all
the profits back to Boston.

By 1740 Boston had grown from a
frontier town to a metropolis of
18,000 souls, "the capital of New England," indeed the capital of the New
World. Where the first generation
had struggled to cut paths through the
briars, hew clapboards for the meetinghouse, and find shoes for growing
children, their grandsons and great-

grandsons walked 60 well-paved
streets and 41 lanes, built three-story
merchant mansions, and traded goods
to all the peoples of the Atlantic. The
fathers of the huckleberry wilderness
had begot the lords of the sea.

Boston was rich, and the aging Puritan fathers were not one bit pleased
about it. "Interest is faith, Money

*Dorchester, Massachusetts, was the home of
America's first chocolate mill on the Neponset
River. In 1765, Irish immigrant chocolate-maker
John Hannon and Milton physician, Dr. James
Baker, collaborated their efforts and soon devel-
oped the Baker Chocolate Factory. General Foods
Corporation moved the company to Delaware in
1963. Courtesy, First National Bank Blotter
Series, Boston Public Library Print Department*

Mr. Shrimpton, Capt. Lidget and others come in a Coach from Roxbury about 9. aclock or past, singing as they come, being inflamed with Drink. At Justice Morgan's they stop and drink Healths, curse, swear, talk profanely and baudily to the great disturbance of the Town and grief to good people. Such high-handed wickedness has hardly been heard of before in Boston.

"*Idleness,* alas! *idleness* increases in the town exceedingly," bellowed Cotton Mather from his pulpit in 1698. Mather, perhaps the greatest of the Puritan divines, saw nothing but evil in this secular turn of events. There were "fortuner-tellers" abroad in the town, he scolded, and bawdy-houses enjoyed their lascivious custom without so much as a peep of protest from godly neighbors. And taverns, too, "an *enormous number* of them," Mather complained, ranting to any who would hear him: "Ale-houses are hell-houses! Ale-houses are hell-houses!" To this grim soul and ardent shepherd, Boston was fast on its way to becoming an "unpardonable town."

Mather exaggerated a little. Even 40 years later a London visitor to Boston marveled at the diligence of the town's Sabbath observance, saying "It is the strictest kept that ever I saw yet anywhere." And, indeed, as soon as the sun went down on a Saturday's eve, Boston shut up tight. Not just taverns, but shops also closed their doors; no money exchanged hands, no toffs strolled the Common; the town's justices themselves patrolled the streets, looking to catch scofflaws engaged in idle conversation. Boston's one gate to the countryside was barred and locked so would-be travelers might more seriously attend to their Bibles and psalters and three-

their God, and Large possessions the only Heaven they covet," complained one Puritan critic of the Boston merchants. The people of Boston had earned a bad reputation. Never a gentle folk, they had turned their rigor from Bible to commerce and had arrived at that Yankee recipe for worldly success that would carry them into the twentieth century: sharp bargains make fat purses. "Their Streets, like the Hearts of the Male Inhabitants, are paved with Pebble," remarked Edward Ward after a visit to Boston in 1699. By the mid-eighteenth century nothing much had changed. "Though they wear in their Faces the Innocence of Doves," wrote a visitor, "you will find them in their Dealings as subtile as Serpents."

Morals, too, were falling all to pieces. Two passages from the diary of Samuel Sewell give a sense of changing times. Here is his description of a blameless outing with his wife:

Carried my wife to Dorchester to eat Cherries and Raspberries, chiefly to ride and take the air; the time my wife and Mrs. Flint spent in the orchard I spent in Mr. Flint's study reading Calvin and the Psalms.

This was Sewell's idea of a high time, good Puritan that he was. Imagine, then, his horror to relate the following report of the escapades of Samuel Shrimpton, a brazier's son turned trade king and land speculator, and the richest man in Boston:

The Boston News-Letter was the first newspaper in America. Beginning in 1704, it was a record of local Boston affairs and ship movements. Courtesy, First National Bank Blotter Series, Boston Public Library Print Department

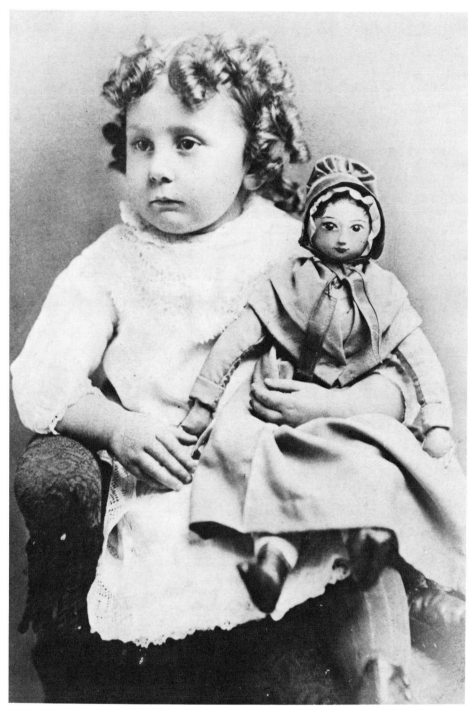

this part of the world." Good peaches sold for but three pence a peck and the rest were thrown to the hogs. The cheese was judged sorry and the beer worse, but milk was plentiful and cheap, as was cider. At more gracious tables, wine and rum and melons were served, brought straight from ships just returned from their tours of Madeira and the West Indian isles.

Entertainment was gay and sometimes lavish. Country outings were popular for hunting, fishing, or picking strawberries, and there was cruising in the harbor. There were teas and soirees and leisurely strolls on the Common most every night but the Sabbath, and one night Ralph Inman entertained 347 guests at a dinner honoring his son's graduation. Leftover Puritan sensibilities would not allow theaters or music halls in the town, it is true. "But ... they don't seem to be dispirited nor moped for want of them," wrote an observer in 1740:

for both the ladies and gentlemen dress and appear as gay, in common, as courtiers in England on a coronation or birthday. And the ladies here visit, drink tea, and indulge every little piece of gentility, to the height of the mode; and neglect the affairs of their families with as good a grace as the finest ladies in London.

The most splendid of splendors could be found at the home of Peter Faneuil, "Boston's Jolly Bachelor" and a true merchant prince if ever there was one in America. Faneuil was a species of those trade-trafficking strangers that the Puritans had tried so hard and unsuccessfully to keep out of town. The eldest son of a French Huguenot immigrant, Faneuil came to

Polly Sumner was a wealthy young woman living in Roxbury when she purchased this doll, imported from England, just a few days before the Boston Tea Party in 1773. The doll remained in her family for four generations, and is seen here in the arms of her great-great granddaughter Mary P. Langley. Courtesy, The Bostonian Society

hour sermons. These were Boston's famous "blue laws," the forerunner of the Sunday closings that are observed in Boston to this very day.

No, Boston was never a frivolous town, but by the mid-eighteenth century Boston had loosened up considerably. The merchants' wealth and the town's new cosmopolitanism brought a measure of grace, elegance, and even splendor that Boston would not see again until long after the Revolution. Drab Puritan garb was packed away. Ladies wearing ruffles and hooped skirts cast jealous eyes on the governor's wife, Mistress Bernard,

quite the lady in her ermine and sables and ball gowns embroidered with silver and gold. The gents sported scarlet breeches, gold braid, and those topping vanities so abominated by the Puritans—powdered periwigs. In matters sartorial, the model was no longer the Kingdom of God, but rather, the Court of St. James.

They ate well, too, in this "Mart of the land." For common fare there was chicken, cornbread, fish, pork, and beef. There were fruits in abundance, for native grapes and berries had been tamed for the table and the people had "run mightily into orcharding in

Above: The Reverend George Whitefield was the English evangelist who led the Great Awakening in New England during the eighteenth century. From Cirker, Dictionary of American Portraits

Right: John Smibert designed Faneuil Hall in 1742 for the prosperous merchant Peter Faneuil. Red brick was used for the building which was two and one-half stories high with arcaded market stalls below and assembly rooms above. Burned in 1761, it was rebuilt and depicted in this 1909 postcard. Courtesy, Private Collection

Facing page: Modern day Faneuil Hall continues to provide the community with both the assembly room and marketplace functions it did over 100 years ago. Photo © Stanley Rowin

Boston as a teenager in 1719 to wait on his uncle, Andrew, an enterprising land speculator and warehouseman. The wait was worthwhile, for in 1738 Andrew died and Peter inherited the greatest fortune in Boston. Peter Faneuil was no slouch himself. From trade he diversified into shipping, operating three vessels of his own, investing in others, and marketing newly built Boston ships abroad. He collected 5 percent on every cargo he handled, and he handled everything—codfish, whale oil, rum and wine, fruit, tobacco, barrel staves, tar, cloth and crockery, sugar, and molasses. What he couldn't legally import or export, he smuggled, and invested his profits in rock-solid assets—$115,000 alone in Bank of England stock.

Profits gladdened Peter Faneuil's heart, and possessions pleased him, too. Faneuil's estate inventory survives, and among his household effects are listed a silver-hilted sword, a full set of delft china valued at $199, 6 lignum vitae chocolate cups lined with silver, 6 silk quilts and 3 feather beds, 224 copper cooking pots, a chariot, and 5 black slaves.

Such was Boston at mid-century, when fortunes were made in sailing and shipping and smuggling and slaving. But by 1743 Boston's Jolly Bachelor was gone, dead of a "dropsical complication." Boston's mercantile glory, too, was soon to founder, the victim of an imperial complication.

For England was once again at war. First King George's War, then the French and Indian War, broke out. The king needed men and ships and a

calculations. If the king was serious about enforcing the customs laws, and he seemed to be, Boston stood to lose $164,000 in revenues a year and $100,000 in Boston shipping would go idle—all for the sake of a motherland few of them had ever seen. From their charter-cherishing Puritan fathers these merchants had inherited an attitude of liberty; with King George's provocation they discovered they had an investment in independence.

So while the rest of the American colonies breathed easier and prospered with the peace, between 1763 and 1775 the citizens of Boston grew increasingly restive and mulish. The Declaration of Independence may have been signed in Philadelphia, but the Revolution was fomented in the streets of Boston, and the voices of freedom that were sounded in her taverns, on her wharves, from her pulpits, in Peter Faneuil's market hall, and under the Liberty Tree all had distinct Boston accents. In the course of 3 acts and 12 years, Boston would draw America into war.

The first act was the Stamp Act, a measure designed to raise revenue for the Crown by requiring the colonists to pay for the privilege of passing any commercial or legal papers. Deeds, newspapers, wills, marriage licenses, vessel permits, import licenses—all would have to be stamped for a fee. Boston received this news badly. "I hear the Stamp Act is like to take place," wrote John Hancock nervously to London in 1765. "It is very cruel. We were before much burthened and we shall not now be able much longer to support trade, and in the end Great Britain must feel the ill effects of it."

Left: When King George repealed the Stamp Act in March 1766, there was due cause for celebration. The Liberty Tree which had been planted at Essex and Washington streets in 1646 was hung with 150 iron, tin, and glass lanterns, including this one. The tree was among those later destroyed by the British soldiers for firewood during the winter of 1775. Courtesy, The Bostonian Society

Below: The Hartt House on Hull Street in the North End, built in 1724, served as the headquarters of General Gage during the Battle of Bunker Hill. In the nineteenth century it was replaced with tenement walkups. Courtesy, Boston Public Library Print Department

war chest, and he looked to his prosperous New England colony to supply them. The toll was heavy, and Boston entered the first of her economic stalls. England and France finally worked out their peace, but the peace brought no peace to Boston. With taxes at 67 percent and West Indian trade already down 80 percent, Boston suddenly found her mainstay shipping industry under attack from the Crown. George III had war debts to pay. He also had a bone to pick with Boston, for he was heartily tired of its flagrant violation of the navigation laws. Boston merchants had been smuggling and evading import and export duties for more than 100 years now. It was time to extract some revenue and obedience from Boston. So, in a packet of trade legislation, he laid down the law.

Boston merchants did some fast

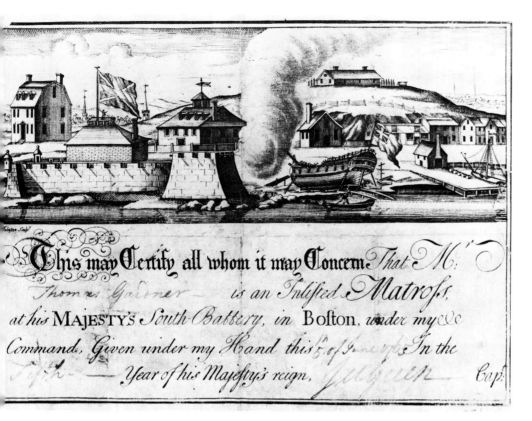

Hancock had reason to be nervous. Just six months earlier, he had inherited nearly $100,000 and a thriving merchant business from his uncle. He was a very rich man. But it was not the rich merchants of Boston who brought Boston's resentment against the Stamp Act to the attention of the Crown. That honor fell to a gang of drunks.

Boston had a long history of mobbish answers to assertions of royal authority. It was a mob that threw Governor Andros into jail after the revocation of the charter in 1689. It was a mob that hurled brickbats through the Council House windows and carted a deputy sheriff off to the stocks when the Royal Navy tried to impress Boston seamen in 1747. Now a mob was descending on the residence of Lieutenant Governor Thomas Hutchinson, great-great-grandson of the antinomian Anne Hutchinson, who herself had been hounded out of town by a mob of inflamed Puritans. This mob was different. Taking courage first from vigorous street protests against taxation without representation, a gang of men looted the house of the customs agent, Benjamin Hallowell, and broke into his wine cellar. Now thoroughly drunk, they interrupted a decorous sermon on the evils of the Stamp Act, then lurched out down the street toward Hutchinson's three-story house in the North End.

The Lieutenant Governor was peaceably taking supper with his children when a messenger arrived with news of the approaching mob. Hutchinson had barely made good his escape, running pell-mell in his housecoat through backyard flower beds to the safety of a neighbor's house, when, he reports, "the hellish crew fell upon my house with the rage of devils and in a moment with axes split down the door and entered." Now in the very seat of Royal Provincial authority, the mob proceeded to tear it down. They ripped off the wainscoting and battered down walls; they climbed on the roof and threw the cupola to the ground; they leveled the garden house and cut down the trees. By morning, says Hutchinson, "one of the best finished houses in the Province had nothing remaining but the bare walls and floors."

Shivering in borrowed clothes the next day, the king's Lieutenant Governor received a delegation of Boston townsmen who came professing outrage and offering their condolences. Hutchinson found their protestations fainthearted. No one offered to pay the stamp tax, and within nine months the Stamp Act was repealed.

In June 1767 Parliament, in a new tactic, imposed import duties on a variety of consumer goods shipped to the colonies from London. Under the terms of these new "Townshend Acts," no glass or lead could be unloaded onto Boston docks until the king's customs agents had inspected the goods and collected the tax. No paper for broadsheets; no tea for afternoon gossip; no powdered paints of Prussian blue, Dutch pink, and Indian red so fashionable for painting colonial parlors. Once again Parliament had levied a tax on the colonies without so much as a by-your-leave.

And, once again, the citizens of Boston turned restive and mulish. The town's merchants, banded together as the "Society for the Encouragement of Trade," agreed to boycott all British goods but necessities. Handbills appeared in the streets threatening the 16 town importers who refused to comply with the boycott. John Hancock got into a snarl with British authorities when the captain of his ship, the *Liberty*, crammed a customs inspector into a steerage hold and kept him there while the crew off-loaded 100 casks of wine smuggled from Madeira. The wharves and taverns rang with the cry "no taxation without representation." Petitions were circulated, and the townspeople marshalled their hometown vigilantes, the Sons of Liberty.

Incensed by these demonstrations of civil disobedience, George III dissolved the Massachusetts legislature and dispatched the Prince of Wales'

A series of harbor forts was used to defend the Boston peninsula. This certificate shows the south battery prior to the Revolution. Courtesy, Boston Atheneum

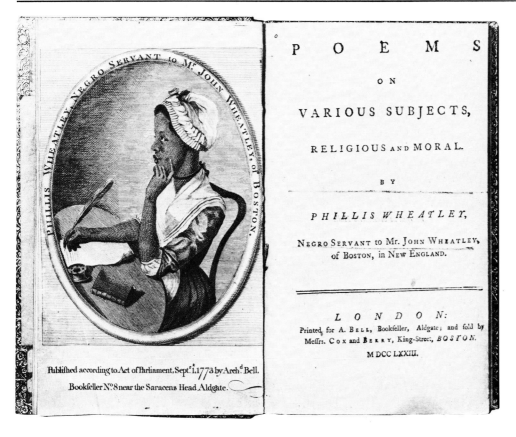

Own 14th Regiment and the Worcestershire 29th to Boston with orders to see the customs laws dutifully executed. With this show of royal force, the dispute between Crown and colony changed utterly. Mercantile insults were one thing, but the presence of warships in the harbor and standing armies on the Common was a menace that the free community of Boston would not abide.

"It is Matter of too great Notoriety to need any Proofs, that the Arrival of his Majesty's Troops in Boston was extremely obnoxious to it's Inhabitants," wrote Thomas Preston, captain of His Majesty's mainguard in Boston, to his superiors in 1770. Captain Preston had good reason for this judgment, for it was he who had commanded the troops seven nights earlier when a nasty street altercation turned into the tragic incident which has come to be called the Boston Massacre.

There had been trouble all week. Armed citizens roved the streets looking for soldiers to bait, and a gang of dockyard toughs had provoked a brawl at Gray's Ropewalk when they invited a British patrol to climb down into a latrine. Three days later, on the night of March 5th, Captain Preston was called out to investigate a report that a sentry was being pelted with snowballs in front of the Royal Custom House. Within minutes, a dozen soldiers had shouldered their rifles and fixed their bayonets on a crowd of 70-100 angry townsmen who taunted the Redcoats, shouting, "Come on, you Rascals, you bloody Backs, you Lobster Scoundrels; fire if you dare, G-d damn you, fire and be damn'd." And, in circumstances which to this day are not very clear, they did fire—killing three men on the spot and mortally wounding two others.

By the next afternoon 3,000 Boston townsmen had assembled at the Old South Meeting House, seeking justice. They can't all have been rabble and ruffians. But taking their authority from the streets, they shouted down Governor Hutchinson and announced to the world what had become evident to the mob in the night: "That it is the unanimous opinion of this Meeting that the inhabitants and soldiery can no longer live together in safety; that nothing can rationally be expected to restore the peace of the Town & prevent Blood and Carnage but the removal of the Troops."

Luckless Hutchinson had no choice; the display of majesty's force had only provoked a mobbish reply, and Boston had wrested in one night of violence what it could not win in two years of petition and civil disobedience. The troops were removed to Castle Island in the harbor, there to await new gambits from the Crown and new trouble from Boston.

It didn't take long. Within the month the Townshend duties were repealed—all but the tax on tea. This utterly British beverage was already provoking toasts to American independence, but Parliament—partly spiteful, partly stupid—stubbornly refused to grasp the point. And Boston always loved a stubborn match.

As soon as the Townshend Act was published, townsmen met in Faneuil Hall and took as solemn a pledge as any Victorian teetotaler's to abstain from drinking the insidious brew. By the next year, 75 percent of Boston's households had joined the boycott, and it became a point of honor in the parlors of the proud Daughters of Liberty to serve only coffee, or tea honestly smuggled from Holland, or home-grown "Liberty Tea," a wretched ersatz brew made of weeds.

The boycott had its intended effect. With the London warehouses

Facing page: The Committee of Public Safety was appointed by the Provincial Congress of Massachusetts in 1774. Paul Revere was a member of the committee which was responsible for stockpiling supplies and preparing for conflict. Courtesy, First National Bank Blotter Series, Boston Public Library Print Department

Above: Phillis Wheatley was the first black poet in America to be published. As a slave for the John Wheatley family, she learned to read and write from the children, wrote poetry before the age of sixteen, and was published in London before the Revolution. Courtesy, The Bostonian Society

The Beaver was one of three ships attacked during the Boston Tea Party. Located on the dock alongside the brig is the Boston Tea Party Museum. Photo © Mark E. Gibson

of the British East India Company crammed with tea left moldering for lack of colonial customers, Parliament, thinking itself clever, embarked on a new plan intended to save face and fortune at the same time. By the Tea Act of 1773, the East India Company was permitted to ship its tea from London without paying the customary export tax. The colonists in America would still have to hand over the import duty of three pence a pound, but British tea would now be cheaper than any smuggled Dutch tea. As one later commentator on this folly remarks, "Not yet had it been borne in upon the stupid ministers of the king that those men in America were contending for a principle, not looking for a bargain in groceries."

What followed is the most celebrated incident of street theater in American history—the Boston Tea Party.

On the night of December 16, 1773, three British ships—the *Dartmouth*, the *Eleanor*, and the *Beaver*—lay at anchor off Long Wharf. Each night for two weeks their nervous captains had inspected the cargoes of tea, fervently wishing they were in some port other than Boston. For in town, Governor Hutchinson and his refractory charges were engaged in their third, and final, struggle. The citizens would not permit the tea to come ashore; Hutchinson would not permit the ships to leave. Three times the townsmen demanded that the tea commissioners resign; three times they refused. Hutchinson ordered up arms at Castle Island and brought two warships into the harbor. Sam Adams ordered up a rally through his Committees of Correspondence and 7,000 men turned out at Old South Meeting House. And there they waited—six, then seven hours, for Hutchinson's final decision on whether to allow the ships peaceably to leave. The word came back: No. Adams, somber for once in his hellfire career, rose to address the assembly, saying only, "This meeting can do nothing more to save the country." And with that solemn pronouncement, a cheer of such raucous acclamation arose that a Boston merchant, unabashedly drinking tea in his house down the street, remarked, "You'd have thought that the inhabitants of the infernal regions had broke loose."

Certainly some demon possessed the crowd. It was not the drunken frenzy that had torn down Hutchinson's house in 1765, nor the accidental rage that had fired the massacre five years later, but a very deliberate demon this time, intent on an errand of rebellion. Marching now, two by two, from the meetinghouse to Griffin's Wharf, 50 men with their faces already smeared with copper paint and their heads wrapped in blankets, descended on the ships, hatchets raised. Three hours work and the deed was done: 342 crates chopped to pieces and $112,000 worth of tea dumped in the harbor, left to wash up on the Dorchester shore in the morning. Their performance over, the "Indians" returned quietly home to their Boston beds.

It was an odd little drama—part shenanigans, part morality play. But with it, Boston finally made its point. Like Hamlet baiting Claudius, the upstart colony had seized the stage and rang the curtain down on the king's own three-act play: Stamp Act, Townshend Act, Tea Act—Boston would have no more of tyranny.

Boston had invited havoc to her Tea Party and she was made to pay dearly for it. Though Boston was not alone in her resistance to the tea tax (New York, Philadelphia, and Charleston, South Carolina, had also had their skirmishes with ship captains and tea commissioners), George III vent his full fury on Boston, naming it specifically in the Boston Port Bill of 1774, a retaliatory and punitive measure aimed at nothing less than reducing the town to "full and absolute submission." The royal agenda had just three brutal items: grind Boston's economy into the ground, squash her firebrand politicking, and cow the defiant citizenry. Leaving nothing then to chance, the king ordered the port closed and blockaded, recalled Governor Hutchinson and installed General Thomas Gage as military governor, abolished the Boston town meeting, filled elective posts

with royal appointees, and sent troopships to enforce a full military occupation of the town. By summer the thriving port of Yankee Boston had become a British garrison. "Surely the People of Boston are not Mad enough to think of opposing us," wrote Earl Percy sailing to America with his regiment of reinforcements in April 1774.

Certainly, the effects of these Coercive Acts were dire. With the perimeter of the harbor tightly sealed with British warships, the port of Boston came to a standstill. "They intend to deprive us of all trade in the future," wrote the merchant John Andrews to his brother-in-law in Philadelphia in June. "Our wharves are entirely deserted; not a topsail vessel to be seen either there or in the harbor, save the ships of war and transport ... Four regiments have already arrived and four more expected." The town fell into an eerie quiet. No carpenters hammering in the shipyards; no oystermen hawking their briny wares; no bawling curse or mirthful shout of sailors glad to be in port. Gone were the sounds of snapping canvas, creaking winches, and crates crashing on the docks. More ominous still, coins no longer clinked in counting houses and merchants' tills—shops and warehouses and dockside taverns all were shut up tight.

With the port closed, all of Boston's dockside laborers were thrown out of work—all the thousands of sailmakers, caulkers, blacksmiths, ferrymen, mechanics, chandlers, stevedores, coopers, ropewalkmen, and sailors. Within a year, the town's population plummeted from 17,000 to 6,500 as the men left with their families to find work in other towns or join up with the patriot militiamen in the countryside. The merchants also felt the pinch as debts mounted and commercial income dwindled to a trickle. "You can have no just conception how sensibly I am affected in my business," Andrews reported to his brother-in-law in August.

When I reflect on the unhappy situation we are in I can't help but be uneasy less the trade of the town should never be reinstated again ...I think myself well off to take cash enough to supply the demands of my family and you may as well ask a man for the teeth out of his head as to request the payment of money which he owes you.

These things Andrews knew well, for though he held £2,000 sterling in debts and another £2,000 in stock, his income during the summer of the blockade had fallen to less than £10 a week.

Boston was down, but not out. Lord Percy, who had so arrogantly predicted Boston's imminent submission from the security of his troop deck, changed his tune soon after docking in town. "This is the most beautiful country I ever saw in my life," he wrote in August from his headquarters

Left: Political satirists such as Paul Revere used cartoons to garnish support for the radical position. This cartoon suggests the effectiveness of the blockade of Boston Harbor. "Printed for R. Sayer and J. Bennett, Map and Printsellers on Fleet Street, November 1774." Courtesy, Boston Public Library Print Department

Above: A teapot hangs against Boston City Hall commemorating the Boston Tea Party. Photo © Gene Peach

Samuel Adams, loyal Patriot and governor of the Commonwealth, was laid to rest in the Granary Burial Ground in Boston, 1803.
Photo © Stanley Rowin

overlooking the Common, "& if the people were only like it, we should do very well." But the behavior of Boston's citizenry could scarcely be called "beautiful." Rash, wrong-headed, cruel, violent in their determinations, quick, and tyrannical—this is how Percy described the defiant townsmen of Boston during the summer and fall of 1774, for the town was doing its best to undermine the occupation. They skirted the blockade by bringing provisions in overland from the country. They would burn straw before allowing troops to use it for bedding, and would let officers and their families starve before selling them food for their commandeered tables. The town's carpenters went out on strike in the fall, refusing to build barracks for the soldiers and leaving them to freeze in flapping tents as winter approached.

Nor had Percy counted on the likes of Sam Adams—Adams, who had taken to the streets after the Boston Massacre, shouting for the removal of the troops, "Both regiments or none!" Adams, who had plotted the Tea Party at the Green Dragon Tavern

and led the "Indians" on their errand of destruction; Sam Adams, that erstwhile brewer, tax collector, and chimney inspector whom Governor Hutchinson called the "master of the puppets." And, indeed, this brooding and impulsive man who had squandered his inheritance, failed utterly in business, and barely kept his family in shoes, was the man of the hour in Boston. For here was a populist and true revolutionary, a man whose mind was so crowded with thoughts of liberty that he was oblivious to poverty and physical danger. It was Sam Adams who kept the town's resolve firm in the summer of 1774; he who haughtily declined a bribe to quit his incendiary provocations and dared upbraid the military governor in the very teeth of the occupation, warning, "Tell Governor Gage it is the advice of Samuel Adams to him, no longer to insult the feelings of an exasperated people."

Firebrand and provocateur, Adams was also a consummate organizer. In the fall of 1772 he had set up his greatest organization, the Committees of Correspondence, a network of patriots who communicated the troubling events in Boston by letter to neighboring towns. The network grew. Committees were formed as far away as New York and Philadelphia.

By 1774, with the Massachusetts Legislature dissolved, town meetings abolished, and Boston cut off from communication by sea, the Committees of Correspondence had assumed a new role. Part horseback newsletter, part clearinghouse of colonial information, Sam Adams' Committees had become nothing less than the underground rebel government. Percy, sharp-witted for once, grasped this point immediately, already warning London in July 1774, "One thing I will be bold to say, which is, that until you make their Committees of Correspondence and Congresses with the other Colonies high treason & try them for it in England, you must never expect perfect obedience & submission from this to the Mother Country."

Percy's warning came too late, for already the Committees had begun organizing for the military defense of Boston. The town itself, under siege, could do little but hide guns and ammunition in cartloads of dung and smuggle them out to compatriots in the countryside. There, hidden armories were working overtime, manufacturing firearms and bayonets to stock the local magazines. Militias were set drilling in earnest, and each town organized a corps of Minute Men, charged with having ready at a minute's notice stores and provisions sufficient to last two weeks.

The Committees of Correspondence had launched a clever campaign to intimidate and so they did. In Boston for the approaching winter, General Gage was growing nervous. To the increasingly alarming reports of his field commanders were added cheeky threats from the countryside. John Andrews reported one of these tall tales to his brother-in-law in Philadelphia in October:

One more anecdote, Bill, and I'll close this barren day. When the 59th [British] regiment came from Salem and were drawn up on each side of the Neck [the narrow land entry to Boston from

By the rude bridge that arched the flood, their flag to April's breeze unfurled, here once the embattled farmers stood, and fired the shot heard round the world.

parliamentary acts void, Warren affirmed that Boston and her neighbors would pay no tax, quarter no troops, nor heed any other English directive. In the face of tyranny, Boston would not stand down.

By year's end Earl Percy was sending grim news home to England: "Things here grow more and more serious every day," he wrote in November 1774, "for ... this place is the fountain from whence spring all their mad and treasonable resolves & actions." He was right. Already Paul Revere, that tireless rider and father of 16, was thundering to the Continental Congress in Philadelphia with the Suffolk Resolves in his saddlebag. In his run-down house on Purchase Street, fiery Sam Adams was preparing to join him, uncomfortable in the new silk hat and decent suit of clothes which his friends insisted he wear for the occasion. General Gage was ordering up reinforcements from London, and trying to accommodate the flood of Tory refugees coming into town on the heels of the patriots' leaving. Fruit trees were blooming in the town orchards, all out of season. Boston was preparing for war.

REVOLUTION AND REBUILDING

Boston was the warmonger of the American Revolution. Furious and deliberate by turns, her rabble crowds and lantern-lighting leaders had dragged the sister colonies into war. It was a war that would redeem Winthrop's shining City on a Hill, create a new nation, and leave the town in a shambles from which it would not recover for 30 years.

In the conduct of the war itself, Boston played little part. It was no battleground. Indeed, after Paul Revere rode off that April night in 1775 to warn the countryside that Colonel

Roxbury], a remarkable tall countrymen, near eight feet high, strutted between 'em at the head of his waggon, looking very sly and contemptuous on one side and t'other; which attracted the notice of the whole regiment. —Ay, ay says he, you don't know what boys we have got in the country. I am near nine feet high and one of the smallest among 'em.

Such nonsense Gage could dismiss in safety, but what of the rumor (also counterfeit, but Gage could not be sure) that the neighboring towns were

preparing to come to the defense of Boston with three brigades of 5,000 men each, ready to take up stations at Charlestown, Cambridge, and Roxbury? Or that in Worcester County to the north, 7,000 men were mustered, drilling twice a week, and polishing their 20 pieces of cannon?

By September Gage had his answer. For in that month Dr. Joseph Warren drafted the 19 articles of the Suffolk Resolves, a sober document that staked out the course of revolution. Declaring royal authority forfeit and

Concord, Massachusetts, is the location of Minuteman National Park. This statue represents those Patriots who fired the "shot heard round the world." Photo © Gene Peach

Percy was mustering his troops on Boston Common, and after the Redcoats answered the insults suffered on Lexington and Concord greens with the horrific battle at Bunker Hill two months later, Boston's military part in the war ended altogether.

For the next 11 months the patriots kept the British-occupied town "under siege," to use the glorifying depiction of the side that won. But really it was nothing but a standoff. The British, under the command of General Howe, held the port and so controlled all access to shipping and the sea-lanes. George Washington, newly elevated to the rank of commander-in-chief of the American army, controlled the countryside from his encampment in Cambridge. And so the two generals dug in, staring at each other across the Charles in bitterness and frustration for nearly a year, as the battles for freedom were fought elsewhere.

The town wasn't itself. The patriots had left en masse, sometimes by the thousands in a single month, so that by July 1775, only 6,573 civilians were counted in Boston. Most of these were Tories who elected to stay under the Crown's protection, outnumbered two-to-one by the soldiers

Facing page: The solid granite Bunker Hill Monument was dedicated in 1843, commemorating the British attack on the nearby Patriot fortification, Breed's Hill. Photo © Justine Hill

Right: Congress established the Continental Army in June, 1775, uniting the militias of each colony under federal control. George Washington took command of the troops of the first United States Army, July 3, 1775, in Cambridge, Massachusetts. Courtesy, First National Bank Blotter Series, Boston Public Library Print Department

Below: Duties of the Washington Guards are reenacted in the Boston Public Garden. Photo © Martha Everson

and their entourages quartered in the town. Some patriots also remained in town, held hostage against rebel attack, but everything had changed for them. British officers had commandeered the mansions lately abandoned by John Hancock and other worthies of the town. British guns fired practice rounds on Beacon Hill, and Redcoats drilled on the Common. For the first time in 140 years, no Thursday lecture was preached from the Congregational meetinghouse. Even the fishing fleet was idle, for the British admiral had imposed an exit fee on schooners headed out to fish the bay. "The present state of the inhabitants of Boston is that of the most abject slaves, under the most cruel and despotic of tyrants," wrote Abigail Adams to her husband, John, at the beginning of the summer.

It got worse. Food was scarce. Even the British officers had to resort to jerky, salt pork, eels, and cod for their dinners. Salads appeared only in dreams, and even such despised stalwarts of the New England root cellar as turnips and lentils were in short supply. Winter set in, blasting and frigid, and the problem became fuel. "The troops and inhabitants are absolutely and literally starving for want of provisions and fire," wrote an observer in December 1775. Fences were dismantled on Beacon Hill, and a fine stand of trees lining the Common was cut down for firewood. When that ran out, 100 wooden buildings, including John Winthrop's old house and the original Old North Church, were pulled down for the fire. The British were niggardly with what fuel they had—so discovered the once prosperous merchant, John Andrews, to the great offense of his proper Bostonian sensibilities, when soldiers refused his bribe of more than one dollar a bushel for coals, leaving him with no recourse but to keep warm with horse dung. This the good Mr. Andrews had to collect, lay, and burn himself, for his two remaining servants were both down sick. Boston was in the grip of smallpox.

The troops themselves were idle, for Washington would not attack them and would not let them leave, so they prowled the empty streets and paraded on the Common—restless, hungry, and sulky—waiting for any command to let loose. None was forthcoming. The soldiers took their vengeance where they could, specializing in entertainments calculated to offend the patriots across the river. They raced horses on the Common, staged satirical plays in Faneuil Hall, and took potshots at the venerable Puritan gravestones in the burying ground on Copp's Hill. In August 1775 a fit of spiteful hilarity overtook them, and they chopped down the Liberty Tree. Earlier they had taken hatchets and crowbars to the interior of Old South Meeting House and turned it into a riding ring where the popinjays of the Light Horse Dragoons would parade round and round under the fluttering handkerchiefs of the admiring ladies in the gallery. All the pews were burned for firewood

Patriots Day ceremonies are held annually at the Old North Bridge in Minuteman National Park, Concord. Photo © Gene Peach

except the elegant carved and silk-hung pew of old Deacon Hubbard, which was carted off for duty as a hog sty. Looting houses was good sport, too, and beyond the power of General Howe to control, though he issued an edict that "the first soldier who is caught plundering will be hanged on the spot."

The tension did not break until the late winter of 1776 when the provisional rebel congress, fearing British reinforcements in the spring, gave an approval that was tantamount to a death sentence for the town that bred the Revolution. At last it authorized General Washington to attack "in any manner he might think expedient notwithstanding the town and property in it might be destroyed."

In the end it didn't come to that. In the dead of night on March 4, 1776, Washington quietly mounted his guns on Dorchester Heights and when General Howe awoke to this fact in the morning, he knew the cause was lost. The Redcoats were permitted to leave quietly to save the town devasta-

tion. By March 17th they were gone—the officers, the troops, the horses and livestock, the camp followers, the supply wagons and baggage carts, along with the 1,000 Tory families with their servants and any personal possessions they could salvage—all packed into 78 ships slinking out of the harbor headed for Halifax.

Boston had been returned to the patriot cause, but it was a long time before the town returned to normal. The war dragged on for another seven years. The people came back slowly to the empty town, to commerce not at all. Houses lay broken and empty for decades. The wharves were idle, except for the occasional excitement when a captured British ship was towed into port, and you couldn't see the bacon on the shop shelves for the dust, but it didn't matter because the bacon cost too much to afford anyway. About the only thing that survived the Revolution intact was Boston's fierce pride in its self-appointed destiny to run things in America. Sam

Adams, for one, didn't mellow much with either age or exposure to other worthy patriots in New York and Philadelphia. After Adams succeeded John Hancock to the governorship in 1793, an observer remarked, "Samuel Adams would have the State of Massachusetts govern the Union, the town of Boston govern Massachusetts, and that he should govern the town of Boston, and then the whole would not be intentionally ill-governed."

Massachusetts did, indeed, send Adamses to the White House (though never Sam), but it was Boston's lot to rule not the nation, but the seas. By the turn of the century the town had mustered its famed determination and had returned to its earlier calling of overseas commerce. "The common people are exceedingly avaricious," General Greene had written meanly

The Monroe Tavern in Lexington dates back to the American Revolution.
Photo © B. & J. McGrath

of his enemy during the Revolution; "the genius of the people is commercial from their long intercourse with trade." In 1805 this genius appeared on the Boston waterfront in the person of Frederick Tudor, a town merchant of no special renown, who had an odd idea and the pluck to carry it through. Tudor saw that overseas trade was in trouble. Boston was short of cash, her manufacturing stores were down, and the old Atlantic trading ports in the British West Indies were closed to American ships. But Tudor also observed two other things: Boston winters were cold and there were other ports of call. He made his decision and it had a certain mad logic: Frederick Tudor would sell ice to the tropics.

And so the enterprise began. Tudor engaged workmen to cut ice on the ponds near his father's house in Saugus. One hundred and thirty tons

Above: Crispus Attucks, the first black person killed in the Revolutionary War, is prominently featured in this work by W. Champney. The Boston Massacre scene was created in 1856 and printed by lithographer J.H. Bufford. Courtesy, The Bostonian Society

Right: Paul Revere was laid to rest in the Granary Burial Ground in Boston. Photo © Stanley Rowin

of ice were carted to Charlestown and loaded onto the brig *Favorite* (whose crew, fearing being swamped once the ship sailed into southern latitudes, had been assembled only with great trouble). Then an expedition was launched to the French colony of Martinique, where the ice was offered for sale at 30 sous a pound. Boston thought him a lunatic, and the enterprise failed utterly, but Tudor was undaunted, writing in his journal these classic words of Yankee philosophy: "He who gives back at the first repulse and without striking the second blow despairs of success, has never been, is not & never will be a hero in love, war, or business."

It could have been a motto for the age, for men who could see a business opportunity in carting ice through the tropics would think nothing of going to China for tea. And it was here, in the famous China trade, that Boston made its first postwar fortune.

The initial problem was finding something to trade. If the Bostonians had thought the British provincial governors were a difficult and arrogant lot, they would revise their opinion when they met the haughty Chinese mandarins. These elegant, arrogant potentates had a high regard for themselves and their ancient

civilization and looked upon the traders who flocked to Canton as ill-bred, unclean, "foreign devils" whose business was best kept at a distance—in this case sequestered 12 miles downstream from Canton in the cramped dockside warrens of Whampoa where the hoppo, or custom man, could keep an eye on them. Such nabobs as these probably weren't going to fall all over themselves for baskets of salt cod and barrels of pitch, the old mainstays of Boston's Atlantic trade. New trade goods were needed, and Boston men found them, first in the woods of New England and then in the waters of the Pacific Northwest.

The New England product was ginseng, a knobby, forked, and aromatic root of the *Panax* family, which Americans had never found much use for, but which the Chinese had prized for centuries as the "dose for immortality" reputedly capable of doctoring the sick, easing old age, and restoring a man's flagging virility. Traders would hire Indians to dig it up in the woods and bring it to Boston in exchange for whiskey and baubles. Indians also provided the second, and far more profitable, China trade item: the lustrous pelts of the playful sea otter. The pelts, which the Chinese used to line their fine silk robes in

beads at two for a pelt, chisels in even trade, brass buttons for the greatcoats they so admired, Jew's harps, and even, on one occasion, a Japanese flag. In this way, more than 10,000 sea otter pelts would find their way to China on Boston ships each year between 1801 and 1803, and though other American cities and European nations would try to break into the Northwest trade, the Indians would come to call all white men "Bostons."

They had spirit, these Bostons, and they needed it for the dangerous crossing to China in the same little boats with the same youthful crews, trying to find their provisioning port of Hawaii in the middle of the ocean and dodging pirate junks in the East Indies. Once in China they needed to be sharper still to manage the shrewd dealings of the Chinese hong merchants, who sometimes felt like trading and sometimes didn't, and who would impose a heavy burden of taxes, levies, gratuities, and duties on the cargoes in either case. The China trade was a buccaneer business, requiring fully as much pioneer spirit from Boston as did the opening of the western frontier from other American cities. And it bred in the China traders a rough-and-ready ethic unlike any seen in Boston before or since. "Always go straight forward," William Sturgis advised his nephew, the great Robert Bennet ("Black Ben") Forbes when he set to sea at the age of 12, "and if you meet the devil cut him in two, and go between the pieces; if anyone imposes on you, tell him to whistle against the northwester and to bottle up moonshine."

The profits were worth the effort of the trade. In Canton the sea otter

winter, brought such profit to Boston that the great China trader, William Sturgis, was moved to remark that "next to a beautiful woman and a lovely infant, a prime sea-otter fur is the finest natural object in the world."

The sea otter pelts were much harder to get than ginseng. They required a long and treacherous voyage from the Boston waterfront south around the tip of South America at hurricane-ridden Cape Horn, stopping at the Falkland or Galapagos islands for provisioning, then north again through the uncharted seas of the Pacific to grateful anchorage at Nootka Sound or the mouth of the Columbia River on the Northwest

coast. It's a wonder the traders made it at all. The vessels were uniformly small, many under 100 tons. The crews were often Massachusetts farm boys more interested in adventure than their paltry wages of eight to ten dollars a month, and on many ships the only aids to navigating the Pacific coast were unfamiliar stars and a geography book called *Guthrie's Grammar*.

But the "Nor'westers" were a hardy lot, and if they didn't always know where they were going, they always drove a hard bargain when they got there. They strode straight into Indian camps, their ship cannon primed just in case, and began to deal. The Indians fancied New England goods—shoes, nails, red and blue cloth, green

In 1784 the state government of Massachusetts adopted the codfish as its emblem, indicating the importance of cod fishing to the welfare of the Commonwealth. The codfish replica hung in the Old State House until 1798, when, with great ceremony, it was moved to the New State House. Courtesy, First National Bank Blotter Series, Boston Public Library Print Department

pelts fetched $20 to $50 apiece, and additional profits could be made on exotic merchandise picked up in ports on the way—sandalwood from Hawaii; shark's fins, sea cucumbers, and birds' nests from the South Pacific Islands (all destined for the mysterious Chinese soup pot); pepper from Sumatra; nutmeg and mace from Batavia; coffee and betel nuts from Java. There were humbler cargoes to trade as well. The Boston merchants encouraged individual, hometown investors to entrust small consignments to the discretion of the ship's "supercargo," the owner's shipboard agent, who would sell what he could of them at 9 percent commission in Canton. These little cargoes, appropriately (if vicariously) called "adventures," were often placed by working men, widows, and schoolboys who hoped that their modest offerings of a box of chocolates or a dozen spermaceti candles or a handful of silver dollars knotted in a

Above: The Massachusetts Charitable Fire Society, established in 1794, was an attempt to minimize the effects of fire within Boston. The Society provided momentary relief for those who suffered following a fire, and stimulated research into better fire-fighting techniques. Courtesy, First National Bank Blotter Series, Boston Public Library Print Department

handkerchief might please a mandarin and so win them a Chinese curio or a small batch of tea to sell on the Boston streets at a profit.

In this way all of Boston became keen on all things Oriental. First and best was the tea—the real stuff for a blessed change after the wretched decoctions of the Revolution—good, strong, smoky Chinese Bohea, Hyson, and Souchong teas by the chestful, nearly 10 million pounds imported to the United States in 1806 alone. But China brought other pleasing things to Boston homes: bolts of silk and crepe, satin slippers for the ladies, satin breeches for the gents, silk gloves and ribbons; paper umbrellas, mother-of-pearl fans, and bamboo and silk window shades to hang in the parlor; lacquerware tea caddies and ivory boxes; scrolls, floor mats, and exotic scenes painted on glass; and chinaware, tons of it, by the crateload.

China also brought money to the State Street counting houses and glory to her merchant princes. The

Below: Eighteenth century medical care was primitive. The Boston Dispensary, opened in 1796 in Bartlett's Apothecary Shop on Corn Hill, provided a central clinic for medical advice and treatment. The Good Samaritan became the Dispensary symbol. Courtesy, First National Bank Blotter Series, Boston Public Library Print Department

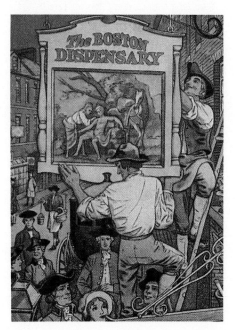

Boston firm of Bryant & Sturgis alone controlled more than half the nation's Pacific trade from 1810 to 1840 (when American exports to Canton averaged more than $3 million a year and imports more than $5 million), and a Boston ship, *Columbia* (for whom the Northwest river is named), was the first American vessel to circumnavigate the globe. When she returned to Boston Harbor, the proud citizenry crowded the wharves and greeted her "with three huzzas and a hearty welcome," but even a greater treat was in store. For on board was a splendid curiosity, a Hawaiian youth named Attoo who had been recruited as cabin boy on the journey to China, and was brought forth on this solemn occasion to call on Governor John Hancock and cement friendly relations between the far-flung trading

Above: The first public high school for girls in Boston was established in 1826, through the support of Mayor Josiah Quincy. Later, Quincy lost political support when he opposed a second girls' high school. The first school closed a short time later. Not until 1870 was public education beyond elementary school available to Boston girls, when Girl's High opened. In 1878, the first public Latin School for Girls opened. Both schools were on West Newton Street in the South End. Courtesy, First National Bank Blotter Series, Boston Public Library Print Department

nations. "Clad in feather cloak of golden suns set in flaming scarlet," reported a dazzled observer, "crested with a gorgeous feather helmet shaped like a Greek warrior's, this young Hawaiian moved up State Street like a living flame." All was bright again in Boston, back on its feet and ruling the waves again and looking for new worlds to conquer.

And what of Frederick Tudor and his madcap ice business? He stuck with it, learning as he went along to double-sheathe the cargo holds of his ships and pack the ice with sawdust, and fill empty spaces in the hold with juicy Boston-grown Baldwin apples reserved for bonuses to good customers. Though wiped out by the War of 1812, he began making money soon thereafter, though he charged just one to three cents a pound for the ice. By 1820 he was trading to Havana, Kingston, and Rio de Janeiro (where he tried to drum up interest in ice cream parlors), and had a flourishing domestic trade in Charleston, Savannah, and New Orleans. The 1830s and 1840s found him taking ice clear around the Horn to Persia and India where he made enough money to pay off old debts of over a quarter million dollars.

The ice-cutting operation had branched throughout the countryside, even to Walden Pond in Concord, where Henry David Thoreau, deep in nature and self-study, observed in 1846, "It appears that the sweltering inhabitants of Charleston and New Orleans, of Madras and Bombay and Calcutta, drink at my well." By this time the skeptics had joined the bandwagon: Tudor had 15 competitors, and 95,000 tons of ice were being floated south from Boston each year. Thus did Boston make her seafaring fortune in the first half of the nineteenth century: by bravery of enterprise, careful reckoning, not disdaining the penny-a-pound cargo, and never taking no for an answer.

But not everyone in Boston was willing to risk all in the China seas.

When the War of 1812 stalled Boston shipping, wary merchants began to look elsewhere to invest their money and they found it, close at hand, on the banks of the Merrimack River. Francis Cabot Lowell had invented the power loom (or rather, reconstructed it from his memory of a tour he had taken of the Birmingham and Manchester textile mills in England), and was using the strong rushing river water to drive it. On the heels of elegant Canton silk came bolts and bolts of good Massachusetts cotton, and soon the manufacturing towns of Lowell and Lawrence were driving Boston business to its second postwar fortune.

Boston in the early 1800s was still a small and familiar city where the rich and powerful had no trouble recognizing each other and had every reason to forge useful alliances. And so it was with the old China traders and the new mill men. Boston's lords of the seas, those rowdies of the waves and purveyors of smelly animal skins, were not the kind to sneer at fortunes made

Early morning fog envelops Walden Pond.
Photo © Gene Peach

on river power, rackety spinning machines, and the sweaty manual labor of others. In no time the merchant elite and the manufacturing elite of Boston were consolidating their fortunes. So when the staid drawing rooms of Beacon Hill held wedding receptions for grooms who were grandsons of privateers and brides who were daughters of mill bosses, it was to everyone's great satisfaction. For here was a sweetheart deal in more ways than one: the boy got the girl, the mill men got markets for their cotton, and the traders got manufacturing profits to funnel back into commerce. By 1835 the Lowell mills were sending $1.5 million worth of cotton to China a year, and about the same time, the shrewd hong merchant, Houqua, entrusted half a million dollars to the Forbes China trade house to invest in New England factories.

In this marriage of trading house and mill the Boston Brahmin caste was made and came to run the Federalist town. They were a dignified and conservative lot—all these tight-knit Lowells, Appletons, Forbeses, Sturgises, Lawrences, Russells, Cabots, and Higginsons—intent, it

would seem, on maintaining standards of social and moral decency in a world which they knew from their business enterprises was plenty rough enough.

Their style was more British than American. Visitors saw no coonskin caps on Tremont Street, no naive primitive art in Boston parlors. The city held no hoedowns. In Boston the gentlemen wore knee breeches and ruffled wristbands as they headed down to the State Street Exchange in the morning, while the ladies wore lace and jewels as they dished out scalloped oysters at their "suppers" for 300 guests. Well-painted oil portraits of august ancestors hung over black marble mantels in the drawing rooms on Beacon Hill, and even waltzing was frowned upon in this town that still danced the minuet. Old Stephen Higginson, who in partnership with a Lowell and a Russell had founded the nation's second bank in 1784, the Massachusetts Bank, and was every inch the Brahmin, could not bring himself to leave the house until he had found his gold-headed cane, fastened his old-fashioned buckled shoes, and caught his powdered hair in a ribbon to form a proper queue.

"He simply felt that it was a part of self-respect, as of mutual respect, to be scrupulously neat, refined, and elegant," remembers his grandson, Octavius Brooks Frothingham.

Other Brahmins felt as Stephen Higginson did and, out of mutual respect and the buoyant enthusiasm for civic improvements that comes with good times, they turned their money and will to fixing up the town. Boston in 1820 was a town of 43,298 souls, and as it neared its 200th birthday it was showing its age. In 1822 the bold step was taken of incorporating the town as a city. The Boston town meeting became a thing of the past, replaced by a mayor and aldermen who were charged with governing the city with due respect for the sensibilities of a populace that had chosen for their new city the prayerful and cautionary motto, "May God be with Us as He was with our Fathers."

Things could be changed, within reason, and they were. Cows were banned from their old pasture on the

Lawrence Heritage State Park pays tribute to textile manufacturing which was once a leading industry in Massachusetts. Photo © Gene Peach

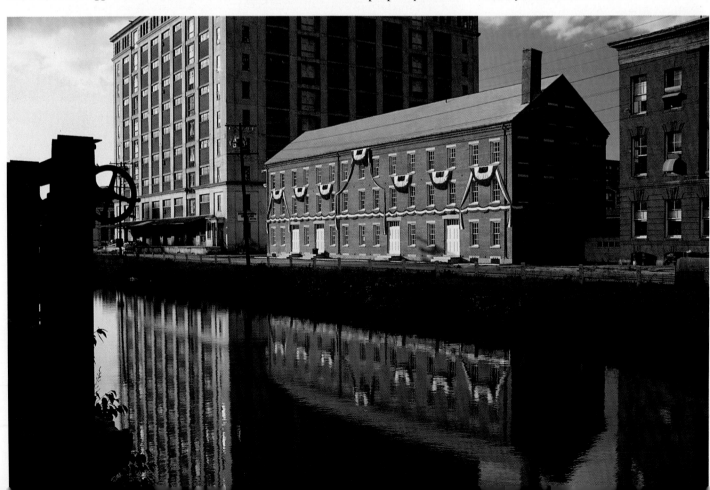

Common. Lights were lit on the newly paved streets, and Faneuil Hall market was expanded to its present form. Under the mayoralty of Josiah Quincy, the streets were swept of 6,000 tons of dirt in a single year, garbage was collected for the first time on a regular basis, and sewer lines were run out far onto the mud flats. There still wasn't much of a police force, but Mayor Quincy took his duties as city father seriously, and so sent out his 18 night watchmen each evening to break up fiddle fests in the dance halls and ride herd on the drinking establishments in the more riotous parts of town. On one occasion, he enlisted the help of the city's draymen to break up a riot. But Quincy's special cause was the fire department. Against strong resistance, he introduced such innovations as hose in place of bucket

brigades, new engines from New York and Philadelphia, and an early hydrant system—a new-fangled idea that was received with nearly universal mockery, but fire insurance premiums promptly fell 20 percent.

As the city was cleaned up, it also made room. The peninsula itself couldn't budge out much, but geography had never daunted the inhabitants of Boston. They had already thrown a wharf out half a mile into the bay and spanned a bridge across the Charles, a river wider than the Thames. This time, Boston merely cut down her hills. Down came the old landmark Trimountain—Beacon, Mt. Vernon, and Pemberton Hills— to provide fill for the old Mill Pond. In the ruins Charles Bulfinch made his distinguished contribution to American architecture. First he built

the Massachusetts State House, whose glittering gilt dome still dazzles visitors and residents alike at the corner of Park and Beacon streets. Then Bulfinch turned his attention to what remained of Beacon Hill, turning the old cow pasture into a stately neighborhood of well-gridded streets lined with the strong, upright, and conservatively elegant townhouses of the Federalist aristocracy.

But if the Brahmins living behind the doors of Beacon Hill were keen on civic improvements, they were suspicious of any kind of social or economic reform. In Boston it had taken only three generations and two

This mill in South Sudbury is located on the grounds of the Wayside Inn.
Photo © B. & J. McGrath

fortunes to change the heady Republicanism of the Revolution into a stodgy Federalist conservatism. There was some pretty rabid anti-democratic feeling among the Boston Brahmins who looked upon "that man" Jefferson in Monticello with alarm and who saw nothing but villainy in the French Revolution. In his stinging essay "The Dangers of American Liberty," Fisher Ames frankly pronounced democracy to be violent, arbitrary, destructive, ferocious, dema-

gogic, and good only for ensuring the wretchedness of mankind. Ames was the whip of Federalism in Boston, and not universally listened to, but nevertheless it was generally counted a good thing in the Federalist press that 2,000 evangelists had flocked to the boom town of Lowell to keep the hearts of the mill workers pure and get their bodies to work on time.

For the Brahmins of Boston were men of property and privilege, and they preferred the common man in their own backyards and sculleries and factories to keep a proper dis-

tance. Though generally upright and generous in their dealings, they were often unwilling to grant that others might be, too, so they kept a firm rein on the city, reserving power to themselves and their kin. By mid-century, the Brahmins had become a hard and immovable lot. A visitor to Boston then remarked on their stony aspect, the cold and lusterless expression of their eyes, the rigid compression of their lips, and pronounced that "of God's creatures they are the least liable to be influenced by circumstances appealing to the heart or imagination." Good men still, the new Boston fathers had fallen into a rigidness very like their Puritan ancestors'. And like them, too, the Brahmins would lose control of Boston, as the "new fangled morality," so loathed by the Federalists, swept them away in the late nineteenth century.

ABOLITIONISTS AND IMMIGRANTS

It was bad enough when young people of respectable families in the 1830s and 1840s went abroad, bearded, robed, and sandaled, eating health food, joining communes, and carrying on about ending wars and liberat-

Above: From the moment Faneuil Hall Market opened in 1826, people called it Quincy Market, in honor of "The Great Mayor," Josiah Quincy, who built the project to serve as Boston's central marketplace. During the nineteenth century, the shoreline was filled in, and the Market now faces a major elevated highway and additional wharves and warehouses. Lithograph by Andrews and Bowen, 1827. Courtesy, The Bostonian Society

Right: The Massachusetts Horticultural Society held its first annual exhibition in 1829. Such exhibitions were part of the Society's efforts to cultivate a knowledge of and interest in horticulture. As the second oldest Horticultural Society in America, it was also responsible for the establishment of Mount Auburn Cemetery, one of the earliest of the "Garden Cemeteries." Courtesy, First National Bank Blotter Series, Boston Public Library Print Department

ing women and marching to a different drummer and finding transcendental routes to the godhead. (And if this all sounds familiar, it's because Boston has been around long enough to see old ideas return, masquerading as new ones but wearing the same old clothes.) It was called "The Newness" then, as it was to be called "Hippiedom" 130 years later, and it caused the same commotion among the Establishment. But the first real assault on the Federalist point of view was abolitionism.

It may seem natural that the town that produced the Sons of Liberty would later become the home of the abolitionist paper, the *Liberator*. But when William Lloyd Garrison set up his presses on Washington Street in 1831, only visionaries would have predicted that Boston would become the center of anti-slavery agitation in America. Boston owned no slaves, but it held strong opinions about rabble-rousers bent on breaking the new nation for which Boston had so cruelly suffered, and overturning an economic order in which Boston money had such a profitable stake. For while it was slaves that picked the cotton on southern plantations, it was factory workers in the mills of Lowell and Lawrence that turned that cotton into

cloth. So when Harvard President Edward Everett returned from a tour of Louisiana plantations and pronounced the slave quarters there to be clean, comfortable, and thoughtfully provided with mosquito netting, Boston was happy to let the matter rest.

Garrison was not, and soon his paper was encountering what he called "contempt more bitter, opposition more active, detraction more relentless, prejudice more stubborn, and apathy more frozen" than any he had met among slave owners themselves. In a celebrated and ugly incident in 1835, a mob broke in on the opening prayers of a meeting of 30 members of the Boston Female Antislavery Society, hounded Garrison out a back office window, and threw a rope around his neck when they cornered him in an upstairs room of a carpenter's shop next door. Deciding lynching was too good for him, the crowd, now numbering over a thousand, paraded Garrison to the site of the old Boston Massacre, where they stripped him half naked and hurled mockery and abuse at him until he was carted off to jail on charges of disturbing the peace. Here he stayed overnight, "safe from my persecutors," he said, "accompanied by two delightful associates, a good conscience and a cheer-

ful mind."

More interesting than Garrison's cell-mates was the nature of the mob. There is little doubt, as Garrison alleged, that the attack was deliberately planned by the businessmen of State Street, "gentlemen of property and standing from all parts of the city." Only four months earlier, a mass meeting had been called in Faneuil Hall to denounce the abolitionists, with mayor Theodore Lyman, Jr., and mill boss Abbott Lawrence presiding, and the king of Boston Federalist society, Harrison Gray Otis, giving a speech. But Federalist Boston had met its match in William Lloyd Gar-

Left: Charles Bulfinch designed these fine mansions along Park Street in the early 1880s. The first house on the corner was built for publisher George Ticknor. Courtesy, Boston Atheneum

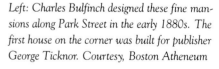

Above: Scrimshaw is the art of carving whale bone or teeth. It was a popular craft in nineteenth-century Boston, as a result of the large whaling industry in both Boston and Salem. This tooth of a sperm whale, about six inches tall, was used to create a familiar household scene. Courtesy, The Bostonian Society

rison, for he was not the sort of man to be deterred. As he wrote in the *Liberator*:

I will be as harsh as truth, and as uncompromising as justice. On the subject of slavery I do not wish to think, or speak, or write, with moderation. No! no! Tell the man whose house is on fire to give a moderate alarm; tell him to moderately rescue his wife from the hands of the ravisher; tell the mother to gradually extricate her babe from the fire into which it has fallen, —but urge me not to use moderation in a cause like the present. I am

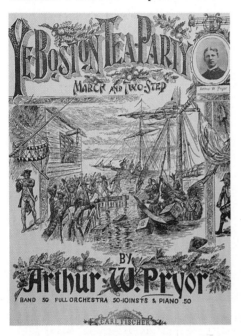

in earnest—I will not equivocate—I will not excuse—I will not retreat a single inch—and I will be heard.

With speeches like these, Garrison was heard, and by the time Harriet Beecher Stowe, the unimpeachable daughter of the minister at Park Street Church, published *Uncle Tom's Cabin* in 1852, Boston had been won over to the abolitionist cause. And in May 1863, Colonel Robert Gould Shaw, son of one of Boston's wealthiest families, led the first regiment of free black men off to war in South Carolina from the steps of the State House, where Governor Andrew hailed them, saying, "I know not, Mr. Commander, where in all human history to any given thousand men in arms there had been committed a work at once so proud, so precious, so full of hope and glory, as the work

committed to you."

But there was other work to do in Boston in the late nineteenth century, and this was to find a place for the thousands of immigrants who began flocking to the city in the 1840s. For Boston the problems of slavery, while stirring, could be kept at a safe remove. They were fought out in the hearts and consciences of the citizenry, in the weaving rooms in Lowell and the countinghouses on State Street, on the battlefields of the South, but rarely on the streets of the city. But immigration brought strangers, desperation, and struggle directly to the doorsteps of the conservative and well-ordered Federalist town, and sparked the kind of social confrontation that has never gone smoothly in Boston.

The simple arithmetic of change was overwhelming. Between 1840 and 1860, 162,200 Irish arrived in

Boston—25,250 in 1847 alone—all refugees of the potato famine. Some moved on, but many stayed, and by 1855 nearly a third of the people living in Boston had been born in Ireland, England, Scotland, and Wales. By 1890, when Italians, Germans, Russian Jews, and others had joined the tide, immigrants and their children accounted for 68 percent of Boston's population.

The immigrants lived hellish lives, but it was make it in Boston or die, and they counted themselves lucky to have a roof over their heads, even if it

Above: In 1868, Boston annexed Roxbury, a predominantly Yankee, Protestant town. The streetcar along such streets as Humbolt Avenue helped bring new people to Roxbury. First upwardly mobile Irish and then Jewish families moved into Roxbury Highlands. Apartment buildings filled the spaces between finer, single-family homes. After World War II, the area would become home for Boston's growing black population. Courtesy, Boston Public Library Print Department

Above left: The Boston Tea Party became part of the popular culture of Boston in the nineteenth century. "Ye Boston Tea Party March and Two-Step" was written by Arthur W. Pryor. The sheet music was published in 1896 by Carl Fischer. Courtesy, Boston Public Library Print Department

Left: Boston City Hall was built on School Street in 1865 in the French Renaissance style. Today, fittingly, as Old City Hall, it houses a French Restaurant which uses the old vaults for dining rooms. From Gillon, Early Illustrations and Views of American Architecture

The Bijou Theater opened in 1882. A broad horse-shoe balcony with Moorish architecture and decoration created an exquisite setting for an audience of 1,000 people. The theater, with ingenious scenery-moving devices and electric lights, was described as the "dainty parlor of the Boston places of amusement." Courtesy, The Bostonian Society

was three or four kids to a mattress in some flooded cellar or deserted warehouse in the North End or Fort Hill, with the garbage piling up in the yard because there was no access to the street, coal and wood too expensive to afford, and just one backed-up outdoor privy for a family of 20 and any passerby with the urge. Cholera, tuberculosis, pneumonia, diarrhea, and dysentery ran through the tenements on Hanover Street, Mechanics Court, and Burgess Alley many times, killing thousands of immigrants

and their children and pushing Boston's mortality rate to double that of the rest of Massachusetts.

Boston was suffering, and the victims were blamed. There were clashes, first between the immigrants and Boston's indigenous working class, who resented the Irish undercutting their wages and who perceived that the newcomers' very desperation would be a threat to the old guard (as, indeed, it was). Already by 1850, the Irish had taken 7,000 of the city's 8,500 laborers' jobs

and two-thirds of the domestic positions. And so the self-styled and self-important "honest and respectable laborers of the State" came to despise the immigrants, who, they complained, were "satisfied with food to support the animal existence alone …while we not only labor for the body but for the mind, the soul, and the State."

In fact, after the first decades of misery, the immigrants of Boston worked hard to find a honorable place for their minds and souls in some respectable cranny of this inhospitable State. This is nowhere more evident than in the settlement houses where immigrants struggled through their English and civics lessons on the way to better jobs and citizenship at the turn of the century. One such settlement house, the Civic Service House, was founded on Salem Street in the North End in 1901 through the philanthropy of a proper Brahmin matron, Mrs. Quincy Agassiz Shaw, and the determination of Meyer Bloomfield, a Rumanian immigrant. Here Russian Jews and Italian dockworkers worked with bright-eyed girls from Simmons and idealistic boys from Harvard, trying to chart a course to the American mainstream.

The immigrants had high hopes. They wanted to be doctors, lawyers, dentists, and pharmacists. One wanted to improve his position at the local delicatessen by buying out his boss; another, a bearded old man in his seventies, wanted only to get married, but his intended bride wouldn't have him until he got his American citizenship. It wasn't easy, becoming an American in Boston at the turn of the century. There were cultural misunderstandings all around. One settlement house hopeful, a tailor by profession, had trouble with the citizenship test when asked to identify Abraham Lincoln. No, the judge

This advertising card was distributed by Avery Lactate Company in the late 1800s.

HECKERS'
BUCKWHEAT.
The Best! The Cheapest!

said, Abraham Lincoln wasn't a tailor. No, he never lived in Chelsea. "Well, then—I guess I don't know him!" replied the applicant in exasperation. On another occasion, Paul Davis, a young White Russian staff member, had to travel clear to Washington by train and call on the Secretary of Labor to prevent a new arrival from being deported. The immigration authorities considered the man too old to practice his profession, which they understood to be that of a butcher. But the old man wasn't a butcher, he was a *mohel*, a Jew trained in the practice of ritual circumcision. When this matter was finally cleared up, the old gentleman was allowed to remain.

In this way the immigrants slowly made their way in Boston and changed the city utterly. By the turn of the century, Boston was no longer a staid, conservative, Federalist town, but a city of mixed ancestry and mixed blessings. Its politics were in the hands of Irish bosses who had wrested control of the wards and city councils. Its money was in the hands of old Brahmin countinghouses on State Street, which were becoming increasingly timid about investing it. Its daily work on the docks, on the streets, in the shops, and in the factories was in the hands of people who 40 years before had never heard of Boston. Boston's future was uncertain.

Above left: The bright, happy face of this chubby baby was fed with Hecker's Buckwheat Cakes. This advertising card was distributed by George Nazio and Howard Knight.

Left: Fishing played an important role in the economy of Boston in 1900. Fishing vessels and work boats are lined up at the granite warehouses and wharves of the waterfront. These same warehouses and wharves have now been renovated to provide luxury apartments and docks for pleasure boats. Courtesy, SPNEA

The Massachusetts State House is the oldest existing building on Beacon Hill. Its cornerstone was dragged into position by 15 white horses on July 4, 1795. The dome was covered with gold-leaf in 1874. Photo © Gene Peach

TRAUMATIC TIMES

The curtain rose on the twentieth century, but Boston's stage was still dark. And the lights would be a long time coming up: the first 50 years of the century were a catalogue of decline, death, and disruption so thoroughgoing that when a commentator contemplated Boston from Beacon Hill in 1928, he wrote, "It is flawless, complete, finished, static, dead; it lies before you in an autumnal sunset splendor, like Rome under the Ostrogoths."

There were bright spots, of course, but you had to look hard for them. A screech owl was spotted on the Common in 1908, and caused a stir. A medium named Margery held seances on Beacon Hill in the twenties, producing bugle calls and glowing ectoplasmic limbs from the other world, to the befuddlement of Harry Houdini and a committee of Harvard scientists who had assembled to investigate. In 1919 the city's first skyscraper was built, a 29-story tower mounted incongruously above the Doric columns of the old customhouse. Grande dame Isabella Gardner died in 1924, to the dismay of all who secretly appreciated a woman who delighted in shocking proper Boston society by becoming a Buddhist and walking a pet lion down Tremont Street. But she willed her fabulous art collection—Rembrandts and Botticellis, Belgian tapestries and Persian carvings, to name but a few of the things that caught her eclectic fancy—to perpetual public view in the Florentine palace she had built in the Fenway. The thirties saw the Raytheon and Polaroid companies launched, and State Street began issuing shares in an obscure new investment vehicle, the Boston fund, now universally known as the mutual fund. The Braves won the pennant in 1948, and though they left for Milwaukee four years later, by then Ted Williams was slugging for the Red Sox, .406 in 1941, the first man to break .400 in 50 years.

The rest of the news was mostly bad. First came the war. Then came influenza, brought to Boston in September 1918 aboard the training ships tied up at Commonwealth Pier, a grim stowaway that would kill four times as many as the battles in Europe. In that year, Francis Russell was in Miss Sykes' third grade class at the Martha Baker School in Dorchester, and 46 years later he wrote about it. The boys, he remembers, were obsessed with the thrill of the war. They swapped torpedo stories on the railing during recess and goggled at posters of helmeted German brutes dragging maidens off to some unspoken doom. Once Eliot Dodds tried to get a rise out of prissy Miss Sykes by coming to class sporting a button that said "To H-ll with the Kaiser," which of course she required him immediately to remove.

But if her unruly charges were oblivious to the advancing plague, Miss Sykes was not. Every day a parade of funeral cars lurched heavily by under the schoolhouse window, headed for New Calvary Cemetery where the coffins piled up in stacks because graves couldn't be dug fast enough to bury them. Sometimes Miss Sykes' composure would snap. "Eyes front!" she would shriek as curious eyes drifted to the window; her ruler then fell smartly on the nearest set of knuckles penning childish scribbles meant to be the elegant Palmer script she loved so well. "The fear was on her," Russell finally understood those many years later. For at the beginning of October, 1918, more than 200 Bostonians died in one day of influenza. By the end of that week, all the Boston schools were closed, and the boys were set loose to watch for themselves the grim goings-on in New Calvary Cemetery and themselves fell ill. By spring 6,000 were dead.

Boston also saw its share of strikes and civil disturbances in the early twentieth century, as the country's social conscience caught up with industrialism and grappled with socialism and depression. At first the protests were decorous. When Mrs. Glendower Evans and Miss Mabel Gillespie of the Women's Trade Union League of Boston were threatened with arrest for circulating leaflets to the factory workers at the Gillette Safety Razor Company in 1910, they behaved as perfect ladies. The arrest-

CHAPTER 2

The Dark Before the Dawn

BY NANCY ZERBEY

ing officer was in a jam. He had already nabbed Mabel Gillespie and had his eye on Mrs. Evans, but was afraid to turn Mabel loose for fear she'd run away. No such thing. Mabel Gillespie was a good Radcliffe girl and Glendower Evans' wife was a proper Back Bay matron. They knew their civic duty, and it didn't include brickbats and insults. So Mabel stayed put as Mrs. Evans was handed into the paddy wagon, then clambered in after her. Duty done, they turned and distributed the rest of their leaflets from the back of the wagon into the hands of the crowd of factory girls

Right: City workers clean trash from streets in the North End, 1901. The neighborhood, home to successive waves of immigrants by 1900, was occupied mostly by Eastern European and Southern Italian newcomers. Courtesy, Boston Public Library Print Department

Below: Following a snowstorm Bostonians sleigh on Beacon Street in the Back Bay. Courtesy, Boston Public Library Print Department

who cheered them on to jail.

Things were not so polite in the summer of 1919 when the Boston police force of 1,544 men in gray, domed helmets and blue frock coats began to voice grievances about meager pay, 12-hour shifts, and dilapidated station houses. Against jail threats from the police commissioner, Edwin Curtis, and the ineffectual mutterings of the mayor, Andrew Peters, they organized themselves on August 11 as the Boston Police Union Number 16B07 of the American Federation of Labor. The ink was barely dry on their charter when, 28 days later, they

Right: Recruiting for World War I on Boston Common in 1917 included promises of protecting American womanhood. Photo by Leslie Jones for the Boston Herald. Courtesy, Boston Public Library Print Department

Below: Boston joined other United States cities during World War I in converting open space into "victory gardens." Here the Boston Common has large garden patches and temporary service buildings. Courtesy, The Bostonian Society

Newsboys from the Boston Globe *pause for a group photograph before fanning out across the city to sell their newspapers. Photo by Lewis Hines. Courtesy, Boston Public Library Print Department*

voted 1,134 to 2 to strike. This didn't sit well with Curtis, Peters, or with Calvin Coolidge, who was sitting as governor in the State House. Before the week was out, Curtis had been dismissed, Peters had attacked Coolidge at the state armory and given him a black eye, and police sympathizers had staged a giant craps game on the Common in one of the first mass demonstrations of civil disobedience since the Boston Tea Party.

If the strike was farcical at its inception, it was tragic by its close. Mischief turned to rioting and lynchings were threatened. The State Guard was called out and upright citizens were issued badges and guns to protect themselves and their businesses from angry mobs. More than a dozen people were killed and the AFL organizers, sensing that public opin-

ion was turning against them, simply melted away. On September 12 the chastened policemen called it quits and reported back to the station houses, only to find that Curtis, reinstated as commissioner, wouldn't have them—then, or ever. In Boston the Brahmins still had a tenuous hold on town government and weren't about to let law be made on the streets or the Common. When Coolidge declared from the State House that "There is no right to strike against the public safety by anybody, anywhere, any time," Boston and the nation applauded, and four years later Coolidge had resigned the State House for the White House.

But Brahmin power would not last into the third decade of the twentieth century, for it had lost its essential grounding on the wharves, in the factories, and at the polls. The boardrooms and investment houses on State Street, already struggling with the timidity of enterprise that had first shown up in the late nineteenth century, now faced a serious decline in the underpinnings of the Yankee economy. The mills were in trouble,

racked by labor disputes like the famous Bread and Roses strike at the Lawrence woolen mills in 1912, and bruised by competition from cheaper factories elsewhere. Manufacturing prices rose and production fell. Soon the textile industry would move south to mills in Georgia and the Carolinas, and shoe manufacturing would go abroad. With the loss of domestic manufactures to ship, Boston's waterfront began to stall. Steamship owners complained they could not meet longshoremen's wage demands in 1909 because their bulk handling business was already in a period of depression. Lumber freightage alone showed an eightfold decline between 1910 and 1918, and in the next decade total exports from the Port of Boston plummeted from 573,489 tons to 303,120 tons. With less and less to carry, State Street sold off her ships, and the docks began to go to seed. The Brahmins were losing their economic grip on Boston.

At the same time it was clear that Boston was no longer a Yankee town. The immigrants who had begun coming in the 1840s had kept coming, and by 1920 there were nearly a quarter of a million foreign-born people in the city, comprising a third of the population and 44 percent of the work force. Taking their Boston-born children also into account, the immigrants' share of Boston's population had reached 73 percent. The immigrants were moving up the occupational ladder, but not very fast. By 1930 about a quarter of the foreign-born workers held white-collar jobs, but twice as many worked as unskilled laborers. Among the native-born Yankees, these percentages were reversed.

It was the second generation of immigrants that perceived this discrepancy and came to resent it. As the docks, factories, enterprise, and government all slipped from the hands of the Brahmins, the immigrants began to consolidate their position. No longer desperate, they were no longer content to share a mattress with three kinsmen in some frigid North End or South Boston attic room, no longer grateful to work long hours at a grueling job for a pittance, and no longer willing to suffer

quietly the indignities of cool Yankee bigotry. These new Bostonians, these *majority* Bostonians, took stock and got moving. They moved straight into ward politics and civil service, the only route of genuine advancement available to them, and the best lever they could find against the Brahmins on Beacon Hill and State Street.

And so it was that the city paid special attention when the golden tones of James Michael Curley rang out with the following pronouncement:

No land was ever saved by little clubs of female faddists, old gentlemen with disordered livers or pessimists cackling over imaginary good old days, ignoring the sunlit present. What we need in this part of the country are men and mothers of men, not gabbing spinsters and dog-raising matrons in federation assembled.

Curley was running for office, as he did off and on for over 50 years between 1898 and 1955, serving 16 years as mayor of Boston, four terms as U.S. congressman, and two years as governor of the Commonwealth.

Curley was one of the immigrants'

own. He knew their stories, grudges, and aspirations well. He was a wharf rat from the Irish slums of Roxbury's Ward 17, the son of a hod carrier and Beacon Hill maid, who quit grammar school to help support the family in a series of dead-end jobs familiar to every immigrant who wanted better: newspaper peddler, grocery bundler, drugstore clerk, and deliveryman. By the age of 23, he had settled on politics. But in politics, as in everything else, James Michael Curley was a rogue. He curried no favor, thumbed his nose as cheerfully at the political machine of the Irish ward bosses as at the drawing rooms of Beacon Hill, and appealed directly to the people in the neighborhoods for support. And, through sheer exuberance of style, he got it.

Haymarket opened at 3 p.m. every Saturday. Fruit peddlers such as these would race to their favorite stalls when the clock struck three. Courtesy, Boston Public Library Print Department

Once installed in City Hall, Curley turned the city on its head. He understood his constituency perfectly. They were not, as is often alleged, a collection of "gimmes" with a chip on their shoulder and an attitude of entitlement. But they were a people with a strong sense of township who saw Boston not as a convenient place to put in a day's work or shop for Easter clothes or dine on food cooked by someone else, but as their home—a community of participants, almost a guild. Willing to put into the city all of their sweat, talent, service, and aspiration, Curley's supporters also expected something back from it—a square deal between Boston and her residents. And it was this deal that Curley brokered so brilliantly.

Curley's politics never amounted to a philosophy, for he was a man not much concerned with ultimates, but Curley understood benefits, and his arithmetic and geography were flawless. He counted up his supporters, mapped out where they lived, and proceeded to dispense benefits where the votes were. The votes were in the outlying ethnic neighborhoods: in South Boston, where Curley built the beaches and the bathhouses; in Charlestown, where he paved the streets; in the North End, where he opened health clinics; in East Boston, where he drove a tunnel; in Roxbury, where he cleared the slums; and in the South End, where he expanded Boston City Hospital. The votes were not on Beacon Hill, in Back Bay, on State Street, or in Scollay Square, and these old downtown neighborhoods, the last of the Brahmin strongholds, Curley let fall into decay.

The doors of City Hall and Curley's mansion on the Jamaicaway were thrown open to all comers without appointment, and Curley saw 200 people a day. They came seeking jobs, contracts, stop signs, playgrounds, promotions, dispensations, food, lodging, coal, insurance, or just a word in the right ear, and they got it. Curley's mayoralty was hugely expen-

sive of course, but Curley had a solution to that too. He ran the city on loaned money and credit, and when those ran out, he simply raised the tax rate and assessments on businesses and homes downtown, where the votes weren't.

James Michael Curley was playing Robin Hood, and he was proud of it, too. If he was padding the payroll, incurring sky-high debts, and maybe

lining his own pockets, at least he wasn't churning portfolios for the idle sons of robber barons, throwing honest workmen off the job, and directing Boston money and manpower to bigger profits out of town. His was a grudge match with the Yankee Establishment, and he said so frankly. "The Puritan has passed," he declared, "the Anglo-Saxon is a joke; a new and better America is here." Everybody

cheered but the Brahmins.

It can be said, in truth, that the Brahmins hated James Michael Curley. Every inch of breeding in them was offended by his brash and taunting mayoral style. Every vote he wooed and every dollar he spent infuriated them. For a while they put up a fight, trying to assert the ancient prerogatives of the Boston social register and State Street to dictate terms to the city. They sponsored candidates of their own, and organized watchdog committees to ride herd on City Hall: the Good Government Association, the Boston Finance Commission, and the Citizens' Municipal League—"Goo-goos" and the "State Street Wrecking Crew," as Curley called them as he barreled right over them. But mostly the old Brahmin establishment just steamed,

Both the North and West Ends of Boston are seen in this photograph dating 1900. The domed building in the upper left corner is Charles Street Jail, and immediately in front of the jail is the West End. To the right of center is the steeple of Old North Church, and to the right of that, the open space of Copp's Hill Burial Ground. Courtesy, Boston Public Library Print Department

for demographics and New Deal politics were against them. There was little choice but to shut up and pay as Curley squeezed the old downtown city tighter and tighter until the tax rate quintupled and State Street banks had collected a stack of worthless city promissory notes. Curley had the Brahmins by the throat.

The man was undeniably a fraud. He got his famous golden speaking voice from elocution classes at the Staley College of the Spoken Word. He got his shamrock-shuttered house on Jamaica Pond (which the city purchased in 1988 for $1.5 million) as a payoff from a contractor. He got many of his votes by tricks—registering "mattress men" from out of town in city boarding houses, spreading rumors that his opponent had a liking for young girls, and paying a Ku Klux Klansman $2,000 to launch a fake campaign against him so Curley could

fulminate self-righteously against the evils of bigotry. ("Politics and holiness are not always synonymous," laughed Curley. "There are times ... when, if you wish to win an election, you must do unto others as they wish to do unto you, but you must do it first.") He got his first jail term for cheating on a civil service exam, his second for bilking investors in a war contracts scheme, and only narrowly escaped a third stretch in the joint in a suit over mismanagement of city funds that ended in his having to pay back $42,629 to the treasury in installments of $500 a week.

In the end, Curley lost both face and power. The Archdiocese of Boston turned its back on him (Archbishop Cushing, later Cardinal Cushing, would not even speak the eulogy at his funeral), and the voters, tired of the growing scandals, abandoned him at the polls.

FORGING AHEAD

There was still a vibrancy to Boston as Curley left the stage after the Second World War, a vibrancy in the quality of life in the ethnic neighborhoods he owned, succored, and held dear. Many Boston oldsters still remember the era with affection, telling stories of babies born in tenement flats with only the help of neighbors, of boys shooting craps in the North End as one stood guard keeping an eye out for the cops, of Irish wakes where the pols turned out and slipped money to the grieving widow. But for all the cozy human dramas and neighborly compassion, Boston at mid-century was a sick city on the verge of bankruptcy. The bustle of the once-thriving seaport, the enterprise and investment of State Street, the rectitude and even dealing of City Hall—all were gone. The gyroscope was broken. Boston had lost her center.

Throughout her history, Boston has been a town obsessed with questions of community and right orderings. Her citizens have engaged in a long

Above: Mayor for a record sixteen years, four terms in succession, Kevin H. White was first elected in 1967. He established Little City Halls in the neighborhoods and a program of youth activities called Summerthing, which became hallmarks of his early years as mayor. Courtesy, Boston Public Library Print Department

Left: Mayor James M. Curley poses with his family. Courtesy, Boston Public Library Print Department

struggle to wrestle people and power into some proper and pleasing relationship. This is what the Puritans were up to when they set their Kingdom of God upon this City on a Hill, and this is what the patriots intended when they fired the shot heard round the world. When the teachers and the immigrants struggled together through lessons in the settlement house, they were working for a new community, and so was William Lloyd Garrison when he braved the wrath of the textile kings by publishing his abolitionist newspaper, the *Liberator,* on Washington Street. In the same way, the Brahmins on Beacon Hill have always held strong opinions about the right of men of property and privilege to run the town, and so did James Michael Curley when he opened the doors of City Hall to all comers from the ethnic neighborhoods and drove the Brahmins out. Bostonians had been wrangling about power, community, and rights for more than 300 years, but through it all there was always the conviction that Boston was worth fighting for.

It was this conviction that began to flag in the middle of the twentieth century. Boston, it seemed, no longer had the strength to command community. The Brahmins were disgusted with Boston and had retired behind their shuttered windows on Beacon Hill while Curley blew them raspberries from the street. The money men had abandoned the city wholesale, calling it too spent and too chancy for their business. By 1959 State Street

was poised to take receivership as the city's credit rating hit bottom. After the war the middle class also began its exodus, alarmed by the deterioration and rising tax rates in the central city and attracted by the green lawns and uncontentious stability of the suburbs. Even the working-class ethnic neighborhoods lost heart for Boston. As the young vets took their families out of town looking for work and cheaper housing, the old-timers remained behind, a thin line of defense against the urban blight and increasing numbers of transients who crept into the neighborhoods, not much caring who held the reins of the city so long as bills were paid and the kids came to visit once in a while. And so Boston began its dangerous skid into becom-

ing yet another of those tired, broken-down, former manufacturing towns of the Northeast—honored, if at all, for her former glories.

And yet, by the late 1950s, Boston began to come back, though not so much from any principled application of will or renewed sense of community direction, but through a sudden and rather surprising infusion of cash. Two things had happened in rapid succession: science came knocking on the doors of State Street, and John F. Kennedy went to the White House.

"It is the deepest conviction of men who praise their practical common sense that industrial activity is man's ultimate economic frontier," wrote the great American economist, John Kenneth Galbraith, from across the river at Harvard in 1980. "It is not

Above: Mayor John Collins receives a check from Bernard L. Boutin for urban renewal. Seated are Senators Kennedy and Saltonstall. Courtesy, Boston Public Library Print Department

Left: On October 5, 1947, political notables joined Archbishop Richard J. Cushing on the reviewing stand of the Holy Name Society parade. From the left are Senator Leverett Saltonstall, Senator Henry Cabot Lodge, Governor Robert F. Bradford, the Archbishop, and Boston Mayor John B. Hynes at the far right. Courtesy, Archives of the Archdiocese of Boston

so," he concluded.

Once people are reasonably supplied with goods, they want them to be better or to work better. And they become concerned with how they look. And, above all, people give attention to where they themselves live. It is the activities that improve operational quality, artistic quality, and the ambience of living that take over and become important. It is this sequence that has saved Boston and Massachusetts, and will save us in the future.

Galbraith is speaking of the now much-vaunted "Massachusetts Miracle," that marriage of business and technology that helped launch a governor of the Commonwealth to the Democratic Presidential nomination in the summer of 1988. But when a

tentative and rather bemused collection of MIT scientists first came to Boston looking for money to finance their backroom inventions after the war, State Street was skeptical. Trade and manufacturing they understood, but science and engineering were untried fields for capitalist venture. They invested, cautiously at first, and were only convinced when such unlikely commodities as radio tubes, optic filters, radioactive isotopes, and electronic modules turned technology into profit for Boston-based companies like Raytheon, Polaroid, Tracerlab, and Digital Equipment Corporation. "People said that it couldn't be done, and that we'd lose all our money," said Georges Doriot, president of American Research and Development Corporation, which

began funding high-tech ventures in the forties. "They said it was too dangerous, and nearly everyone thought we would fail." But they were wrong.

Science was the first source of ready cash for the recovery of Boston; federal money was the second. It started with Franklin Roosevelt's New Deal subsidies, then exploded with the social programs inaugurated under President John F. Kennedy. These programs continued, with the generous and helping hand of Boston's own House Speaker Thomas P. ("Tip") O'Neill, Jr., through the administrations of Lyndon Johnson.

This National Historic Site was the boyhood residence of President John Fitzgerald Kennedy. Photo © Gaye Hilsenrath

Suddenly there was federal money for all the helps and services needy Bostonians used to petition for, cap in hand, at City Hall—apartments, groceries, insurance, retirement benefits, legal advice, and medical care.

But most particularly there was money for urban renewal, both private money and federal funds. With this, downtown was salvaged and Boston regained her center. The ratty burlesque joints in old Scollay Square fell to make way for the new, no-nonsense, concrete-and-glass monuments to bureaucracy that were raised in Government Center. The old wharves and warehouses on the Waterfront were rescued for housing, shops, restaurants, excursion boats, and the New England Aquarium. Commercial development marched up and down Washington Street, luring shoppers back in from the suburbs. And in the old railroad yards of Back Bay rose the granddaddy commercial project of them all, the $200-million Prudential Center complex, so bold and so momentous that the *Globe* was moved to declare in 1958, "All the daring and imagination in this country today is not being spent on launching space missiles. Boston and Prudential are shooting for their own moon."

Not all of Boston's urban renewal projects rocketed off so bravely. While the downtown area was carefully and extravagantly revitalized, the outlying ethnic neighborhoods either continued to decay or were slated for the bulldozer in wholesale projects of "slum clearance." Neglect would have been the happier solution, as the residents of the West End were soon to find out. In February 1958 the wrecking crews arrived, and this once vibrant and colorful neighborhood of 23,000 immigrant Irish, Italians, and Russian Jews—no longer vibrant, but still home to 7,000 people—was gone. In its place rose luxury apartment towers, parking garages, and a

multi-screen cinema. The poor were just out of luck in Boston.

The outcry against the West End debacle was immediate and sobering. Not everyone, it seemed, shared this vision for Boston's glorious future—anyway not in their own backyards. Under threat of displacement and destruction, Boston's community spirit returned to the neighborhoods. Further renewal projects were stopped dead in their tracks, and the Boston Redevelopment Authority was sent packing to rethink its priorities.

Community activism spread beyond issues of slum clearance as the neighborhoods relearned the knack of voicing their varied concerns. In 1967 welfare mothers from Roxbury staged a sit-in at the Welfare Department, with the honest complaint that they were "tired of being treated like criminals ...of having to depend on suspicious and insulting social workers and at being completely at the mercy of a department we have no control over." Reasonable and effective words, these, from a black neighborhood so rough and tumble that it had shocked and entranced young Malcolm X on his first visit to Boston. "I spent my first month in town with my mouth hanging open," he remembers in his *Autobiography.*

I had never tasted a sip of liquor, never even smoked a cigarette, and here I saw little black children, ten and twelve years old, shooting craps, playing cards, fighting, getting grown-ups to put a penny or a nickel on their number for them, things like that. And these children threw around swear words I'd never heard before, even, and slang expressions that were just as new to me, such as "stud" and "cat" and "chick" and "cool" and "hip." Every night as I lay in bed I turned these new words over in my mind.

Above left: Senator Ted Kennedy holds a press conference. Photo © Gaye Hilsenrath

Left: Speaker of the House Tip O'Neill addresses an issue. Photo © Gaye Hilsenrath

But the welfare mothers wisely kept their neighborhood words to themselves, and while they could not move the Welfare Department, 1,000 people rallied to their cause in a demonstration on the Common several weeks later.

A year later, Italian housewives in East Boston demonstrated that they, too, knew something about neighborhood activism when they sat down in the middle of Maverick Street in their housedresses, and stopped the trucks that were carrying the fill that would transform the mudflats of Bird Island into another runway for Logan Airport. When slapped with an injunction, Anna De Fronzo, grandmother of 15 and organizer of the rebellion, uttered the classic words of community defiance of authority, "I don't give a damn. Let them arrest me. People have taken too much. They're fed up to here." And the city and the Port Authority backed off.

But in other neighborhoods, the mood was uglier as racial tension swept through Boston in the sixties and seventies in response to court-ordered busing. The old Irish neighborhoods of South Boston and Charlestown resented it, reviled it, fought it in cruel demonstrations of violence, and lost. "It's a tough time to be a senior in high school," said Kevin White, Boston's mayor at the time. "It's a trying time to be the mother of an elementary-school child in Boston. And it's not the greatest time to be mayor of this city, either. But, it is our time, and we must make the best of it." Boston was forging a new community, once again.

In Boston, history is inescapable. In the burying grounds rest the bones of Puritans so fierce their skull-and-crossbone headstones still send shivers down the spine. At your feet are the brick paths and red lines thoughtfully painted on the sidewalk to lead you along the Freedom Trail to sites of Revolutionary War significance. In the ethnic neighborhoods, foreign tongues and exotic merchandise recall 150 years of immigration to a city rarely willing to welcome newcomers, but always, in the end, making room for them. On the waterfront, the granite warehouses of the China Trade still hulk importantly among the gleaming shops and restaurants of new commercial ventures. And all around are the strong, upright, red brick and brownstone buildings announcing Boston's nineteenth-century pride in town and citizenry.

The wonder of it all is that Boston has not become a museum piece, has escaped becoming some self-congratulatory bit of set decoration on the stage of former glories. The city has tried several times in its history to rest on its laurels, but its people are too cussed and contrary to permit it. As it enters the second half of its fourth century, Boston still pursues money unabashedly, as it always has. It still struggles with questions of community and right ordering, as it always has. It is a prescription that will take Boston strongly into the twenty-first century, where it will not rest quiet either, because it doesn't know how.

Left: City Hall Plaza was built atop the site of Scollay Square, a notorious, honky-tonk district of ill repute. Photo © Peter H. Dreyer

Facing page: The rotunda of the State House is superbly detailed. Photo © Ulkrike Welsch

*The graceful arches supporting Rowes Wharf
frame the eclectic architectural style of the Boston
waterfront area. Photo © Martha Everson*

How the Puritan fathers would shudder to find themselves in downtown Boston today. For here, smack in the middle of their shining city on the hill—where Winthrop lived and John Wilson preached, where coins were proof of devil-dealings and hymns were considered amusement enough —is Boston boasting worldly boasts with no apology at all. "Welcome to the New Downtown—Financial Center and Midtown Cultural District—New England's capital of Enterprise and Entertainment."

From Washington Street east to the Waterfront, and State Street south to Chinatown, downtown Boston clamors with solicitations. You feel it at Downtown Crossing, where the retail giants, Filene's and Jordan Marsh, wage their window dressing wars; in the Theater District, where bright lights and greasepaint draw crowds to every show; on the Waterfront, where the aquarium lures you with fishy promises and cruise boats invite you on bracing excursions into the bay; down through the sleazy streets of the Combat Zone, where hookers hustle junkies and junkies hustle drugs; and on into the offices of the Financial District, where bankers tender offers and brokers option stocks. "Let us clothe you, amuse you, make your fortune, or tickle your fancy" —all through downtown Boston, Boston is busy making deals.

So much is going on downtown, and in such a small space, that it's difficult for the visitor, and even native Bostonians, to sort it all out. For downtown Boston is not so much a neighborhood as an arena. It is the city's countinghouse and playground, a jumble of activity with people making money, spending it, and getting away from the cares of all that dealing.

Downtown is Boston's most public district and its character has been forged by city fortunes and public tastes. But times change. Fortunes falter. Tastes get reconsidered. In Boston's 350-year quest after all that is profitable and pleasing in public life, downtown has seen many enterprises come and go, pleasures offered, pleasures scorned, and the mark of changing times is clear throughout the district. There is so much to see and ponder!

Downtown you will find eighteenth-century warehouses, a nineteenth-century customhouse, and twentieth-century investment houses—all within a few blocks of each other. There are stolid granite wharves built for the lumbering ships of the China trade, and sleek concrete-and-glass skyscrapers built for the fragile circuitry of the microchip trade. Bicycles, elevators, looms, clipper ships, telephones, and shoe machinery all have been built here, for Boston has put its money anywhere it could turn a profit.

But successes and failures abound in downtown Boston, and they often seem capricious. Boston's eminent architect, Charles Bulfinch, built his elegant Tontine Crescent townhouses downtown in 1796, then promptly went bankrupt and eventually landed in Court Street jail in the same year as he was chairman of selectmen and commissioner of police. But 14-year-old Eben Jordan arrived in Boston from Maine in 1836 with only change in his pocket, sold some cherry-colored ribbon to Boston's admiring housewives, and launched the Jordan Marsh department store to his everlasting fortune. Then in 1872, 67 acres of Boston business literally went up in smoke when the Great Fire broke out behind Beebe's dry-goods store and spread and spread until the entire area bounded by Washington Street, Milk Street, Summer, and Broad was completely destroyed. (But Jordan's luck held true; his store was spared.)

Morals have changed, too, in downtown Boston. On Milk Street the International Trust Company Building makes a bold statement of Boston's public values, circa 1893, with four chastely draped figures standing guard over the entryway, representing the sober virtues of commerce, industry, security, and fidelity. In 1988 the Financial District witnessed a bold statement of a different sort when the Transportation Building in Park Square mounted a daring exhibition of modern public art: six real-life toilets draped in black velvet

CHAPTER 3

The Bright Lights of the City

BY NANCY ZERBEY

squatting in the lobby. (Even today, in the New Downtown, Boston was shocked.)

There have been skirmishes over the morality of theater downtown, too. The Puritans forbade playacting of any kind, and even in 1792, the sheriff was called out to put an end to the frolic taking place on Hawley Street where citizens were staging *The School for Scandal*— "a serious crime" —under the guise of an improving moral lecture.

But thespians prevailed in Boston, and by 1935 downtown had built 24 of the finest theaters and concert halls in the country. Many of these buildings still stand in the Theater District, centered today on the intersection of Tremont and Stuart streets, where old classics like *The Nutcracker* and new classics like *Les Miserables* are staged. Just around the corner is the Naked I Cabaret in the heart of the Combat Zone, where Boston's preeminent stripper, Princess Cheyenne, used to strut her not inconsiderable stuff. But now Princess Cheyenne has retired from the stage to pursue a career as a personal body trainer, and the Combat Zone is being cleaned up (at least on the drawing boards of city planners and in the minds of arts committees, dreaming dreams of urban renewal and cultural renaissance in the newly named Midtown Cultural District).

Today's downtown Boston bustles in every direction where money and frolic can make a deal.

There is no "Money Trail" to lead you through the streets of downtown Boston, but there should be. For the

Mounted police are a common sight amidst the bustle of the Downtown Crossing. Photo © Justine Hill

area is renowned as the capital of conservative money management in America, the place where Brahmin merchant nabobs entrusted their fortunes to their Brahmin banker kin and watched their money grow in the nineteenth century when New York, Chicago, and Los Angeles were still upstarts in the world of finance.

Boston money has been made in occupations honorable and not-so-honorable ever since the Puritans found themselves short of change and so commenced coining their own, in defiance of British law reserving such privileges to the Crown, in 1652. (The coin was the famous "pine tree shilling," minted by John Hull on

Essex Street at the edge of today's Financial District. King Charles II mistook the scrubby New England pine for the mighty royal oak, and so the Puritans got away with it.) From that point on, you couldn't keep Boston money down. British warships couldn't strangle it out when they blockaded the harbor in 1774. Hurricanes couldn't drown it out, even when Cape Horn howlers swamped the Boston clipper ships carrying cash to the emperor in Canton during the China trade. The Great Fire of 1872 couldn't smoke it out, though it consumed the modern equivalent of one billion dollars of downtown business. No, Boston money doesn't quit; it just

grows and grows. And downtown's seen it all.

The Money Trail would begin at the head of State Street, near the Boston Stock Exchange Building at number 53. The Exchange was not a new idea when it was built in 1889 (a portion of the original facade still stands under the gleaming glass sky-scraper that now towers above it), for Boston money men had long discovered that mercantile association is good for commerce, and trading information is every bit as important as trading goods. (Not surprisingly, it was a Boston merchant, Edward Filene, who organized the United States Chamber of Commerce and opened the first one, on Milk Street, in downtown Boston.) In the eighteenth century the money men would meet at the Royal Exchange, later called the Exchange Tavern, at the corner of State and Congress streets. Here merchants and shipowners

Above left: The Old State House poses an anachronistic presence among the sleek and modern downtown office towers of the city. Photo © B. & J. McGrath

Above: Known locally as the "Lollipop" building, this prestigious structure at 100 Summer Street provides whimsical, aesthetic relief in the downtown area. Photo © Sarah Hood

would get drunk on flip, argue the best route to the Indies, and cook up schemes for avoiding import and export duties collected at the custom-house just down the street.

For the Money Trail links State Street to the Waterfront, for 200 years the dynamo and treasure house of Boston money. The wharves are downtown's special legacy, now carefully preserved and recycled after years of neglect, making Boston's Waterfront one of the most attractive and exciting in the nation.

There is Long Wharf, at the foot of State Street, begun in 1710 and once stretching half a mile out into the Bay, where the West Indian traders crammed their tropical fruits and molasses into red brick warehouses

Left: A high-rise building forms a towering abstraction in downtown Boston.
Photo © B. & J. McGrath

Below: The downtown district has been forged by the city's fortunes and public tastes.
Photo © Martha Everson

and smuggled Madeira and Dutch tea ashore. When Britain's colonial wars put a crimp in the West Indian trade, Long Wharf men did not lose heart, but turned to privateering, capturing enemy merchantmen at sea and disposing of the spoils in town. All the best families did it. In 1748 a Quincy family ship tied up at Long Wharf and offloaded 163 chests of silver and gold stolen from a gullible Spanish captain who believed his treasure ship was under attack on the high seas. But those weren't cannons trained on his ship, they were logs, hastily brought up on deck from the holds to intimidate the Spanish captain into surrender. The booty was carted up State Street and deposited in the Quincys' wine cellar to the acclamation of the Boston privateers who lined the street. ("Pirates,"

explained Godfrey Lowell Cabot, speaking of the ancestors who also built his family's fortune on privateering. "They were pirates, but now we're so refined we call them 'traders.'")

The Money Trail leads on to Central Wharf, at the foot of Milk Street, built according to plans drawn up by Bulfinch in 1816-1817 to accommodate the overflow of the China trade. The Revolution had nearly sunk the Boston fleet and bankrupted State Street. But Boston money men were not afraid to travel far to turn a profit. Soon Nootka Sound, Hawaii, Manila, and Macao were ports of call for Boston ships, and the granite warehouses of Central Wharf were crammed with iron tools and Jews' harps, which the Indians on the Pacific Coast fancied and would trade for

sea otter pelts, which the Chinese fancied and, in turn, would trade for silk and tea, which the whole world fancied, and soon Boston men were rich again.

Being rich, Boston merchants turned their attention to other ventures downtown. They banded together and built Broad Street, for example, as a speculative real estate development, and rented out the fine brick stores and warehouses to up-and-comers bullish on the China trade. But Francis Cabot Lowell had other ideas. In 1812 he rented space at Number 64 Broad Street, a building that still stands, and began fiddling

The Harbor Towers form nearly natural lighthouses for passing watercraft as they reflect the early morning sun along Boston Harbor.
Photo © Gene Peach

with spindles and bobbins and spools. Soon he had it. "I well recollect," wrote Nathan Appleton, one of Lowell's investment partners, "the state of admiration with which we sat by the hour watching the beautiful movement of this new and wonderful machine." Francis Cabot Lowell had perfected the power loom, and Boston's fortune in textiles was launched.

Francis Cabot Lowell was not a Cabot and Lowell for nothing. The offspring of privateers, Lowell stole the design for the loom from the British. Nothing actually *illegal,* mind you—no outright violation of Britain's strict embargo on the export of textile machinery and mechanical designs. Lowell just happened to be in England recovering from a nervous condition and merely toured a num-

Above: These craft are moored near the Union Wharf. Photo © Martha Everson

Right: The financial district offers much unique office space. Photo © Lee C. Hauenstein

ber of Birmingham and Manchester cotton mills and asked a lot of questions that the machine operators, being good sports, obligingly answered. No one suspected that poor, nervous Lowell was a mechanical genius who had little trouble keeping the loom's specifications under his hat until he could return to Boston and re-create it, piece by piece, on Broad Street.

With the booming textile industry, the character of downtown changed. By the 1830s, the Waterfront had regeared for the domestic trade, with twice as many ships visiting coastal ports as were sailing off to foreign climes. Nathaniel Hawthorne witnessed the boom and hated everything to do with it. But 1839 was a bad year for Hawthorne. His writing wasn't going well. His wedding plans were stalled for lack of marriage money, and, at the age of 34, he was still living with his mother in Salem. In desperation Hawthorne took an inspector's job at the old customhouse at the foot of State Street— "that unblest Custom House," he wrote, "that makes such havoc with my wits." There he buckled down to the work of inspecting holds, weighing cargoes, and breaking up seamen's fights on the docks.

How Hawthorne loathed the entire Waterfront trade! "Long Wharf is devoted to ponderous, evil-smelling, inelegant necessaries of life," he complained to his fiancee: bales of cotton from New Orleans, barrels of molasses, vats of linseed oil, casks of nails, barges of coal that grimed his face and salt that encrusted his very handsome wavy locks. It was no job for an aesthete. But these "inelegant necessaries of life" brought Hawthorne $1,500 a year—enough to get him out of the customhouse in 1841 to marry Sophia Peabody and retire to

Balloons released from the Customs House rise past the Clock Tower in this view of the downtown area. Photo © Kathy Tarantola

the utopian community at Brooks Farm.

And these same "inelegant necessaries of life" were making Boston richer still; so rich, that even as Hawthorne toiled away in the old customhouse, a grand new customhouse was being built nearby because the old one was not big enough to keep up with Boston money. This astonishing building, in the style of a Greek temple with thirty-two 46-ton fluted Doric columns standing guard over the treasures within, is a famous Boston landmark that still stands in McKinley Square. It is surmounted now by a 495-foot-high tower, Boston's first skyscraper, built in 1911 to provide more office space for the booming business at the customhouse.

From the customhouse the Money Trail would follow Boston business

99 High Street (left) is one of the institutions lining Boston's Financial District.
Photo © Kenneth Martin

away from the Waterfront and deeper into downtown, up State Street again, to the Cunard Building at Number 126. Here figures of Neptune cavort on the facade, announcing the site where Samuel Cunard opened the Royal Mail Steam Packet Company in 1839 to the everlasting gratitude of the thousands of immigrants who boarded his transatlantic steamships and swarmed to this premier port of America in the 1840s.

Next door, at Number 114 State Street, stands the Richards Building, a distinguished cast-iron building built for shipping firms engaged in yet another Boston business venture. For, in 1849, Boston's money men had caught the scent of gold clear from California. The Gold Rush was on, and enterprising investors rushed straight down State Street to the Waterfront again. They loaded up their clipper ships with beef and biscuits to feed the miners, added picks and shovels for clawing out the gold, and guns to fend off bad guys in the

rowdy streets of San Francisco, then sent their Boston ships around the Horn again to make another fortune. The profits were enormous. Flour sold for $44 a barrel in the mining towns; eggs fetched $2 a dozen; and lumber brought a 1,000 percent return. Boston's first clipper ship, the *Surprise*, paid for herself and cleared $50,000 for her investors—all on her maiden voyage.

But Boston money is never caught by surprise, and by the time the Gold Rush petered out in the 1850s, the investment houses on State Street had already turned their attention from trade to other promising ventures. Western railroads, Denver stockyards, Kansas real estate, Nevada silver mines, Pennsylvania coal mines, Michigan copper mines—Boston was making money out of town and bringing it all back home to State Street. State Street was America's nineteenth-century Wall Street, and the money men weren't too proud to boast about it. "When-

ever any coal mines are made accessible, or ill-managed Rail Roads made available, or indeed any scheme that requires Capital & intelligence they come to Boston for help," observed John Murray Forbes, a founder of the Boston investment dynasty that began with "Black Ben" Forbes peddling opium to the Chinese and continues today with Malcolm Forbes fondling Fabergé eggs in the offices of the business magazine that bears the family name. "And those that take hold do it on such terms that they play with sure cards."

The surest cards were on the western railroads. Boston money had never shrunk from long journeys if there was profit at the end of the line. So, by 1845, State Street had already mustered $30 million from the China trade and textile mills and put it into railroad building, thus securing nearly a quarter of the total national railroad investment. The investment was knowing, shrewd, and lucrative. "The Boston people are certainly the only Community who understand Rail Roads," remarked the railroad analyst J.J. Stackpole in 1845. "At the present time they have more money than they know what to do with."

Business was also brisk elsewhere downtown at mid-century, though the enterprises were more homegrown and more mundane than in the investment houses on State Street. In fact business was so good that it was invading former residential districts. If it could, our Money Trail would lead us down Franklin Street to Tontine Crescent, Bulfinch's elegant townhouse debacle, which was torn down in 1858 to make way for the stores and warehouses of Boston's flourishing wool industry. It would continue on down Franklin Street to Winthrop Square, where Eben Jordan and James M. Beebe had their imposing dry-goods stores, and on to Church Green, on Summer Street, then "the handsomest street in Boston" and soon to become the leather and shoe-making district. This was

downtown in its heyday of commerce and finance, but the Money Trail won't show us any of these prosperous sites, for in 1872 everything in Boston's booming downtown was laid to ashes.

By the time the watchman turned in his alarm at Call Box Number 52, still standing in grim memorial at the corner of Lincoln and Summer streets, the Great Fire of Saturday, November 9, 1872, was already burning out of control. It had started, historians believe, in a wooden elevator shaft in a dry-goods warehouse at the corner of Summer and Kingston streets. It spread, inexorably, from one building to another, for the old mansard roofs of the downtown district were made of wood and provided perfect tinder. "I saw tall buildings catch in their roofs like huge matches, and blaze there," recalled Henry Cabot Lodge, who stood watching, with much of Boston, in helpless wonder as 67 acres and 767 buildings burned completely to the ground.

Bucket brigades were of no use, nor streams of harbor water pumped from

Architecture in the Financial District is visually striking. Photo © Judith Canty

fire tugs in the bay, nor relief engines clanging in from stations as far away as Providence and New Haven, nor even dynamite and gunpowder set to level buildings in the path of the inferno in hopes of creating a fire break. The fire just raged on and on, taking with it the accumulated stores of downtown: felt hats and leather gloves, workmen's boots and bolts of cotton, woolen trousers in one building and suspenders in another, food and groceries from the stores of provisioners who catered to the workers of the district. On State Street, nervous merchants and investors mobbed the offices of the Union Safety Deposit Vaults, calling for their railroad stocks and real estate bonds and insurance certificates. On the Waterfront, coal barges went up in flames and fish

Office workers pass beneath the decorative portals in the lobby of One Financial Center.
Photo © Martha Everson

caught fire on the docks, for the fire did not stop until it ran into the waters of the harbor.

By Monday thousands of Bostonians were out of work, merchants had lost $60 million in merchandise, and the insurance companies were bankrupt. "DEVASTATION," blared the *Globe* headline. "The city weeps in dust and ashes," wrote a contemporary observer, "and the wealthy are made poor."

But Boston money had seen trouble before, and in time downtown Boston bounced back again. Almost all the buildings seen today were raised after the fire, on faith that Boston money would endure, and it did. It got some help from Alexander Graham Bell, who arrived in Boston the year of the fire and set about inventing the telephone in a fifth floor attic room overlooking Scollay Square. His famous call to his assistant Watson was placed in Bell's rented apartment at 3 Exeter Street, now the site of the

Lafayette Plaza shopping mall, on March 10, 1876.

State Street was quick to answer the call to profit. Within two years the fledgling Bell Telephone Company was scooped up by William Forbes, who fended off an attack by New York-based Western Union, and by 1880 the nation's telephone system was a monopoly of Boston investors. Monopoly was profitable in the days before antitrust actions and divestiture; from 1880 to 1884 alone this new blue-chip telephone stock paid out $25 million in dividends, more than half of it into Boston portfolios. Today the New England Telephone Company building stands across Franklin Street from the 34-story State Street Bank building in the heart of the Financial District, a fitting testament in modern concrete and glass to that nineteenth-century partnership of banking and invention that propelled Boston money into the twentieth century.

But it wasn't enough. By 1930, Boston business and the downtown district had stalled. New York had grabbed away the lion's share of East Coast shipping and commerce, and was fast becoming America's financial center. On State Street Boston's enterprising spirit flagged as the money men became more concerned with protecting old fortunes than making new ones. In this era of family trusts and fiduciary responsibility, opportunity had became suspect and risk was shunned. Robber barons were not welcome here. Boston had become a cautious town of money managers, not money makers.

Above: The architecture of Rowes Wharf provides the waterfront area with timeless beauty.
Photo © Martha Everson

Left: An eclectic blend of architecture is found in the Downtown area. Photo © Kathy Tarantola

The Brahmin establishment had lost more than heart. It had also lost political control of Boston to the Irish bosses. James Michael Curley was mayor, and his was an era of extravagant municipal spending (but not in downtown). Curley's political base lay in the ethnic neighborhoods, many of them recently annexed to Boston, and when there were streets to mend or parks to dedicate or buildings to raise, the city's tax money went to Dorchester, Charlestown, East Boston, Roxbury, and South Boston, where the votes were. And when the treasury dwindled, taxes and valuations

Above: Many different styles of architecture can be found on a stroll through South Boston. This scene is on East Broadway. Photo © Gene Peach

Left: These charming homes are located in Dorchester. Photo © Kenneth Martin

were simply raised against the business properties downtown.

Curley was playing Robin Hood, and downtown, already in a business slump, began to suffer from neglect and abandonment. There was trouble up and down the Money Trail. The once-bustling waterfront was now home port to a fleet of derelicts rotting at the spavined wharves. Companies began moving out in search of more congenial business climates elsewhere. There was little new building.

Right: Charlestown was one neighborhood targeted for renovation funding due to its large voter base. Photo © Stanley Rowin

Below: The prestigious Fenway neighborhood features these residences. Photo © Stanley Rowin

And Scollay Square, the once-respectable, tree-lined residential neighborhood at the intersection of Tremont and old Court streets, had become a notorious precinct of saloons, tattoo parlors, fleabag hotels, and hock shops.

Run-down as it was, there are those who remember Scollay Square fondly from their salad days as undergraduates and servicemen-on-leave in the first half of this century. For here was the Old Howard theater, that "sink of sin" where a rollicking good time could be had, sitting pie-eyed in the balcony watching a repertoire of lowbrow acts that included sword swallowers, fire eaters, a human fly scrambling across the ceiling, boxing matches, and that perennial favorite, Dainty Violet Mascotte and Her

Thirty Merry Maids. State Street sniffed and ladies' morality societies fumed, but the entertainment was lively and the pitch was pure downtown salesmanship. "You Boys in the Know will Get a Wallop out of Violet Mascotte and her Merry Maids," trumpeted the advertisements:

Thirty, Count Them; Lovely, Lively, Artery Softeners, Good for That Tired Feeling, With their Bear Skins, and Oh, My! But a Word to the Wise is Enough, and the Wisenheimers know There is Always Something Doing at the Old Howard from 3 to 11.

All good fun, perhaps, but downtown had not seen such dismal days since the Puritan founding. By 1959 the city's credit rating was in the cellar, and State Street business leaders had organized a coordinating committee to steer Boston through what seemed to be certain bankruptcy and receivership. Fortune did not return to the Money Trail until the 1960s, when a combination of new business opportunity, new capital, and urban renewal rescued the district. The catalyst came not from the venerable Boston money-makers of trade, textiles, and

Above: The Aquarium is a central fixture of the commercial waterfront area. Photo © Justine Hill

Below: Old Scollay Square was razed to make way for the new Government Center, home of the town's City Hall. Photo © Gene Peach

trusts, but rather from an upstart enterprise—technology.

State Street was leery at first when MIT scientists came looking for money after the war. It seemed a little, well, *risky* to put conservative trust money on all these newfangled inventions and futuristic brainstorms that kept turning up at the door—radio tubes, optic filters, missile guidance systems, and electronic circuit boards. But in time the new high-tech companies and research and development firms were making solid names for themselves—names like Raytheon, Polaroid, National Research Corporation, Itek, Digital Equipment Corporation, Prime, and Wang—and in time they were making solid profits for a new breed of venture capitalists

on State Street. Boston money was back in the game, and the downtown boys had a new spring in their step.

Physically, too, downtown began to assume the air of prosperity, confidence, and diligent hard work seen here today. First old Scollay Square was razed to make way for the new Government Center. Now bureaucrats toil where Dainty Violet used to do whatever it is she did so well with the bear skins. The Waterfront was reclaimed for shops, condos, restaurants, and recreation. Washington Street saw new commercial development at Downtown Crossing and Lafayette Place, Boston's answer to the retail challenge of the suburban malls. And now plans are afoot to bring culture back downtown by restoring the Theater District and luring museums like the Institute of Contemporary Art to new downtown quarters.

Today Boston money rallies as it always did, turning pretty deals and tidy profits in downtown, because you can't keep Boston money down. "Boston money is the best money," said Serge Semenenko, the Boston banking genius who reportedly arranged

$5 billion worth of loans for First National Bank of Boston without suffering a single loss in the 1960s, "for we stay with it through thick and thin."

No visit to downtown would be complete without a contemporary stop on the Money Trail, a pilgrimage to Downtown Crossing where one will find the "World Famous Filene's Automatic Markdown Basement Store," known to bargain hunters everywhere simply as "The Basement." This is the quintessential downtown, where enterprise *is* enter-

tainment, and great deals are the order of every business day.

This is no ordinary discount store. Here the merchandise comes rolling in, half a football field of trailer-length a day, from Brooks and Saks and Neiman Marcus and some stores you never heard of, and out it goes again in shopping bags, sometimes 18,000 dresses in a single day, $90 million worth of business a year. You can take your bargain right off the racks as the stock boys push them down the aisles from the loading platform, or you can wait. And here

the gambling fun begins. (*If* you can stand the suspense and if some other shopper doesn't beat you to the cash register). Because after 12 shopping days the bargain price is reduced 25 percent, then another 25 percent after six more days, until by the 24th day on the floor that knock-out dress or camel hair coat is sold for 75 percent off the original Basement price.

Faneuil Hall, Quincy Marketplace, and the Custom House Clock Tower figure prominently in this photo of the commercial waterfront. Photo © Justine Hill

This gazebo in Belmont, is surrounded with the colors of autumn. Photo © Kenneth Martin

It's a game true shoppers relish, and a carnival no visitor should miss. It begins in the Washington Street Arcade, a brick-paved outdoor mall closed to traffic and thrown wide open to the public. There are street musicians playing calypso on genuine 55-gallon steel drums, beggars cadging quarters, pushcart vendors hawking Red Sox caps and *Cheers* sweatshirts, and shoppers planning strategies at cafe tables under gaily striped umbrellas. ("Just let me find where the sweaters are," says one to another, "*then* we'll go back to the hotel.")

Their game plans set, they enter. They sail right past the salesclerk offering a squirt of Estee Lauder's lat-est fragrance, and march straight down the stairs. One stop at the automatic teller machine (thoughtfully placed at the entrance for shoppers' convenience), and out onto the floor.

There's nothing like it anywhere in Boston: mountains of sneakers, heaps of shorts, jackets, and blouses askew on hangers (when they're not dropped on the floor). The Brooks Brothers shirts stay neat in their plastic envelopes, but the Marshall Field slacks are all tangled up in the center aisle.

And there they are—a tumble of sweaters! Next to them is a special purchase of overstocked dhurrie rugs from Lord and Taylor, dumped, unaccountably, on the floor in Children's World. Designer names, brand names, no-names: one can get most anything at The Basement.

And, in a typically Bostonian twist, the shark hunt of commerce gets a civilizing dose of philanthropy in Filene's Basement. Any merchandise not sold after 30 days is donated to charity. Or, shoppers can take it with them at the 75 percent markdown price by making out a check to the charity of their choice among the list of more than 20 worthy causes supported by the store. Old William Filene, the German immigrant capmaker who started all this madness in 1909, who organized the U.S. Chamber of Commerce in 1912, and who knew a good deal when he saw one in Boston's downtown, would be proud.

Yes, downtown is much more lively than one might expect of stodgy old Boston. There is old money invested in trust funds and mad money spent on chorus girls. You'll see tough guys smoking marijuana on the street corner and old boys smoking cigars in private clubs. There's a former Federal Reserve Bank turned into an elegant French hotel (the Meridien) which hosts a "chocolate bar" each weekend afternoon, and a new Federal Reserve

Bank that hosts fine arts exhibitions in its sky-lit gallery every day of the year. You can have a proper Boston lunch with your banker in a private dining room at Locke-Ober's famous restaurant in Winter Place, or you can dine on dim sum in Chinatown.

Soon you will be able to visit the old customhouse, purchased by the city from the federal government in 1987 for $10 million. (If only the city can figure out what to *do* with it.) The skyscraping tower will house luxurious offices and the old Greek temple base will house some sort of museum—this much is known. But rival developers are still pitching their museum schemes, and whether you'll be treated to a history of maritime commerce, New England sports, or Boston civic enterprises will depend on who makes the best deal. Downtown there's a little of everything. You'll find wheeler-dealers and drug dealers, fine arts and martial arts, pushcart peddlers and flesh peddlers, real-estate promoters and sports promoters, stockbrokers and pawnbrokers. There is Boston established, Boston gone-to-seed, and Boston up-and-coming. Downtown Boston doesn't quite know where it's going, but it keeps heading there, nevertheless, straight into the twenty-first century.

Left: The Oriental architecture of Chinatown is a continuation of the variety of cultural decoration in the city. Photo © Gene Peach

Below: A nineteenth century partnership of banking and invention propelled Boston into the twentieth century. Photo © Judith Canty

Narrow buildings line narrow streets in the North End of Boston. Photo © Kenneth Martin

NORTH END

No neighborhood of Boston has seen such a parade of inspired purposes, grim resolutions, and lunatic ideas as the North End. The Puritans came there in 1630 seeking nothing less than the Kingdom of God on earth, and they got it. Then there was John Childs, a genial madman who, in the summer of 1757, got a notion to fly. And so he did, by strapping on wings of uncertain design and launching himself from the steeple of Old North Church, firing a pistol in the air as he sailed triumphant into the crowd of admiring North Enders below. Eighteen years later, as every schoolboy knows, Paul Revere crept through these North End streets, hung his lanterns high in the same church tower, and dashed off on his midnight ride to free Boston from the English king who would squelch such strange and wonderful ambitions. The North End is Boston's inspiration and its soul.

It is also Boston's "ethnic quarter," for in the nineteenth century the Cunard Steamship Line brought thousands of immigrants to the port of Boston and dumped them, dazed and full of the hope of last resort, into the brutal tenements of the North End. First came the Irish, men of brawn and brag, who built the city stone by stone and then seized control of the political machine and bossed the city for a hundred years, vote by vote. Then came the Jews from Russia with their scissors and cloth, opening hab-

erdasheries and dry-goods stores on Salem Street and setting the ark of their covenant in a synagogue around the corner, just two blocks from where the Puritans, in a sectarian rage, had nailed shut the door of the Baptist meetinghouse in 1680.

The immigrants did not come to the North End for the bracing seaside air and charming cobbled streets. They came to the North End because it was a horrid place and this was all they could afford. Hemmed in by a brawling, stinking, and dangerous waterfront, they worked 16-hour days for starvation wages and crammed their families into any warehouse, coal bin, barrel storeroom, or hunchover attic they could find. No decent Bostonian would stand to live there. No bank would lend money on North End property. The newcomers were despised, and they had the neighborhood all to themselves.

But the immigrants were every bit as resolute as the Puritans and patriots who preceded them in the North End. The Irish and the Jews were determined to get out, and they did. But then the Italians came and stayed to work the docks and feed the town. Today the Russian synagogue is a Knights of Columbus Hall. There are no more groggeries and gin mills, but Hanover Street is lined with innumerable cantinas, tavernittas, cafes, and ristorantes. And each summer during festa time, rollicking Italian bands parade with statues of their patron saints

through the streets of the old "Black Hole" and "Murder District," where sailors used to bed the whores and wager in the rat pits.

Today's visitor to the North End is likely to be following the Freedom Trail from the marketplace at Faneuil Hall. He has come dutifully, prepared to be edified at the many worthy patriotic stations of the neighborhood. There is Paul Revere's house to visit, and a bust of George Washington to contemplate in Old North Church. There is a Bulfinch church to admire (Saint Stephen's), and Copp's Hill burying ground, where the Reverends Mather have their tomb at a safe distance from the monument to Prince Hall. Hall, a former slave turned Revolutionary War hero, was a leader of Boston's free black community when this section of the North End was known as New Guinea, or less politely, Nigger Hill.

The Freedom Trail through the North End is an educational tour, all right, and not to be missed. But it's the present energy of the place that most captivates the visitor. Eat! Drink! Dance! Pray! Parade in the streets; hector the reluctant shopper; argue with all comers. The North End is a neighborhood that lives in the active voice and rings with the imperative mode. The enthusiasm is contagious, and many a dogged Freedom Trailer is astonished to find himself carrying home some exotic merchandise pressed upon him by one

CHAPTER 4

A Tour of the Town

BY NANCY ZERBEY

of the North End's very persuasive Italian shopkeepers: some kitchen contraption for the wife, a tomato grinder or expresso maker perhaps, or frankincense tears and marzipan rabbits, or confirmation dresses—those fairy tales of lace and veil that capture the hearts of little girls and their fathers everywhere, never mind that they aren't Catholic. Here in the neighborhood where freedom was hatched, there is freedom to do as you please.

By all means start at the Paul Revere House, which 200,000 people visit each year. Most come away with the wrong impression, for Paul Revere's house is not at all what one would expect. Mr. Revere, it appears, was no struggling revolutionary. He was a shrewd and prosperous businessman, a man not above stealing other men's designs for the copperplate engravings on which he made his first fortune. On that fortune he bought this house and decorated it according to his vibrant and rather elegant tastes. There is a feather bed in the master bedroom, imported fabric on the wing-back chair, a stunning inlaid highboy in the corner, and brightly patterned hand-blocked wallpaper. The place looks like a decorator's showplace·on a house and gardens tour. There is no hint here of toddlers bashing into things, no sense of the exhausted horseman stamping about in muddy boots, anxiously awaiting some clandestine meeting of traitors to the Crown.

In Paul Revere's house there is the same eerie sense of unreality that too often marks Boston's presentation of its venerable history and landmarks.

Left: Schoolgirls parade through the streets of the North End during an Italian festival. Photo © Kenneth Martin

Below: In this aerial view of the North End, the white steeple in the center background is the Old North Church. Photo © Stanley Rowin

Everything is solid, sure, and larger than life—full of heroic inevitability. Just walk around the corner to the Paul Revere Mall and take a hard look at the statue of our hero. Was there ever a more muscled steed or more large and confident rider? Stroll to the other end of the mall and feast your eyes on the soaring spire of Old North Church. Surely God Himself was there that night to bless those beacons of liberty blazing high in the tower. And listen, my children, one more

Above: During Italian festivals, food vendors sell steaming hot sausage and peppers, fried mozzarella, calzone, and delicate Italian pastries. Photo © Kenneth Martin

Right: Italian festivals celebrate Roman Catholic saints. A shrine is erected for the saint whose day is being celebrated, and devout individuals make donations and pray for special blessings. Photo © Kenneth Martin

time to Longfellow's epic verse with its galloping, inexorable cadences:

One if by land and two if by sea
And I on the opposite shore will be
Ready to ride and spread the alarm
Through every Middlesex village and
farm.

Can any patriotic heart fail to stir at this paean to America's rightful destiny?

In reality, Paul Revere very nearly didn't make it to the opposite shore. The British had discovered the lanterns, and while Revere's co-conspirator, Captain John Pulling, Jr., hid out under a wine barrel in his cellar on Ann Street, Revere himself made

Above: The Paul Revere House located at 19 North Square has been renovated and is currently open to the public. Photo © Justine Hill

Above right: The Old North Church, built in 1723, was made famous by the Longfellow poem "Paul Revere's Ride." Today its belfry holds the church's original bells that were cast in 1744. Photo © Stanley Rowin

good his escape across the Charles in a heartstopping row directly under the guns of the warship *Somerset* with a full moon rising over the exceeding danger of his enterprise. Once across, he did succeed in rousing Sam Adams and John Hancock from their slumbers in Lexington (Hancock had been out late spooning with his sweetheart, Dorothy Quincy), only to be ambushed by a British patrol in a cow pasture. There was nothing in the least heroic about the encounter. As Revere himself tells us, "Major Mitchell of the 5th Reg. Clapped his Pistol to my head, and said he was go-

ing to ask me some questions and if I did not tell him the truth he would blow my brains out." A sergeant then appropriated Revere's good horse, drove off his own, and left Revere to walk back to a tavern in town to inquire after the news he had meant to deliver himself. The news, of course, was dire: 10 men dead on Lexington Green, 5 more at Concord Bridge, and the British already plotting their revenge at Bunker Hill.

The Old North is a beautiful church, graceful and strong and true. But it, like Paul Revere's house, is another piece of set decoration in

Boston's self-congratulatory memorial to itself and to American freedom. Standing in the tower today, looking out past the USS *Constitution* and the Bunker Hill monument, it is hard to appreciate how much was at stake that night more than 200 years ago. When Boston starts looking like a museum piece (and it does, all too often), it is time to hit the North End streets again to drink in the very human determinations and frailties of its residents.

In the North End everyone comes to the coffeehouse to watch the world go by. You can't miss it, because the life of the North End is conducted in the street. Old sailors shuffle off to the Mariner's House, two doors down from Paul Revere's house, where a bed can still be had for $3.50 a week. Then come the teenage girls strolling home from mass at Saint Stephen's. The tradesmen are out in force, too, and the streets teem with their energy and wares. Pyramids of oranges topple onto the sidewalks outside the fruit sellers' shops on Hanover Street. The Anastasi Brothers' gaily painted trucks rumble by, carrying bananas to the market under the expressway where they're sold under a banner urging, "Go Bananas!"

The abundance of the marketplace finds its way to the tables of the North End's many restaurants. The mainstay is hearty southern Italian fare, nothing fancy. For the first course you'll get a dish of olives and celery, or maybe a hunk of bread to dip in olive oil—some simple, chewy, stomach-starting stuff prepared by Mamma in the kitchen. For the main course, there's manicotti or lasagne or meat balls or fish. The fish is served alla siciliana or alla romana if you prefer,

Left: The ride of Paul Revere is commemorated with this statue of Revere on horseback in front of the Old North Church. Photo © Stanley Rowin

Below: Tranquility is found in the Peace Garden on Hanover Street. Photo © Kenneth Martin

and if you're the type to quibble over what kind of fish, then you're better off down the block where the menu is more elaborate and pricey. It's still Italian food, but here it is called cuisine. The nappery's pink, there are dates on the wine labels, and the pasta gets dressed up as "tagliatelli verde portofino" —that's green fettucini with mushrooms and prosciutto and peas. The proprietors are proud of the newfangled fare and happy to serve their upscale clientele, but on Easter Sunday, when the restaurant is closed to the public and Mamma herself is the guest of honor, the family sits down to ziti and tomato sauce, with anchovies on the side. Food, just food, and lots of it.

In the coffeehouse the conversation turns to changing times in the old North End. There is bad news: old Grande, the barber, is closing up shop—after 82 years there are no Grandes left who want to cut hair. Rents are going up again. That is good, if you own some property, but listen to this. Those new condos chiseled out of old Lincoln Wharf are selling for $181,090 for two bedrooms and $299,390 for three. That is $118,000 for a bedroom! But who's surprised? It said in the *Globe* the other day that the Highway Department wants another *billion* dollars to fix up the expressway that rattles along the Central Artery. A fancy new road to carry fancy new people into the old North End. But the Italian North Enders are a generous people. "I don't mind the new people," a woman is overheard to say. "But don't make us feel like nobodies."

No, they are not nobodies. They have much in common with the momentous history that preceded them in the North End. Paul Revere was a businessman. And John F. ("Honey Fitz") Fitzgerald galvanized the North End immigrants on the promise of "A Bigger, Better and Busier Boston" over 75 years ago. All came to the North End from somewhere else, demanded respect and a piece of freedom, and got it. This is what is so stirring about the North End. More than any other neighborhood of Boston, the North End has the energy and life that reminds us that history is made on the dreams and determination of ordinary people.

Above left: Caffe' Pompei offers only the finest Spumoni and Espresso. Photo © Justine Hill

Above: Ristorante Lucia gathers a crowd on a summer evening. Photo © Kenneth Martin

BACK BAY

When the object is to give a good impression, the visitor to Boston is taken to Back Bay. It is a stately neighborhood of fine old houses and upscale commerce, stretching west along the Charles between Beacon Hill and the Fenway, and marching south through a blessedly well-gridded street plan to Boylston Street and Copley Square, where it gives way to the South End. The Back Bay is Boston in the deliberate mode, all monumental elegance and self-conscious style, calculated to impress. And so it does.

Here is beautiful Commonwealth Avenue, a mall as grand and broad as any Paris boulevard, where retired gentlemen go to read their weekly Barron's and lift their hats to ladies walking afghan hounds. Here is Emmanuel Church, whose congregation mounts a full-scale Bach cantata each Sunday as part of the 11:00 liturgy. To Newbury and Boylston streets come blushing about-to-be brides trying on gowns at Priscilla's of Boston and sizing tiaras at Shreve Crump and Low. And soaring above it all is the Hancock Tower, 60 stories of shimmering blue glass thrust like a knife into the stone heart of Copley Square, where tourists and townsmen alike flock to the observation deck for

breathtaking views of the city and harbor.

But the most impressive part of all Back Bay lies beneath your feet. Dig down under the asphalt and you'll find horseshoes, skirt hoops, tons and tons of gravel, and the remains of a railman's lunch. Dig down further and you'll find clamshells and eel skeletons oozing up through the mud. Back Bay's solidity is only apparent. One hundred fifty years ago, Back Bay was a swamp.

Boston has never suffered its topography gladly. The Puritans had not been here many years before they corralled the tidal waters of the North End to make the Mill Pond. Nor were the colonial merchants and shipwrights content to huddle meekly on Boston's ragged shoreline; they threw their granite wharves and jetties out half a mile into Massachusetts Bay. While San Francisco ordered cable cars to climb her famous hills, Boston took up pick and shovel and simply cut hers down. And so, when Boston's population grew beyond the bounds of Shawmut's strangling peninsula in the nineteenth century, Boston's antlike instinct for civil engineering struck again, and the Back Bay was filled in.

Every 44 minutes, night and day, for more than 20 years, a train of 35 rail cars would pull into the gravel pits in Needham, nine miles away. There that amazing new invention, the steam shovel, would load the cars— "Two scoops, you're done, move on!" —and send them back to Boston to dump their loads on the smelly tidal flats of the Charles. And so the Back Bay grew acre by acre, ton by ton, 2,500 cubic yards a day through civil war and assassination, centennial celebration and Great Fire, until the job was done. By 1882 this former garbage dump and sewage field had been transformed by sheer human will and industrial might into 450 acres of

Above: Beacon Street blossoms each spring. Photo © Kathy Tarantola

Left: Marlborough Street is a vision in pink when the Magnolia trees bloom. Photo © Sarah Hood

Facing Page: With each new season color comes alive on Commonwealth Avenue. Photo © Gene Peach

Page 91: The John Hancock Tower, home of the John Hancock Mutual Life Insurance Company, stands tall over Copley Square. Photo © Ulrike Welsch

new land for the asking. And here the most fashionable of Bostonians commenced to build.

No visitor is in Back Bay very long before he finds himself looking upward, heedless of the baby carriages and messenger boys in his path. He is gazing in astonishment at the architecture. Few can put names to what they see, but it doesn't matter what you call them—these oriel windows and mansard roofs; porticos, pediments, pilasters, and portes-cochere; turrets and towers and gargoyles. It is enough to recognize that something truly amazing is going on here. Some

architectural genius, something eloquent and grand and sometimes flatly ridiculous, once whirled through these streets and left its stony stamp upon the city. Not a handful of houses, but the entire Back Bay is enshrined in the National Register of Historic Places. It is the most remarkable example of Victorian architecture in the country.

The Victorians had eclectic tastes, less modesty than we're led to think, and fewer scruples. A wrought-iron balcony graces the Palladian window at 32 Hereford Street; it was carried off from the Tuileries Palace after

Paris erupted in riots in 1871. An Italian Renaissance Revival mansion stands at 150 Beacon Street. Its stately Ionic columns and fierce stone face proclaim the uprightness of its owner, Alvan T. Fuller, governor of the Commonwealth, representative to Congress, and a man whose instinct for up-and-coming profit resulted in the Fuller Cadillac Company. Fuller didn't care much for the double brownstone row house that first was raised on this spot, so he simply tore it down. Or perhaps he didn't care for the former occupant, Isabella Stewart (Mrs. Jack) Gardner, that

marvelous scandal of a woman who walked down Tremont Street with a lion at her side and received her guests on Beacon Street while perched in the branches of a mimosa

Below: Darkness falls on Boston's Back Bay. Photo © Gene Peach

Right: By day or night the John Hancock Tower and Trinity Church are readily recognized. Photo © Judith Canty

Below right: Christmas in Boston is celebrated with the annual lighting of a tree at the Prudential Center complex. Photo © Stanley Rowin

tree like some gleeful spider monkey god receiving tribute at the Taj Mahal. Her neighbor, Oliver Ames, railroad tycoon and another Massachusetts governor, built a sixteenth-century-style French chateau at 355 Commonwealth Avenue, the largest and most lavishly appointed mansion in Back Bay. But then a fit of humility seized Mr. Ames, who hedged his extravagance behind a frieze on the facade that features blameless little cherubs engaged in scenes of humble domesticity—eating, reading, and playing the flute.

These Boston Victorians wanted everything: mercantile respectability and domestic virtue, a dash of shock and whimsy, and all the glory, honor, and attention due their lofty station. But most particularly they wanted nothing to do with riffraff, those lower sorts so recently arrived from

Left: Brownstone and brick adorned with seasonal flora is characteristic of most Back Bay homes. Photo © Sarah Hood

Below: Boston's Back Bay was constructed on landfill during the mid-nineteenth century. Newbury Street parallels the Charles River. Photo © Judith Canty

Ireland and Russia and other un-washed, brutish places. In their stately Back Bay houses—all upright brick and granite-sure, as sure as railroad stock and Bell Telephone shares—these doyens of Victorian Boston Society drew their heavy velvet drapes and turned their backs on the whores and slumlords and abortionists trafficking openly in the North and West End neighborhoods that quality folk had lately abandoned. In this new Back Bay, so lately built on garbage and sewage and immigrant labor, proper Bostonians looked out across the tree-lined streets, so perpendicular and true, to admire the houses of neighbors who had passed inspection. They ventured out to promenade the boulevards, bowing gravely, greeting only one another. Boston never saw such smugness.

But life was grand behind the doors of old Back Bay. A visit to the Gibson

Above: Joggers take to the paths along the Esplanade. Photo © Sarah Hood

Right: Flowers and pottery brighten this Newbury Street windowsill. Photo © Kenneth Martin

House Museum on Beacon Street, opened to the public by the New England chapter of the Victorian Society of America, gives a rare opportunity to see Victorian Boston from the inside. In such houses as these, the very rich and middling rich somehow got through the daily business of living among incredible collections of *stuff*: figured carpets and French gilt chairs in the drawing room; chandeliers and Chickering pianos in the music room; horsehair chairs in the parlor, all fringed and antimacassared, perhaps to disguise the fact that they were utterly unsittable. There were stuffed owls in the game room, camellias in the conservatory, and

peacock feathers in madam's bamboo sitting room. Everything about these houses was overstuffed and over-wrought, prompting Henry David Thoreau to remark pointedly in *Walden*: "We have built for this world, a family mansion, and for the next, a family tomb." But *Walden* was out of print by 1859, so little did Victorian Boston regard his admonition to simplify, simplify.

Instead the Back Bay gentry entertained themselves in lavish style. There were sumptuous banquets, dig-

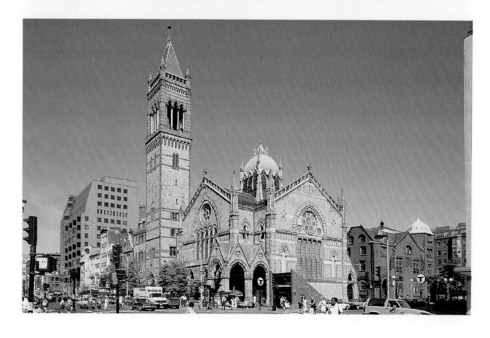

nified musicales, and dazzling balls to attend most every week of the year. "The whole procedure was accompanied by a certain gorgeousness and parade, which used to terrify me," wrote John Jay Chapman, recalling fondly his undergraduate days in the mad social whirl of Victorian Boston.

Evening receptions were regarded as a natural form of amusement; people stood in a pack, and ate and drank, and talked volubly till midnight. And they enjoyed it too. There was a zest in it ... That age was an age of witticisms and of personal hits, which were recorded and handed down. To-day the taste for bon-mots has waned, and if anyone should bring such a

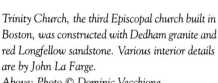

Trinity Church, the third Episcopal church built in Boston, was constructed with Dedham granite and red Longfellow sandstone. Various interior details are by John La Farge.
Above: Photo © Dominic Vecchione
Above right: Photo © Gene Peach

Right: Copley Square is central to Trinity Church, Boston Public Library, and the New Old South Church, seen here. Photo © Gene Peach

thing as a witticism into a drawing-room, people would balk at it and regard it as an old snuff-box ... I don't know why the world has become so dull of recent years, and society so insipid. People in Boston in the Eighties knew how to enjoy themselves.

But not all of them knew how to enjoy themselves. Charles Francis Adams, for one, was only too glad to abandon his elegant brick house at the corner of Gloucester Street and Commonwealth Avenue for the simpler pleasures of suburban Lincoln. This descendant of two presidents and mogul of the Pacific Union Railroad had tired of Boston Society. "I have tried Boston socially on all sides," Adams wrote. "I have summered it and wintered it, tried it drunk and tried it sober; and, drunk or sober, there's nothing in it—save Boston!"

But that, of course, was its appeal, for this was Boston in its glory days— Athens of America! Hub of the Universe!—and Back Bay was its capital. There was more culture per square inch in Copley Square than anywhere on earth, except maybe Rome. Here was Trinity Church, H.H. Richardson's masterpiece of Episcopal self-assurance, its glorious Romanesque hulk resting on 4,500 wooden piles kept constantly submerged in water lest the whole magnificent edifice slide ignominiously back into the swamp. The Museum of Fine Arts and the Museum of Natural History also crowded in on the Square. So did the Boston Public Library, which opened in 1895 to the delight of the cooped-up children at Chauncy Hall School, who were shepherded on periodic field trips across the Square to view such worthy acquisitions as John Eliot's Indian Bible and the Bowditch collection of mathematics. (But not, most emphatically *not,* the statue of the prancing nude "Bacchante," intended for the library's interior courtyard, but declined by the horrified trustees and

shipped off instead to the Metropolitan Museum of Art in New York.)

And in Copley Square was held the grandest Victorian cultural extravaganza of them all, the Peace Jubilee of 1869 celebrating the end of the Civil War. The Grenadier Guards band steamed over from London to join the 1,000 drummers and tooters handpicked from auditions held all over the United States. Kaiser Franz's Grenadier regiment band came, too, with La Garde Republicaine from Paris, the Emperor's Cornet quartet

from Berlin, and dear old Johann Strauss himself, lately arrived for the occasion with his waltz orchestra. President Grant attended, escorted by 3,000 militiamen. For four glorious days in June, 50,000 flushed Bostonians crowded into the three-acre

Mary Baker Eddy founded the First Church of Christ Scientist in 1879. The Christian Science Center on Massachusetts Avenue is a major complex of buildings serving as a home for the Church. Photo © Mark E. Gibson

professionals have a lunch hour free, they head straight for "The Street." That is Newbury Street, Boston's combination Fifth Avenue and Left Bank that stretches eight blocks down the middle of Back Bay from the Public Garden to Massachusetts Avenue. Here on the street there are people to watch, art to inspire, clothes and toys to lift the spirits, and plenty of money to burn. This is Boston at its most fashionable, parading the signature style that thrills the hearts of the chamber of commerce and proud residents alike with equal parts old Brahmin manners and new establishment affluence, and a dash of funk and hip thrown in for fun. Back Bay flashes a bright and prosperous present built on a solid foundation of quality and class.

You cannot merely stroll along to window shop on Newbury Street; you must go up and down. This is because the storefronts are built into nineteenth-century townhouses, whose front doors were located up a flight of stairs to keep visitors at a decent distance from the horses tramping mud in the street and from tradesmen barreling down another flight to service entrances in the basement. So it's up

Coliseum erected in the Square, and listened rapt beneath the bunting and flags and coats of arms of the unsundered states as a cacophony of joyful noise erupted praising God, country, industry, and Boston, queen of the Union. Opera diva Madame Parepa Rosa delivered a moving rendition of Gounod's "Ave Maria," accompanied by a select ensemble of 200 violins, and was warmly received, though there were murmurs that the selection was awfully *Catholic*. But the "William Tell" overture perked up the crowd, and there wasn't a steady pulse in the house when the 20,000-voice chorus launched into "The Spangled

Banner," with every church bell in the city chiming the melody and artillery cannon booming the bass line. By the time 100 Boston firemen were done hammering out the "Anvil Chorus," Boston was fairly faint with an excess of patriotism, civic pride, and culture. Not *high* culture, truth be told, but a wondrous occasion nonetheless. For this was Back Bay Boston, so lately built on a swamp, capital of a nation so lately saved from strife, where anything was possible and everything was monumental.

One hundred years later, Back Bay still bustles and crows behind its elegant facade, and when Boston's young

Above left: Braving the snowstorm, a solitary woman walks along the tree-lined park which runs down the center of Commonwealth Ave. Before her is the statue of William Lloyd Garrison. Photo © Kathy Tarantola

Above: Beacon Street is delicately dusted with snow. Photo © Kathy Tarantola

and down you go. Up to the window of the decorator's shop to cluck over the pair of Chinese cloisonne rooster urns, circa 1810, and $2,500 apiece. Then down to the window of the art gallery across the street to frown over the Jackson Pollack paintings.

Up and down, up and down—it's enough to make you hungry. You'll be hard pressed to find a sub or pizza on Newbury Street, but sidewalk cafes invite you to sit down to trendier fare. And then there's tea at the Ritz. Head for the blue awnings of this glittering hotel at the head of Newbury Street, overlooking the Public Garden. Past the doorman busily obliterating the fingerprints from the revolving door, up the curving staircase, past the satin settees and French gilt chairs, and on into the Lounge. There are original nineteenth-century oil paintings on the wall and a rose at every table. A harpist plays prettily in the corner, and your only care is whether to take Earl Grey or Tio Pepe with your cucumber sandwich. The guests do tend to linger, admits the maitre d'. And who wouldn't?

BEACON HILL

Codfish and baked beans, Brahmins and Beacon Hill—everybody knows this recipe for quintessential Boston. The codfish and baked beans part is bunk, but Boston cherishes the

Brahmin enclave on Beacon Hill for the sheer beauty of its manners and the unswerving certitude of its convictions. The convictions have often been misguided and snobbish, and sometimes lowdown and mean, but here on Beacon Hill, "where the Lowells talk only to Cabots, and the Cabots talk only to God," there has always been a template for right living. And Boston, ever mindful of right and rights and ready at a moment's notice to argue which is which, appreciates the example, if sometimes for no other end but to scorn it.

Left: This Beacon Hill monument was erected in 1899 marking the site of the original Bulfinch column, which stood as a beacon at the summit of the hill before the peak was leveled to its present height. Photo © Martha Everson

Below: The Charles River comes alive with sailing enthusiasts during the lush, green summer months, in full view of Beacon Hill residents. Photo © Gene Peach

Beacon Hill is named for a beacon that no longer stands on a hill that was cut down 175 years ago. The beacon had been set soon after Winthrop's arrival, a grim guardian of Puritan determination, standing "like a gibbet against the sky" to warn the citizens of danger from fire, or storm, or enemy attack. The beacon towered above the town, for in those days Beacon Hill rose 130 feet high, the middle crest of a three-hill ridge called the Trimountain, for which Tremont Street is named. The land had been purchased from Boston's first eccentric, the Reverend William Blaxton. A refugee from the abortive Gorges colony in Weymouth, Blaxton didn't suffer company kindly and so retired to the Shawmut Peninsula and

Above: The Massachusetts State House sits atop Beacon Hill. Photo © Martha Everson

Right: Charles Street shopowners cater to the local Beacon Hill market. Photo © Gene Peach

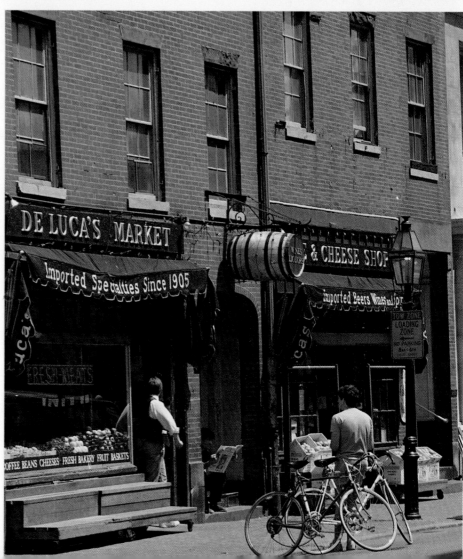

claimed it for his own. He spent five contented years there among his books and vegetable garden and apple orchard on the west slope of Beacon Hill, with no one to bother him. Then the Puritans turned up from Charlestown, looking for fresh water, in 1630. Blaxton recognized a high-handed, interfering lot when he saw one, and knew it was time to move on again. "I came from England because I did not like the Lord Bishops," he explained to the Puritans as he packed his bags, "but I will not join with you because I do not like the Lord Brethren." Graciously selling his wilderness retreat to the newcomers for 30 pounds, he left town for Rhode Island, riding away, it is said, on a brindle bull.

Louisburg Square is privately owned. The first house was built in 1834, and the last, completing the square, was built in 1847. Photo © Gene Peach

The Hill remained unoccupied, save for the beacon and some cows owned by John Singleton Copley, John Hancock, and their neighbors. Then in 1810 the Hancock heirs seized on a money-making scheme and commenced cutting off 60 feet of the crest. The gravelly earth was loaded into wagons and carted away to the Mill Pond, where it was dumped, load after load for twelve years, to make new land for real estate development.

But it was the decapitated Hill that became the height of residential style in Boston. Here Charles Bulfinch, Asher Benjamin, Alexander Parris, and other skilled architects transformed the lowing pasture and scarred landscape into a neighborhood of great stillness, dignity, and charm. Brick townhouses line the narrow streets, their brass door knockers gleaming and their windowboxes cascading joyous colors at street level, while tall, stately shutters (scru-

pulously painted only in authentic period colors by order of the Beacon Hill Architectural Commission) flank the drawing rooms on the second floor. Narrow passageways lead round back to cobbled carriageways and old stableyards. The sidewalks are brick and the streetlights are gas lamps. Bootscrapers and hitching posts and the serenity of Louisburg Square (perpetually composed behind its wrought-iron railing and off-limits to the general public) remind us of an era when it wasn't necessary to rush about pell-mell and mingle with the hoi polloi to rule the roost in Boston.

For Beacon Hill was the refuge of Boston's Brahmins, those blue-blooded, high-caste "sifted few," as Oliver Wendell Holmes called them, who, through money and marriage, luck, and talent, orneriness and noblesse oblige, shaped the course of Boston from the Revolution well into the twentieth century. Adamses, Appletons, Russells, Otises, Cabots,

Lodges, and Cabots Lodge—all have directed the political, financial, social, and philanthropic life of Boston from their homes on Beacon Hill.

They were an odd lot, the Brahmins—a breed as close to aristocracy as America has ever produced. Many found them stuffy, touchy, and fish-cold, though proper in every inch of their bearing. Here is the portrait of an archetypical Boston Brahmin as drawn by the always penetrating observer George Santayana, in *The Last Puritan:*

Every Tuesday and Friday at half-past eleven the front door opened and gave exit to a lank and rigid gentleman in black, with a small head and pinched features and little steel-blue eyes, blinking. He was young, but had put on old age in his youth, was cautious and nervous in his movements and made sure from time to time that his hat was firm on his head, his scarf pinned, his gloves buttoned, and his umbrella tightly rolled. He always turned to the left, for never, except to funerals, did Mr. Nathaniel Alden walk down Beacon Hill.

Others, like John Jay Chapman, who hobnobbed with Boston Society at the turn of the century, were dazzled by the goings-on on Beacon Hill:

Boston was a family—a club—and is so still. Some people resent the family atmosphere of Boston; but I always liked it. The people there speak of "Cousin John" and expect you to know to whom they refer. But this is charming! Someone has said that Boston is the only city in the world where when two ladies meet on the street, one says, "How is he?" ... It was

Boston's foible to set metes and bounds to everything: that was the game which we played; but it was a good game, and the players were among the best-hearted people in the world.

James Michael Curley, for one, didn't think so. This rabble-rousing Irish pol, who made his mayoral career scoffing at everything Brahmin in Boston, would lead crowds of supporters up Beacon Street on election nights, stopping gleefully outside the drawn curtains of the private Somerset Club, to make rude noises at the

stodgy Hill men seething sulkily within.

By the time Curley got around to giving the raspberry to Beacon Hill, Brahmin Boston was already in decline. Today the Hill sees more new rich and glitz than old guard and tweeds. But the inhabitants and mer-

Above left: The Boston Brahmin Cabot family mansion was built on Mount Vernon Street. Photo © Gene Peach

Above: Beacon Hill homes are accented with many varieties of flora. Photo © Sarah Hood

chants still aspire to something of the old Beacon Hill manner. There is a 7-11 on gaslit Charles Street, but you'd scarcely recognize it behind its mock Corinthian columns and dentilated window cornices. Other shops tend toward the precious and expensive—teddy bear stores for adults, deli-markets where the outsized produce carry no price tags, a florist who specializes in Victorian bouquets. But no one with a Brahmin's respect for budget comes to Beacon Hill to shop. People come here rather to admire and be calmed.

There is no better way to see Beacon Hill than on the Hidden Gardens Tour. This annual springtime event is sponsored by the Beacon Hill Garden Club and raises money for their numerous projects of civic betterment

and neighborhood beautification. The self-guided tour takes you past the purple-paned windows and fanlights of the houses that front on the public thoroughfares and into the alleyways and kitchen yards behind the venerable Beacon Hill streets: Mount Vernon, Spruce, Walnut, West Cedar, and Chestnut. Here is a world long suspected but rarely glimpsed. It is a private world of old brick courtyards and ivied walls, lead fountains and stone statuary, wrought-iron furniture and marble benches. The gardens are mostly shady, offering a cool backdoor retreat for the residents of this sometimes sweltering city, but a riot of flowers have been coaxed to bloom here by generations of Beacon Hill matrons accustomed to getting their way. You'll see lilies, clematis, wisteria, and lilacs that have been in the ground for years; tuberous begonias and camellias brought out from the conservatory where they've been pampered through the winter; and masses of geraniums and impatiens, bought by the hundreds from commercial growers, and hastily potted up for the occasion in fine old urns and Italian terra cotta ware. If this isn't one of the "ribbon gardens," primly tied off for viewing only at a distance, you'll be allowed to poke around. Pretend you need a closer look at a climbing hydrangea, and you can sidle up to a kitchen window and peer right in for a glimpse of Boston's

modern Brahmin class at home. But a glimpse will have to do, for the press of the crowd and good manners insist you move on to the next garden gem, and the next.

On the Beacon Hill garden tour, you won't be invited in for tea. You are welcome to admire the hidden gardens—so fine, well-tended, and closely guarded—but your curiosity about the gardener inside is firmly turned away at the back door: "Private," "Keep Out," "Don't Touch." It's never spelled out that baldly, because that would be rude, but Beacon Hill extends its welcome on its own terms. And so, for refreshment you'll be directed down the Hill to the Advent Church Garden, where the worthy ladies of the Garden Club have set out tea and coffee for the horticultural hordes at a goodly distance from the shuttered drawing rooms on Beacon Hill.

Doorways and window boxes on Beacon Hill are each as unique as they are old.
Photos © Sarah Hood

Following page: Only ten feet wide, Acorn Street on Beacon Hill is paved with cobblestones. These humble abodes once housed servants who were employed at the finer mansions on the Hill.
Photo © Sarah Hood

BOSTON COMMON

But you won't make it to the church, because on your way, at the foot of Beacon Hill in the other direction, bounded on six sides by Beacon, Park, Tremont, Boylston, and Charles streets, spreads Boston's beloved Common. You'll be waylaid here, as thousands of townsmen and visitors are each day, by scenes of Boston in the public mode. There are pushcart vendors selling pretzels at the Park Street Metro kiosk, demonstrators reviling injustice on the steps of the State House, hustlers hawking three-card monte games, frat brothers toss-

Right: George Washington presides over the Boston Public Garden. Photo © Gene Peach

Below: Sunbathers and tulips enjoy this springtime afternoon in the Public Garden. Photo © Kathy Tarantola

ing Frisbees, toddlers wading bare-bottomed in the Frog Pond, and Hare Krishna devotees jangling their way to Nirvana right before your eyes. And here you'll stay until more urgent matters than tea with the garden club tear you away. Because, for all its charm for the visitor, Beacon Hill is a closed society where the admission fee is steep and the credentials committee particular. But Boston Common is an open public space and a free-for-all commotion, sister to that other great New England democratic institution—the town meeting—just as lively and just as old.

In other American cities, eager young urban planners have just recently discovered the salutary virtues of "open space." They are faced, now late in the twentieth century, with the monumental task of clawing out some cracks in the cramped and asphalted cityscape in which to squeeze some fresh air, pansies, and a little bit of elbow room. But Boston is blessed with a wide-open, 50-acre park. It has been here ever since the founding Puritans (whose spiritual hunger put them in the habit of arranging eternal rewards) purchased the plot from crazy old Reverend Blaxton and set it aside for the use of

Swan boats at rest, swan boats at play, the Boston Public Garden operates swan boats everyday!
Above: Photo © Judith Canty
Above right: Photo © Justine Hill

the citizenry, decreeing that "henceforth there shalbe noe land granted eyther for housplott or garden to any person out of the open ground or Comon Field."

And so it has remained, unparceled and untrammeled, for 348 years—not just a park, or a green, or a preserve—but a *Common.* The Common is a place that belongs to everybody and is owned by no one, whose superintendency rests not with the Parks Commission but with the people, and where townsmen and visitors go to sit down, sound off, goof around, and breathe freely of the democratic air.

In the early years, cows, not people, had the run of the place. They were pastured there under the watchful eye of a cowherd hired by the town at two shillings a beast, with only the frogs for company. But they were mighty fine frogs in those days. "Some, when they sit on their breech, are a foot high," remarked John Josselyn in the middle of the seventeenth century, "and some as long as a child one year old." (Josselyn exaggerated, and the frogs are long gone, but the Frog Pond remains as a favorite gathering spot for summer waders and winter skaters.)

In time the town became less bucolic, and as Boston became preoccupied with the knotty questions of might and right, the Common saw fewer cows and more soldiers and preachers. For a long time the soldiers

George Whitefield, brought his Great Awakening to Boston in 1740, he had to repair to the Common because, in the excitement of his preaching, several people were trampled to death in the confines of New South Church. The open air of the Common had a temporarily calming effect on the crowd of 20,000 people, but by the time he was done hellfiring and brimstoning, several faithful had been admitted to Boston hospitals under the terse diagnosis: "Rendered insane by listening to Rev. Whitefield."

But passions have always run high on Boston Common, where people have come for 300 years to settle their scores. Sometimes the results have been fatal. In 1728 Benjamin Woodbridge sought an honorable solution to dishonorable dealings. He caught a buddy cheating at cards, challenged him to a duel on the Common, and was run through the chest with a sword for his troubles. In 1919 concerned Boston citizens turned the formula around when they thought they saw a dishonorable means to an honorable end. To show support for striking Boston police officers, they staged a massive craps game on the Common. It was one of a long line of Boston exercises in civil disobedience and a forerunner of the angry demonstrations to be held on the Common during the Vietnam War, but the authorities didn't buy it. The Massachusetts Guard was called out to the old militia ground, and 20 demonstrators were killed just steps away from where Woodbridge had been laid to rest in the Old Granary Burying Ground at the corner of Boylston and Tremont streets.

Yes, Boston Common is a true "people's" park. It is a place where Boston greats have gone about their ordinary rounds. This is where Ralph

Park Street Church, located on the corner of Tremont and Park streets overlooking Boston Common, was built between the years 1794 and 1828. Photo © Justine Hill

were hostile. When the colonists set aside the Common as a training field and parade ground for militiamen, they probably didn't have Redcoats in mind, but that's who they got in 1768 when Boston's pre-Revolutionary unruliness finally snapped King George III's patience. The Redcoats were bad guests who specialized in gestures calculated to offend Boston's touchy sensibilities. They held horse races on the Common, cut down trees for firewood, and generally tore up the place with their trenches and fortifications. They piped a taunting version of "Yankee Doodle" outside the meetinghouse doors on Sundays, and

suckered a farmer into an illegal gun trade so they could tar and feather him and parade him around the Common with a placard reading "American Liberty, or a Specimen of Democracy." But democracy prevailed, and when the Redcoats finally overstayed their welcome and were forced to retreat from the town in 1776, they cut down all the trees that remained along Tremont Street in spite.

Preachers have been more welcome on Boston Common. When Pope John Paul II said a mass there in 1979, 100,000 people turned out in the pouring rain. And when the Church of England's thundering revivalist,

Waldo Emerson drove his cow to pasture; where Louisa May Alcott rolled her hoop one girlhood day and got lost; where young Francis Parkman conducted his first nature experiments, catching pouts in the Frog Pond and frying them up in his garden to serve to his cousin, with cinnamon, in a recipe that is probably best forgotten; and where Oliver Wendell Holmes, for once at a loss for words, muttered his bumbling proposal of marriage to his schoolmistress sweetheart—three times—on the Long Path before she finally got the point, and accepted him.

And, in the democratic nature of things in Boston, the Common is also a place where ordinary Bostonians have gone about tackling great things. This is where desperate mothers spread their children's blankets in hopes the sun would banish the smallpox virus breeding there; where a jostling crowd of winded boys organized themselves as the Oneida Club, played a harum-scarum game, and so invented football; where householders trundled their belongings and watched while downtown burned in the Great Fire; and where free black men from "Nigger Hill"

Right: Couples enjoy the peace, quiet, and the willows in the Public Garden.
Photo © Judith Canty

Below: Christmas lights decorate the trees on Boston Common, framing Park Street Church.
Photo © Sarah Hood

volunteered to set their Southern brothers free in the Civil War, and marched off under the command of Colonel Robert Gould Shaw to their deaths in South Carolina.

But the Common is perhaps best known for its massive civic celebrations. Whenever Boston has had a general to salute, a victory to celebrate, a death to mourn, or some municipal achievement to acclaim, its citizenry has headed for the Common. George Washington, the Marquis de Lafayette, General Ulys-

ses S. Grant, Charles Lindbergh, Andrew Jackson, and the Prince of Wales have all been feted here. After Lincoln was assassinated, his log cabin was shipped to the Common from Illinois and set up on the baseball field to the great satisfaction of the mourners. In 1837 Chief Black Hawk, fresh out of prison after the failed Sac and Fox Indian War, led his braves in a war dance on the Common. ("A clatter and a frightful show," pronounced one observer. "Their hideous and grotesque manoeuvres, their wild onsets, their uncouth motions in the dance, and their unearthly yell, made them a most impressive spectacle.")

Eleven years later Bostonians flocked to the Common for the most impressive spectacle of them all, the Great Waterworks Celebration. At last the line from the Lake Cochituate reservoir was complete, and water flowed freely into Boston's horse troughs, hydrants, privies, sculleries, and fountains—plenty for everyone in the booming town. This was truly an achievement of great civic import, and the town turned out in force to mark the occasion. A parade of floats wound through the streets in praise of the industry and commerce that this reliable supply of water was sure to promote. There was a printing press from downtown, a war sloop manned by sailors from the North End, a market shop from Faneuil Hall, and, though no one knew quite what it signified, an oriental palanquin borne by the men of the Salem East India Society. The procession ended at the Common, and as the crowd pressed in around the Frog Pond, a fountain of water shot 75 feet into the air. What a glorious sight! Grown men shouted; women wept. Schoolchildren sang an ode composed for the occasion and were rewarded with a school holiday. Boston loves to throw parties for itself, and where better than the Common?

"The Common was the beauty and pride of the Town, ever suggesting the lighter side of life," wrote an observer as early as 1663. It is still that way today. On the Common there is earnestness and nonsense side by side, and always the air of the school holiday. Lovers engaged in private spats glower past placards vilifying the mayor, the governor, the president, the Pentagon; Arabs, Israelis; God and the Antichrist; the rich and the poor. Everybody has a beef. Nobody pays much attention. Jugglers and chalk artists compete with slush vendors and Bruins boosters for space on the sidewalk. On the corner of Park

and Tremont, a bearded young man in an odd hat—part Amish elder, part cowboy dude—belts out a rousing version of "Come Thou Almighty King," with full rhythm section and choir provided by the boom box at his feet. No one is rendered insane, but a couple of grizzled black men have joined him, nodding kindly as the would-be revivalist offers a new selection, an upbeat rendition of the Lord's Prayer. "That's fine son," they assure him, "just fine."

There is an optimism and a confidence here on Boston Common. It isn't necessary to wrap identity and

resolve tight around you in order to negotiate this park. On the Common you fall in with the common crowd, sharing its pleasant enthusiasm for the everyday and the happy conviction that life is well enough ordered and will turn out all right, no matter the baggage foul-ups at the airport or the morning's alarming stock market quotations. On the Common, Boston takes its ease.

Wishes made at the fountain on Boston Common have been known to come true! Photo © Sarah Hood

An apertif, a new purse, or simply an afternoon stroll are available at Quincy Market.
Photo © Gene Peach

Boston's economic future seems assured. In particular, the ascendancy of business and professional services and the renewed vigor of retailing bestow on the city unequalled advantages over other urban economies which have been less adroit in adapting to a quickly evolving world.

According to figures from the Boston Redevelopment Authority, the Massachusetts economy will create almost 450,000 new jobs between now and 1995. This 15.8 percent growth rate almost mirrors the national rate of 15.9 percent. More than half of these projected jobs—87,500—will be in the services sector. Business services are defined as advertising, building maintenance, personnel supply, computer and data processing, and protective, management, and consulting services. Professional services include engineering, accounting, law, health, and others.

Meanwhile, retail trade industries employ roughly 656,000 workers, accounting for more than 23 percent of the state's employment. Between now and 1995, eating and drinking establishments, the largest retail trade sector in the state, will grow by 51,700 jobs, an increase of 31 percent.

In Boston there seems to be no end in sight for the boom in both the service and retail sectors. "The service and retail parts of the Boston economy are growing like crazy," said James Howell, chief economist of First National Bank of Boston, "and I don't envision that stopping." Employment in the city ballooned by more than 85,000 between 1976 and 1986. By the turn of the century, Boston businesses of all types are projected to employ an additional 150,000 workers, an average increase of 10,000 new jobs every year over 15 years. Among the industry groups that have grown and are expected to keep expanding, services and retailing are the fastest-growing industries.

Economic self-reliance and industry mix have always been among Boston's greatest strengths. In the late eighteenth century, the city was the most vital port in the American colonies and its merchants became increasingly rich through trade to Virginia, the West Indies, and England. As Boston developed a wealthy merchant class, its advantage over other colonial cities became anchored not only in its fortuitous geographic location as an international port but also in the web of financial and institutional relationships that served as its economic infrastructure. That diversity and independence is a legacy still apparent today.

Michael Dukakis, Democratic governor of Massachusetts, loves to tell voters that he engineered an economic "miracle" in his state. Whether he was directly responsible or not, the numbers are truly remarkable. More than 350,000 jobs have been created in the state since 1983.

In 1975 the state, saddled with a crumbling and outdated manufacturing base, had an unemployment rate of 11.2 percent, the highest among the nation's 11 major industrial states. Unemployment now stands at 3.8 percent, the lowest of any industrial state. Since 1982, personal income has risen to 20 percent above the national average.

So, too, has Boston gone from basket case to showcase. Together with the much-vaunted high-technology sector located on Boston's Route 128, the service and retailing sectors have been in the vanguard of the city's resurgence.

Of the various economic sectors in Boston that have grown in the last decade, business and professional services accounted for 58,000, or 70 percent, of the net new jobs. Retail trade was moribund until 1982, when the sector finally started to bloom again, and has since added more than 6,000 new jobs. The stunning gains in these two sectors alone—services and retailing—far outweighed the net loss of 11,000 jobs in the city's declining manufacturing sector.

Roughly three of every ten employees in Boston work in privately leased office space. Business and professional services account for 70,000 jobs, or 37 percent of all office employment. By the year 2000, workplaces in Boston could support an additional 152,000 employees, based on the optimum capacity of existing office space.

CHAPTER 5

Miracle on State Street

BY JOHN F. PERSINOS

Below right: Governor Michael Dukakis announces his candidacy for president at the Massachusetts State House in Boston. Photo © Martha Everson

Right: Kitty Dukakis watches attentively as her husband Michael announces his presidential candidacy in a press conference at the State House. Photo © Martha Everson

Employment is projected to grow from approximately 600,000 today to 746,000 in 2000, a growth rate every city in the country should envy. Services will lead this expansion in magnitude and growth rate with 110,000 additional jobs, or about a 50 percent increase above the current level.

Retail trade, meanwhile, will expand by another 9,000 jobs or so. In large part, the strong performance of both services and retailing is due to the city's inherent market advantages: its core of financial and service establishments, ties to other major national and international centers, and the well-planned and orderly construction of office space. To be sure, Boston is fast losing its reputation for small-scale parochialism, as the breakneck speed of office development transforms its skyline into something that more closely resembles Manhattan than the quaint Bean Town of old.

"Boston's enormous economic expansion has turned economic theory on its head," said James Sullivan, president of the Greater Boston Chamber of Commerce. "Economic theorists used to assert that a city couldn't have healthy service and retailing sectors without a strong manufacturing base. But Boston has proven that wrong. Business and professional services, in particular, are at the city's economic core, while many old-line manufacturing companies have simply faded away."

Sullivan pointed out, however, that many aspects of Boston's economy are unique:

Boston has 250,000 students—more

students per capita than any other city in the nation. Moreover, Boston is the birthplace of venture capital and is awash in sources of financing. When you combine money and brains, you come up with something like Boston. Those are powerful qualities, when you put them in the context of our information and services-based society.

He emphasized that Boston's economic boom is not a temporary phenomenon, and would probably weather a national recession should one occur. "The city has unique structural resources that ensure a stable and long-term prosperity," he said. "The healthy nature of its service sec-

Right: Along the wharves of Boston Harbor, one will find quaint cafes and outstanding restaurants. Photo © Mark E. Gibson

Below: Charles Square in Cambridge is the location of the Charles Hotel and shopping mall. Photo © Gene Peach

tor is an inherent strength that it can draw on for some time to come."

In Boston's retailing sector a lively recent boom in sales activity has reversed decades of grim decline. Led by eating and drinking establishments and specialty-goods stores, the city's retail employment has increased more than 10 percent since 1982, compared to 6 percent growth for all employment in the city. Several factors have contributed to the increase in retail trade. First, Boston has been in the throes of a mind-boggling expansion of retail space since the doldrums of 1982. Of all the new retail space constructed since 1975, more than 61 percent was completed after 1982, including two new massive and glittering retail complexes, Copley Place in the Back Bay and LaFayette Place in the central business district. Second, the volume of daytime shoppers has expanded, largely due to the growth of Boston's employment base by almost 40,000 jobs during that period. Third, the population of

people who actually reside in Boston has increased, supplying a steady stream of shoppers to stores within walking distance. Like other historic cities in the Northeast, Boston is a "public" city with a European flavor. It is amply bestowed with parks, fountains, and brick-lined sidewalks, making it a joy for pedestrians who love to stroll and browse.

Above: Copley Place is an extraordinary retail complex with a walkway adjoining both the Westin and Marriott hotels.
Photo © Judith Canty

Left: Snowflakes adorn the atrium of Copley Place during the Christmas season.
Photo © Gene Peach

The future of retail trade in Boston is bright, due to projected increases in daytime and resident population, growing personal income, and rapid construction of new retail space through the end of the 1980s and well into the 1990s. Perhaps the catalyst for the rebirth of retailing was the now-famous renovation of Faneuil Hall marketplace in 1976. Private developers turned the patch of decrepit and abandoned warehouses on the harbor waterfront into a myriad of retail shops, boutiques, and eateries imbued with a festival atmosphere. The concept has since become a trend among urban planners and development firms, and other cities (notably New York and Baltimore) have renovated declining waterfront property in similar fashion. In Boston, the success of Faneuil Hall's renovation created a platform for the revival of retail trade in the nearby distressed downtown area that will continue far into the future. Moreover, recent public and private investment in neighborhood retail districts and the ever-increasing buying power of residents have heightened the prospects for retail activity throughout the city.

In 1978 the City of Boston, under former mayor Kevin White, launched an audacious plan for revitalizing its retail core by eliminating virtually all vehicular traffic from a 12-block area of downtown Boston bordering the Combat Zone, the city's notorious and dangerous red-light district. Named Downtown Crossing, the new area has become a symbol of retailing's revived fortunes in downtown Boston. Since 1978 Downtown Crossing has experienced huge gains in pedestrian volume and retail sales. Perhaps more importantly, though, the creation of the area fostered a climate of cooperation between the public and private sectors that the retailing industry will be able to tap into again in the future.

In essence, Downtown Crossing is a landscaped pedestrian shopping mall. With the financial and moral support of the city's leading department stores and retailers, the city upgraded buildings and created a strong central business district. Faneuil Hall and the new white-collar employment base have created a growth market for downtown department stores. Office workers in the city currently account

Right: Samuel Adams is a popular brew in Beantown.

Below: Harbor cruises are available along the commercial waterfront. Photo © Gene Peach

for about 45 percent of Downtown Crossing's sales. To solidify the gains already made in Downtown Crossing, the incumbent administration of Mayor Raymond Flynn plans to beef up residential development, particularly along Tremont Street facing the venerable Boston Common, to create more residential traffic, which translates into more shoppers. About 70 percent of Boston residents shop in the city's retail stores, including those in Downtown Crossing.

Robin Reibel, spokesperson for William Filene's and Sons Company, commented: "We're looking forward to the continued development of retail space in Boston to sustain the vitality of retailing in the city. There are more and more shopping possibilities opening up here all the time."

Especially gratifying, Reibel said, is the fact that retail construction has diminished the territory occupied by the Combat Zone.

Filene's, with 19 stores throughout New England and New York, maintains its flagship store in downtown Boston. A major player in the city's

retailing market, Filene's had roughly $400 million in sales in 1986—the best year in the history of the company.

In a recent survey conducted by the accounting firm Touche Ross & Company, 59 percent of the retailers questioned said retail competition is increasing in Boston. Nevertheless, most predicted more good times ahead. That has not always been the case. In the early 1980s the prospects for Boston's retail stores looked grim indeed. While the Boston metropolitan area had a history of modest growth in the retail trade before 1982, adverse demographic trends began to take their toll. Population shifted toward the suburbs, and huge, sprawling shopping malls proliferated, causing Boston to lose scores of establishments, sales, and jobs in the retail trade sector from 1967 to 1982. Sales in automotive, furniture, apparel, general merchandise, and food stores fell steadily. It became a common scenario in urban areas throughout the country.

Since 1982, however, retail sales have posted an almost miraculous rebound, reversing a 15-year trend of steady decline. Since then, the city's retail employment has increased more than 9 percent. Each major retail business category, with the exception of apparel, gained employees. Eating and drinking establishments and miscellaneous retail accounted for nearly 80 percent of the additional jobs. Retail sales totaled almost $4 billion in 1987, making Boston one of the top 10 retailing centers in the country. Many other cities have not been

Left: If it's entertainment, fine food, or drink you seek, visit Quincy Market. Photo © Kenneth Martin

Below: Colorful Quincy Market is a favorite attraction of tourists and locals alike. Photo © Justine Hill

Above: From the Neck Up is a charming little boutique on Charles Street catering to those with a penchant for hats. Photo © Gene Peach

Right: Located on the corner of Washington and School streets, the Globe Corner Bookstore was built in 1711 for an apothecary and then converted to a bookstore in 1828. Photo © Gene Peach

Below right: For the antique enthusiast there are shops such as the East India Trading Co. all about town. Photo © Lee C. Hauenstein

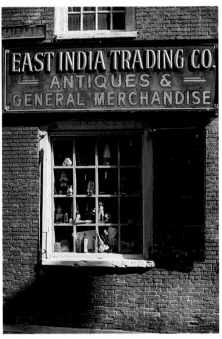

as fortunate, having permanently lost the retailing war with the ubiquitous suburban malls.

As stated previously, the rebound is in large part due to the unprecedented increase in retail space within the city itself. The frenetic pace of retail space construction has dovetailed with an overall construction boom that has made Boston one of the hottest real estate markets in the nation. From 1983 to 1985, for example, developers invested a total of $163 million in retail construction projects in the city, an amount that exceeded the $161 million spent on retail construction during the entire seven years before 1983.

From 1986 through 1989, scheduled construction projects will add 985,200 square feet of new retail floor space in Boston. The development is occurring, for the most part, in the downtown area, Back Bay, and Charlestown.

Boston's revival as a tourist destination has also boosted the retail sector. Annual visitors to the city numbered 2.9 million in 1970 and today total well over 6 million. Many of these visitors, of course, purchase goods in the city. Retailing activity is also stimulated by Boston's reputation and prominence as a cultural center—the "Athens of America." The city is dotted with evening attractions, including professional sporting events, theaters, and retail centers.

Boston, with roughly 600,000 in population, has been gaining resi-

John Gillis, spokesperson for Reebok International Ltd., based in Canton, Massachusetts, said the healthy retailing climate in Boston has nurtured his company and others like it. "As it pertains to our business, the fast growth of the retailing sector in Boston has been a big plus," Gillis said. "The kind of product we make and sell—athletic footwear—gets a good reception here. The growth of the local economy in general is a big plus. There is low unemployment and more disposable income, and that helps companies like ours that make consumer goods."

Reebok, a manufacturer and seller of athletic footwear, is one of the state's most salient success stories. Like many companies based in Canton, a once-moribund city on the outskirts of Boston, Reebok has received copious amounts of state aid. In 1983 the Massachusetts Industrial Finance Agency (MIFA), a quasi-government agency that provides low-cost financing to promising start-ups, lent $700,000 to Reebok when it was a small and obscure manufacturer and retailer. In 1983 Reebok was a strug-

gling start-up company that was badly strapped for cash. In 1986, however, Reebok racked up $919 million in annual sales, and in 1987 sales exceeded $1.4 billion.

The MIFA has invested more than $4 billion in 2,100 businesses. The agency raises its funds by issuing taxable bonds, including industrial development bonds. It is one of many funding vehicles created by the Dukakis Administration to nurture companies, especially those in such up-and-coming sectors as retailing and services.

Boston is at its heart a city of neighborhoods. Workplaces are spread across 16 diverse neighborhoods, each with a distinct ethnic mix and strong sense of community. The outlook for

Left: Local farmers and merchants sell their produce, meats, and cheeses every Saturday at the infamous Haymarket along Blackstone Street. Photo © Gene Peach

Below: A study in red: these strawberries, peppers, and tomatoes are just a few varieties of available produce at the open-air Haymarket. Photo © Justine Hill

dents for the first time in 30 years. In 1990 total employment in the city is projected to be 652,000, compared to the current employment level of roughly 600,000 within the greater Boston population of more than 3 million. Retail employment is also projected to increase during that period, from about 64,000 to 67,500. From 1990 to 2000, retail employment is likely to expand by 93,700. In similar fashion, retail sales for Boston are expected to grow to $4.4 billion in 2000. Retailers are cautiously predicting a 4 percent to 6 percent increase in sales in 1988.

retailing in these neighborhoods has improved dramatically. Recent public improvements and renovation projects have enhanced several once-seedy districts. The national "Main Street Inc." program channeled $1.6 million in public and private investment into Roslindale Square in 1985 and 1986. In the last five years, the City of Boston's Commercial District Program leveraged $17 million for renovations in 15 commercial districts. In addition, gains in population and income have recently improved and will keep improving the prospects for neighborhood retail establishments.

As a result of the new boom in retailing, rents for retail space in revitalized areas have risen dramatically in recent years. As rents go up, retail outlets that have relatively high sales per square foot of space or low operating costs are more likely to occupy more expensive space. In the last three years or so, changes in the kinds of businesses occupying storefronts seemed to favor high-volume businesses that cater to the commuting daytime population. For example,

establishments that sell gourmet food, sometimes known somewhat derisively as "cute food," have multiplied like mushrooms in the rain. Meanwhile, some low-volume jewelry and clothing stores have been forced to move out of the downtown area or go belly-up. This trend toward high-volume gourmet items, common in other cities, continues to shape the complexion of the downtown area. In addition, Faneuil Hall is increasingly catering to tourists, suburban visitors, business visitors, and young professionals.

As alluded to earlier, another source of strength for Boston's retailers is the large student population in the city. Boston is home to more than 60 colleges and universities, some of them among the most prestigious in the country. In the 1985-1986 academic year, personal spending by students reached $137 million.

Fast and diverse population growth, the greater attractiveness of Boston's

new retail complexes, revitalized shopping districts, and the increase in consumer purchasing power have all converged to give the city's retail trade a huge lift that will last into the next century.

In the final analysis, however, the retailing sector owes its good fortune to the Massachusetts economic renaissance. Rick Gureghian, spokesperson for the Massachusetts Office of Economic Opportunity, pointed out that the state has evolved from being the Appalachia of the Northeast to a powerhouse of prosperity and innovation. "Other states look to us," he said. At the center of this evolution

Above: Shay's sidewalk cafe is a popular retreat for weary Harvard Square shoppers. Photo © Gene Peach

Left: During lunchtime hours, office workers flock to the Faneuil Hall food stalls, perhaps for a slice of pizza or a deli sandwich and a can of pop. Photo © B. & J. McGrath

has been the state's shift away from manufacturing and toward service-oriented businesses. This shift is reflected in national trends as well, but nowhere has it occurred more starkly than in the Bay State. Historically, the state was a key manufacturing center, particularly in textiles and shoes. Today, however, the strength of the state's economy derives largely from a host of dynamic, service-oriented businesses.

Well over half of Boston's total private employment is located in Central Boston, the Back Bay, and Beacon Hill. Most of the jobs in services are clustered in these downtown areas. About 40 percent of the total employment in Boston is in the service-producing rather than the goods-producing sector; the former will be the dominant source of job growth in the state and the city through 1995. The 10 fastest-growing Massachusetts industries are dominated by services, including computer and data processing services and service to buildings and offices.

Ironically, the rapid growth in services has created a problem. Many service-oriented jobs are going begging. Boston, a city reborn after a deep recession in 1982, is now struggling to find enough workers to keep the economy chugging along. It's the sort of dilemma many cities would love to share.

Changing demographic trends and the service sector's insatiable appetite for new workers are posing new challenges in Boston. Even those service professions that do not generate a large number of openings—paralegals, occupational and physical therapists, physician and medical assistants—are causing recruitment problems for service employers. The crunch in health services is especially worrisome. Boston is a world-renowned medical center, and its hospitals are an essential source of jobs in the city's service economy. Among the city's largest employers, hospitals make up 27 percent of the employ-ment among companies with more than 500 employees each. Health services are projected to grow by almost 23 percent through 1995, but finding adequately trained people to fill the available slots is no easy task for hospital administrators.

Below: Brilliant neon signs lend appeal to this Chinese restaurant. Photo © Kenneth Martin

Below (bottom): Diners are currently enjoying renewed popularity. Photo © Sarah Hood

Nevertheless, the Commonwealth's history of leadership in education and training is proving to be an effective resource in the worker shortage. Scores of companies are already devising ingenious ways of coping with the shrinking pool of employable people. They are putting increasing emphasis on recruiting; they are automating or improving employee perks; they are paying higher salaries and advertising positions that need to be filled; and they are digging deeper into the pool of minority workers. For example, fast-food restaurants are paying more than six dollars an hour, almost double the national minimum wage. And in 1987, help-wanted

advertising at the region's paper of record, *The Boston Globe*, amounted to roughly 15.5 million lines, up 15 percent from 1984.

In 1975 few businesspeople were optimistic about Boston's economic future. With high unemployment, state government deeply in the red and teetering on the brink of bankruptcy, and rising oil prices, the city's prospects looked quite bleak. In hindsight, however, it is clear that the city was well positioned in the mid-1970s for the changes that would wrack the national economy during the next decade. Boston has been blessed with a diverse economic mix since colonists first set up shop there three centuries ago. The city's inherent strengths truly came into play as Massachusetts gradually and sometimes painfully reduced its reliance on mill-based manufactured goods and increased its reliance on high-technology manufacturing and the service sector.

Rapid growth in business-related services has played an important role

Above: Things are looking up for the construction industry in Boston. Photo © Kenneth Martin

Left: Construction sites are numerous within the city limits of Boston. Photo © Kenneth Martin

in generating prosperity since 1975, proving that employment in high technology is not the only locomotive of the city's growth. Not only did service employment grow rapidly, but it also contributed to the state's economic base by attracting new companies and financial resources into the Boston area. Between 1975 and 1983 alone, employment in business services in the state grew by an astounding 95 percent.

Boston's unparalleled position as one of the world's leading educational and medical centers has generated a huge variety of service-sector jobs that are simply nonexistent in many other

Right: A horse-and-carriage ride around the city is an enjoyable way to see the sights, provided the horse is cooperative. Photo © Sarah Hood

Below: Built in the shape of a pyramid, the Hyatt Regency Hotel enjoys its location beside the Charles River in Cambridge. Photo © Gene Peach

cities. Openings abound, for example, for data managers who also possess a certain amount of medical training. Businesses in the city are also spending more on so-called "intermediate" services, such as management consulting and accounting. Further, because of the increasing complexity of operating a business, growing numbers of firms are using specialized services such as guidance in government regulations and international marketing to remain competitive.

As new technology inundates businesses with a bewildering amount of information, accounting, advertising, and consulting are expected to prosper. In particular, employment in computer and data processing services will surge ahead. One-third of Boston's large corporations are located in the downtown area, among the ever-expanding stacks of glass-and-steel office towers. Boston's service companies benefit greatly from their location in the state capital and the region's largest city. Downtown, with

its wide variety of industries, provides them with customers, clients, suppliers, and contacts within a small radius. Routes 93, 95, and the Massachusetts Turnpike all lead into the city, providing everyone with direct access to the central business district. The subway—the world's first—unites four extensive lines downtown, and efficient commuter trains transport suburban commuters to their offices in the city. Logan International Airport, one of the country's busiest and best, is less than two miles from

downtown. A central location, extensive mass transit, and a well educated and increasingly affluent workforce are a natural attraction for service companies.

Theoretically, the massive expansion of the service sector in tandem with the decline in traditional manufacturing industries should translate into lower productivity and earnings growth for the city's economy. But this has not happened. Economists who warn of the "deindustrialization" of America point out that some ser-

vice jobs require little skill and pay close to the minimum wage. That is true enough. But in Boston, where higher education is an entrenched tradition, the service jobs tend to be concentrated in law, medicine, engineering, advertising, accounting, data processing, and the like, not in flipping hamburgers. Those jobs, moreover, tend to have high productivity and earnings growth.

The numbers seem to bear that out quite clearly. According to *New England Business* magazine, New Eng-

land's top 100 service companies in 1986 posted a collective 13 percent increase in revenues and a 118 percent increase in net income compared with the 100 companies listed in the magazine in 1985. In fact, service

Above left: Local broadcasters from WBZ-TV4 in Brighton pose for this still photograph. Photo © Sarah Hood

Center left: WBZ-TV4 local sports announcer Bob Lobel relaxes in the stands. Photo © Sarah Hood

The headquarters of the Polaroid Corporation is located in Cambridge, Massachusetts.
Photo © Stanley Rowin

companies, with $52.3 billion in revenue in 1986, grew the most of any business category. The majority of those companies are based in Boston, which its denizens have appropriately nicknamed "The Hub."

"Boston has a lot of advantages as a central business area, as the nexus of the regional boom," said Sullivan. "It provides proximity to other firms, and a lot of new convention space. Face-to-face networking continues to be vital among the kinds of businesses that dominate the city, despite the improvements in telecommunications."

Sullivan added that Kevin White's famous description of Boston—the "livable city" —remains true. "There's a great quality of life here that attracts management types," he said. "Just ask any corporate personnel director. The city is high on most people's list of desirable places to live. It has good schools, a relatively healthy environment, plentiful recreational resources, and an active intellectual life."

Boston's success story is perhaps best summed up by Robert Reich, professor of political economy at Harvard University's John F. Kennedy School of Government. "It's one of the most exciting economic stories this country has seen since World War II," Reich said.

It's pretty hard to top that.

*Boston's Prudential Center tower, a city landmark,
was designed by Charles Luckman & Associates,
architects. Photo © Stanley Rowin*

Boston was the commercial capital of post-Revolutionary America. As the port closest to Europe, commerce and trade naturally settled in the city with three hills. With its superb natural harbor and abundant educational resources, Boston seemed a natural to develop into a center for finance. But there was one obstacle: the city, and indeed the country, had no organized financial system. The British, in one of their many failed attempts to keep the colonists under their rule, made sure that an independent American financial system did not develop.

Thus it was that the founders of the Massachusetts Bank—the nation's second chartered bank—turned for assistance to the Bank of North America, based in Philadelphia. Thomas Willing, president of the Philadelphia bank, had these encouraging words: "The world is apt to Suppose a greater Mystery in this sort of business, than there really is ..." The Massachusetts Bank opened its doors on July 5, 1784, and was soon financing world trade. Still, modern consumers would find many of the bank's early practices mysterious in their own right. The bank initially charged interest on deposits. Loans, called discounts, were made only two days a week, and they had to be repaid in full within 30 days. And directors voted on discounts by placing either a white or black ball inside a small box. If the latter was chosen, the loan was "blackballed."

The early days of Boston banking were quaint, but the growth of trade and commerce were soon to fuel the expansion of financial services in town. As Russell B. Adams writes in *The Boston Money Tree,* Boston was the first American city to make large amounts of money—and it soon became the first city preoccupied with conserving it.

A large part of the early banking consisted of factoring—short term lending to finance shipping and trade. And Boston was more closely associated with the China trade than any other American city. From the late 1700s through the middle of the next century, the great tall ships from Boston sailed 22,000 miles around Cape Horn to pick up loads of highly prized sea otter pelts in the American Northwest. They then traveled to China to exchange the pelts for ginseng, chinaware, silks, and, especially, tea. The Massachusetts bank was both a financier and a participant in this trade. Of the seven owners of the *Columbia,* the ship that virtually established the China trade, six were customers of the Massachusetts Bank. In 1787 the *Columbia* landed in Canton and traded 1,050 otter pelts for $21,410, which, after expenses, bought 21,462 pounds of Bohea tea. During its first 90 years of existence, all of the Massachusetts Banks' presidents were both merchants and shipowners.

But the quickly growing economy

of Boston was to prove a fertile ground for numerous other banks—not all of them tied to shipping. For in many ways the participants in Boston's first banking boom in the 1800s used strategies similar to those of today's niche-crazed marketers. Each bank was positioned to appeal to a particular clientele. In 1816 the first savings bank in the United States received its charter, and it opened its doors the following year. James Savage envisioned The Provident Institution for Savings in the town of Boston as a place where people of modest means could build their assets. Since commercial banks did not yet pay interest on deposits—they had only recently halted the practice of *charging* interest on deposits—The Provident was one of the first alternatives to speculative investments or stuffing currency in mattresses. Today, there are 140 savings banks in Massachusetts alone.

Other early banks included The Hibernia Bank of South Boston, which appealed to new Irish immigrants who experienced discrimination in other institutions. The Suffolk Bank for Seamen and Others set itself out as the first place a crewmember from a trade ship should stop: "When you came off the ship, you tried to save a penny before you went into the saloon," explains Robert Fichtor of the Massachusetts Bankers Association. At the Roxbury Penny Bank, notes Fichtor, a penny was considered a respectable weekly deposit.

CHAPTER 6

Money in The Bank

BY JEFFREY O. KRASNER

From the very start, says Fichtor, Boston bankers developed a reputation for loyal but unexciting service. "Boston banking was the most old-fashioned in the country," he says. "It never tried anything new. The fashionable thing to do was to be unfashionable." But, he notes, the reputation did little to hurt the growth of the banking industry. "Through bad times and good times, Boston has always been perceived to have a certain quality—integrity and trustworthy service. A little dull, but trustworthy."

Today Boston is one of the strongest regional banking markets in the country. There are nearly 400 banks and credit unions in Massachusetts, with combined assets of $125 billion and more than 68,000 employees. By far the largest is the First National Bank of Boston, which merged with the old Massachusetts Bank in 1903.

It now has assets of more than $25 billion and deposits of more than $17 billion. Other major regional banks include Bank of New England, descended from the Merchant's Bank, with assets of $13.3 billion; Boston Safe Deposit and Trust Co., with assets of $12.7 billion; and Shawmut Bank, named after the Indians' word for the small peninsula of land later settled as Boston, with $7.5 billion in assets.

In the past two decades, the character of Boston banking has begun to shift. To be sure, it isn't visible to the naked eye; Boston bankers still wear the same traditional blue and gray suits. But two pieces of legislation have combined to change the way Boston banks do business. The Bank Holding Company Act of 1956 gave commercial banks a way around geographical branch restrictions by enabling them to own many individual banks through a parent firm. Then, in

Left: Money is the driving force behind Boston businessmen. Photo © Stanley Rowin

Below: Activity is constant during trading hours at the Boston Stock Exchange.
Photo © Stanley Rowin

1982, savings and cooperative banks were given the power to convert to stock ownership structure. Both legislative changes have fueled a massive wave of mergers and consolidations among New England banks. As a result, there are fewer banks of more equal size competing for business in the robust New England economy. Robert Mahoney, head of the Bank of Boston's Massachusetts banking division, sees it as a positive development:

It makes the challenge more interesting. Instead of having six or seven medium-sized banks with one giant, you now have four very-good-sized banks. The indicators of competition are good; there are more automatic teller machines per capita in Massachusetts than any other industrialized state, the credit card rates are lower in Boston, and the deposit rates in Massachusetts, with the possible exception of Houston, are the highest in the nation. That's banking competition.

Mahoney adds that competition has forced Boston bankers to change some of their stodgy ways:

Our bank is unexpectedly innovative. The expectation is that the Bank of Boston is staid, mature, and conservative, but the stock analysts and our more aggressive customers think of us in a different way. We really go after people. We're very aggressive when it comes to the creation of risk assets. We find winners early on and we run much longer with them than other banks might.

Mahoney sees it as a good time for all of Boston's banks:

We've got everything—low unemployment, high employment; it's darn concentrated. There's a lot of wealth concentrated in a small area. Plus, there's been almost uninterrupted economic growth since 1979.

In life insurance, as in banking, Boston lays claim to the second-oldest company in the nation. The New England Mutual Life Insurance Company received its charter from Massachusetts Governor Samuel T. Armstrong on April 1, 1835. It was the first to be issued to a mutual life insurance company. But the charter contained an unusual provision: one-third of the company's profits were to be donated each year to the fledgling Massachusetts General Hospital. This requirement concerned prospective

Above: Inside the main branch of the Bank of New England customers wait in line patiently for the next available teller. Photo © Stanley Rowin

Above left: Robert M. Mahoney is president of Massachusetts Banking, Bank of Boston. Courtesy, Bank of Boston

investors in the new company. It took lawyer, schoolteacher, and scholar Willard Phillips several years to persuade investors that the profit-sharing provision would not materially affect his venture. But by the time New England Life issued its first insurance policy in February 1844, Mutual of New York had been in operation for over a year.

Nevertheless, Phillips is considered the father of U.S. life insurance. He is credited with pioneering the mutual insurance company structure, wherein the firm is operated for the benefit of its policyholders, not its shareholders. New England Life, now known

Right: Shawmut Bank provides its patrons with automatic teller machines inside the bank lobby. Photo © John Coletti. Courtesy, Stock Boston

Below: Copley Square is the location of both old and new Hancock towers, as well as the Prudential building. Photo © Martha Everson

simply as The New England, served as an example for many others. State Mutual Life received a charter in 1844; Berkshire County Mutual Life and Massachusetts Mutual Life received charters in 1851. A decade later, a group of Massachusetts businessmen attempted to secure a charter for an insurance company using Benjamin Franklin as the firm's figurehead. They were turned down. But a year later they applied again, using another famous patriot for their logo, and the John Hancock Mutual Life Insurance Company was officially sanctioned.

Today the 10 surviving life insurance companies in Massachusetts (including The New England, John Hancock, Berkshire, State Mutual, and Massachusetts Mutual) make up one of the most powerful economic forces in Boston and the state of Massachusetts. In 1987 the companies employed 20,000 people, paying $564.8 million in payroll and $14.2 million in state corporate income

taxes. More importantly, the life insurance industry in Massachusetts had more than $3.7 million invested in the state and made $5.2 million worth of charitable contributions.

Another significant contribution of the insurance industry to Boston are some of the largest and most renowned structures on the Boston skyline. The Prudential Center, a mixed-use office, retail, hotel, and residential development built by The Prudential Insurance Company of America, is perhaps the best-known symbol of Boston's rebirth and devel-

opment after decades of decay in the first half of this century. The tower, which was dedicated in 1965, rises nearly 60 stories over the Back Bay, the proper and historic neighborhood created on landfill in the mid-1800s. Just a few blocks away rises the gleaming John Hancock tower, a $160 million project that opened in 1976. Almost adjacent to the Hancock is the old Hancock tower, a fitting symbol of the old Boston. The elder Hancock sports a stone facade, a gabled roof, and a neon light that changes color to indicate the weather. Hancock recently announced a seven-year, $100 million project to restore the weathered, 26-story beauty to its original grandeur.

Boston's glory days of international trade did more than just stimulate the development of regional banking and insurance. The China trade, at least indirectly, gave birth to a completely new industry: money management. In the early 1800s, prosperous sea captains were able to embark fully financed and insured. But they were faced with a new problem: they needed responsible firms to manage their assets while they were at sea. Their need gave birth to the Boston trustee—a firm made up of lawyers and professional money managers that provided public fiduciary services.

It was not until 1830 that the role and responsibilities of these trustees were fully defined. In that year Justice Samuel Putnam of the Massachusetts Supreme Judicial Court heard the case of *Harvard v. Amory.* Wealthy John M'Lean had died in 1831 and

Above left: Built between 1945 and 1949, the old John Hancock Building on the corner of Berkeley and Stuart streets was, for two decades, the tallest structure in Boston. Here the Art Deco style building is reflected in the new John Hancock Tower. Photo © Stanley Rowin 1988

Above : The 33-story Federal Reserve Bank which looms above Boston Harbor is located at Atlantic Avenue and Summer Street. Photo © Martha Everson

Above: A banking tradition is The Boston Five Cents Savings Bank. Photo © Richard Pasley

*Right: The 60-story, new John Hancock building was designed by I.M. Pei & Partners in 1968 and construction was completed in 1976.
Photo © Gene Peach*

left $50,000 to be managed by trustees Jonathan and Francis Amory. Upon the death of his wife, the money would be split between Harvard College and Massachusetts General Hospital. But the Amorys invested the $50,000; its value soon shrank to $38,000; Harvard and the hospital sued, and Justice Putnam handed down his famous Prudent Man rule, declaring that holding the trustees responsible for the investment's loss of value was harsh and unfair. The justice wrote:

All that can be required of a trustee to invest is that he shall conduct himself faithfully and exercise sound discretion. He is to observe how men of prudence, discretion and intelligence manage their own affairs, not in regard to the permanent disposition of their funds, considering the probable income, as well as the probable safety of the capital invested.

The Prudent Man ruling quickly became the standard for professional money management, and the role of the Boston trustee flourished. Three old-line trust firms dominated the industry: Old Colony Trust Co., now a part of the Bank of Boston; Boston Safe Deposit, a predecessor of the Boston Company; and New England Trust Co., since purchased by the

Bank of New England. Chris Flanagan, director of sales for the investment management and personal trust department of the Bank of Boston, says the role of the Boston trustee often went far beyond that of merely managing money. "Trustees attended weddings, baptisms, and funerals," he says. "They would help the children in the families get into the right schools. They maintained an intimate but professional relationship with the family—a highfalutin servant, like the family lawyer." Flanagan notes that early family trusts sought to pre-

serve wealth over several decades, and the trustees' fiduciary role often emphasized safety over growth. "As long as you preserved the money, nobody got mad at you."

It was this tradition of money management that led in 1925 to the formation of a revolutionary new investment: the mutual fund, an organization that pools the money of many individuals and then invests it in stocks, bonds, or other instruments, thereby giving each investor greater diversification and lower costs. It was George Putnam, the

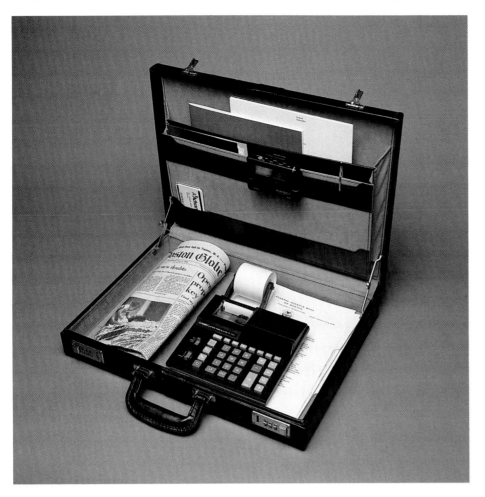

great-great-grandson of Justice Putnam, who founded and managed
Incorporated Investors, perhaps the
first all-stock growth fund. Putnam
left Incorporated in 1933, dissatisfied
with that fund's investment strategy.
He envisioned a balanced fund—a
mixture of stocks and bonds that
would give small investors greater
stability through volatile economic
times. In 1937 he founded the George
Putnam Fund of Boston. Incorporated
Investors later merged with Putnam
in 1966.

Putnam is one of several Boston
firms that today dominate the mutual
fund industry. The Putnam Companies, led by Chairman of the Board
George Putnam, Jr., offer a family of
about 40 mutual funds, which have
assets of about $40 billion, including
institutional accounts.

Other Boston firms with significant
contributions in the mutual fund industry include Fidelity Investments,
which has nearly 140 mutual funds
with more than 4.5 million customer
accounts and $80 billion in assets; the

Keystone Group, with $15.8 billion
in assets, 40 funds, and 520,000
shareholder accounts; and The Colonial Fund, founded in 1931, which
claims to have started the first mutual
fund in 1924, Massachusetts Investors
Trust.

Fidelity Vice President Michael
Hines says that Boston's mutual fund
industry is in many ways an outgrowth
of Boston's old Revolutionary tradition of democracy and independence.
"In Boston, people are more challenging of authority and more likely to
take matters into their own hands,"
says Hines. "The Fidelity family of
funds is designed so people can think
for themselves. It's been made democratic, and it's a good value." Hines
adds that some of Fidelity's contributions to the industry include building
a complete family of funds; direct sales
to investors, eliminating the need to
pay brokers' commissions; and introducing checkwriting privileges on its
money market funds.

Despite the innovation, there are
some things that just won't change,

say Boston money managers. One is
the traditional Boston money manager's uniform: a brown Brooks Brothers suit, with pant legs about two
inches too high, and a well-worn pair
of cordovan oxfords. The garb certainly isn't stylish, but it is in keeping
with Boston's 200-year-old tradition
of financial service. Says William
Rice, founder and president of
Anchor Capital Advisors: "There's a
general perception that Boston is a
bastion of conservative money management. Some people carry this image to the point of thinking that Boston isn't aggressive enough. We don't
have too many firms in Boston at the
lunatic fringe. In Chicago, with the
commodity exchange, there's more of
a gambling mentality."

*Above left: Essentials of the trade are found in this
briefcase. Photo © Stanley Rowin*

*Above : Assistance is provided by a loan officer
to a woman who seeks credit. Photo © Dawson
Jones, Inc. Courtesy, Stock Boston*

Massachusetts is the leading producer of cran-
berries in the United States. The cranberries are
harvested along coastal lowlands of the South
Shore and Cape Cod. Photo © Stanley Rowin

For all the attention and accolades lavished on Boston's booming service sector, manufacturing remains an important part of its economy and the region as a whole. Roughly 24 percent of all workers in New England hold manufacturing jobs, compared to 20 percent nationwide. In Boston, manufacturing and wholesale trade make up about 11 percent of total employment. These seem like counterintuitive statistics in light of the constant talk and hoopla about the area's shift from manufacturing to services. As many economic analysts point out, however, a service sector without some sort of manufacturing base is a house built on sand.

"You can't have a healthy service economy without manufacturing serving as a foundation," said Martha Bernard Welsh, spokesperson for Boston-based Associated Industries of Massachusetts, (AIM) the state's major manufacturing trade group, representing more than 2,800 companies. "Manufacturing wages, for example, tend to be higher than in the service sector. And sectors like retailing are dependent on consumer buying power."

But despite its prevailing importance in the Boston area, the manufacturing sector has lost a lot of ground. From 1985 to 1986, for example, New England lost about 42,000 manufacturing jobs—almost 3 percent of the total. By comparison, the country lost four-tenths of one percent, according to the U.S. Bureau of Labor Statistics.

The picture is even grimmer in Massachusetts. From 1985 to 1987, the state lost an estimated 60,000 manufacturing jobs, according to AIM. Indeed, Massachusetts is shedding manufacturing jobs faster than any other state, except for the severely depressed oil-patch states of Oklahoma and Louisiana. In 1987 manufacturing jobs in the Bay State were down to approximately 597,000, compared to 673,000 in 1984.

The good news is that manufacturing has nowhere to go but up. Despite its unremitting decline over the past decade, non-high-technology manufacturing remains, and will remain, a key player in the city's economy. In fact, some experts say manufacturing posted a small rebound in 1987, a mild surprise that has brightened a typically gloomy subject. One reason for the renewed optimism over manufacturing is the devalued United States dollar, which makes the prices of American goods more competitive and the cost of goods from the state's factories more attractive. In particular, durable products—a mainstay of the city and state economies—have benefited greatly in the ferocious fight against foreign competition.

American manufacturers as a whole, of course, have been going through the same travails as those in Boston. In Boston, however, the painful transformation from manufacturing to services has served as a stark symbol of worldwide dislocation. That is because modern manufacturing was, in essence, born in the city. The enormous wealth of the colonial merchant class, in the form of disposable investment capital, and the nascent machine tools industry formed a unique economic convergence that gave birth to the first factories in the New World. By the Civil War the largest industries in the state were shoes, leather, textiles, machine-building, and metal working. As the number of mills and factories proliferated, new cities sprouted up around them—Lowell, Lawrence, and Fall River, to mention the more prominent ones. But after World War II, the decline in footwear, textiles, and leather goods began a downward slide that has continued unabated to today.

About a decade ago, 17.8 percent of all workers in the state were employed in non-high-technology factory jobs. They now account for less than 11 percent. Although each industry has its special problems, the common denominators are the same: increased foreign competition, increased labor costs, and slimmer profit margins. The state's major manufacturing industries are projected to lose more than 10 percent of their employment base, with textiles losing more than 25 percent. These industries are dominated by blue collar jobs that have traditionally paid well, but have required less educa-

CHAPTER 7

Made in Boston

BY JOHN F. PERSINOS

tion, making them perfect havens for the waves of immigrants who came to the shores of Boston and New York.

There are signs, however, that demand is picking up and the tide is turning. Moreover, the tough times have made manufacturing companies leaner and quicker on their feet when competing with foreign companies. Nobody is Pollyannaish enough to predict that the Massachusetts "miracle" will extend to shoemaking and textiles in the Boston area, but some companies, especially those in durables, are anticipating an upsurge in business. Commented Martha Bernard Welsh of Associated Industries of Massachusetts: "Don't forget the fact that this is still an industrial state."

Unlike the economic geography of the late eighteenth century, today's economic geography finds most manufacturers in Massachusetts located outside Boston's city limits. The most important local industry related to manufacturing, defense, is clus-

tered around the city's outskirts. Because of the high level of military spending in Massachusetts, the manufacturing sector will always be critical (which is also true for the entire East Coast). Massachusetts and Boston are not the only places to have staged an economic comeback. From Maine to Maryland new businesses have sprouted up and longtime unemployment rates have plunged. This is mainly due to the region's dependence on huge infusions of defense spending. Massachusetts receives more than 6 percent of the nation's defense procurement budget, even though it is home to only 2 percent of the country's population. When President Reagan went on a defense spending binge, Massachusetts and the defense contractors located in and

Fisheries have maintained a significant role in the economy of Boston since the earliest settlements. Photos © Kenneth Martin

around the state's capital were flooded with lucrative contracts. In 1986 the state's defense contracts totaled $7.7 billion, an increase of roughly 60 percent from 1980.

Part of the reason for the steady stream of defense money into Massachusetts is pork barrel politics. The state's congressional delegation is among the most influential on Capitol Hill, and it makes sure its constituents are well cared for. The prime reason, however, is the historical strength of the state's high-tech and manufacturing sectors. Defense spending has always provided a stimu-

Above: Telephone company workers test equipment on site. Photo © Kenneth Martin

Right: Set builders at WBZ-TV4 create ambience. Photo © Sarah Hood

Institute of Technology in Cambridge. Military spending affects non-high-tech manufacturers as well, as it creates demand for jet engines from General Electric Company in nearby Lynn and machine tools from the various small machine shops that dot the landscape in Boston's working-class neighborhoods. Today defense firms in the Boston area account for 6.6 percent of the state's entire economic output.

The era of blank checks for the military is coming to a close, however, and Massachusetts will undoubtedly feel the effects. No matter what Congress does to the military budget, though, the defense industry in Boston is likely to do well in the immediate future. Most companies are still trying to whittle down their backlogs. In addition, the increasing emphasis on military electronics helps the scores of small electronics firms in the city's environs. Nurtured by the presence of research institutions such as MIT, a sophisticated electronics industry has long been a specialty in the

state. As the Pentagon tries to save money, it will build fewer big ticket items, such as planes, tanks, and ships, and spend more on making existing weapons better—"smarter" in Pentagon lingo—by incorporating electronics. It's called getting "a bigger bang for the buck," and it's a trend that will bring handsome profits to local firms.

"Massachusetts is not overly dependent on defense spending, but defense is not insignificant either," said Christopher Anderson, spokesperson for the Massachusetts High Technology Council, a Boston-based lobbying group comprised of nearly 100 of the state's leading high-tech CEOs. "It's a yin-yang situation, one of balance. There will be a decline in defense spending, we can all count on that. It

lus to the city's economy, dating back to companies in Boston that made rifle parts during the Civil War. During World War II, the United States government signed major military contracts with metalworking and electronics firms and research organizations, including the Massachusetts

General Electric in Lynne, Massachusetts, provides the U.S. Department of Defense with jet engines and parts. Courtesy, General Electric Corporation

won't even keep pace with inflation. But it will affect Massachusetts less than other major defense states, because of the diversity of high tech here. Our companies are involved in electronics, software, robotics, you name it."

Defense systems, electronics, hardware, software, robotics—those words all spell "Route 128." A horseshoe-shaped highway leading through Boston, Route 128 was begun in 1951 and exerted a profound and permanent change on the state's economy. By 1961 more than 300 companies,

most of them producing electronics and instruments, were located along the highway. Inevitably, suburbanization gathered steam, and soon the highway was clustered with new housing tracts and shopping centers.

Most of the state's high-tech companies are now headquartered along this famous stretch of road. At one end of Route 128, heading away from Boston and toward the tiny suburban enclaves of the North Shore, a large sign tells it all: "Route 128—America's Technology Region." A major reason for the technological and

entrepreneurial fecundity of the area is its proximity to Cambridge, located adjacent to Boston on the opposite bank of the Charles River. Cambridge is home to Harvard, MIT, and some of the nation's best medical and educational establishments. These ivy-covered walls have produced and nurtured dynamic, innovative companies that form the backbone of the state's prosperity. Taken as a whole, Route 128 constitutes a high-tech center as important as California's Silicon Valley.

Today, roughly 700 high-tech companies are within 30 miles of Boston, employing more than 250,000 people. According to a 1988 survey conducted by the Massachusetts High Technology Council, the state's high-tech community is bullish on the future. The survey of 193 CEOs of high-tech companies showed that 72 percent of the respondents felt that

Left: The recently constructed Silver Building reflects the growth of high technology along the Route 128 corridor. Photo © Kenneth Martin

Below: Route 128 through the town of Needham is the center of high-tech growth in the Boston area. Photo © Gene Peach

the Boston area is a good place in which to engage in high-tech manufacturing. Concerning the future, 64 percent of those questioned felt that the climate will remain steady. The CEOs cited several factors in the Boston area that made it a prime location for technology—the abundance of high-quality universities, as well as cultural, physical, and geographical advantages.

Many analysts concur with this sanguine assessment. It is widely believed among industry insiders that the high-tech industry has weathered the nasty downturn that lasted from 1984 through 1986, when many fledgling computer makers went belly-up. The firms that were left standing are leaner, meaner, and more competitive with the Japanese. The Massachusetts High Technology Council projects at least double-digit earnings growth for Boston's high-tech firms.

The key firms in the area are familiar corporate names: International Business Machines Corporation, Digital Equipment Corporation, Data General, Wang Laboratories, Prime Computer, and Honeywell. IBM,

based in upstate New York, has extensive operations in the Boston area. DEC, based in Maynard, Massachusetts, is the second-largest computer maker in the country and the arch rival of first-ranked Big Blue. The competition between these two titans is especially intense in the market for midrange systems, often referred to as minicomputers. That competition heated up in the first half of 1988 as IBM shipped its new midrange system, the model 9370, designed to regain the market share it lost to DEC's highly-touted "VAX" midrange line.

Another major player is Wang, founded by Dr. An Wang, a Chinese scientist and entrepreneur. Wang, family-owned and operated, specializes in office automation and has done much to revive the once-moribund mill town of Lowell, where it is based. Governor Michael Dukakis, a master practitioner of the art of quid pro quo, has persuaded many recipients of state aid to expand their operations into economically depressed areas of the state. Wang Labs, for example, received a $5 million unsecured loan from the state in 1978, partly in

return for expanding its facilities in Lowell. It's all part of Dukakis' emphasis on public-private cooperation, and it appears to have worked—at least among Boston's high-tech firms.

Despite the plethora of innovative state programs and quasi-public agencies that the Dukakis administration instituted to nurture high tech, nothing has aided the sector more than the area's inherent factors, notably its research institutions and ready availability of venture capital. In the Boston metropolitan area, there is a conglomeration of research and training institutions unrivaled anywhere in the world. Thirty-seven institutions of higher education in the area have engineering programs; Massachusetts ranks among the top five states in handing out degrees in engineering. Defense procurement meshes with this solid academic foundation to broaden the high-tech industry's research and development base. MIT, for example, is the state's fifth-largest defense contractor.

Research and development are extremely important in the industry. Every fiscal year the key to high tech's

vitality is the percentage of sales companies spend on R&D. Typically,
non-high-tech manufacturers spend
about 5 percent of sales on R&D,
while high-tech companies view
R&D as their lifeblood, spending up
to 10 percent or more. For example,
DEC spends about 10 percent of sales
on R&D; Wang, more than 7 percent;
Data General, 11 percent. In addition, the state receives far more than
its proportionate share of federal
R&D grants for military as well as
non-military purposes.

The availability of risk capital is
also vital. Venture capital companies
provide equity capital and management advice to the young entrepreneurs who leave the local research
labs to form their own companies.
These technologically based companies are often high-risk, but also
high in potential, and they find

plenty of venture capitalists willing to
listen to them when traditional banks
have given them the cold shoulder.
California, Massachusetts, and New
York account for nearly 60 percent of
the country's venture capital spending, and Massachusetts accounts for
nearly 25 percent of that figure. One
reason for the availability of risk capital in the state is the cornucopia of
marketable inventions and ideas.
These interrelated factors feed each
other—venture capital makes its
home in Boston because of the abun-

*All: Prevalent industries within the Greater Bos-
ton area include electrical machinery: specifically
computers, aerospace guidance systems, and electrical components. Also, nonelectrical machinery
includes machine tools and accessories, and products such as power transmission equipment. .
Photos © Sarah Hood*

entrepreneurs who start these companies tend to stay close to their alma maters, and they maintain close personal and professional ties with their former colleagues. It's an amazingly fertile climate for technological innovation.

In fact, the first truly important venture capital firm in the United States was American Research and Development (ARD), founded in Boston in 1946. Two of its three key founders were a Harvard Business School professor and the then-president of MIT. ARD's most notable and successful investment was $72,000 in the late 1950s to Kenneth Olson, a researcher in an MIT laboratory, to start DEC in Maynard. Olson is still president of high-flying DEC, and the founding of the firm has become an archetypal story that occurs again and again in Boston.

Software companies, in particular, thrive on the symbiosis of financial and intellectual power in Boston. Highly innovative companies that develop and sell communications links, specialized programs, and programming aids have done the best in the software market. The biggest and best-known is Cambridge-based Lotus Development Inc., the maker of Lotus 1-2-3, the industry standard for spreadsheets. Lotus, one of the

dance of entrepreneurial companies, and additional entrepreneurial companies are spawned by the abundance of venture capital.

"Venture capital has been an invaluable stimulus to the high-technology community in Boston over the years," said George Kariotis, founder and chief executive officer of Alpha Industries Inc., a $70 million manufacturer of microwave components in the Route 128 area. "The availability of funding has allowed a lot of promising start-ups to get off the ground. In terms of venture capital disbursed to high technology, the Boston area is rivaled only by Silicon Valley."

Kariotis, a former state secretary of economic affairs, also pointed out that venture capitalists tend to have the same risk-taking mentality as high-tech entrepreneurs. "A lot of venture capitalists are willing to give money to these entrepreneurs because they understand where they're coming from."

Anderson of the Massachusetts High Technology Council, however, emphasized that venture capital is only half of the city's allure:

The other half is brain power. Since 1980, a lot of new firms have been spun off from the labs at local universities. The

Above left: Storrow Drive is a heavily traveled road running alongside the Charles River. Photo © Gene Peach

Above: Boston's Callahan Tunnel services the main thoroughfare to Logan Airport. Photo © Stanley Rowin

mass transit. From 1870 to 1900, both the city's landmass and its population doubled, and new forms of transportation were needed and quickly devised.

Concentrated in Boston are government, business, and public service institutions, and the largest central business district in all of New England. Today more than one million people using cars, trucks, buses, planes, and trains enter the 2.2 square miles of downtown Boston every single day. Because it is a regional center, Boston's transportation needs are highly complex and crucial to its economic vitality. Adequate transportation in and out of Boston is also important to the economic vitality of surrounding communities. Over the years Boston has risen to its transportation needs, and for the most part has maintained an orderly flow of goods and people. Its subway system, while nowhere near the gargantuan size of New York City's system, is nevertheless one of the best in the nation and also America's first. It has received serious commitments in funding in the last five years in order to keep pace with Boston's economic boom.

That boom has put strains on the system. As office buildings have gone up, for example, traffic has increased,

fastest-growing start-ups in history, controls about 70 percent of the worldwide market for spreadsheets. Lotus' customers are primarily those who are looking to improve office productivity on existing hardware systems, a growing corporate need that will ensure good business for Boston's software makers for some time to come.

It is, however, Boston's built-in attributes, rather than public policies or private management practices, that have put the city in a class by itself. Almost as important as the city's edu-

cational and financial resources are its assets as a transportation center. More than half of the state's population lives in Boston, and getting in and out of the city is vital. Boston has always been a city of motion. A century ago its residents, then numbering roughly 300,000, made their way through a haphazard network of streets that could be traced back to accidental cowpaths formed during Boston's beginnings in 1630. But the late nineteenth century heralded a burst of construction in transportation that propelled the city into the forefront of

The Central Artery through downtown Boston is a convergence of Route 1, Interstate 93, and the Massachusetts Turnpike.
Above left: Photo © Stanley Rowin
Above: Photo © Kenneth Martin

Above: A Massport Shuttle boat from Logan Airport crosses Boston Harbor. Photo © Gene Peach

Left: Construction and maintenance materials and their transport are of concern to transportation authorities. Photos © Kenneth Martin

forcing public officials to scramble for new transportation initiatives. Logan Airport, the world's eighth-busiest, continues to expand apace. It serves approximately 20 million air travelers a day, and increasing congestion has led to traffic and parking problems on the ground. In fact, the number of vehicles registered in Massachusetts has grown from about 3 million in 1974 to about 6 million in 1986, and much of the increase has centered around Boston. Almost 70 percent of the jobs in Boston are held by residents of other cities and towns who commute into the city on a daily basis. In addition, 6 million tourists visit the city every year. On the average, well over a million people travel into or through Boston every day.

Throughout its history, though, Boston's economic growth has gone hand in hand with the development of transportation, and the city has always maintained a commitment to transportation that few American cities have ever matched. Colonists settled in Boston primarily because of its secure and convenient harbor, and the town grew into an international center with foreign trade brought from clipper ships. Today Boston Harbor handles more than 22 million tons of cargo.

Another transportation advantage is the convergence of the regional

entity in Boston is the Massachusetts Port Authority, which oversees Logan Airport and the Boston Harbor. Since Massport was founded in 1959, Logan Airport has grown tremendously. In the past decade the growth of New England's economy has produced an increase in passenger use at Logan of more than 80 percent. The airport has experienced an especially large growth spurt since 1982, due to the combined effects of airline deregulation, a decline in the price of aircraft fuel, and the comeback of the regional economy. Logan presently serves 47 air carriers, making it possible for travelers leaving Boston to fly to every major city in the United States.

"Logan Airport is an extraordinarily important resource to the region's economy, and we're taking steps now—not later, but now—to make sure that the airport is ready for the

highway system in Boston. The Central Artery, which passes directly through the downtown area, is the nexus of Interstate 93, Route 1, and the Massachusetts Turnpike. The merging of these roadways also places a heavy burden on the city. Boston's narrow and meandering streets provide the city with a unique historical quaintness, but they also frustrate city planners—to say nothing of the hapless motorists who must navigate them. In 1986, for example, city officials responded to the increasing

traffic crunch with the Traffic Relief Program, which among other things created strict parking restrictions and new loading zones. More importantly, the Massachusetts Bay Transportation Authority, which oversees most of the state's transportation facilities, plans to widen the Central Artery and participate in a federal and state program to create a third harbor tunnel. The new tunnel is anxiously awaited, and it promises to pull 40,000 cars off the streets.

Another important transportation

Above: Environmentalists clean up an oil spill in Boston Harbor. Photo © B. & J. McGrath

Below: A boat breaks ice in the Charles River locks. Photo © B. & J. McGrath

year 2000," said David Davis, executive director of Massport. "Sure, there's increasing congestion at Logan, but you can say that about every major airport in the country. We're trying to exercise some foresight in dealing with it. If we don't, there will be a serious price to pay."

According to Davis, there will probably be a 120 percent increase in the number of people traveling in and out of Logan by the year 2010, or more than 45 million people compared to the current annual rate of 21 million. The third harbor tunnel, however, scheduled to be completed in a little less than 10 years, is expected to connect with Logan's roadway system, thus alleviating much of the strain. Massport has commissioned a $6 million study to find a way for the airport to make optimum use of the tunnel.

Logan is also a major regional employer, with more than 10,000 employees commuting to the airport every day. More than 75 percent of these workers get to the airport in their own cars. In addition, the closeness of Logan to Boston is a great asset, especially when compared to the distances between other major cities and their airports. Cab fare from downtown Boston to Logan, for example, costs about $10, while the cab fare from midtown New York to La Guardia is almost $30.

Boston is the sixth-largest gateway in the United States in terms of the value of import and export products shipped through it. In 1960 international shipments accounted for less than 4 percent of Logan's air-cargo

business. Today, air cargo represents more than one-quarter of that business. Most interesting, and telling, is that each of the top three export categories—electronic computers and parts; measuring, testing, and control instruments; and broadcasting and communications equipment—were linked to the city's vital high-tech industry. In the exports category, electrical machinery was first in terms of dollar value and business machines ranked second. In terms of volume, photographic, optical, and consumer goods were first, followed by the city's old standby of fish and shellfish.

Davis said the kinds of products produced by the local economy "are those that like to travel. It stands to reason that international air cargo plays a very important role at Logan."

Since the early 1980s, Logan has been developing the Massachusetts Technology Center, a concept that is new in airport development. Located near one of Logan's main cargo areas,

Logan International Airport, situated at the Port of Boston, provides the transportation link which is so vital to the Boston economy.
Above left: Photo © Justine Hill
Above: Photo © Martha Everson

adjacent to Boston Harbor, the Massachusetts Technology Center is a privately financed commercial building that allows firms that ship by air to maintain spare parts and service areas on the airport's premises. With more than a third of its space leased to technology-related companies, the Massachusetts Technology Center enables its tenants to avoid off-airport trucking costs and delays. The center, located on 20 acres of airport land, is being expanded by Massport to eventually house one million square feet of manufacturing and warehouse space in eight buildings. Also in the planning stage is a 270-room conference center complex. And, as a federally designated Foreign Trade Sub-zone, the center allows businesses located there to realize savings on import-export operations. Under the special exemptions of an FTZ, a company can import or export goods involved in international trade duty-free for processing, manufacturing, or value added procedures. Once processing is

completed, the goods can be imported into the United States or re-exported to a foreign country without having to pay United States duties or excise taxes.

More symbolic of Boston's history as an economic center than Logan Airport is the Port of Boston, located within Boston Harbor. The port was important even in the days before the Boston Tea Party, and is valued to this day for its natural deep-water berth. Boston's economy has undoubtedly changed in the last 350 years, but the city still gazes toward the ocean for its future prosperity.

More than two dozen steamship lines haul general cargo between Boston and 175 ports around the world. Every year the six-state New England region generates more than 2 million tons of shipborne cargo. At more than $4,500 per ton, Boston handles the highest value cargo in the entire country and twice the national average. More than one million tons of cargo worth almost $4 million pass

through the port annually. General cargo, most of which is containerized, is shipped through the public terminals of the port, which are owned and operated by Massport. Those terminals are Moran Terminal, which handles about 45,000 containers every year; Conley Terminal, which handles containers, lumber, automobiles, and other types of cargo; and the Harbor Gateway Terminal, an automobile import and distribution center.

Not all of the terminals, however, are run by the state. There are also 23 private terminals in the Port of Boston that handle commodities such as fuel oils, scrap metal, and cement. The value of this cargo also approaches $4 million.

All of the port's busy terminals are easily accessible by rail or road. The interstate highway system and the compactness of the New England

Shipping activity is constant in Boston Harbor. Photo © Kenneth Martin

market make it possible to deliver cargo from Boston to any point in the region virtually overnight, handing local shippers a savings of more than $25 million. Numerous common carrier trucking firms are available, as well as rail service via the Boston and Maine and Conrail, with tracks leading directly into the loading terminals.

Most residents of Boston, however, are more familiar with the MBTA and the city's internal system of transportation. Starting at 5 a.m. every day of the week, hundreds of thousands of workers, businesspeople, students, shoppers, and tourists wend their way through the city on buses, streetcars, trackless trolleys, commuter trains, commuter boats, and

Above: Large quantities of cargo are transported by container vessels such as this one in Boston Harbor. Photo © Judith Canty

Left: The Port of Boston ships cargo from six New England states to various ports around the world. Photo © Martha Everson

rapid transit subways. The MBTA, known by the locals as the "T," serves countless points throughout the city. The MBTA also carries people to the city's recreational areas along the North and South shores—a feature that makes the city attractive to professionals in search of a high quality of life. The MBTA runs four interconnected and color-coded subway lines and more than 150 bus routes. Its fleet of more than 1,000 buses transport more than 400,000 passengers each day over more than 700 miles of routes.

In the last few years, as Boston's economy has taken off, the MBTA has taken great pains to keep step with increasing office construction and population growth. Between 1983 and 1985, for example, the authority invested more than one billion dollars to improve its transportation facilities. Commuter rail service in the city alone includes more than 270 miles of track on 8 lines and serves about 85 stations. According to the MBTA, commuter ridership on all its lines has increased about 50 percent over the last three years.

State and city officials are nevertheless worried about the region's mounting transportation needs, and want to make sure that transportation problems do not constrain the area's economy. For example, developers are being asked by Boston Mayor Raymond Flynn to "contribute their fair share," in such ways as proposing transportation access plans to city government to reduce the effect their projects have on traffic. Major employers are also devising remedial measures of their own, such as carpools or the subsidization of "T" passes for employees. In general, efforts to promote car or van pooling have produced fairly good results.

Caravan, a nonprofit agency that assists companies in arranging commuting pools for their employees, operates about 250 vans daily. About half of them travel the Route 128 area. Meanwhile, the state Department of Public Works is planning to

Below: This Red Line car approaches Charles Station from Beacon Hill. Photo © Gene Peach

Below (bottom): A Massachusetts Bay Transit Authority (MBTA) car drives off into the sunset on Commonwealth Avenue. Photo © Lee C Hauenstein

spend $60 million to widen the well-traveled Route 128 corridor.

Even commuter boats have gotten into the act. In 1984 the MBTA started commuter boat service as an experimental alternative. During that year, about 600 daily riders made the voyage on two boats between Hingham on the South Shore and Rowes Wharf in the heart of downtown Boston. The service has become extremely popular. Ridership has skyrocketed to 2,200 riders, making 30 trips per day on six boats.

Amtrak's Northeast Corridor represents the bulk of noncommuter rail service in Boston. Amtrak, working with the state, recently instituted rail service from New York to Hyannis, on Cape Cod. The new line will relieve

traffic congestion at roads leading from Boston to Cape Cod, and is expected to generate new economic activity on the Cape in the process. The Boston-Cape Cod Railroad is another convenience cherished by residents who seek to escape the city in the summer and visit the Cape's famed stretches of pristine beach.

The importance of transportation to the vitality of any urban economy should not be underestimated. Just ask city officials in the overcrowded and overbuilt cities of Houston, Denver, Los Angeles, Orlando, and elsewhere. In cities such as these, economic growth has been pursued for its own sake, with little thought given to mass transit or other transportation alternatives. The result has been chronic traffic jams that threaten to choke economic growth. City planners are just beginning to recognize the limitations of the American "car culture," and even fiscally conservative businesspeople are exhorting their state and local governments to make large commitments to mass transit. But as other great cities inch towards the twenty-first century, Boston will already be there waiting.

Above: Trains provide a traditional mode of transportation to and from Boston.
Photo © Kathy Tarantola

Right: The importance of transportation is not underestimated in Boston.
Photo © Kathy Tarantola

The Memorial Church spire at Harvard University rises above snow-covered treetops.
Photo © Gene Peach

Home of prestigious universities, progressive public schools, and a racially mixed population, Boston is a mecca of education that challenges students and teachers alike.

The strength of the educational system in Boston, both public and private, goes back three centuries to the Puritan settlement. Boston Latin School, the first public school in America, was established in 1635 and is still one of Boston's outstanding high schools. Harvard College, founded one year later, was the nation's first and only college for 57 years.

Add to the city's list of education firsts that Boston established the first public tax-supported school system in the nation. In 1647 the Massachusetts Bay Colony ordered all towns with more than 50 families to hire and pay teachers of reading and writing, and towns with more than 100 families were ordered to establish Latin grammar schools to prepare students for university study.

In 1837 the nation's first state board of education was established in Massachusetts, largely through the persistence of Horace Mann, who became its first secretary. Mann made Massachusetts a model of education reform, and his efforts influenced education not only in other states but also in Europe. He improved individual schools, lengthened school terms (which were often as short as eight weeks), began teacher training

schools at a time when teachers were often college students on vacation or high school graduates at best, and tried to ensure a free public education to many more children than were being schooled. Through his efforts the Commonwealth introduced the nation's first compulsory school attendance law in 1852, established the first state school for the retarded, and opened the Perkins School, which was the country's first school for the blind.

When a public school for the deaf in Boston opened in 1869, Massachusetts led the nation in working with people unable to hear. One of the state's foremost teachers of the deaf, Alexander Graham Bell, experimented with electrical hearing aids while a young professor of physiology at Boston University and, out of his experiments, invented the telephone.

The Boston Public Library was the first major tax-supported library in the United States, freely providing books to all classes of citizens. Between the Harvard College Library, which was the first in the American colonies, and the Boston Athenaeum, a private library, Boston in the 1800s already had more books than any other city in the country. But in 1850 a local statesman reasoned that a new library, supported by the city, "would put the finishing touch to that system of education that lies at the basis of the prosperity of Boston." Four years later the Boston

Public Library opened. Today the Boston Public Library houses more than 10 million materials within its main library and 26 branches.

The greater Boston area is home to 65 institutions of higher learning that draw nearly a quarter of a million students to the city each year. Harvard University, the oldest institution of higher learning in the United States, celebrated its 350th anniversary in 1986. Located in Cambridge, across the Charles River from Boston, Harvard College was established in 1636 by vote of the Great and General Court of the Massachusetts Bay Colony. The university is named for its first benefactor, John Harvard of Charlestown, a young minister who, upon his death in 1638, left his collection of books and half his estate to the new institution. Founded just six years after the Pilgrims landed at Plymouth, the university has grown from 12 students with a single master to an enrollment of some 17,484 degree candidates, including undergraduates and students in 10 graduate and professional schools and an extension school. Six United States Presidents—John and John Quincy Adams, Theodore and Franklin Delano Roosevelt, Rutherford B. Hayes, and John Fitzgerald Kennedy—have been graduates of Harvard. Its faculty has produced 30 Nobel Laureates and 29 Pulitzer Prize winners.

In 1879 Eliza Cabot Cary Agassiz

CHAPTER 8

First in Education

BY LISA PONIATOWSKI

created the "Society for the Collegiate Instruction of Women" that ultimately became Radcliffe College. The college was named for Ann Radcliffe, Lady Mowlson, whose gift of $100 in 1643 established Harvard's first scholarship fund. From being an annex in which separate instruction was given by members of the Harvard faculty to 27 women in rented rooms, Radcliffe College has become an integral part of Harvard. Today undergraduate women are admitted to Radcliffe College (which remains a separate corporate institution) and through their enrollment in Radcliffe they are also enrolled in Harvard. Radcliffe holds unique resources for research and scholarship by and about women.

Above: Harvard College, founded in 1636, was the nation's first and only college for 57 years. Photo © Gene Peach

Right: The Charles River flows past Elliot Tower at Harvard University. Photo © Gene Peach

Wellesley College, another of the "Seven Sisters" (as the seven oldest women's colleges are affectionately known), and a newer college for women, Simmons College, continue to admit female undergraduates only, as opposed to several of the "Sisters" that now admit men as well.

Massachusetts Institute of Technology was the brainchild of four brothers from Philadelphia—all scientists—who decided to settle in Boston because they liked its intellectual climate. MIT admitted its first students in 1865, four years after approval of its founding charter. The event marked the culmination of an extended effort by William Barton Rogers, a distinguished natural scientist and the school president, to establish a new kind of private, independent educational institution relevant to the needs of an increasingly industrialized America. Rogers believed that professional competence was best fostered by a coupling of teaching and research and by focusing attention on real-world problems. Located on 142 acres extending more than a mile along the Cambridge side of the Charles River Basin, today MIT is an independent, coeducational, privately endowed university that is recognized as one of the world's outstanding research universities.

Tufts University was incorporated on the land of a farmer and bricklayer

Left: The Widener Library at Harvard University is the largest university library on earth. With 3 million volumes, only the New York Public Library and the Library of Congress have more books in America. Photo © Judith Canty

Below: Six presidents of the U.S. have graduated from Harvard University. This is the Harvard Business School. Photo © Gene Peach

in 1852. Tufts boasts of having one of only two private veterinary schools in the country, in addition to well-respected graduate and professional schools for students of dentistry, medicine, law and diplomacy, engineering, nutrition, occupational therapy, environmental management, and the arts and sciences.

The establishment of Boston University (BU) in 1869 was chiefly due to a boot and shoe man, a fish peddler, and a cloak and suit maker. Today Boston University is a sprawling, urban, teaching and research university with approximately 28,000 full-time and 11,000 part-time students. The College of Liberal Arts forms BU's backbone. Eight professional schools enable students to pursue career paths in management, communications, engineering, education, the arts, music, and the allied health professions.

Boston College was the creation of a South End Jesuit. Since its founding in 1863, Boston College has developed graduate schools that make it a university in fact, if not in name. From rather humble beginnings, Boston College has grown and evolved to become one of the nation's leading Catholic universities.

Northeastern University, founded in 1898, offers what is called the cooperative plan. Students alternate terms of study with work at an outside job. Northeastern is today the largest cooperative-plan university in the United States.

The establishment of Brandeis University in Waltham in 1948 sprang from the same kind of motives that caused the Puritans to found Harvard, the Methodists Boston University, and the Jesuits Boston College, says historian Walter M. Whitehill, for it was due to "the

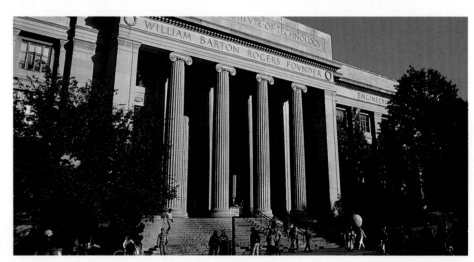

Massachusetts Institute of Technology, located on 142 acres which extend for more than a mile along the Charles River, is a private, co-educational university recognized as one of the world's outstanding research centers.
Below: Photo © Stanley Rowin
Below (bottom): Photo © Gene Peach

desire of American Jewry to make a corporate contribution to higher education in the tradition of the great American secular institutions that have stemmed from denominational generosity." The nonsectarian character of Brandeis is emphasized by its provision of Jewish, Catholic, and Protestant chapels for its students.

Students of the arts will find a plethora of opportunities in Boston. The New England Conservatory of Music is one of the foremost U.S. centers of professional music training, as is its neighbor, Berklee College of Music. Boston's Museum of Fine Arts School, the Art Institute of Boston, and the Boston Architectural Center are three of the city's academic institutions for visual artists.

Left: The grounds of the Harvard Business School are beautifully maintained. Photo © Gene Peach

Below: This student hits the books on the grounds of Radcliffe College which, although a separate institution, maintains a symbiotic relationship with Harvard University. Photo © Gene Peach

Boston's health care industry, with its 114 hospitals, including such world-renowned medical centers as Massachusetts General Hospital and three major medical schools, provides some of the finest opportunities in the world for students of medicine and the allied health professions.

The largest unit in the public higher education system is the Uni-

versity of Massachusetts, founded in 1863 as an agricultural college in Amherst. Since 1947 the agricultural college has grown into the huge University of Massachusetts. UMASS's sizable Boston campus, begun in 1965, received national attention in 1986 when *TIME* magazine rated UMASS/Boston as one of the nation's "hot colleges." The UMASS/Worcester campus houses the medical school.

A system of two-year community colleges was inaugurated in 1960, and Governor Michael Dukakis recently initiated a seven-year, $954 million capital plan to modernize, expand, and upgrade the state's public colleges and universities. These, together with a myriad of Catholic and Protestant colleges, junior colleges, and professional and vocational schools too numerous to mention, have made education Boston's greatest continuing industry.

The founding of Boston Latin School in 1635 was, in effect, the cre-

ation of the first public school in America. To this day it continues to function, along with the Boston Latin Academy, as a college preparatory school. Illustrious alumni include Benjamin Franklin, John Adams, Paul Revere, John Hancock, and more recently, Leonard Bernstein and Joseph Kennedy.

In keeping with the history of local responsibility for education, the operation of the state's public schools is decentralized among more than 320 city and town school systems as well as district systems and special schools. School costs are provided in part by local property taxes and partly by state assistance to the city and town

Left: The Longfellow Bridge and the MIT campus are seen in this view at sunset. Photo © Gene Peach

Below: Crew racers on the Charles River glide past the Boston University chapel. Photo © Kathy Tarantola

governments. More than 60,000 students enroll in Boston's 120 public schools. An alternative to public education is provided by 78 parochial and private schools.

Pooling arrangements, or collaboratives, are increasingly being made between school systems in small neighboring communities. One approach is for two or more small towns to hire the same superintendent. Another allows two or more towns to establish regional schools and vocational institutions that provide better facilities than either town could afford on its own.

Public school education was negatively affected statewide by legislation aimed at reducing property taxes. Proposition 2 1/2, enacted in 1980, stopped the increase in per capita spending on public school students. In 1981-1982, the first year under Proposition 2 1/2, total spending by cities and towns fell by 2 percent. But, in contrast, school budgets decreased by an average of 6 percent, with many plummeting nearly 25 percent.

Many parents and educators had spoken out against the tax reduction law, although these protests were doomed to failure in the face of demands for lower taxes. Concerns that Massachusetts students would suffer if fewer tax dollars were available for state schools were well founded. There was simply not as much money available to cities and towns after this tax limit law passed.

Prior to the passage of Proposition 2 1/2, the period roughly from 1976 to 1980, 242 schools were closed and 1,000 teaching positions were eliminated due to dropping enrollments. During the first year of 2 1/2, school districts were forced to close an addi-

Right: Studies in computer science are available at Boston College. Photo © Martha Everson

Above right: A finance class is held at Boston College Business School. Boston College is one of the nation's leading Jesuit universities. Photo © Martha Everson

tional 262 schools, severely reduce children's food programs, decrease textbook budgets, cut back on athletics, and shut down many evening and adult education programs. In addition, more than 7,800 teachers—mostly teachers of reading, foreign languages, art, drama, and music—lost their jobs.

Attempts to repeal Proposition 2 1/2 have been unsuccessful. Many of the state's poorer communities have been forced to eliminate numerous school programs, such as interscholastic and intramural sports, advanced elective courses, drama, orchestra, student newspapers, and even yearbooks. But wealthier communities, with tax bases that have broadened in

the past eight years by soaring residential real estate values and new commercial development, have not felt the impact of Proposition 2 1/2 as strongly.

In the early 1980s a number of national studies revealed the sad state of U.S. public education. One study found that in school year 1980-1981, only 77 percent of all students who entered the ninth grade graduated. In Boston less than half—only 47 percent—of those students entering ninth grade graduated.

Responding to these staggering statistics, in July 1985 the Massachusetts legislature approved a massive two-year education reform program, by far the most comprehensive (and expensive) in the state's history.

Above (top): Simmons College for women is located along the Fenway in Boston. Photo © Stanley Rowin

Above: Emmanuel College, also a women's school, is located along the Fenway as well. Photo © Stanley Rowin

Above right: Massachusetts College of Art is just one of Boston's academic institutions for the creative. Photo © Stanley Rowin

Costing $211 million, the package included $75 million in grants to poorer school districts, $69 million in teacher raises and bonuses, and $12.7 million in direct grants to local schools. The law is designed to close the gap between the state's rich and poor school districts, at least in terms of student test scores and high school dropout rates. Funds distributed under the reform program are intended to augment, not replace, current and future spending at the local level, and are targeted to reach children in low-income communities. The state funds have allowed schools to redress some of the effects of Proposition 2 1/2 by hiring new staff in areas such as art, music, and physical education, and by purchasing new equipment and supplies.

Contributing to the quality of Boston's public education is its close relationship with the area's colleges, universities, and business community. Today some 100 degree-granting institutions are involved with public school systems. For example, MIT is an active member of the Cambridge Partnership for Public Education, a cooperative effort between the Cambridge public schools, business, and higher education communities. Northeastern annually offers scholarships to 100 Boston high school students and extends the use of its facilities for dozens of activities involving Boston students. Brandeis University's Career Beginnings program is a national network of colleges and businesses that helps disadvantaged urban youth, including those in Boston, gain admission to college. Boston University's proposal to manage the troubled Chelsea public school system would be one of the city's most innovative university-public school system collaborations.

Close ties between private industry and public schools have also improved the quality of secondary education in Boston. The Boston Compact, a three-tiered school improvement effort that involves the Boston School

Department, members of the business community, local colleges and universities, and the Boston trade unions, has been used as a model across the country. First signed in 1982, the Compact aims to improve education, work preparation, employment opportunities, and college attendance prospects of students in Boston's public schools. Businesses pledged to hire qualified graduates; in return, the school system agreed to improve attendance, increase math and reading scores, reduce the high school dropout rate, and increase the placement rates of graduates for post-secondary education and employment.

The Compact appears to be working well. Modest increases in test scores were reported on local standardized tests and the Scholastic Aptitude Tests; daily student attendance is up from the low of 82 percent in 1980-1981 to 88.7 percent in 1986-1987; more Boston high school graduates are going to college, up from 45 percent of the graduates in the early 1980s to 55 percent in 1986.

In 1987, five years after the Compact was created, the Greater Boston Chamber of Commerce reached its goal of recruiting the 400th Compact company participant, and 3,010 students were placed in summer jobs through the Boston Summer Jobs Pro-

gram, the placement component of the Compact operated by the Boston Private Industry Council. In addition to supporting the Compact, a number of Boston businesses have made major financial contributions to establish scholarship and grants programs. These include a $15-million education endowment fund called The Boston Plan for Excellence in the Public Schools.

Boston is not only a city of prestigious universities and innovative public school systems. Boston is a city of neighborhoods, a city vulnerable to the problems inherent in absorbing ethnic and racial changes in its population. In particular, the Boston public schools have faced challenges posed by various immigrant groups for years.

According to historian Judith Freeman Clark, author of *Massachusetts:*

Left: A newly constructed building gleams in the warm afternoon sun at the University of Massachusetts. In 1986, Time magazine rated UMASS as one of the nation's "hot colleges." Photo © Martha Everson

Below: This view of the Connecticut River Valley overlooks Amherst, the site of the agricultural college founded in 1863 which eventually grew into the University of Massachusetts. Photo © Gene Peach

From Colony to Commonwealth, older white Anglo-Saxon residents of Boston were threatened early in the nineteenth century by the large numbers of Irish Roman Catholic immigrants who moved into the Boston area. The new arrivals brought their own customs, customs that often clashed with established traditions of longtime Boston residents. Among the bases for these confrontations was the education of children, which Irish Catholics often left to the Roman Catholic Church. This led to violent anti-Catholic riots, and, in some cases, to attacks on the nuns who taught in Catholic schools.

But among the most pervasive and disruptive problems facing Boston as a community in the latter years of the twentieth century was court-ordered busing of black children into predominantly white neighborhoods. Most of this busing focused on South Boston schools, an area of some isolation from the rest of the city.

"Southie," as it has been known for generations, is a predominantly working-class, Irish Catholic area. Geographically, it is part of Boston but is set off by the Southeast Expressway, by railroad lines, and by its staunchly parochial identity. Nonetheless, this strictly homogenous group displayed some of the most severe reactions to school desegregation that had yet occurred anywhere in the United States.

It might seem that racially provoked violence would be more common to areas where racial segregation had been first accepted and then later legally denied continuance. But in states where all-white or all-black restaurants, public transportation, and schools were no longer legally supported, school desegregation had been effected with relative ease (after initial attempts to block it). The positive results of the 1954 Supreme Court ruling in *Brown v. Board of Education* were clearly evident in Southern school desegregation. Such positive changes were not easily wrought, however, in Boston in the 1970s.

Boston's Irish Catholic mayor, Kevin White, had been elected in 1967. Less than a decade later he

The Boston area boasts 65 institutions of higher learning, perhaps the most famous of which is Harvard University. Photos © Gene Peach

faced the almost insurmountable challenge of persuading a recalcitrant school committee to accept busing of black students to white schools. It was no simple task for him to persuade his ethnic peers to comply with a law that seemed to threaten their heritage.

White himself was skeptical about forcing the desegregation of Boston's schools, stating openly that "it's a lousy law." But by 1974 even schools in cities like Charlotte, North Carolina, and Jacksonville, Florida, where racial tensions had been extremely apparent, complied with federal laws concerning racially integrated student

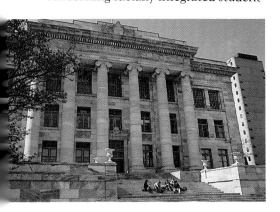

populations. Boston residents, on the other hand, continued to reject desegregation outright. They rejoiced that the Boston School Committee refused to fall into line.

In June 1974, U.S. District Court Judge W. Arthur Garrity, Jr., ruled that the Boston School Committee must approve a citywide desegregation plan for all public schools by September 1975. The committee refused to cooperate. It filed a court appeal, but was defeated when Garrity's decision was upheld.

The public nature of the school authorities' defiance gave Southie residents, their children, and others with anti-busing sentiments an excuse to take their anger and frustration into the schools and onto the streets.

Riots in and around South Boston schools became commonplace throughout the early part of the 1974 academic year. Yet it soon became clear that violence would not solve the deadlock concerning desegregation. Arch-foes of desegregation, like

School Committee member Louise Day Hicks, grew fearful as incident after incident erupted in the schools and in the streets. Yelling racial epithets, thousands of parents gathered when black students were bused into the previously all-white school district. In December 1974 an 18-year-old white youth was stabbed at South Boston High School, and a black was charged with the crime. This provoked more violent demonstrations. And a few months before, a black Haitian immigrant had been the innocent target of a severe beating.

Southie residents traditionally relied on their church and on the police force (largely Irish Catholic) for

Left: Founded just six years after the Pilgrims landed in Plymouth, Harvard University now offers ten graduate and professional schools. This is the Medical School. Photo © Stanley Rowin

Below: Rowers are a common sight along the Charles River. Here, they glide past the Radcliffe boathouse. Photo © Judith Canty

protection and guidance. But on this issue, the neighborhood priests failed to give their approval. After being denied help by federal marshals, Mayor White turned to city law officers to protect schoolchildren before, during, and after school. Mayor White even suggested closing South Boston High School as a way to prevent further violence. This was no idle threat, since federal support for all Boston public schools was at risk due to the city's noncompliance with desegregation laws.

Southie parents felt betrayed. They could no longer rely on their police force, and the Church failed to help. Not one priest would participate in anti-busing activities.

Gradually the violence abated. After months of anguish, mothers from both South Boston and Roxbury (home for most of the black students) offered to form patrols in school buildings. They hoped their presence might reduce hostility and violence. Black and white high school students formed biracial committees to investigate causes of their mutual difficulties. And parents from both black and white areas of the city agreed to sit on a biracial peacemaking council.

In the face of threats to their children's welfare and serious disruption of the educational process, parents in Southie began to look beyond their initial distrust of change. School authorities gave in and complied with

The Boston University Law School building can be seen through this arch; the university, established in 1869, is now a sprawling, urban, teaching and research facility with more than 28,000 full-time and 11,000 part-time students. Photo © Dominic Vecchione

desegregation plans, keeping the schools open and operating in a more or less orderly fashion. By the early 1980s Boston schools were different. They had grown more responsive to the needs of all students. Anti-busing factions were, for the most part, absent from the school committee. A professional administrator had been hired to upgrade the educational system and make it accountable to parents and to the city. By signing the Boston Compact, the corporate community provided support for education in the form of guaranteed hiring priorities for Boston high school graduates in entry-level positions. This gesture of confidence helped turn around the previously high dropout rate.

To talk of the past, or to enumerate numbers of buildings and bodies, is not to begin to describe the catalytic effect of Boston education. There is an incredible energy sparked by "town-gown" interfaces.

Left: Northeastern University provides the largest work-cooperative system in the country. Photo © Martha Everson

Below: This MIT student works on a 3-D hologram. Photo © Stanley Rowin

A comprehensive effort is underway in Boston to improve the public schools and the academic preparation of the students, to encourage students to finish high school and go on to higher education, and to expand employment opportunities for local graduates. This effort reflects an unusual and exciting synergy between the education and business communities, and is an important facet of Boston's current dynamism.

From the excellence of Boston's scientific laboratories springs an easy discourse between university and business. This dialogue, perhaps more than any other factor, has brought the state to the cutting edge of what may become the state's future principal business—the conceiving, making, and marketing of laboratory technologies.

The beginnings of the high-tech industry in the greater Boston area, especially along its highways of high tech, Routes 128 and 495, can be traced to the electronics and defense firms that spun off from MIT and nearby universities several decades ago. By 1986, for example, MIT alone had spun off at least 400 companies, most of them since 1950.

The crucial role played by academia in providing people and research to spawn entrepreneurial activity is clear. Digital Equipment Corporation (DEC) was started by two employees leaving MIT's Lincoln Labs in the 1950s. Wang Laboratories was founded by Dr. An Wang in 1951 after he finished post-doctoral study at Harvard's Applied Physics Labs.

Advances in academe have continued to provide ideas for new products, improved processes, and entirely new industries. Biotechnology, for example, which has potential for application in a broad spectrum of industries, evolved from basic research in the life sciences. And the diversity of companies that started up in the area to make electronic devices, sophisticated medical equipment, advanced computers, and software at-

test to the importance of the academic backdrop. The 65 colleges and universities in the greater Boston area have also provided a critical source of professional labor, including physicians, managers, and lawyers as well as engineers and scientists. Figures show that half of the state's 2,000 annually graduated Ph.D.'s remain in Massachusetts after completing their studies.

As competition stiffens and technology changes, high-tech companies must take advantage of every innovation that can step up their productivity. Effective application of some of the new methods and machines demands new work skills that can only be learned by going back to school. This national problem finds

particularly fruitful resolution in Boston's educational environment.

In greater Boston alone, adult learners will find more than 7,000 offerings of academic, vocational, and recreational courses. Currently, adults can work toward undergraduate degrees through special programs at Boston College, Tufts, Boston University, Harvard, and Northeastern. Northeastern's huge cooperative work-study program is the national pacesetter in continuing education.

Other institutions, such as the Boston Center for Adult Education, offer courses for fun and personal enrich-

Dana Barrows moves down court for the Boston College Eagles. Photo © Christopher Lauber

ment. Choose from such classes as "Swing Dance," "Antique Hunting in Boston," and "Personal Financial Planning."

The quality as well as the quantity of opportunities in the Boston area, combined with the city's long history of commitment to learning, have earned Boston its well-deserved reputation for excellence in education.

Above: Doug Flutie, playing for Boston College, faces an assault from the Army team. Photo © Christopher Lauber

Left: College sports in Boston are supported enthusiastically. Photo © Christopher Lauber

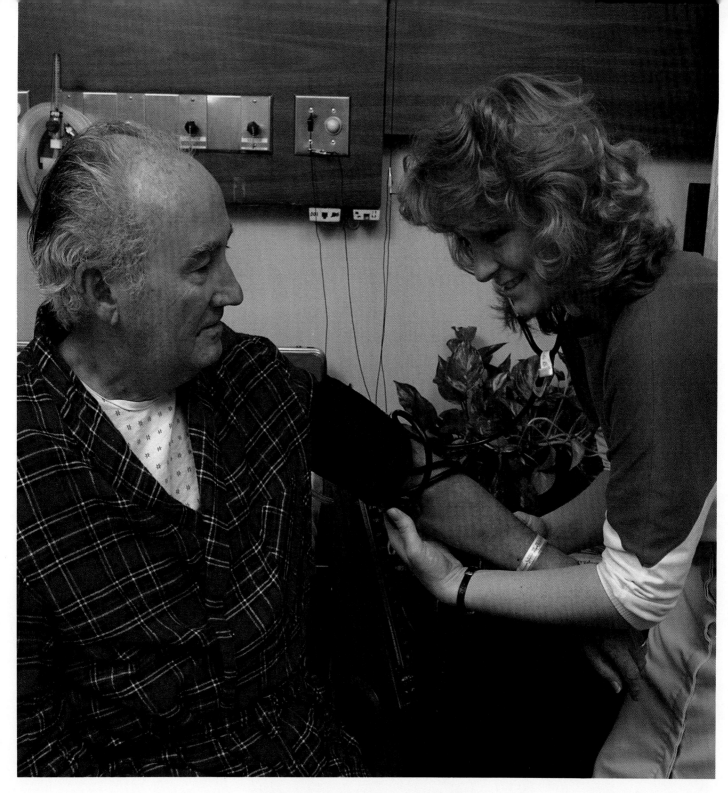

The quality of nursing care in Boston is excellent.
Photo © Shelly R. Harrison

John Collins Warren was "a spare man," according to Oliver Wendell Holmes, Sr., "with strongly marked features, of austere expression, authoritative manners, sometimes careless, occasionally aiming at elegance in personal presentment." Holmes considered him "one of the best educated medical men of his generation," and stated that "he commanded allegiance and obedience... always deliberate, always cool, with a grim smile in sudden emergencies where weaker men would have looked perplexed and wiped their foreheads." Another medical colleague, James Jackson, was described by Holmes as "a pure and noble character, of serenely cheerful aspect, pleasant, inspiriting manner, always neat and plainly dressed, exact in all his habits, punctual as the morning sun [and] full of sober wisdom of experience." Together in 1812, Drs. Warren and Jackson founded the oldest continuously published medical journal in the world—*The New England Journal of Medicine.* Harvard graduates, Bostonians through and through, these two medical mavericks also obtained the charter for the Massachusetts General Hospital in 1811, and Dr. Warren in 1846 participated in the making of medical history in this same hospital.

On October 16, 1846, Dr. Morton entered the surgical amphitheater of Massachusetts General. He was 15 minutes late and the small crowd of doctors and observers were growing impatient ("All is ready—the stillness oppressive"). The stage was set for the most important medical event of the nineteenth century—the administration of ether. Once the doctors were assembled, the experiment was completed and the brave patient, Mr. Gilbert Abbott, survived his surgery, declaring he had "suffered no pain." Dr. Warren, a participating doctor, turned to the observers and declared, "Gentlemen, this is no humbug." No humbug indeed. Surgical practices, historically excruciating, usually fatal, turned a corner and never looked back.

"The disease known as puerperal fever is so far contagious as to be frequently carried from patient to patient by physicians and nurses," declared Oliver Wendell Holmes, Sr., in a paper delivered to the Boston Society for Medical Improvement in 1843. Holmes' controversial ideas—ideas that suggested a need for new standards of sanitation in medical care—were ahead of their time and forerunners to the much-heralded introduction of the germ theory. The enormously positive impact of acceptance of the germ theory on medical care was further to revolutionize surgical survival. No humbug here either.

Boston, in the forefront of medical progress, found itself in a spotlight that continues to shine on exciting and diverse innovations in the field of health care.

Boston proper today boasts 17 hospitals with more than 100 facilities in the greater Boston area. In these hospitals, many combining direct care with the latest in biomedical research, we find patients who have come from every corner of the country and the globe seeking help in "the health care capital of the world."

Massachusetts General Hospital (MGH), perhaps Boston's best-known medical center, is certainly its oldest (1811) and one of its largest. From its original building designed by and named for the architect Charles Bulfinch, the hospital has expanded to approximately a score of buildings. Today more than 31,000 patients are admitted each year, and there are an estimated 2,500 patient visits per day. It is no wonder that people flock to this institution when in need of care—an institution that the *Boston Observer* has called "the center of the medical constellation ... of the whole Boston system." This central role stems from a long history of trailbreaking discoveries. Aside from the ether episode mentioned previously, doctors at MGH were the first to solve problems of bladder stones (1878); abdominal surgery (1886); lead poisoning (1926); endocrine disorders (1929); the use of radioactive iodine (1937), influential in the development of nuclear medicine; methods for freezing blood (1964); and, in the early 1980s, the invention of artificial skin for burn victims. This tradition continues with contributions too

CHAPTER 9

The Hub of Health Care

BY ALEXANDRA DUNDAS TODD

numerous to list here. The current research in dermatology on the removal of various vascular lesions of the skin such as "port-wine stains" with laser technology is one example of past glories continuing into the present.

John A. Parrish and Rox Anderson, two doctors working at the Wellman Laboratory at MGH, are conducting research in this area with Candela Laser Corporation of Wayland, Massachusetts. While the use of laser technology in dermatology is not new, Candela's pulsed dye laser system is in the vanguard of laser surgery.

Treating skin lesions without damaging surrounding tissue or causing scarring of the skin has been the goal. The pulsed dye laser system dramatically increases this possibility. The researchers and Candela Laser Corporation have published clinical results showing that "the Candela laser operates within predetermined parameters of laser-tissue interaction and selectively targets oxyhemoglobin within the lesion. Clinical studies have shown reduced thermal damage to the skin and functionally normal skin immediately after treatment." FDA approved, this laser system is being

used with increasing frequency in dermatology, and future applications in the fields of ophthalmology, cardiovascular medicine, and gastrointestinal disorders are being developed. The collaboration of high-tech industry and biomedical research, corporate development and the medical community—a young, growing business (with a revenue increase of 280 percent from 1986 to 1987) and a

Below: An interesting architectural mix is created by the Grey building and the Ambulatory Care building at Massachusetts General Hospital. Photo © Gene Peach

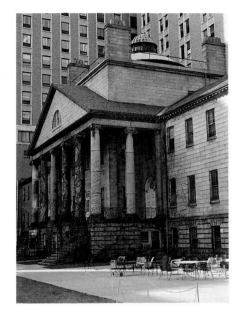

historically honored hospital—is a collaboration offering infinite possibilities for our health.

Founded in 1869 with 20 beds, The Children's Hospital today, with 344 beds, is another old and prestigious hospital important for health care in the Boston area. It is the largest pediatric hospital in the United States. Approximately 14,000 children are admitted each year, and the more than 100 outpatient clinics see over 168,000 patients annually.

In 1983, eight-year-old Ben was one of these patients. First diagnosed at the University of Massachusetts Medical Center as having a malignant brain tumor, Ben was referred to Children's. His chances of survival were slim. After careful consideration of the limited options for treatment combined with limited chances of a cure, Ben was chosen to undergo a new, experimental treatment—Children's first radioactive brain implant.

The procedure was a success. Both his doctor, Nancy Tarbell, who says "Ben is doing great," and his mother, Maureen, who "felt Ben's recovery was a miracle. We had been told that his chances for survival were very low," are optimistic about Ben's future.

Louis M. Kunkel's research group, making significant progress toward unraveling the mysteries of muscular dystrophy, is one more example, among many, where research holds great promise to save children's lives. By identifying a protein needed for proper muscle development, the

Above left: The use of ether was pioneered at Massachusetts General Hospital in the mid-nineteenth century by Dr. John Collins Morton. This is the Bulfinch Building at Massachusetts General Hospital. The Ether Dome can be seen at the top of the photo. Photo © Gene Peach

Below: The Ether Dome at Massachusetts General Hospital was so named for the early discovery and demonstration of ether use at this facility. Photo © Stan Rowin

Below: These nurses at University of Massachusetts Medical Center are taking a patient's EKG. Photo © Shelly R. Harrison

Right: This young man receives therapy. Photo © Shelly R. Harrison

group has made treatment a foreseeable possibility for many children the world over.

This is a hospital dedicated to the health of children, but medical research for all ages is done here. Roger Madison, a neurobiologist, has spent recent years working on nerve guides, seeking a better understanding of the nervous system. While much of his funding is from the government, his team also enjoys sponsored research. American Biomaterials Corporation (ABC) of New Jersey came to Boston seeking medical experts to work with them on collagen products, drawn by the hospital's reputation for expertise in this area. Dr. Madison and ABC are working together on testing collagen in

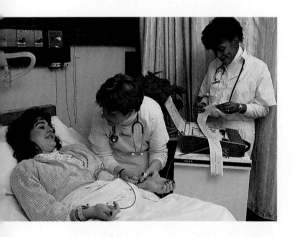

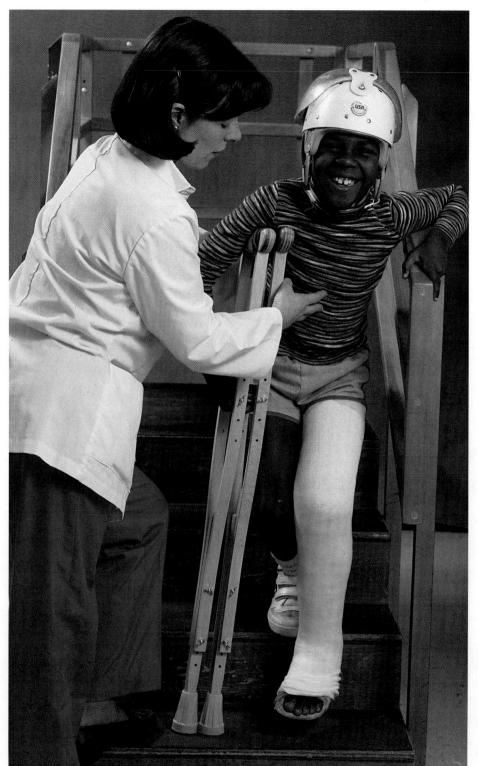

nerve guide tubes, with the immediate hope of treating peripheral nerve injury and the long-term goal of correcting spinal cord trauma.

The New England Deaconess, another hospital with a long history, opened its doors to the sick in 1896. A group of women, church deaconesses concerned that the poor and indigent of all ages needed quality care, were the founders. Throughout this long history many changes have occurred, making the Deaconess today a prestigious teaching and

research hospital. One aspect that has not changed is its commitment to personal, caring accommodations for the sick.

Especially known for research in cancer and radiation, the Deaconess' computer-controlled radiation therapy is finely tuned to radiate a "large tumor-bearing area while sparing normal tissue." This technique has introduced a radiation therapy more sophisticated than any in the world.

Also specializing in "tracking the silent killer," heart disease, Dr. Robert Lees is discovering resources for undermining the nation's number one cause of death. "Atherosclerosis is the most common cause of death in this country," says Dr. Lees. "It leads to 40 percent of all deaths and is far ahead of cancer, which is number two with about 25 percent of deaths."

Lees is working on metabolic imaging, using a radioactive substance to image plaques (such as cholesterol) in blood vessels. Trouble areas can be targeted and treated *before* hardening of the arteries, stroke, and heart attack occur. Dr. Lees emphasizes the importance of research in this area because heart disease kills so many people, especially relatively young people. "Atherosclerosis is a very nasty disease that takes away people in their most productive years."

The best in technology, an interest in such central health issues as cancer and heart disease, and a caring atmosphere reflect a historical progress

that continues to make patients very satisfied customers at the Deaconess.

Brigham and Women's hospital also has an enthusiastic following, especially those using its extensive obstetric and newborn medicine services. Brigham and Women's delivers the sixth highest volume of live births in the United States and provides the most comprehensive obstetric services in the state. But while best known for these specialties, Brigham and Women's is a leading medical center in other areas as well. For example: (1954) the first successful kidney transplant was performed; (1959) the first clinical reports appeared on the efficacy of birth control pills; (1973) abdominal electrocardiography, or monitoring of the fetus during labor, was developed; (1984) the first heart was transplanted in New England.

This rich, innovative history continues today in such areas as rheumatology and immunology. Dr. E. Frank Austin's studies of drugs that suppress joint inflammation offer hope in a

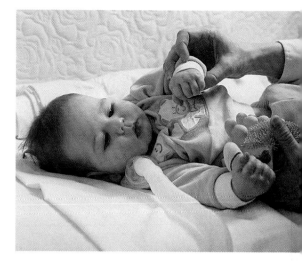

field that is receiving much attention, yet still holds many mysteries.

Research on AIDS, a disease so frightening to people that the very word holds threat, is a major research interest at Beth Israel Hospital. Dr. Clyde Crumpacker and his associates are testing drugs that may "ease suffering and prolong life" for those afflicted.

Cancer, another highly charged topic, is also in the forefront of research and treatment at Beth Israel. In the past year Dr. Eric Fossel, Dr. Justine M. Carr, and Dr. Jan McDonagh have developed an experimental blood test that could potentially detect a wide range of cancers in early stages of growth—detection that could save lives through earlier treatment and prevention.

More specifically, colorectal cancer is being fought in a collaborative effort to implement "The Test You Can't Fail." Beth Israel, WBZ-TV4, CVS Pharmacies, and Smith/Kline Diagnostics have developed a public service campaign supported by the American Cancer Society to encourage the detection of hidden blood in

Children's Hospital

Above: Babies receive extra TLC. Photo © Shelly R. Harrison

Above left: For this psychologist, a small toy is a useful tool. Photo © Shelly R. Harrison

Left: The Children's Hospital in Boston is the largest pediatric hospital in the United States: approximately 14,000 children are admitted each year. Photo © Stanley Rowin

the stool—another preventive technique through early detection.

The Dana-Farber Cancer Institute is also internationally known for research and treatment of cancer. In 1986 this institute commemorated its 40th anniversary, "celebrating a heritage of hope," with pride in its past accomplishments and optimism for future breakthroughs. While some cancers continue unchecked and some, even more alarmingly, are growing (those of the breast, lung, and colon), progress is being made in understanding the immune system and cell pathology, as well as stemming the tide of specific cancers. Leukemia in children, a major research

Right: The New England Deaconess Hospital is today a prestigious teaching and research facility, specializing in cancer and radiation research. Photo © Stanley Rowin

Below: AIDS research is currently a primary concern at Beth Israel Hospital, and doctors here are testing new drugs to ease the suffering of those afflicted. Photo © Stanley Rowin

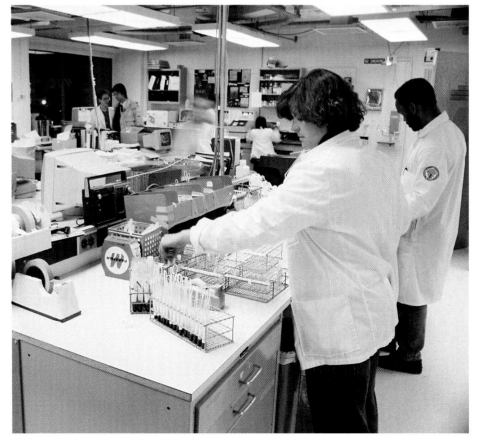

interest of founder Dr. Sidney Farber, has undergone dramatic progress. Osteogenic sarcoma, a tumor in the knee joint most often affecting adolescents, and cancers of the head and neck have also changed from prognosis negative to increased survival rates.

Most hospitals have wards or specialists that cater to mental health needs. McLean Hospital, however, owned by the Massachusetts General Hospital Corporation and affiliated with Harvard Medical School, is ex-

Above: The Brigham and Women's Hospital provides extensive obstetric and newborn medical services. Photo © Gene Peach

Left: These laboratory technicians busily working at the University of Massachusetts Medical Center are one indication of the high level of collaboration between high-tech industry and biomedical research. Photo © Shelly R. Harrison

clusively concerned with psychiatric care. It is the third oldest psychiatric hospital in the United States and, in 1818, became the first in New England. Today McLean treats approximately 3,500 patients annually in the hospital, in outpatient clinics, and in community residences. As well as extensive treatment and research to help people with psychiatric problems, McLean has a long history dedicated to preventive care. The staff works in community schools and offers employers consultations on in-house programs to promote mental health.

McLean Health Services (MHS) is a corporation that combines McLean Hospital and American Medical International, Inc., to provide high-quality psychiatric services throughout the United States and abroad. According to a McLean brochure:

Current efforts... focus on the development and/or management of: community residential treatment programs, employee assistance programs, psychiatric services in acute care hospitals, and educational programs for professionals and the general public.

In terms of research programs, McLean has more than any other psychiatric hospital in the United States. For example, in 1985 it spent $8.5 million on research. Always trying to unravel the perplexing questions about the causes of mental illnesses, who is likely to suffer from them, and how most effectively to treat them, McLean does extensive research into psychotic illnesses; neuroanatomical, neurochemical, and genetic investigations; substance abuse; psychopharmacology; geriatric problems; and

The medical facilities in the Boston area contribute greatly to our understanding of human health and disease. Photos © Bob Krist

psychosocial/environmental influences on mental health.

These hospitals and many others in the Boston area are primarily noted for their extraordinary research contributions to medical science. It is these findings that we read about in our daily newspapers and hear about on the nightly news. Less discussed, but equally important, is the dedication of these hospitals to teaching and patient care. The medical and nursing students in the area receive fine clinical training in the hospital setting, and enjoy classroom instruction from many of the world's finest experts. Major researchers at area hospitals are also usually on the staff of local medical schools. Given the tremendous variety, it is no wonder that people from all over the nation and world vie for the medical school spaces available.

The same reputation for quality that attracts students also attracts patients. Quality of care is a trademark at the hospitals previously mentioned as well as at the many other notable institutions in the area. Recovery and health, increasingly tied to caring as well as curing, receive thoughtful attention. For example, James Carroll in the *Boston Observer,* describing the excellent diagnostic and surgical procedures his brother-in-law experienced at MGH, stated, "I was not surprised that doctors there were able to treat his illness, but I was surprised at how well they treated him." Similarly, patients in Boston's Beth Israel Hospital, when responding to questionnaires evaluating their experiences, are most likely to remark on the nursing service—a service that promotes the same primary nursing assignments to patients for the length of their hospital stay, providing a model of caring being adopted by medical centers around the country.

THE NEW MEDICINES OF MIND AND BODY

Just as Boston is a leader in modern conventional medicine, a variety of

Above: The Dana Farber Cancer Institute is internationally known for its campaign against cancer and for its studies of the human immune system. Photo © Gene Peach

Below: Highly-trained specialists review a skull x-ray. Photo © Shelly R. Harrison

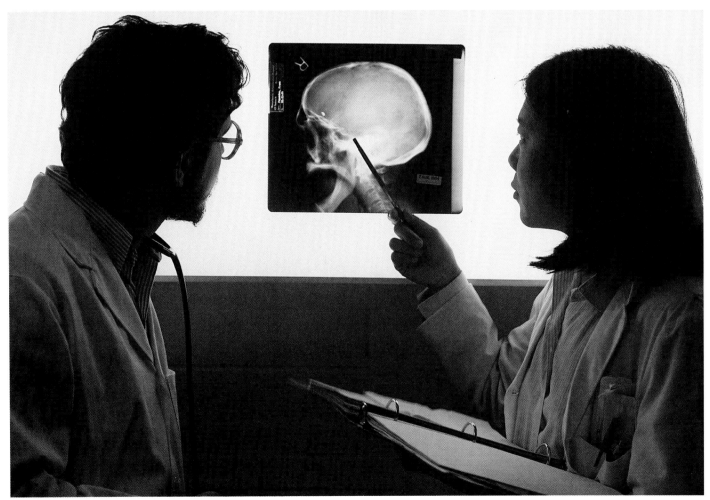

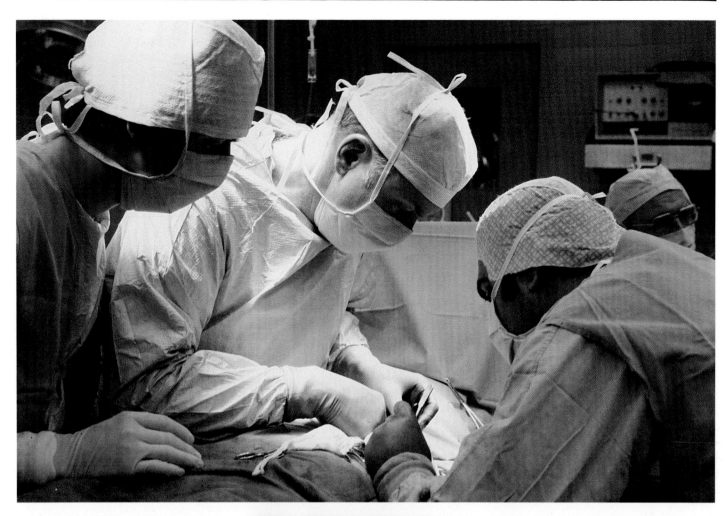

innovative medical practices interested in the mind/body connection are also available—another example of progress in Boston health care.

Herbert Benson, M.D., author of *The Relaxation Response*, first organized his mind/body programs in Behavioral Medicine at Beth Israel Hospital. Today, located at the New England Deaconess and still affiliated with Harvard Medical School, Dr. Benson and his associates integrate radically new concepts for understanding disease and health with the best that conventional medicine has to offer. Their 20 years of research on stress management, based on the relaxation response, have set the tone for an entirely new modality in American health care. The current climate of prevention, wellness, and mind/body connections is in large part due to the innovative efforts of this group. Known most widely for work with hypertension patients, the mind/body approach offers programs to encourage preventive and general

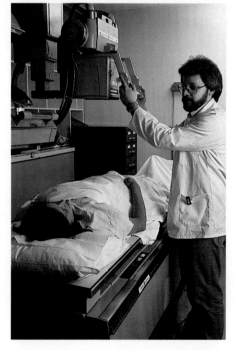

Quality of care is a trademark at Boston area hospitals. Photos © Shelly R. Harrison

health for cancer patients, for those with infertility problems, for people with AIDS/ARC, and others. Relaxation techniques, stress management, nutritional counseling, and exercise are all advocated and discussed in small group settings.

People from all walks of life come

to take advantage of these techniques. The business community in particular has utilized the mind/body programs. Executives and managers, long targeted as high-risk, high-stress groups, come from around the country and the world to learn to relax, to use relaxation as an antidote to stress-related disease. The goal is to help people take control of their health and their lives. Medications are used as needed, but the hope is that lifestyle changes will reduce or eliminate the need for drug and surgical therapies. For example, the mind/body brochure points out that:

A study of 100 patients who completed our program showed that 80 percent significantly reduced their blood pressure or

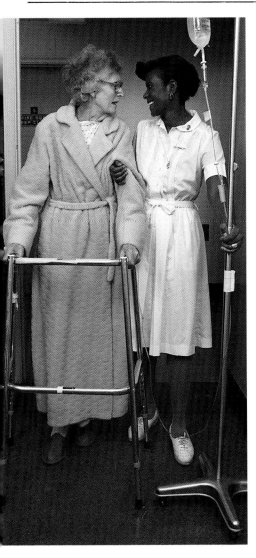

ers under one roof. Centers such as the Health Alliance bring together into one group practitioners such as an M.D., chiropractor, psychotherapists, muscular and physical therapists, a Chinese herbalist, and more. This group was founded "in order to provide high quality, comprehensive health care in an environment that actively promotes well-being of the body, mind, and spirit. The Health Alliance is based on... collaborative healing." Its interest is to provide "care to the community; individuals, couples, special populations and industry" (Health Alliance brochure).

While alternative medicines differ tremendously, themes of self-help and environmental change run through many of the philosophies. This em-

phasis on self-help is especially relevant when looking at health care in Boston because the city is home to two nationally and internationally known self-help organizations. The Boston Women's Health Book Collective was started in 1969. The latest edition of their book, *The New Our*

Left: Boston hospitals provide personal service to patients of all ages. Photo © Shelly R. Harrison

Below: The hospitals in the Boston area are primarily noted for their extraordinary research contributions to medical science, and are dedicated to the training of new physicians.
Photo © Shelly R. Harrison

decreased their need for medications. These people also reduced their overall risk of cardiovascular disease by lowering their blood cholesterol levels, reducing weight and body fat, improving cardiovascular conditioning and reducing anxiety.

Outside of the hospital, health centers emphasizing some of these same ideas abound in the Boston area, as well as other approaches such as acupuncture, clinical ecology, herbal therapies, and chiropractics. *The Directory of Holistic Practitioners for the Greater Boston Area,* edited by David I. Weiss, John R. Boynton, and Marcia Guntzel, includes holistic physicians, nurses, counselors, chiropractors, acupuncturists, homeopathy, biofeedback, spiritual healing, rolfing, and the Alexander Technique, among others. Also listed are health centers where one may find many of these different health work-

Bodies, Ourselves, published in 1985,
has sold copies in the millions around
the world with at least 14 foreign
translations. Another example of a
self-help movement is the Independent Living Movement, started in
Boston and Berkeley in the early
1970s by and for the disabled and/or
chronically ill. Today there are centers around the country providing
consumer resources to turn chronic
"patients" into active participants,
both within and outside of conventional medicine. One such center in
Boston offers advocacy, education,
counseling, training in peer-counsel-
ing, resources to the disabled community, and consultation on issues of
disability to government and the
larger community. Publications such
as "The Disability and Chronic Disease Newsletter," from Dr. Irving Zola
of Brandeis University, provide information for research that serves to further people's understanding and re-
sourcefulness. Both organizations are
interested in helping people to take
care of themselves when possible and
to utilize medical facilities when
needed.

It is this combination of fine, established medical communities, increasingly meshing with new, or old but renewed, understandings of health care
that makes Boston one of the most
lively and prominent medical centers
in the world today.

GIVE ME YOUR POOR...
Boston, like all major American
cities, is faced with the problem of
poverty. Pockets of poverty exist
throughout the United States, and
the need for health care for these
populations looms large. Recently
Massachusetts has, more than any
other state, been grappling with this
old problem in new ways. If Boston is
in fact the health care capital of the
world, then it is perhaps exactly the
place to find insights into how to
achieve first-class health care for all.

Boston City Hospital, like most
large American city hospitals, is so

busy and moves so fast that the observer hardly knows where to look. It
opened its doors in 1864, and open
they have remained. Boston City
offers emergency medical services and
ambulance services for the city, runs
25 neighborhood clinics, has programs for the homeless, treats 90 percent of penetration trauma in the city,
has one of four neonatal intensive
care units in the city, has enormous
patient turnover, but has also seen
some families for generations, and
never turns anyone away.

More unusual, but part of a growing
national movement, is the Community Health Worker Program, a Boston organization affiliated with New
Alliance Community Services based
in New York. According to Gwen
Lowenheim, the director, the importance of finding out what the community wants before setting up programs
or developing policy is one of their
primary goals: "We are not assuming
we know what it is the community

needs." This is a door-to-door project
in deprived neighborhoods where
health professionals ask residents
what they think the community
needs, what would help *them.* Preventive care in the following areas
seems to be called for: how to handle
stress, hypertension, pregnancy,
parenting, family violence; how to
develop self-esteem in a poverty environment. Unexpected approaches
can turn up—such as "cultural
work," talent shows, drawing on the
strengths, often hidden, of a community—that increase self-esteem and
community pride, and have eventual
impacts on physical and mental
health. A broader model of health
than we usually think of is being
developed. Ms. Lowenheim emphasizes that this is a practical project

*The Joslin Diabetes Center is one segment of a
massive medical community in the Boston area.
Photo © Stanley Rowin*

working for a partnership among communities and professionals, with the hope of increasing wellness and well-being.

What makes Massachusetts unique in this area, however, is the current universal health bill first introduced by Governor Michael Dukakis and continued by the chairperson of the state senate Ways and Means Committee, Patricia McGovern. Surrounded by controversy, subjected to several major revisions, this bill is a first attempt in the nation to assure health coverage for nearly all working people. Implementation of the bill will require not only additional legislation and regulation, but also significant funding. Massachusetts will be closely watched to see if this much-heralded plan will work. If successful, it could serve as a model for programs in other states and ultimately for national health coverage.

NEW PATHWAYS IN MEDICAL EDUCATION

Equally unique in the Boston area is medical education. In 1636 the Great and General Court of the Massachu-

setts Bay Colony founded Harvard College. The school was named for its first benefactor, John Harvard of Charlestown, who bequeathed his library and half his estate to this institute of higher learning in 1638. Over a century later, in 1782, President Joseph Willard and the fellows of the college voted to open Harvard Medical School.

Today this prestigious institution is affiliated with numerous hospitals and health care establishments in the Boston area: The Beth Israel Hospital, Children's Hospital, The Dana-Farber Cancer Institute, Massachusetts Eye and Ear, Massachusetts General Hospital, Mount Auburn Hospital, New England Deaconess, West Roxbury and Brockton Veteran's Hospitals, The Center for Blood Research, Harvard Community Health Plan (an HMO), Joselin Diabetes Center, Massachusetts Mental Health, McLean Hospital, and Spalding Rehabilitation Hospital. Few medical students in the world today have such an extensive and impressive community in which to pursue their interests.

Always a trailblazer in medical education, Harvard Medical School, like the Commonwealth of Massachusetts, is breaking new ground in innovative health care. Steeped in tradi-

Above: The Boston Women's Health Book Collective meets for group discussions. Photo © Gaye Hilsenrath

Left: Boston City Hospital offers emergency medical services, ambulance services for the city, runs 25 neighborhood clinics, and has programs for the homeless. It never turns a patient away. Photo © Gene Peach

tion, Harvard Medical School is also taking a giant step into the future.

In 1980 Daniel C. Tosteson, Dean of the Faculty of Medicine at Harvard, in a speech to the Assembly of the Association of American Medical Colleges (AAMC) challenged the community of medical educators to reexamine the education of physicians in light of the overwhelming changes in biotechnology and biomedical knowledge facing medical professionals in the 1980s. Students needed a shift in perspective away from an enclosed learning experience during their school years to the open classroom that would prepare for lifelong learning.

This talk set in motion a revision of the form and content of medical education at Harvard. In 1985 a small group of incoming medical students set apart from those taking the conventional curriculum started on an exciting, experimental journey, a journey that has proven to be very successful.

In 1987 this New Pathways curriculum, renamed the Oliver Wendell Holmes Society, has been integrated and adopted into the general medical education and all incoming students are now educated in the new format. Small groups work with a faculty leader and then develop independent self-study programs. Educational methods also include lectures, seminars, laboratory instruction, clinical training, computer-assisted learning, and problem-solving based tutorials. Instead of being passive recipients of large bodies of knowledge, students actively participate in the educational process. They will study preventive methods as well as disease processes, social influences on health and illness as well as the biophysiological, and communication skills as well as technical expertise. As stated in the Oliver Wendell Holmes 1987-1988 *Program Guide:*

A primary goal is to exercise the student's capacity to think and discover at the same time that facts are learned. The responsibility for learning lies with the student. We seek to make this process challenging and deeply satisfying. We have tried to design an educational process that guides, stimulates, and challenges rather than directs.

The emphasis is on caring as well as curing. The changes enhance rather than replace. Such innovative reorganization is yet another example of an experimental program in the Boston area where the medical community of the nation turns its gaze, expectantly, to observe the results.

A HEALTHY ECONOMY

It is no wonder that Boston, with such a long history and illustrious record, attracts business and private research interests to the area. Private interests come from all over the world to work with experts here on improved products and health procedures as mentioned in examples above. Companies endow prestigious professional chairs such as the Johnson and Johnson Professor of Surgery at Harvard Medical School, currently held by Dr. William Silen, who is doing research on aspirin and ulcers. Health-related

A trailblazer in medical education, Harvard Medical School is breaking new ground in innovative health care. Photo © Ulkrike Welsch

businesses also move to the area to be close to so many medical resources.

Massachusetts is being touted as an economic phenomenon in America today. Employment is up, business is booming. This economic health has in part been created by an influx of new industry which in turn attracts yet more growth. Between 1976 and 1983 the highest job growth industry in the city of Boston, amidst this economic expansion, was in hospitals. Today, while hospitals around the country are experiencing some decrease in patients, Boston's facilities, due in part to the large teaching hospitals, are maintaining or increasing their patient load. High-tech industry has become central to Massachusetts' economic well-being. Within a 30-mile radius of downtown Boston, there are more than 700 high-technology firms, many of them biotechnology companies creating new medical tools and pharmaceutical products. Businesses are continuing to grow, and are increasing so

quickly that the Massachusetts Office of Business Development points out that its figures are dated before they can even be reported.

Pharmaceutical companies in the area, which numbered 30 in 1978, grew to 54 by 1985. These companies manufacture products ranging from allergy medicines to veterinary pharmaceutical preparations to fertility drugs to standard drug preparations to high-tech, biotech, animal, and human therapeutic research.

Biogen Corporation, a company specializing in "human therapeutics," is currently involved in three biotech treatments: AIDS-related drugs, anti-inflammatories, and selected cancer therapies. Started by Walter Gilbert of Harvard and Phillip Sharp of Massachusetts Institute of Technology, this is an example of a locally founded company. Biogen draws on the wealth of medical facilities as well as its own laboratories for research, and then markets its products through Schering Corporation.

Medical equipment companies, such as those specializing in optical instruments and lenses in medical and dental instruments and supplies, are another example of a growth group. There were 149 in 1978 and 188 in 1985. These companies make diverse products that include every imaginable (and unimaginable) kind of optical equipment, dialysis equipment, electron microscopes, surgical instruments, gynecological supplies and appliances, orthopedic and prosthetic devices, and lasers, and often offer services to help use these products.

Spectro Film, Inc., is an example of a large, well-established company in the Boston area that is anything but local. Serving an international clientele, this firm manufactures and markets optical interference filters that read substances through the use of stacks of glass and beams of light. Useful in many medical procedures, such as the analysis of blood, this product has been used in AIDS research.

Whether local or international, whether drawing on or contributing to the medical community (or both), private industry plays a vital role in Boston's economy and the city's status as "the health care capital of the world."

The rich history of health care in Boston—like the Old North Church, the cobblestone streets of Louisburg Square, or the homes of Louisa May Alcott and Paul Revere—is a regional and national treasure, yet this chapter only reveals the tip of the iceberg. There are many other fine hospitals, medical staffs, research projects, alternative practices, social service efforts, educational facilities, and business enterprises that contribute to the spirit of medicine in Boston. Its prognosis is excellent. As Dr. Warren would say, "This is no humbug."

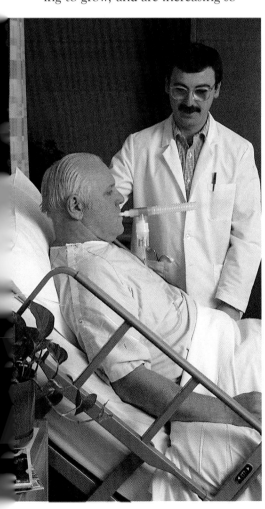

Above: This pharmacist must maintain an accurate inventory. Photo © Shelly R. Harrison

Left: A patient receives respiratory therapy at Brookline Hospital. Photo © Shelly R. Harrison

*Abstract lines of a glass atrium characterize the
Kennedy Library. Photo © Stanley Rowin*

Charles Dickens had a marvelous time seeing Boston. He went on a carriage ride through Mount Auburn cemetery. He dined on the Harvard campus and at the Parker House. He walked on Beacon Hill. He met with Henry Wadsworth Longfellow. Then, back home in England, Dickens wrote nostalgically in his 1842 *American Notes:* "The city is a beautiful one, and cannot fail, I should imagine, to impress all strangers favorably."

Has there ever been a visitor from a foreign land who was not enamored of Boston? Outsiders invariably love the traditional architecture, the easiness getting around. Above all, they are impressed with Boston's European-like dedication to culture. While many American cities seem desperate to import writers, artists, musicians—anything to bolster their precarious cultural credentials—Boston stands truly secure, like Paris or London. Many Bostonians share the proud, almost haughty perspective of Ralph Waldo Emerson, who once observed: "Boston commands special attention as the town which was appointed by the destiny of nations to head the civilization of North America."

For two-and-a-half centuries those who write and paint have flocked to Boston and found favor. They have been joined by those who dance and produce drama and make music—classical, folk, jazz, and pop. Also, photographers and filmmakers have made their homes in Boston environs.

Lastly, Puritan Boston has been transformed into a national center for raucous, irreverent stand-up comedy.

Boston cultural history ranges from the dour sermons of Cotton Mather to the upbeat jokes of comic Jay Leno. That's skipping past Benjamin Franklin and Mother Goose, Henry James and Louisa May Alcott, Emerson and Hawthorne and Thoreau, John Singer Sargent and Henry Wadsworth Longfellow, Harvard and MIT, the Boston Symphony Orchestra and the Museum of Fine Arts, and hundreds of other cultural signposts. There are cultural attractions every day and night, and most are taken for granted. They go with the territory. Boston's greatest landscape architect, Frederick Law Olmsted, once bragged about his town's abundance of "...schools, libraries, music and the fine arts. People of the greatest wealth can hardly command as much of these in the country as the poorest working girl is offered here in Boston ..."

With no further ado, let's explore what's available in Boston.

The first colonial newspaper came out in Boston, on September 25, 1690, edited by Benjamin Harris, an English exile. *Publick Occurrences Both Foreign and Domestick* included news of a holiday called "Thanksgiving," the sad story of a suicide in Watertown, and a horrific tale of children in nearby Chelmsford being carried off by Indians. This spicy three-sheet was promptly censored and

stopped. In 1704 America's second paper, *The Boston News-Letter,* emerged and continued for 72 years. But lively journalism really began with a genuine opposition paper, the *New England Courant,* started in 1721 by James Franklin. The printer's 16-year-old brother slipped a satiric sketch under the *Courant* door and signed it "Silence Dogood." For six months, before James Franklin discovered the identity of the anonymous writer, "Dogood" letters appeared in every issue. By that time, Benjamin Franklin could not be silenced. He fled to Philadelphia and started his own *Pennsylvania Gazette.* The rest is American journalism history.

Back in Boston, the future Revolutionary leaders—Samuel Adams, James Otis, John Adams—used the pages of *The Boston Gazette* to protest the Stamp Act and other colonial taxation. British sympathizers countered with articles and letters in Loyalist-minded Boston papers such as the *Newsletter.* A precedent was established. Boston print media would be found on all sides of significant issues of the day.

The Boston newspaper world has shrunk from the 11 dailies which, in 1900, battled it out on Beantown's version of Newspaper Row. Still, Boston is among the few American cities that offers its citizens a clear choice of political positions and ideologies with its current newspapers. The liberal-

CHAPTER 10

The Finer
Things of Life

BY GERALD PEARY

minded *Boston Globe,* a staunch supporter of the Kennedys, Michael Dukakis, and other Democrats, has been published since 1872 by the Taylor family. The energetic conservative tabloid *Boston Herald* was owned until recently by the Hearst Corporation. Then Rupert Murdoch bought it, raised the circulation, and made the *Herald* increasingly profitable.

If the choice of the *Herald* and *Globe* isn't enough, Bostonians turn to the weekly *Boston Phoenix*—a long-running and now-established alternate paper which specializes in arts coverage—and, for international news, to the much-respected *Christian Science Monitor.*

As for magazines, Boston is, before all else, the home of *The Atlantic Monthly,* a revered national institution. These days the competition is urbane, slick, and upscale. Among others are *Boston Women, Running Magazine, New Age Journal, Bostonia, Harvard Magazine,* and the immensely successful *Boston Magazine.* The latter, founded in 1962, stands at the top of all city magazines for ad revenue.

To introduce Boston's incredible literary heritage we start with the undeservedly little-known Phillis Wheatley. Born in Africa, sold a slave in Boston in 1761, but taught to read and write by her masters, Wheatley published, at 19, the first book of poetry in America by a black woman. In it she chronicled her tribulations two centuries before Alex Haley's *Roots:* "I, young in life, by seeming cruel fate/Was snatch'd from Africa's seeming happy seat."

Mention should also be made of Mother Goose. Yes, she was a real person, a bonafide Bostonian named Elizabeth Foster, who married Isaac Vergoose. Her son-in-law, Thomas

This well known trompe l'oeil can be found on Newbury Street. Photo © Kenneth Martin

Fleet, a printer, published her immortal work, *Songs for the Nursery, or Mother Goose Melodies.* There is a gravestone in the Old Granary Burying Ground on Beacon Hill for a "Mary Goose." Is this the tomb of the matriarch of nursery rhymes? It's a scholar's puzzlement.

And not many people realize that Fannie Farmer really had a cooking school in Boston. It was located at 40 Hereford Street, in the Back Bay, where she tried out the recipes that became the basis of the *Boston Cooking School Cook Book.* That volume, published by the Boston firm of Little,

Brown, and Company, might be the all-time Boston best-seller, with more than 4 million copies read around the world.

And for all-time fiction favorites, a basic bookshelf of Boston literature with stories set locally, try these 10 for a good beginning: Henry James' *The Europeans* and *The Bostonians;* Esther Forbes' *Johnny Tremain;* Jean Stafford's *Boston Adventure;* Nathaniel Hawthorne's *The Blithedale Romance;* John P. Marquand's *The Late George Apley;* Edwin O'Connor's *The Last Hurrah* and *The Edge of Sadness;* George Santayana's *The Last Puritan;*

and any of Robert B. Parker's Boston-set Spenser detective novels.

But invariably the best way to get a feel of Boston's literary heritage is by a walking tour of the city. Begin at the Parker House. No hotel in America holds so many prestigious literary ghosts, not even New York's Algonquin. It was here in the private dining room that the "Saturday Club" feasted in the mid-nineteenth cen-

Left: Boston Architectural Center's trompe l'oeil is a prime example of design diversity throughout the city. Photo © Martha Everson

Below: This mural depicts children as being the force of the future. Photo © Gaye Hilsenrath

tury, a group including Emerson, Longfellow, Oliver Wendell Holmes, John Greenleaf Whittier, Richard Henry Dana, and Hawthorne. It was here, in 1859, that *The Atlantic*'s founders met to launch the new magazine. And it was here that Dickens stayed for his 1867 Boston tour, hiding out from autograph-seekers, practicing before a large mirror a speech to be delivered to Hub admirers. Check the Parker House mezzanine; Charles Dickens' mirror has been moved there.

Next, there should be a neighborhood stop in the King's Chapel Burying Ground at the grave of Elizabeth Swain, supposedly Hawthorne's inspiration for *The Scarlet Letter*'s heroine, Hester Prynne, and then a walk over to Cornucopia, a restaurant on West Street. Imagination is required to think past the svelte decoration to

The Granary Burial Ground on Beacon Hill draws tourists year round. Photo © Gene Peach

this space as a pre-Victorian literary parlor. Here, the great nineteenth-century magazine *The Dial* was published, and here Hawthorne was married. The latter event occurred in the back, now Cornucopia's formal dining room.

But real literary Boston means a trip up Beacon Hill. A nineteenth-century *Who's Who* inhabited these sublime, brick-faced townhouses looking over the city, seconds away from a walk in the Common, and 10 minutes from the Parker House. Louisa May Alcott owned 10 Louisburg Square, where her father, Bronson, the experimental educator, died. The author of *Little Women* also resided at 20 Pinckney Street, and there she did most of her writing. Hawthorne's home was 54 Pinckney Street, and the Jameses—novelist Henry, psychologist William, and diarist Alice—lived at times at 131 Mt. Vernon Street. William Dean Howells owned 4 Louisburg Square in the 1890s, after his Cambridge days as editor of *The Atlantic Monthly*.

Number 50 Chestnut Street was the home of Francis Parkman, author of *The Oregon Trail*. Interestingly, 33 Beacon Street is the made-up fictional address of Nathaniel Alden, the Brahmin protagonist of philosopher George Santayana's best-selling 1930s novel, *The Last Puritan*. To make matters more confusing, that is next door to the real-life home of the prestigious Boston publishing house, Little, Brown, and Company, at 34 Beacon Street, and a block from Houghton-Mifflin at 1 Beacon Street. Also, writer Edwin O'Connor dwelled at 48 Beacon Street after the success of *The Last Hurrah*. And today, somewhere on Beacon Hill, resides Robin Cook, author of the well-received potboilers *Sphinx* and *Coma*.

Take a walk across the Common for a peek into the Ritz-Carlton Hotel bar. As the legend goes, that is where poets Anne Sexton and Sylvia Plath went for three-martini afternoons following their rigorous Boston University writing class under Robert Lowell. (Native Bostonian Lowell, who

died in 1977, was considered America's preeminent post-war poet.)

That's all for downtown Boston.

For the second major literary stop, it is necessary to cross the bridge into Cambridge. Most nineteenth-century luminaries who rejected Beacon Hill did so to be closer to the appealing environs of Harvard University. Robert Lowell's great uncle, nineteenth-century poet James Russell Lowell, almost always lived in Cambridge. While serving in exotic lands as a foreign ambassador, he dreamed of his neighborhood Cambridge druggist. Lowell said, "I'd rather see Ramsay's in Harvard Square than Rameses the Great in Egypt."

Other intellectuals swore similar allegiance to Harvard Square, like those who occupied the glorious mansions on Brattle Street and nearby. Among them were John Bartlett, author of *Familiar Quotations;* Longfellow; Santayana; Margaret Fuller; Howells; and, in the twentieth century, T.S. Eliot, Robert Frost, and John P. Marquand. There were also those who worked on the Harvard *Lampoon:* Santayana; Owen Wister (*The Virginian*); Robert Benchley; even John Reed (*Ten Days that Shook the World*). In addition there were those who studied at Radcliffe College, including Gertude Stein and Helen Keller, and those in Professor George P. Baker's famous 47 Workshop at Harvard, including Thomas Wolfe, Eugene O'Neill, Philip Barry, and Sidney Howard.

Literary-minded tourists in Cambridge should stroll past the eccentric castle exterior of the *Lampoon,* then pass through Harvard Square to the Blacksmith House Bakery and Cafe, once owned by Dexter Pratt, the

Above (top): Famous Patriots of the Revolution are buried in the Granary Burial Ground. Photo © Judith Canty

Above: Legendary authors and playwrights have walked the cobblestone paths of Harvard Square. Photo © Gene Peach

Left: Author of Little Women, *Louisa May Alcott rests here, in peace. Photo © B. &J. McGrath*

melodramas or eloquent British classics. Between 1860 and 1880 a stock company played in repertoire at the Boston Museum, and the city gave the world at least one great actress, Charlotte Cushman. Born in the North End, she toured America and England as Lady Macbeth, but also assumed the male parts in Shakespeare. Romeo was Cushman's most acclaimed role, the talk of several continents.

For much of the twentieth century, Boston was famous as a pre-Broadway tryout stop, where plays on the way to New York detoured for previews and fix-ups and tried to avoid the diligent

eponymous smitty of Longfellow's famous poem, "The Village Blacksmith." Further down Brattle Street is the Longfellow House, a 1759 Georgian mansion in which the white-bearded poet wrote for 45 years and died in 1882. Operated by the National Park Service, this is the only Boston home of a literary personage open to the public. It's worth a peek at Longfellow's study where he penned "Evangeline" and "Hiawatha."

Cambridge's other major literary site is the Mt. Auburn cemetery. If a cemetery can be beautiful, restful, and spiritual, this is the place. And it's possible to see the graves of Longfellow, James Russell Lowell, poet Amy Lowell, and publishers Little and Brown.

Nobody arriving in Boston for the literary excitements, however, can fail to make a day's visit to nearby Concord, where, at various times, Thoreau, Emerson, Hawthorne, and Louisa May Alcott resided. Concord is a

feast of open-door visitation in the spring and summer months: Orchard House, where Alcott thought up *Little Women*; The Wayside, Hawthorne's final domicile; the Ralph Waldo Emerson Home, where the guides tell funny stories about Thoreau, the dinner guest; and, of course, Walden Pond, which is not only great history, but also a transcendental spot for a swim.

In the beginning the Puritan church leaders had their way by banning theater in Boston. In 1686 Increase Mather railed from the pulpit against the decadent "discourse now of beginning stage plays in New England." There were occasional private performances in people's homes. But even in 1750, a theatrical performance in public could be fined a severe $20. The American Revolution brought many freedoms, and by the 1790s Bostonians could see renditions of *Othello* and *Hamlet* in the New Exhibition Room on Hawley Street. Drama only became respectable after Boston's great architect, Charles Bulfinch, designed the lavish Boston Theatre at Federal and Franklin streets in 1794.

Boston, like other nineteenth-century cities, was treated to touring thespians offering a choice of rickety

Above: The great Henry Wadsworth Longfellow once lived here. Photo © Kenneth Martin

Right: Fall colors surround Walden Pond in Concord. Photo © Gene Peach

city censors. (There was much truth to the phrase "Banned in Boston.") Performers John Gielgud in *Hamlet* and Mary Martin and Ezio Pinza in *South Pacific* came to the Wilbur, Colonial, and Shubert, the three sumptuous, proscenium arch theaters built before World War I and still active in the 1980s. But these days the cost of mounting a Broadway show is too prohibitive for a full-scale New England tryout. Instead, Boston gets the best of New York shortly after the original run, and with authentic Broadway casts for such shows as *Cats, Evita,* and *Les Miserables.* Perhaps the all-time Boston favorite is

Richard Harris in *Camelot,* which set box-office records for America.

But for those whose taste runs to more esoteric fare, more off-Broadway, Boston boasts two superior repertory companies that move deftly between new plays by important writers and imaginative reworkings of theater classics. The first is the American Repertoire Theater (ART), founded by critic Robert Brustein and housed since 1966 at the Loeb Drama Center on Brattle Street in Cambridge. The ART is most famous for its adventurous renditions of Chekhov and Pirandello and other modern playwrights-as-thinker, and for its col-

laborations with such avant-garde figures as director Peter Sellars, playwright Robert Wilson, and composer Philip Glass. ART productions of *'Night, mother* and *THE CIVIL WARS* won recent Pulitzer Prizes for drama.

The Huntington Theatre Company, at Boston University since 1982, mounts five ambitious productions per season by major playwrights from Stoppard to Shakespeare. The Huntington is best known for its world premieres of dramas of black American life by August Wilson, developed under the sensitive hand of director Lloyd Richards.

Boston has little theaters galore, some very experimental, some just old-fashioned satiric fun. In the latter category, mention must be made of *Shear Madness*, Boston's all-time theatrical hit. *Shear Madness* became, at its 3,225th performance during 1987, the longest-running non-musical play in American theater history. This semi-improvised comedy/murder mystery set in a rowdy hair salon has brought laughter to seemingly every second Bostonian, and almost every tourist.

Right: Broadway plays appear on many stages in Boston. Photo © Martha Everson

Far right: The longest-running non-musical play in American theater, Shear Madness, has brought laughter to many Bostonians. Photo © Gaye Hilsenrath

Below: The Museum of Fine Arts is a vast store-house of fine treasures. Photo © Stanley Rowin

Long before there were art galleries or museums, Boston was known throughout the colonies for its superb portraitists. The first famous name is John Smibert, who emigrated from Scotland and, in 1730, opened a studio overlooking Scollay Square to paint New England's renowned. His portraits of Judge Edmund Quincy and Jonathan Edwards hang in Boston's Museum of Fine Arts, but his most formidable achievement is in public sight—Faneuil Hall, of which Smibert was the architect.

John Singleton Copley was probably America's greatest pre-Revolutionary painter, a realist admired for his sculpting, his subtle coloring, and

his chiaroscuro. Before leaving America for permanent residence in England in 1774, Copley executed portraits of John Adams, John Quincy Adams, and John Hancock, earning enough to purchase a 20-acre farm at the top of Beacon Hill. Many of his best works are in the Museum of Fine Arts collection, but important por-

traits were destroyed in the Boston fire of 1872.

The MFA also showcases the portraits of Rhode Island-born Gilbert Stuart, who settled in Boston in 1805. He painted Jefferson and Madison, but he is most famous for his four portraits of George Washington, one of them used as the model for the dollar bill.

Two painters of note in pre-Civil War times resided in Cambridge. Washington Allston, sometimes called "the American Titian," died without completing his masterpiece, *Belshazzar's Feast*. It hangs, unfinished, in the Boston Athenaeum. Winslow Homer observed nature for his rustic watercolors while fishing on Cambridge's Fresh Pond. He sketched his older brother playing football in Harvard Yard. Homer opened a studio in 1857, but moved away forever when he went to New York to illustrate for *Harper's Weekly*.

The genius of Boston's greatest nineteenth- and twentieth-century artist, John Singer Sargent, can be appreciated in his magnificent biblical murals on the walls of the Boston Public Library. But his more personal work on canvas is entwined with the world of his patron and benefactor, Isabella Stewart Gardner. In 1903 she turned her Venetian-style private palace in Boston's Fenway into the world-famous Isabella Stewart Gardner Museum. This museum is a must for visitors to Boston, both for its extraordinary decor, including a Spanish courtyard, and for its nonpareil painting collection. With consultation from art expert Bernard Berenson, Gardner bought masterpieces from around the world at then-affordable prices. Among the prize items in the museum are a Botticelli *Madonna*, Titian's *Rape of Europa*, his most important painting in North America, and Vermeer's superlative *The Concert*. And finally, there are the featured works of Sargent, including *El Jaleo*, of a Spanish flamenco dancer, and a once-scandalous 1888

portrait of Mrs. Gardner in a bold, low-neckline black gown.

One bit of museum trivia: over the years some of the Gardner collection has been proven fake by art historians. Yet the fraudulent pieces stay on display with the great works. According to Mrs. Gardner's will, everything must remain intact.

It may be surprising to learn how few major twentieth-century artists made their careers here. Many simply passed through Boston on the way to paint in the sun of Truro and Provincetown on Cape Cod: Edward Hopper, Hans Hoffman, Ben Shahn,

Red Grooms, Franz Kline, and Robert Motherwell are just a few painters associated with the Cape, but not with Boston.

Avant-garde artists, particularly before the 1970s, stayed away because of rational Boston's traditional antipathy toward abstract imagery. While New York's Museum of Modern Art (MOMA) heralded abstract art movements, Boston's Institute of Contem-

The Isabella Stewart Gardner Museum houses exquisite masterpieces from around the world. Photo © Kenneth Martin

Along with the ICA, visitors to Boston invariably tour the three magnificent Harvard University Museums: the Fogg, Busch-Reisinger, and Sackler. The Fogg collection is especially mandatory because of its Rembrandt drawings, its permanent display of important French impressionist and post-impressionist paintings, including a Van Gogh *Self-Portrait*, and its first-rate American abstract expressionists. This collection began in 1895. The Busch-Reisinger was founded as a modest Germanic museum for reproductions, but it became, during the 38-year curatorship of Charles Kuhn, a major depository for original works of German art, especially by those fleeing the Third Reich. The museum has the largest collection of Bauhaus work outside of Germany, and the invaluable personal archives of artist Lyonel

porary Art (ICA), founded in 1936, broke from MOMA by championing figurative work. It especially favored Northern European expressionism, offering the first American shows of Oskar Kokoschka and Edvard Munch. In the 1940s local artists Jack Levine and Hyman Bloom, influenced by the Europeans, pioneered their own highly successful brand of "Boston Expressionism."

Recently, Boston has become much more open and democratic about all kinds of art. The ICA has initiated a "Boston Now" show of the best local

artists among its annual exhibits. Under the adventurous directorship of David Ross since 1983, the ICA has devoted its energy to "Currents" exhibits, samplings of post-Modernist artists from throughout the world. Also, the ICA has built a new theater in its basement for performance art and for its serious-minded video program. The biggest problem of the museum is lack of exhibit space, but there are plans afloat for a new building on the Boston waterfront to replace the ICA's current squeezed home in a converted firehouse.

Above left: Founded in 1936, Boston's Institute of Contemporary Art has broken the city's traditional antipathy toward imaginative art. Photo © Gaye Hilsenrath

Above: Contemporary sculptures and other works of art are housed at the Harvard Science Center, Harvard University. Photo © Kenneth Martin

Feininger and architect Walter Gropius. The new Arthur Sackler Museum specializes in Eastern and Oriental Art, from Chinese ritual bronze vessels to antique Japanese hand scrolls.

Save the most essential Boston art museum for last. The gargantuan Museum of Fine Arts is second only to New York's Metropolitan for possessing the most important art collection in America. A visitor to Boston must leave time for several extended visits. The Asiatic Collection is reputed to be the best on earth, and the Egyptian and early American collections are likewise hard to match. The greatest painters in the Western world—Velasquez, El Greco, Franz Hals, Van Gogh, and so on—are represented at the MFA with bonafide masterworks. The Chinese and Japanese art collection is the finest in the West.

The only reasonable criticism made about the MFA is that it has been remiss with post-war art. The MFA has attempted to correct itself with the construction of a glorious new I.M. Pei-designed West Wing in 1981, which continually exhibits up-to-date paintings by world-renowned contemporary artists.

If the museums don't offer enough art, visitors should saunter down chic Newbury Street to see the galleries. The best are Barbara Krakow, Stav-

aridis, and Nielsen. Among the friendliest to visit is the Bromfield, a group gallery of up-and-coming local artists. Also, some important galleries have moved to a lower-rent area near South Station: Thomas Segal, Harcus, and Liz Harris, the last devoted to black American and African artists. A visit to the Harris should be complemented by a tour of the Museum of the National Center of Afro-American Artists.

Or visit one of Boston's hundreds of professional artists in his or her studio. Boston has suffered the same problem as other cities: nobody can afford to rent apartments large enough to make art. But innovative solutions are being implemented. The Brickbottom Artists Group, with help from the First Mutual Bank of Boston, recently rehabilitated an A&P warehouse, turning the Somerville property into 91 live-in artists' lofts and 53 non-artists' condominiums. The condos, sold at a much higher price, help subsidize the lofts. Boston Arts Administrator Bruce Rossley said of Brickbottom, the largest artists' cooperative in America: "This has broken new ground among banks. Brickbottom will be a prototype for other rehabs and for new construction."

A case could be made that Boston's strongest twentieth-century visual art is photography. Certainly the most celebrated young artists in any media are the Starn twins, Doug and Mike, Boston Museum School graduates whose cut-and-paste photographic collages are de rigueur in art exhibits around the world. (The *Boston Phoenix* art critic, David Bonnetti, noted that the Starns are the most famous Boston artists in Europe since John Singleton Copley, 200 years ago!) After all, Cambridge was the home of Edwin Land, inventor of instant photography. In 1937 Land founded the Polaroid Corporation, which maintains its corporate headquarters along the Charles River.

Spiritually minded photographers found an impressive guru in the late

Minor White, who taught at MIT and spread his message about the otherworldliness of the photographic image. But as a city of acute social consciousness, Boston has been represented also by White's philosophical antithesis—muckraking street photographers focusing on the ills of America. A third kind of photography, the elaborately staged studio setup, has been facilitated by Polaroid's development of its patented 20 x 24 camera. Many of the world's greatest photographers have come to Boston's 20 x 24 Studio in the last few years to try the large-format camera, which prints, in color or black-and-white, one minute after pictures are taken.

At the Polaroid Museum Replica Collection, view Polaroid's latest

*Above left: Indian sculptures are on display at the Peabody Museum, Harvard University.
Photo © Kenneth Martin*

*Above: The faces of Boston are depicted upon this sculpture alongside the Lechmere Canal.
Photo © Stanley Rowin*

innovation: state-of-the-art reproductions of paintings by a process combining ultra-large-format photography and digital image processing.

Bostonians are fortunate to have three full-time photography galleries—Clarence Kennedy, Vision, and Robert Klein. The Photographic Resource Center (PRC), situated at Boston University, provides exhibits, lectures, a library, and a critical magazine called *Views*, and houses the slides of New England photographers. The nonprofit PRC, which operates on a $250,000 annual budget, had its 10th birthday in 1987.

In addition to its wealth of still photography, Boston has been at the forefront of independent filmmaking since the 1960s. The city is known internationally for its 16mm cinema verite documentaries by Richard Leacock, Ed Pincus, Robert Gardner, John Marshall, and, above all, Frederick Wiseman, whose exposés of American institutions (*High School, Titticut Follies*, etc.) premiere every year on PBS. Young filmmakers can learn at half a dozen local colleges, each with its own aesthetic philosophy and style. Outside of school, the nonprofit Boston Film and Video Foundation is where thousands of locals have learned all phases of making movies.

As for viewing films, Boston is a haven for serious lovers of cinema.

New foreign films are given extended runs at many movie houses, and it is possible to see long-lost pictures in new prints at such exemplary locales as the Brattle Theatre in Cambridge and the Carpenter Center at Harvard. Also, there are at least three huge, great, full-sized screens in the Boston area that make going out to the movies an old-fashioned pleasure: the Coolidge Corner Moviehouse in Brookline, the Somerville Theatre in Somerville, and the Charles Theatre in downtown Boston.

Finally, if one's taste runs to Eddie Murphy and Cher, there's no need to worry. Boston's vast USA Cinemas chain brings to town the newest pictures from Hollywood, normally the same day they open in New York. Also, USA Cinemas has begun an excellent annual Boston Film Festival each September in its Copley Place multiplex.

As for television in Boston, there are approximately 10 stations available even without cable. Two of these, WGBH (Channel 2) and WCVB (Channel 5) are notable. Many of Public Broadcasting's finest programs have originated from WGBH, the PBS affiliate, including

Above: The Photographic Resource Center, with Stan Trecker (left) at the helm, provides an invaluable resource to the local community. Photo © Stanley Rowin

Right: Dance as an art form in Boston had its beginnings at the turn of the century, and has since diversified into many forms, such as jazz and modern dance.

"Zoom" and "Masterpiece Theatre"; while WCVB, the ABC affiliate, has won countless national prizes including two George Peabody Awards and citations as "The Best Station" in America for its sophisticated local programming.

Dance as art in Boston dates from the beginning of the century when, in 1906, Isabella Stewart Gardner invited Ruth St. Denis to perform her Hindu dances at Gardner's Fenway home. Proper Bostonians were scandalized, but no matter. Modern dance had arrived. St. Denis married Ted Shawn, and they performed often in Boston before they moved their influential Denishawn troupe to Jacob's Pillow. Martha Graham also danced locally with Denishawn.

In the 1980s, of course, Boston is filled with modern dance groups, though even the best—Danceworks, the Dance Collective, and the Concert Dance Company—must struggle financially. One local choreographer to achieve national recognition is Beth Soll, whose dances have been described in the *New York Times* and other prestigious publications as a phenomenal amalgam of Martha Graham and Merce Cunningham, and beyond.

Boston's true dance success story is the Boston Ballet, founded in 1965. Its exceptionally solid financial base (there are about 40 skilled dancers on the payroll) is established in part through its astoundingly popular *Nutcracker Suite* each Christmas holiday. The Ballet has access to the huge stage of the Wang Center for the Performing Arts and manages to attract a large, faithful audience for its repertoire of both obscure and well-loved dance works.

"The C-Minor Symphony of Beethoven was played in the Odeon in 1840," Van Wyck Brooks wrote in the picturesque *The Flowering of New England*. "The young men walked in from Cambridge, in parties of three or four, thrilled by the darkness of the road." But Boston music, beyond psalm-singing, begins officially with William Billings (1746-1900), a tan-

ner by trade who became America's first significant composer. Billings' native music was not the kind favored by the Boston Handel and Hayden Society, which started up in 1815 to do choral works by Europe's esteemed composers. By the 1850s the Society expanded its repertoire to include compositions by Americans. In the 1980s the Hayden and Handel Society survives and thrives as the oldest music organization in the United States. It puts on several instrumental and choral concerts a year under the musical directorship of Christopher Hogwood.

Back in 1850, opera sensation Jenny Lind came to Boston, sponsored by P.T. Barnum, to sing at the Fitchburg Railroad Station. She liked the Hub so much that, when she married her accompanist Otto Gold-

Attending the ballet is an uplifting experience.
Photo © Sarah Hood

schmidt in 1852, they moved to 20 Louisburg Square on Beacon Hill.

The New England Conservatory was founded in 1867, and it remains today, along with the Berklee School of Music, a key force in Boston for the training of young composers and musicians. In general, those with a career interest in pure jazz attend Berklee (guitarist Pat Metheney is a famous graduate), and those who desire a convergence of classical music

and jazz (so-called "Third Stream" music) study at the New England Conservatory under such world-famous musicians as French hornist Gunther Schuller and pianist Ran Blake. Both schools offer free concerts by students and faculty for the Boston community.

Historian David McCord has stated, "Boston's chief glory in music is the Boston Symphony Orchestra." Currently under the music director-

ship of Seiji Ozawa, the BSO presents 250 concerts annually to live audiences of 1.5 million, and on an annual budget of $20 million.

It all began in 1881 with the BSO's inaugural concert under conductor George Henschel. But the BSO's halcyon days started with the 1900 opening of the magnificent Symphony Hall, where they still hold forth. British writer H.G. Wells attended a concert there in 1906 and came away extremely impressed: "Boston has in her symphony concerts the best music in America ... I heard Beethoven's Fifth Symphony extraordinarily well done."

In 1917 the BSO made the first recordings by any orchestra, at the Camden, New Jersey, offices of RCA. In 1918 the French conductor Pierre Monteaux became the BSO's conductor, bringing a subtle French repertoire to the symphony. In 1924 began the enlightened 25-year reign of conductor Serge Koussevitsky. He intro-

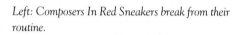

Left: Composers In Red Sneakers break from their routine.

Below: The stage is set at the Berklee Performance Center. Photo © Kenneth Martin

Above: The resplendent Symphony Hall opened in 1900 with the Boston Symphony Orchestra performing under the direction of George Henschel. Photo © Dominic Vecchione

Right: The Boston Symphony Orchestra is currently directed by Seiji Ozawa. Photo © Sarah Hood

duced new and unfamiliar music into the symphony repertoire and commissioned American composers such as Aaron Copland and Samuel Barber to write music especially for the BSO.

It was in 1956, at the height of the Cold War, that the BSO, conducted by Charles Munch, finished a European tour with an unprecedented visit to Moscow and Leningrad. As the legend goes, they were paid for their concerts in ruples, but then were not allowed to take the money out of the Soviet Union.

Seiji Ozawa, formerly artistic director of the Tanglewood Festival, became the BSO's 13th music director in 1973. He has reconfirmed the

Symphony's commitment to new music, and he has expanded the BSO's recording activity to many prestigious labels. Also, Ozawa has brought the BSO an Emmy for PBS' "Evening at the Symphony."

Since 1885 the BSO has balanced its highbrow program with lighter music in the summer months. What

were first called "Promenade Concerts" became the "Boston Pops" series, conducted for 50 years (1929-1979) by Arthur Fiedler in the Esplanade on the East Bank of the Charles River. When Fiedler died, the baton was handed in 1980 to Juilliard-trained John Williams. By popular demand, he has added his world-

famous scores for *Star Wars* and *Close Encounters of the Third Kind* to the repertoire of what is now called the Boston Pops Esplanade Orchestra.

The BSO is only the most visible force in Boston's classical music world. There is also the much-praised Pro Arte Chamber Orchestra, founded and conducted by a Harvard University minister, Larry Hill. It specializes in works by Boston composers, offering world premieres of 24 works in its first 9 years. In addition, the Boston Camerata, started in 1954, is an internationally celebrated ensemble of singers and instrumentalists who bring alive the music of the Middle Ages and Renaissance.

Fans of early music swear by Boston's baroque orchestra, the Banchetto Musicale, and also its Cantata Singers and John Oliver Chorale. These fans count the months eagerly for the biannual Boston Early Music Festival and Exhibition, an event which precipitates pilgrimages from around the world.

Of course, there is the great Boston Opera Company, begun auspiciously in 1907, bankrupt two years later, then raised from the dead in 1958 by Sarah Caldwell. This dynamo is still the Opera's director and conductor. Caldwell is praised for bringing demanding works such as Alban Berg's *Lulu* into the repertoire, for her brilliant stagings, and for attracting such greats as Joan Sutherland and Beverly Sills to sing with the Opera.

And for those who barely tolerate classical music, Cambridge was where it all began for BU student Joan Baez, who sang folksongs at Club 47, now Passim's. There is also the *Boston Globe*'s annual spring Jazz Heritage Festival, a week-long gala event in clubs and concert halls all through town.

As for rock and roll, there are clubs galore for dancing and listening. The Hub is the hometown of Donna Summer, the J. Geils Band, and the Cars.

Finally, there is Boston comedy. Boston's comedians have been neigh-

borhood boys who share a junior Archie Bunker iconoclasm expressed in the street lingo of Richard Pryor and Redd Foxx. Their favorite targets are the "haves" of Boston—Brahmins, yuppies, joggers, vegetarians—and their hilarious jokes can be heard seven nights a week at half a dozen local clubs. Amazingly, these indigenous comedians break out nationally. Jay Leno was first, then Steve Wright and "Bobcat" Goldthwait. It's fun to be there in the crowd, wondering which of these uproarious talents will be next on *Saturday Night Live* and *David Letterman,* or making Hollywood movies.

Can there be any doubt that culture thrives in Boston? According to the January 6, 1988 issue of the *Boston Globe,* arts groups attracted 7.6 million people to their events in 1987, more than twice the 3.4 million who

This crowd gears up for the Boston Pops 4th of July concert on the Esplanade.
Photo © Lee C. Hauenstein

saw professional sports. Art patrons brought $500 million into the city's economy. Also, the cultural industry has grown astoundingly (with 4,188 full-time or part-time workers) to qualify as the city's third largest non-government employer, behind the Bank of Boston and John Hancock Mutual Life Insurance Company.

Lawrence Murray, director of ARTS/Boston, praised cultural activities for having "fueled Boston's economic miracle." Bruce Rossley, Boston's Arts Commissioner, was even more excited. The 1987 statistics demonstrate conclusively "the interdependence of city and state, arts and business ... Supporting the arts is not something that's 'nice to do.' It is enlightened self-interest for all sectors."

A cultural institution, the main branch of the Boston Public Library (BPL) on Boylston Street, with its 2 million books, attracts high school students with term paper assignments and avid readers. It also provides a

complete cultural experience, from weekly screenings of classic Hollywood films to readings by famous authors, to touring photography exhibits, to book discussion groups, to storytelling for children.

The BPL is, before all else, an architectural and artistic treat. The first public library in America, its McKim "Old" Building on Copley Square was finished in 1895 from a magnificent design by McKim, Mead, and White. Twenty-five kinds of stone were utilized, and the floors, walls, and vaulted ceilings are of pink Knoxville marble. The great twin lions at the turn of the Main Staircase

are by Louis St. Gaudens; the second floor corridor is decorated with mural paintings by the notable French artist Puvis de Chavannes. Undoubtedly, the real crowd pleaser is the set of murals titled *The Quest for the Holy Grail* by American artist Edwin Austin Abbey, which surrounds BPL denizens with the Arthurian legend in dazzling Venetian Renaissance colors.

The "Old" BPL houses the wealth of research materials, including the Rare Books and Manuscript Department, while the adjacent "New" Building, the 1972 work of architectural maestro Philip Johnson, is where the circulating books are found. Here the crowds gather day and night. Any Boston-area resident can secure a library card for the BPL's more than 30 branches.

Above: Comedian Steve Allen heads the line-up at the Comedy Stop. Photo © Martha Everson

Below: Night clubs are numerous in Boston. Photo © Sarah Hood

The Boston Athenaeum, on the other hand, is a proudly private library on Beacon Hill. Founded in 1827, it possesses a collection of 700,000 rarer-than-rare books, including the personal library of George Washington and publications

A cultural institution, Boston Public Library attracts avid readers, and offers weekly screenings of classic Hollywood films and readings by famous authors. Above left: Photo © Mark E. Gibson. Left: Photo © Kathy Tarantola. Above: Photo © Ulkrike Welsch

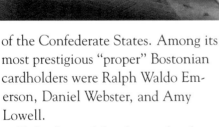

of the Confederate States. Among its most prestigious "proper" Bostonian cardholders were Ralph Waldo Emerson, Daniel Webster, and Amy Lowell.

Today limited family memberships are available, and tours of the Athenaeum occur Tuesdays and Thursdays. Reservations are required.

Researchers with serious, worthy projects may get special permission to use the Houghton Library at Harvard, which specializes in early American manuscripts such as those by Emily Dickinson and Louisa May Alcott.

Most treasured of all is access to the nonpareil Widener Library at Harvard, the largest university library on earth with its 3 million volumes. Only the New York Public Library and the Library of Congress have more books in America.

The granddaddy of Boston museums, and the ideal place to start a tour, is the Museum of Comparative Zoology (1859) on the Harvard University Campus. Begun by the esteemed nineteenth-century scientist Louis Agassiz, the museum is known far better by its unofficial, less impos-

ing title, the "Agassiz Museum." It is visited yearly by myriad scientists and non-scientists, who discover a Cambridge equivalent (though on a much smaller scale) of New York's Museum of Natural History.

The Agassiz is, before all else, a teaching and research institution for Harvard. As such, the public sees

Above: Trees shade the entrance to the French Library on Marlborough Street in Back Bay. Photo © Kathy Tarantola

only a tiny portion of the museum's 10 million mollusk specimens, 6 million insects, and 250,000 bird specimens. What is behind closed doors is truly legendary. A recent visitor reported being shown a "mermaid" in a drawer, an enigmatic thing that was a gift from the late showman P.T. Barnum.

On view for the public, among many wonders, is a 42-foot marine reptile skeleton of *Kronosaurus Queenlandis*, the world's first mounted specimen of this elusive sea creature from 120 million years ago; extinct birds such as the Great Auk, passenger pigeons, heath hens, and a Labrador Duck; remains of the largest turtle to crawl the earth (beneath a 7 foot 2 inch shell), 5 million years ago; a 75,000,000-year-old dinosaur egg; and the "Harvard Mastodon," from an 1844 excavation in Hackettstown, New Jersey.

Four Harvard museums lead into each other, for a single admission. So, before one knows it, the Agassiz has turned into the Museum of Mineralogy and Geology, home of rocks, emeralds, and diamonds, and then into the Botanical Museum, containing perhaps the most spectacular sight in all of Cambridge. It is the world-famous Ware collection of glass flowers, 700 species re-created with uncanny realism by two German artists in Dresden between 1877 and 1936, a lifetime's devotion. (There are glass insects, too, for cross-pollination.) The Dresden process remains secret. The glass was softened by heat, not blown, and the radiant colors never fade. Finally, the corridors lead into the Peabody Museum of Archeology and Ethnology, with its Hall of the North American Indian and Pre-Columbian Gallery. Highlights

include wonderful figurines from Mayan excavations, Hopi Indian musical instruments, and an enthralling generic collection of Indian kachina dolls, gifts to children to bring rain and healthy crops. It is essential to visit the Peabody's museum shop and handle the strange and eccentric folk art items from around the world, available for purchase at extremely

Above: The Widener Library, the first library in the American colonies, was the forerunner of the Boston Public Library. Photo © Judith Canty

Facing page (above): A tugboat passes in front of the Museum of Science. Photo © Gene Peach

Facing page (below): The spacious Museum of Science Omni Theater atrium is seen here. Photo © Gene Peach

reasonable prices. As the shop manager aptly describes the store, "It's a museum in itself."

The final Harvard Museum to visit is the Semitic Museum, a block away from the Agassiz, with its array of artifacts from the Near East of both Jewish and Moslem life. And while in Cambridge stop by the MIT Museum. Founded in 1971 to preserve material associated with the Massachusetts Institute of Technology, it houses microscopes, magnetrons, computer parts, and the Hart Nautical Collections of shipbuilding memorabilia.

The first museum stop across the bridge into Boston is the fabulous Museum of Science, where one can climb aboard a replica of the Apollo capsule or stare up at a 20-foot-high, moving and "breathing" model of a Tyrannosaurus Rex. A more subtle favorite of museum goers is the Theory of Probability model, in which marbles dropping randomly from the air inevitably fall along a bell-shaped curve, mostly in the middle. But those who savor melodrama opt for the twice-daily Theatre of Electronics. There, lightning charges, produced by a Van De Graff generator, strike and strike again. Children romp through the museum's Discovery Room, filled high with shells, rocks, bones, even a human skull. A variety of attractions, including a 45-minute interplanetary show projected in the Hayden Planetarium, lure everyone at every hour.

The next sojourn is to Museum Wharf in downtown Boston, home of the Children's Museum and its adjoining neighbor, The Computer Museum. The Children's Museum is, justifiably, a world-famous showcase for its progressive, hands-on pedagogic approach. The museum is like *Sesame Street* and *Mr. Wizard* and the best day-care center and playground rolled into one, as children race through a maze of sensorially appealing and always congenial environments. By touching and exploring, the children grasp basic lessons in science, math, and civics, and most important, they learn that museums are friendly places. It is also delightful for adults to observe the children at active, imaginative play: crawling over giant telephones and gargantuan eyeglasses, making Zoetropes, moving a skeleton by pulleys, tossing golf balls on special tracks that illustrate formulas of Newton and Galileo. And there are important lessons too, such as a non-sexist sign, "People Working," and a notification on a Native

Facing page (above): This girl tests her skills during the Kids Computer Fair at the Computer Museum. Photo © Martha Everson

Facing page (below): The Mathematica Exhibit is one of the many attractions at the Museum of Science. Photo © Gene Peach

Below: Museum Wharf is home to the Computer Museum as well as the Children's Museum, seen here. Photo © Kenneth Martin

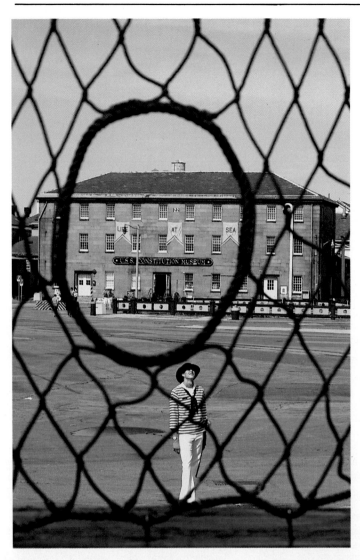

American abode, "This Indian home is not a teepee. It's a wigwam."

The next-door Computer Museum is a one-of-a-kind carnival of today's most advanced technology. Visitors stroll inside a vacuum tube computer, a part of the AN/FSQ-7 built for the United States Air Force and one of the largest in the world. Then it's off to the delightful robot exhibit, including a show in the Robot Theater, where the purveyors of artificial intelligence come on like Rockettes! There are many hands-on machines (this time for adults) to experiment with ways of putting information into computers. A Computer Timeline traces the development of the computer from the bulky, unwieldy 1950s to the latest compact technological wizardry.

Nearby is the Boston Tea Party Museum, a replica of the unfortunate British ship that tried to deliver tea to the American colonies before Ameri-

can Revolutionaries dumped the unwanted load in December 1773. And several miles away, in the Charleston Navy Yard, the USS Constitution Museum tells the story of the War of 1812, and celebrates the American victory of the USS Constitution, "Old Ironsides."

There are more museums elsewhere in the Boston area. The Museum of Transportation in Brookline has a prize collection of early twentieth-century American cars. The Museum of Afro-American History on Beacon Hill shows how black people have made a significant contribution to the culture of downtown Boston. The Museum of Our National Heritage in Lexington concentrates on the icons of American history, including Revolutionary-period antiques and the silversmith works of Paul Revere. And last, but hardly least, the Museum at the John F. Kennedy Library in Dorchester contains nine sequential

exhibits that vividly trace the life and death of the late great Boston-bred American president, from his birth in Brookline to his assassination in Dallas. The museum also covers the history of the Kennedy clan and pays homage to Robert F. Kennedy. A special highlight is JFK's presidential desk from the Oval Office in the White House. Finally, upstairs in the JFK Library are 7 million presidential papers, an archival feast forever for professional and amateur American historians.

Above left: The USS Constitution Museum at the Charleston Naval Yard celebrates the American victory of "Old Ironsides" during the War of 1812. Photo © Ulrike Welsch

Above: The Boston Tea Party Museum should be visited by all interested in the events leading to the Revolution. Photo © Justine Hill

The Museum at the John F. Kennedy Library in Dorchester traces the life of the Boston-bred president and Kennedy family members. Photo © B. &J. McGrath

The "Red Coats" are coming to the "First Night"
celebration on Boston Common.
Photo © Paul Corkum

As late as the Civil War Bostonians had only one central locale, the ancient Common, set aside for public recreation. It was so crowded that, even by 1877, those who came to play were warned off by ominous signs: "Keep off the grass!" No wonder a frustrated city councilman lectured his puritanical male peers for forgetting that "we were ever boys, that we ever loved to play and run and jump, and that we had a place to do these things in."

The councilman's oratory anticipated Boston's future. He foresaw a model city in which its hardworking citizenry could make good use of their off hours, with ample planned space provided for every kind of healthy recreation. None of this was possible without a park system, and Boston had yet to develop one.

A "park movement" took hold in the city, backed by medical doctors, settlement workers, famous writers such as Oliver Wendell Holmes, and even some forward-minded ministers, who insisted that recreation was essential for the spirit as well as the body. Rallies were held in the Common, and finally the city council passed the 1875 Park Act. Bit by bit, the city of Boston bought up undeveloped land and then hired the great landscape architect Frederick Olmsted to plan and oversee its park system, something he personally accomplished through the 1890s.

The twentieth century opened far more promisingly for Bostonians who wished to enjoy the out-of-doors. The park system surrounding Boston was virtually complete. Frederick Olmsted's famous "emerald necklace" constituted an 18-mile corridor of continuous parkland, including the Boston Common, the Fenway, Jamaica Pond, the Arnold Arboretum, Franklin Park, Columbus Park, Marine Park, and Castle Island. By 1910 the city offered its people 14 public bathing and beach areas and 7 public gymnasiums. By 1915 the city had established 26 public playgrounds.

Moreover, the city had adopted Olmsted's wise philosophical division of recreation into two types, both necessary, to encourage and cultivate: "exertive recreation" such as sports, hiking, and bicycling, both mentally and physically active, and "receptive recreation" where one finds pleasure in the aesthetic of ocean, harbor, tours, public gardens, and so on, without special physical effort. Today Boston provides both types of recreation.

Because Boston is amazingly compact for such a large city, walking is the most practical form of exertive recreation. Yes, it is perfectly reasonable to walk into town from Charlestown or Cambridge on a spring day, enjoying the charmed view across the Charles. It makes sense to stroll to Fenway Park for a baseball afternoon. In fact, tourists who enjoy Boston the most seem inevitably to have taken a trek along the Freedom Trail, a leisurely jaunt along a clearly demarcated path through Boston's historical past. A walk through the Arnold Arboretum can be equally glorious.

Those who wish a more vigorous exercise should try racewalking, an increasingly popular local sport. Myrna Finn, who racewalks the Boston Marathon, says, "Anyone with latent athletic ability can rise to a level of accomplishment they never dreamed of." Of course, racewalking can be non-competitive too. The Brookline Racewalkers Club meets each Sunday morning for a friendly five-mile hike.

In addition to walkers, there are joggers everywhere in Boston. There are also half-marathons, "milk runs," "fun runs," and "health runs" for people of all ages. The Greater Boston Track Club offers organized workouts and weekly long runs, and the avowedly anti-Puritan Barley Hoppers Running Club, an irreverent local institution, advertises a weekly social run of two or three miles with a midpoint stop for refreshments. The far more serious Liberty Athletic Club is a competitive running club strictly for athletic-minded women.

Bicycling is a fine form of recreation in Boston. In the nineteenth century bicycles were said to be a favored means of transportation for proper Bostonians, both female and male. Today bicyclists are everywhere. Boston is amazingly flat, and

CHAPTER 11

A Plethora of Pastimes

BY GERALD PEARY

except for Beacon Hill, riders can pedal through their city using only a couple of gears.

The chain of parks surrounding the lower Charles River makes a long, safe bike route. The 18-mile ride along the Dr. Paul Dudley White Bike Path begins and ends at the Charles River Dam by the Museum of Science. The rider stays on the Cambridge side of the ride for the out-

Below: All of Boston may be viewed from the observation deck at the John Hancock Tower. Photo © B. & J. McGrath

Below (bottom): This mural accents the Boston Garden. Photo © Kenneth Martin

bound way, passing MIT and Harvard, finally circling about and coming close to Boston University on the way in.

The Metropolitan District Commission has established two other bikeways. These are the Stony Brook Reservation Bike Path, 3.7 miles along Turtle Pond in the Hyde Park-West Roxbury area, and the 3.5-mile Mystic River Reservation Bike Path.

If one prefers bicycling as a social, group activity, the Boston Road Club sponsors Sunday morning rides for beginning, intermediate, and advanced bicyclists, and a racing club in Newton. The Charles River Wheelmen Bicycle Club has Sunday

social rides all through Eastern Massachusetts. Serious cyclists should make contact with the Boston Area Bicycle Coalition, a nonprofit organization that puts out a cyclists' newsletter, *Spoke N' Word,* and lobbies for a safe bicycling environment in Massachusetts.

For the more socially inclined resident, dancing may be the perfect form of recreation. These days, it seems that every other Bostonian is taking dance classes, whether modern, jazz, or tap, to keep in shape. There are also dance parties held nightly at

fancy Boston area hotels, and many meet, mix, mingle, mambo, and sometimes marry.

In addition, Boston is a folk dancing capital. There are weekly meeting places for contra and square dances, English country dancing, Israeli folk dancing, Scottish country dancing, and even advanced Scandinavian dancing. Boston is most famous for its Dance Free nights in several locations, where single people who *don't* want to meet anyone can whirl themselves about all night, barefoot, in alcohol-free, smoking-free environ-

ments. The music and the moving about are the *raison d'etre,* and children are welcome too.

If half of exercise-obsessive Boston takes dance classes, the other half runs to its employment in sneakers, fielding a squash or racquetball racket for a quick workout. The largest racquetball facility in the Boston area is the Cambridge Racquetball Club, just over the Longfellow Bridge in Cambridge, a 10-minute walk from downtown Boston. There are 10 climate-controlled courts, a club pro available free to new members, and

wild Wallyball games organized for adventurous teams. Additionally, the club offers a Nautilus/Fitness Center, an ambitious aerobics program, and an in-house restaurant. No wonder that many high-level professional tournaments are played out on the club's glass-walled "showcase" courts.

In Boston the Back Bay Racquet Club has 10 courts. Two other splen-

Above: "Pink Creatures and Kids" is the theme of this attraction at the annual Kids Fair.
Photo © Paul Corkum

did facilities in the area are the Brookline Racquetball Club and Cambridge Racquetball.

As for squash, an ideal place to find a skilled match is on the five courts of the Mount Auburn Club in nearby Watertown. Though this club is for members only, Bostonians can also play squash at excellent public facilities at the Boston Racquet Club or the Squash Club Allston-Brighton Nautilus in close-by Allston.

The City of Boston has 64 tennis courts at 21 locations open to the public, first come and first serve. Informed tennis buffs know that even

Chinese New Year celebrations are colorful and crowd pleasing events.
Photos © Kenneth Martin

on a crowded weekend, courts can be found in the Hyde Park neighborhood, at the Charles E. Welder Playground, the Francis D. Martini Music Shell, and the John H. Dooley Memorial Playground. Because of demand, permits from the city are required to use the Charlesbank Park Courts on Charles Street in downtown Boston.

Locating open courts in a busy metropolis can be difficult on a sunny spring day. Many Bostonians turn to private clubs such as the Blue Hill Tennis and Racquetball Club in Braintree, the Belmont Tennis Club in Belmont, and Norfolk Tennis Club Associates in Woburn.

Best of all, there is the Longwood Cricket Club in Boston, a paradigm location for great tennis, with its 17 grass and 9 clay courts. It is here that America's first grass court was put in 1878, and it is here that the United States Pro Championship is played

Right: Boston comes alive with Fourth of July celebrations. An outstanding concert and fireworks display is available to the public along the Esplanade. Photo © Paul Corkum

Below: Brian Boitano performs for "An Evening With Champions" at Harvard's Bright Hockey Center in Allston. Photo © Paul Corkum

each July. Longwood hosts the unique Rogers Bowl Tennis Tournament each September, which is open to competitors at least 70 years of age.

The Massachusetts Badminton Association offers lessons and information on places to play badminton. Check out badminton activities on Saturdays and Sundays at the Natick Sports Club and Sunday mornings at the Jewish Community Center in Brookline.

For those who wish to swing a seven iron, the Boston area is filled with public and private golf courses. Among the many public 18-hole courses surrounding Boston are the Cape Cod Country Club in Falmouth, the Glen Ellen Country Club in Ellis, the Middleton Golf Course in Middleton, the Sandy Burr Country Club in Wayland, and the George Wright Golf Club in Hyde Park. A fine, close-in place to start up is the nine-hole Fresh Pond Golf Club in Cambridge, where lessons are available from clubhouse pro Jack Sullivan. And though Boston is slightly off the PGA trail, the Brookline Country Club hosts the National Open every few years, most recently in 1988.

For others, there are miniature golf courses in Natick, Lenox, Stoughton, South Weymouth, and Stoneham.

For bowlers there are 50 lanes at

Boston Bowl in Dorchester, the KC Bowling Lanes in Somerville, Granada Lanes in Malden, and Lucky Strike Lanes in Dorchester. Most of Boston's bowling activities are registered with, and monitored by, the Massachusetts Bowling Association in Arlington, which will gladly answer bowlers' questions.

Children in the Boston area wisely join candlepin leagues rather than struggle for strikes and spares with a full-sized bowling ball. For example, Lanes & Games in Cambridge overflows with 36 candlepin lanes, and there are 20 such lanes at the Kenmore Bowladrome in Downtown. In truth, candlepin bowling is more popular even among adults in Boston than in other American cities. College students from Boston's many universities are often seen at these lanes.

As for skiing, the area close to Boston is superb for cross-country skiing with its snowed-in golf courses, state parks, and state reservations. A favorite cross-country historic spot is the Walden Pond State Reservation, where one can take a guided tour of where Henry David Thoreau once lived, walked, and wrote.

The Blue Hills Ski Area in Canton is among the closer downhill locales to Boston, a trek 14 miles south of the

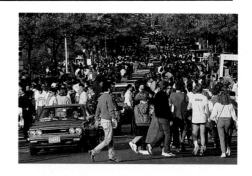

city to its three trails and two slopes. Boston Hill in North Andover is 22 miles north, and the Nashoba Valley Ski Area is 25 miles west. For demanding skiers, Western Massachusetts, home of the Berkshire Mountains, is a better place to go. There, downhill aficionados can find resorts such as Brodie Mountain in New Ashford, the largest ski area in Massachusetts, with 26 trails and slopes and 6 lifts.

A Ski Train leaves each Saturday in the winter from Boston's North Station to Fitchburg in the west, taking skiers to Mount Wachusett or Mount Watatic. In nearby states, the world-

Below: Throngs of fans picnic along the banks of the Charles River while watching the Head of the Charles Rowing Regatta. Photo © Judith Canty

Above: Following the conclusion of the annual Head of the Charles, there occurs a massive migration of individuals heading homeward. Photo © Sarah Hood

class ski spots are Sugarloaf in Maine; and Killington, Mount Snow, and Stowe in Vermont.

Skiing tours can be arranged through the Boston Ski and Sports Club. Free ski clinics for adults are available at Boston Hill, and the Massachusetts Junior Ski Club in Needham specializes in lessons for youth. The New England Handicapped Sportsmen's Association offers free ski instruction and equipment upon request.

Those who prefer water sports can check out Community Boating, the oldest and largest public sailing program in the country. There are 120 sailboats available, with free instruction for those who pay the tiny membership fee. One can register and sail the same day. For this nonprofit corporation, which has operated on the Charles since 1950, volunteer instructors teach basic skills to new sailors, a member-teach-member method that has proven very successful. There is even a 10-week summer program for youth 10 to 17, for a total cost of one dollar. On the other hand, experienced sailors who pass a test can begin sailing at once.

As for swimming, the Metro Parks Division operates more than 16 miles of beaches, from Nahant to Nantasket, and all can be reached by bus or subway. Beaches are open from the end of June to Labor Day, and lifeguards are on duty during daytime work hours.

Of course, those with cars can travel easily to many fine beaches further north of Boston, such as Crane's Beach in Ipswich, Plum Island in Newburyport, and Singing Beach in Manchester. South of Boston there

Above right: The Boston Aquarium provides both an educational and entertaining experience with its many exhibits and shows. Photo © Mark E. Gibson.

Right: A ranger welcomes visitors to the Charlestown Navy Yard. Photo © Kenneth Martin

are Cape Cod's National Seashore beaches, two hours away. And in historic, white-duned Provincetown many of America's greatest writers and painters have spent time, including Eugene O'Neill, Edward Hopper, Norman Mailer, and Robert Motherwell.

Those who wish to make beach trips can get precise information from the North of Boston Tourist Council or, south of the city, the Cape Cod Chamber of Commerce.

For swimmers who want to avoid the beaches, the Metropolitan Recreation Division operates 16 public pools from the end of June to the beginning of September. The local YMCA and YWCA also have convenient indoor pools. For the competitive swimmer, the New England Masters Swim Club holds meets every two weeks, while the Greater Boston Swim Club offers training for all ages, with evening practice in Dedham and Neponset.

For those interested in hiking, the city of Boston has designed hiking trails at the Blue Hills Reservation in Milton, the Beaverbrook Reservation in Belmont, Breakhart Reservation in Saugus, and the Middlesex Reservation, which runs through Medford, Malden, Melrose, Stoneham, and Winchester. Of these, the Blue Hills Trail is probably the most popular, with its color-coded trails covering different distances. The Red Trail is a mere quarter of a mile, but the Blue Dot Trail is almost 10 miles long, so secluded and delightfully rustic one

can almost forget that Boston is close by.

Bostonians with a serious and lasting interest in hiking usually join the Appalachian Mountain Club and/or the Sierra Club. The Appalachian Club encourages visitors to come to its Beacon Hill headquarters for detailed information about hiking, camping, and backpacking throughout New England.

The Sierra Club, environmental advocates since 1892, have a New England chapter of more than 18,000 members. Its activities calendar is immense, with such offerings as snowshoe hikes, cross-country ski trips, workshops on bird and animal life, and nights celebrating spring by gazing through a telescope at the stars. The Greater Boston chapter plans additional activities, such as an all-day exploration of the Blue Hills Reservation.

Many members of the Sierra and Appalachian Mountain clubs also be-

Left: It's a romp through the daffodils for this young man at the Arnold Arboretum. Photo © Paul Corkum

Below: Tulips are indicative of springtime in Cambridge. Photo © Kenneth Martin

long to the Massachusetts Audubon Society, which owns and protects over 12,000 acres of land in the state. Wildlife comes first at such close-to-Boston spots as the 577-acre Broadmoor Wildlife Sanctuary in South Natick, where woodland, field, marsh, ponds, and nine miles of marked trails are preserved for nature-lovers. In all the Society's sanctuaries, dogs, fires, hunting, and firearms are prohibited.

The Audubon Society's Trailside Museum in the Blue Hills reservation has lectures, courses, and nature

Above: Fall colors accent this country road near Concord. Photo © Sarah Hood

Right: Selecting a pumpkin may prove to be a difficult decision. Photo © Sarah Hood

hikes, and admission is only one dollar for adults.

Though Boston is not exactly a wide open, cowpoke kind of town, those who ride horses or wish to learn have a choice of more than a dozen stables in the area. Two typical stables are the North Shore Equestrian Center in North Revere, which offers group lessons in its 180-by-80-foot indoor ring, and the St. Moritz Equestrian Center in Quincy, which provides private instruction in "balance seat" riding and jumping. The more advanced riders at St. Moritz are let loose on the 300 miles of trails at the Blue Hills Reservation.

Although freshwater fishing is extremely limited in Boston, there are those who cast their reels into the Charles River. Probably a better spot ecologically, however, is at Turtle Pond in the Stony Brook Reservation in Hyde Park. Also, Jamaica Pond in Jamaica Plains is nearby, and rowboats are available. A Massachusetts fishing license is required for those 15 years and older from the State Division of Fisheries and Wildlife.

No licenses are needed for ocean fishing, and the best piers are found in South Boston at Castle Island and City Point. Half a dozen reputable fishing fleets are willing to transport

you out to sea for the day, such as Bigfish II, Boston Harbor Fishing, Captain Lou Inc., and Quincy Bay Flounder Fleet.

Whale watching is a favorite activity of tourists to the Boston area, the irresistible chance to closely observe whales, often families of them, riding the waves at the side of the boat. This exhilarating ocean adventure is a peak experience for the ecologically minded. Usually the excursions are led by learned naturalists and oceanographers who talk about marine ecology and mankind's responsibility to save endangered ocean species.

Trips take place from May to Octo-

Below: Cape Cod is characterized by its sand dunes. Photo © Kenneth Martin

Right: A single kayak is moored near the dock at Duxbury beach. Photo © Gene Peach

Center right, below right: Local beaches set the perfect tranquil scene. Photos © Gene Peach

ber and last for four or five hours. From Boston, AC Cruise Lines, Boston Harbor Cruises, and the New England Aquarium run ocean trips to see the whales. Those visiting Provincetown can choose from several daily tours aboard the *Dolphin III*, *Dolphin IV*, and *Ranger III*.

Boston's two city zoos, at Franklin Park and Stoneham, will be revital-

Left: A sailboat makes for open water, passing through the Gloucester drawbridge. Photo © Paul Pavlik

Center left: Clouds begin to scatter above Mt. Greylock in the Berkshires. Photo © Gene Peach

Below left: Many fishing boats anchor at Rockport Harbor. Photo © Gene Peach

ized in the near future. The zoos' new executive director, Mark Goldstein, has outlined a master development plan for more species, more types of exhibits, and, specifically, the unveiling of a tropical rain forest at Franklin Park. Goldstein also is making sure that the health and well-being of the animals comes first. "I'm dedicated to making the zoos as exciting and enjoyable as they can be, but not at the expense of the animals," he told the *Boston Globe*.

In the meantime, Boston's more active zoo is the pocket-sized facility in Stoneham, actually an enormously pleasurable way to spend an hour. Visitors can view lions, gorillas, orangutans, and sea lions bellowing and sunning themselves. Best of all is a free-floating aviary as tall as a drive-in movie screen.

For those interested in aquatic creatures, there is the New England Aquarium. If Bostonians of every age, class, and profession were polled about their favorite recreation spot, the New England Aquarium would undoubtedly finish at the top of the list. Everybody adores the aquarium. Everybody seems to visit there several times a year.

Founded in 1969 on Boston's harborfront, three blocks from Faneuil Hall Marketplace, the private, nonprofit aquarium succeeds in bringing its philosophy to life: "to make known the world of water" to the general public. Oceanic treats include a 288-seat sea theater for films and talks, the Ocean Tray, 131,000 gallons of water at ground level for penguin life, and the spectacular 187,000-gallon, four-story ocean tank filled with eels, sea turtles, and other underwater animal exotica. The huge tank is surrounded by 70 other exhibition tanks containing more than 2,000 fish.

A 1984 addition to the aquarium was a 24-foot tropical coral reef atop the giant ocean tank. This top-floor exhibit features 3,000 individual corals and sponges representing 35 Caribbean species.

Boston is known for its variety of boating opportunities. Photo © Gene Peach

Three-time American League batting champion
Wade Boggs plays with the Red Sox.
Photo © Christopher Lauber

Historians agree that Bostonians always have been sports-crazy. In the eighteenth century, bowling greens were established about town, and there were cricket and boxing matches, and a bit of horseracing. In the nineteenth century, this port city became a yachting capital for the rich (organized regattas occurred by the 1840s), and a rowing capital for seemingly everyone else, with fierce rivalries between teams of Irish immigrant longshoremen and old-time Yankees.

Harvard University led the way after the Civil War with its intercollegiate crew, track and field, baseball, and football teams. Then other local universities—Boston College, MIT, Boston University—followed with sturdy teams of their own. Bostonians James Dwight and Richard Sears dominated early lawn tennis in the 1880s, and helped to organize the United States Lawn Tennis Association.

When the first modern Olympics were held in 1896 in Athens, Greece, Boston sportsmen from the Suffolk Athletic Club and the Boston Athletic Association proved the superstars of the American team. James Brendan Connolly captured the first event ever of the renewed Olympics, the hop, step, and jump, and he led the triumphant Bostonians when they returned home to greet thousands awaiting them at downtown Providence station.

John L. Sullivan, the legendary nineteenth-century heavyweight boxing champion, was also a local lad. He was born in Roxbury in 1858 and studied for a time at Boston College. Then, after knocking out champion Paddy Ryan in New Orleans in 1882 with his bare knuckles, Sullivan toured the country for a decade of fisticuffs, declaring "I will strive to return to the place of my birth with a reputation unsullied and undiminished." On August 8, 1887, 4,000 spectators at the Boston Theatre joined Mayor Hugh O'Brien for a celebration that far exceeded the traditional key to the city for Sullivan. The pugilist-in-residence was given a gold belt with 387 diamonds, valued then at $8,000. Yankee Brahmins howled at the extravagance, but Boston's Irish-Americans were thrilled, for Sullivan was one of them. There are those, a century later, who still mourn Sullivan's debilitating loss of the championship in 1892 to Jim Corbett.

Mention need be made of Francis Ouimet of Brookline, who, by his humble and gentlemanly disposition, turned the little-regarded game of golf into a respectable American sport. When he won the United States Open in 1913 at the Brookline Country Club, the *Boston Globe* wrote enthusiastically:

We have seen, in other sports, the hero of the day cheered to the echo and hoisted upon the shoulders of his admirers, for a jerky ride of fame ... But such enthusiasm has been generally foreign to the golf links until the modest ... Francis Ouimet carried the gallery completely off its feet at The Country Club yesterday afternoon.

Before all else, Boston is a baseball town. The Boston Red Stockings won four pennants in the 1870s, and Mike "King" Kelly of the Boston Beaneaters of the 1880s was probably the most popular baseball player in America. As Irish as John L. Sullivan, Kelly would race about the bases to the standard cry from the crowd: "Slide, Kelly, Slide." When he died of pneumonia in 1894, the *Boston Herald* reported that 5,000 persons attended his wake.

The American League was begun in 1901, but the team now called the Red Sox was stuck with the stuffy name, the Boston Pilgrims. Still, the team struck gold immediately with pitcher Cy Young's heroic 33 wins, and attracted twice as many fans to the Huntington Avenue Grounds as their rivals, the Boston Nationals. (The Nationals eventually became the Boston Braves, then, in the early 1950s, the Milwaukee Braves, and finally today's Atlanta Braves.)

In 1903, 36-year-old Young's 28 wins thrust the Pilgrims into the first World Series, where they defeated the Pittsburgh Pirates. (Young won 193 of his still-record 511 victories in a Boston uniform, over eight seasons.) In

CHAPTER 12

Home, Sweet Home Run

BY GERALD PEARY

lose the 1986 series to the New York Mets.

Still, Bostonians have far better memories of the Red Sox than the ignominious fades in September. Among the amazing team records: Jimmie Fox's 50 home runs and 175 RBIs in 1938; Dick Radatz's 79 games in relief in 1964; Jim Rice's 677 at-bats and 406 total bases in 1978; Carl Yastrzemski's totals of 3,308 games, 11,988 at-bats, and 3,419 hits; and, an extraordinary major-league record, pitcher Roger Clemens' 20 strikeouts in a single game in 1986.

Finally, attention must be paid to the greatest Red Sock of them all, Ted Williams, six times the American League batting champion and, of course, in 1941, the last major-league player to bat over .400. He hit .406. The proud Red Sox star once put it this way: "When I walk down the street, I want people to say, 'There

goes the greatest hitter who ever lived.'" Many Bostonians skip past Ruth, Ty Cobb, and Joe DiMaggio, and say exactly that.

The Red Sox were owned for 44 years by the late Tom Yawkey. Since 1976, his wife, Jean Yawkey, has served as president, with ex-catcher

1907 the Pilgrims changed their name at last to the Red Sox. In 1912 Fenway Park was completed just in time for what some consider the Red Sox's most remarkable season ever. Pitcher Smokey Joe Wood went 34-5, including 16 straight wins, taking the Sox into the World Series. There, future all-time all-star centerfielder Tris Speaker led the Red Sox to a victory over all-time all-star pitcher Christy Mathewson and the New York Giants.

The Sox won another World Series in 1915, but sent Speaker to Cleveland in the off-season. A consolation on the Sox roster was a portly, muscular pitcher who also could hit the ball a country mile: George Herman "Babe" Ruth.

Faced with Ruth's stupendous seasons as a New York Yankee, including the 60 home runs in 1927, it's easy to bury his earlier seasons as one of the Red Sox. But a solid argument could be made that Ruth was even more remarkable in Boston, because he was brilliant both as a pitcher and as a batter. In 1916 and 1917 he won 23 and 24 games, respectively, for the Sox, and also World Series games for the team in 1916 and 1918. In 1918 Ruth hit 11 home runs as a part-time Sox

outfielder, leading the pre-"lively ball" American League.

Complacent 1918 Red Sox fans took winning the World Series for granted. After all, the team had won 3 of the last 4 series, and 5 of the 15 played. But who in Boston would know that the Sox would never win a series again, at least through 1988, and not for lack of trying? What old-timer doesn't still groan at infielder Johnny Pesky's infamous "held ball" in 1946 that allowed Enos Slaughter to score from first on a double and give the series to the St. Louis Cardinals? Or what about the heartbreaking loss in the 1957 series? Or, still a deep wound today, was the ball that scooted through Bill Buckner's legs to

Above left: Red Sox second baseman Marty Barrett attempts to tag out California Angel Wally Joyner in Fenway Park. Photo © Christopher Lauber

Above: The Boston Red Sox games always sell out at Fenway Park. Photo © Paul Corkum

Left: Oil Can Boyd is one of the many superstars in the American League working for Boston's favorite ball club. Photo © Christopher Lauber

Haywood Sullivan as Red Sox general partner and the club's chief executive officer. James "Lou" Gorman runs the baseball operations as vice president and general manager. As a group, these executives are responsible for putting together today's Red Sox, potentially the most exciting team in several decades. Playing as always at intimate, comfortable Fenway Park (Bostonians agree unanimously that this is the best stadium in the majors), the Red Sox are capable of American League pennants. That's because they are led by twice Cy Young Award pitcher Roger Clemens and three-time American League batting champion Wade Boggs. As for a World Series victory, everyone agrees that it's been a long, long wait since 1918.

The Boston Celtics have had no problem with championships. They have topped the NBA 16 times, including the truly extraordinary 8 consecutive titles from 1959 to 1966. But the team certainly began unceremoniously in 1946. Among 11 teams lumped to form the Basketball Association of America, the Celtics fielded a less-than-formidable starting lineup averaging 6 feet 1 inch, and they tied the Toronto Huskies for last place in the East at 22-38. The team averaged a woeful 60.1 points a game, and, the ultimate insult, no Celtic ended in the top 20 in scoring. Chuck Connors, later the TV star of *The Rifleman,* was the Celtics' starting center. He admitted of the first Celtics: "We weren't much of a basketball team. We were the worst."

Three years later, 1949-1950, the Celtics were still losing and losing. They were 22-46, despite the stupendous hook shots of Tony Lavelli. But at the end of the season the Celts got a new coach, who traded Lavelli away. "He's gone," Arnold (Red) Auerbach, 32, said. "He's not tough enough to play pro ball, and I've no time for sentiment." Red Auerbach has been Mr. Celtic ever since.

The Celtics promptly drafted all-American Walter Brown of Duquesne, a black, and ended the NBA color line. Then in a special National Basketball Association lottery (the league had altered its name), the Celtics acquired NBA star "Easy Ed" Macauley and Holy Cross star Bob Cousy. The Celtics of 1950-1951 enjoyed their first winning team at 39-30. Said Macauley: "We changed the Boston fans' image of pro basketball. They began to appreciate the sport in general and the team in particular."

Still, the newly hopped-up Celtics, led by dribbling-and-passing maestro Bob Cousy and sharpshooting Bill Sharman, kept missing out on the playoffs. In 1955-1956 the team averaged a league-leading 106 point average, yet finished six games behind Philadelphia in the East. But Red Auerbach had a plan. He maneuvered the NBA draft to acquire University of San Francisco center Bill Russell.

Bill Russell could leap and rebound and block shots and play magnificent defense. Auerbach said later: "He was the guy we desperately needed ... the greatest of them all, the best basketball player who ever lived." The Celtics won their first division crown at 44-28 in 1957, and their first NBA championship over the St. Louis Hawks. In 11 Celtic seasons, Bill Russell scored more than 14,000 points.

Adding in such Celtics immortals as Tom Heinsohn and K.C. Jones and Sam Jones, the "green and white" won 11 championships in 13 years, an unparalleled achievement for all professional sports. When Red Auerbach

Above left: The Boston Celtics have changed the city's attitude toward the sport of pro basketball. Photo © Stanley Rowin

Below: Recently, the Celtics have acquired some towering talent in the likes of Kevin McHale, Danny Ainge, Robert Parrish, and Larry Bird. Photo © Christopher Lauber

retired from his coaching in 1966, he had guided the Celts to nine of these championships and far more victories (1,037 in all) than anyone in NBA history.

The 1970s had redhead Dave Cowens replacing Russell at center, and no giant man has ever run the basketball court from end to end better. The 1970s also meant, of course, the ascendancy of John Havlicek, who averaged 20.1 points a game over 16 mighty Celtic seasons and world championships in 1974 and 1976. The 1970s also brought the inspired play at guard of JoJo White. And for real basketball devotees, the "night to remember" was June 4, 1976, the triple-overtime 128-126 victory over the Phoenix Suns in the sixth game of the NBA championship. Thousands of words have emanated from sportswriters attempting to describe the game's magical conclusion, when each team kept matching the other with literally impossible passes and baskets. As many newspapers ex-

claimed the next day: "The Greatest Basketball Game Ever!"

And the 1980s brought more championships for the Celtics—in 1981, 1984, and 1986. The quiet, steady, and gentlemanly coaching since 1983 of K.C. Jones sent the Celtics into the NBA finals in each of

his four seasons. The shrewd executive dealings of now-Celtics President Red Auerbach brought the team starters Danny Ainge and Kevin McHale and led to the acquisition of Robert Parish, Bill Walton, and Dennis Johnson in lopsided trades. Best of all, Auerbach made a bold gamble and drafted a talented forward from Indiana State who was only in his junior year in 1979—Larry Bird. Bird, a member of the all-NBA all-star team for eight years, was the league's MVP three seasons in a row, in 1984, 1985, and 1986. An amazing competitor for running, passing, free throws, rebounding, and three-point shots, Bird is the challenge to Red

Left: Larry Bird hoops it up for the Boston Celtics, who have topped the NBA 16 times.
Photo © Christopher Lauber

Below: In 1986, the city of Boston honored the Celtics with this celebration.
Photo © Christopher Lauber

Auerbach's famous remark that Bill Russell is "the greatest of them all."

Now Auerbach can smile in his belief that the two greatest basketball players of all time wore the Boston Celtics green and white. On September 20, 1985, Red's 68th birthday, the city of Boston said "thank you" by unveiling a life-sized statue at the Faneuil Hall marketplace.

As for hockey, the Boston Bruins were born in a Montreal hotel room in 1924, when the National Hockey League voted to grant the first American franchise to New England's grocery king, Charles Adams. But the 1924-1925 season ended with the Bruins on the bottom of the six-team league at 6-24. However, the Bruins quickly turned into a winning team behind "the Edmonton Express," Eddie Shore, a seven-time All-Star and a very tough player, who immediately set an NHL record for penalty minutes. And the Bruins became identified, seemingly forever, as rough-and-tumble hockey players, the alter egos of what Canadian author Peter Gzowski called:

the lusty saloon-tough seaport of the shanty Irish … Although every team in the NHL … has come to personify its home city, none has held more consistently to a single style, over the years, than the Bruins. They are as delicate as stevedores … The Bruins have played the game with a joy-through-brawling that is as Boston … as a last hurrah.

The Bruins also have played hockey with immense skill and finesse. They are five times Stanley Cup Champions (the last time in 1972) and divisional champions 19 times. The Bruins have had a winning record for 20 years in a row, the longest streak

Above right: The New England Patriots are a talented football team. Photo © Steve Lipofsky

Right: Irving Fryar does his stuff for the Patriots. Photo © Steve Lipofsky

above .500 of any professional team. Twenty-eight Hall of Famers have worn Bruin uniforms, including Shore, five-time scoring leader Phil Esposito, and the best of them all, Bobby Orr.

Orr revolutionized the sport of hockey, becoming the first defenseman ever to lead the league in scoring. He was the league MVP three times, and he won the Norris Trophy for outstanding defenseman eight consecutive seasons. Knee injuries led to a forced retirement after 10 years, but Orr had done everything. Many of the skating rinks that sprang up around New England can be attributed directly to Orr's immense popularity.

In the late 1980s, Bostonians find the Bruins doing what they always do—winning games, getting into the playoffs, and trying their hardest to skate past the Montreal Canadiens. No talk of the Bruins is complete without a mention of professional sports' most uncanny jinx. In 1943 the Bruins faced the Canadiens and came out on top for the Stanley Cup. After that the Bruins lost 18 straight series to the Canadiens, until 1988. The Ray Bourque-led squad ended the

dreaded curse, winning the eastern playoffs over the stunned Canadiens.

Football fans wonder when Boston's beloved New England Patriots will manage to take the Super Bowl. A colorful and inevitably talented football team, the Pats have only squeezed into the playoffs twice since they joined the National Football League in 1965, when the AFL merged with the NFL. In 1979 the Pats were the victim of a controversial roughing-the-passer penalty in a playoff loss to the Oakland Raiders. In 1986 they became the first wildcat

playoff team to win three playoff games on the road on the way to the Super Bowl. Boston went wild, but the ecstasy was short-lived when, in Super Bowl 20, the Patriots were mightily trounced by the invulnerable Chicago Bears.

The finest Patriot in the team's first two decades is probably John Hannah, who played his whole career for New England and was chosen by *Sports Illustrated* as "the greatest lineman of all time." The most tragic figure is wide receiver Darryl Stingley, who was paralyzed for life when tackled in an exhibition game.

Until recently the Patriots have been owned by Billy Sullivan and his family, who paid a bargain-basement $25,000 for the Boston Patriots of the AFL. In 1971 the Sullivans spent $15

million to buy and modernize a stadium in Foxborough, for which they renamed the team the New England Patriots. In 1988 the Sullivan family sold its majority stock to Paul Fireman, 44-year-old head of Reebok International, Inc. Good luck to the Pats and their new owners.

Although the United States Open occurs every few years at the Brookline Country Club, Boston would never claim to be a major center of professional golf. Similarly, Bostonians' favorite racetrack, Suffolk Downs, is a funky and amusing place to spend the afternoon. Though it's hardly the gentrified Kentucky Derby, it has been going full speed since 1935. Bostonians look proudly to the Head of the Charles race each October, the largest single-day rowing event in the world. Thousands of rowers in 700 shells race three miles up the Charles River, from the Boston University Bridge to the finish line on Soldiers Field Road in Brighton. Meanwhile, many thousands of fans picnic on the banks of the river, then cheer on their favorites rushing through the waters below. Magnificent fun.

And of course there is the Boston Marathon each April, among the oldest annual sporting events in

America. The marathon has been sponsored by the Boston Athletic Association (BAA) since the first race in 1897. Then, 15 runners started, and 10 finished the course. In recent years, around 7,000 official runners complete the race, including race walkers, persons in wheelchairs, and, inevitably, Boston's Mayor Ray Flynn.

Every Bostonian has a favorite marathoner, from popular Bill Rodgers, four-time men's winner from nearby Melrose, to Joan Benoit, the only woman to take first in both the Boston and Olympic marathons. Then there's Portugal's Rosa Mota, champion in 1987 and 1988, who makes time at each visit to meet with Boston's proud Portuguese immigrant community. Interestingly, the runner with the fastest marathon time of all, 2 hours and 7 minutes in 1986, is one of the least-recognized champions: Australia's Robert de Castella. He ran the 25-mile track, from suburban Hopkinton into downtown Boston,

Above left: The Bruins are five-time Stanley Cup champions and divisional champions 19 times over. Photo © Steve Lipofsky

Below: Suffolk Downs has been the Boston horse-racing venue since 1935. Photo © Steve Lipofsky

Above: The Boston Marathon is the oldest annual sporting event in America; the first race was held in 1897. Photo © Martha Everson

Right: These cyclists compete in the Mayor's Cup Pro Cycling event. Photo © Christopher Lauber

Below right: Portugal's Rosa Mota was the champion of both the 1987 and 1988 Boston Marathons. Photo © Gene Peach

45 minutes faster than John McDermott's winning time of 2 hours 55 minutes in 1897.

Come out to Boston on Patriots Day! The Marathon Official Program explains why:

Think ahead to the cheering crowds of well-wishers that line the route and the thrill of accomplishing a feat of mythic proportions. If you're not a marathoner, you can participate in the excitement without having to meet the physical demands: by joining those throngs of spectators who gather with family and friends ... in one of the best street parties around.

Finally, there is a splendid museum for avid sports fans—the New England Sports Museum, which opened its doors to an all-star's all-star audience including Dave Cowens, Bruins coach Terry O'Reilly, and Bobby Orr.

The sports museum is practically new, erected in 1987 in an admittedly squat space in Christian Herter Park. However, it is looking to expand soon to downtown Boston, maintaining its current headquarters as a video and print library and archive center. In the meantime there have been impressive exhibits, including celebrations of many landmarks discussed earlier: the Bruins of Eddie Shore and, later, Bobby Orr; the 16 Celtics championship squads; the Patriots Super Bowl squads. The museum also is committed to projects of almost-forgotten sports history, such as a Boston Braves seminar and exhibition in conjunction with the 40th anniver-

sary of the 1948 Braves National League baseball championship.

The museum's proudest acquisition is a life-sized statue of Larry Bird by sculptor Armand LaMontagne, who did similar tributes to Ted Williams and Babe Ruth for the Cooperstown Hall of Fame.

Boston's Enterprises

PART II

*The skyline of Boston Harbor is illuminated with
the first morning rays of light.
Photo © Gene Peach*

Hill and Knowlton Advanced
Technology Practice,
238-239;

WNEV-TV, Channel 7,
240-241;

The Christian Science
Publishing Society, 242;

Xenergy, 243;

Boston Thermal Energy
Corporation, 250;

Cablevision of Boston, 251;

AT&T, 252-253;

Houghton Mifflin Company,
254-255;

Massachusetts Bay
Transportation Authority,
260-261;

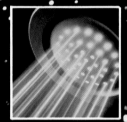

MCI, 262-263;

WMJX-FM/WMEX-AM,
264-265;

Bay State-Spray Provincetown
Steamship Inc., 266;

CHAPTER THIRTEEN

Networks

Boston's energy, communication, and transportation providers keep products, information, and power circulating inside and outside the area.

Photo © Judith Canty

HILL AND KNOWLTON ADVANCED TECHNOLOGY PRACTICE

In the murky and magical world of computers, robots, and other high-technology gizmos, the businesses that produce them have enough on their hands keeping up with the day to day. Buffeted by constant scientific innovation and ever-changing markets, advanced technology businesses are particularly vulnerable to the perceptions of consultants, security analysts, media executives, and a host of others. Keeping tabs on how the company is viewed by the financial world, trade, and consumer press—even its own employees—is something many business executives do not have time for, or lack the resources to do. Developing strategic communications programs to enrich or shift these market perceptions is a challenge that nearly every technology company faces today.

In Waltham, just off America's Technology Route—Route 128—a division of Hill and Knowlton tackles the essential communications and marketing support programs that can spell the difference between a powerful position or a defensive one for these fast-moving companies. In Boston and in Silicon Valley in Santa Clara, California; Chicago; Washington; and London, the Hill and Knowlton Advanced Technology Practice employs nearly 100 professionals to monitor the pulse of the technology industry, report results to businesses in need of this information, and develop strategic plans, messages, and delivery systems that help give its clients distinct competitive advantages.

Included in its corps of public relations experts are consultants, engineers, technical experts, former corporate executives, communications specialists, technical writers, and journalists.

These professionals research opinions and markets; write press releases, brochures, and books; coordinate trade shows; and conduct numerous programs to inform business leaders of technology trends at large. They represent businesses to critical opinion makers in this young and volatile industry.

James A. Baar, executive vice-president, develops quality assurance and professional performance standards for Hill and Knowlton's global technology practice.

They also have access to the immense resources of Hill and Knowlton, Inc., a 60-year-old public relations firm with 56 offices located worldwide.

The Waltham office also serves as headquarters for Hill and Knowlton's technology division, created when Hill and Knowlton, Inc., consolidated its related operations with Boston's Strayton Corporation. Early on in computer history, when computer manufacturers began to envision applications for the business, in addition to scientific uses, the Strayton Corporation began specializing in public relations services for these emerging businesses. Some early Strayton clients included GE, Raytheon, Wang, and NEC. All together, the firm worked with more than 300 computer and other advanced technology businesses between 1969 and its 1984 merger with Gray and Company, which was acquired in 1986 by Hill and Knowlton. Founder Robert G. Strayton currently serves as president and general manager of Hill and Knowlton Advanced Technology Division.

Today this practice is aimed at clients from a broad spectrum of the

worldwide advanced technology industry. This spectrum includes computer technology, semiconductors, data/telecommunications, aerospace, manufacturing technology, electro-optics, biotechnology, materials engineering, energy, and technology-related professional services for accounting, law, architecture, health, financial services, and management consulting.

Communications services include public relations; advertising; research; direct marketing; corporate, marketing, and internal communications; financial and consultant relations; and public and business policy. Many of these skills have been developed into packaged programs designed to meet the special needs of the advanced technology industry and all are developed within the context of a broad-based strategic communications master plan.

Programs for top management, for example, are used by Hill and Knowlton to assist executives in managing communications during periods of rapid change. Hill and Knowlton helps top management to think ahead about issues of management vision, product service, policy differentiation, and the audiences who should know of future development. Through regular meetings with the client, the firm's senior-level consultants discuss advanced technology trends and market development to provide early warning on potential opportunities and crises. For executives changing geographies or responsibilities and for those entering the advanced technology industry for the first time, Hill and Knowlton has developed an Executive Networking Program to tie these individuals into relevant peer groups in the industry.

To help clarify communications goals within the company, Hill and Knowlton performs corporate positioning reviews, polling managers, shareholders, customers, vendors, consultants, and financial analysts, and measuring their perceptions against current objectives. The Databank Management Program lets executives know what researchers, consultants, and the media are reading about them through a number of commercial databanks.

Databanks are monitored, corrected, and updated in all matters of fact. Hill and Knowlton also assists businesses to tailor communications and promotional programs to the many different distribution channels that exist for technology products.

Three other programs help advanced technology businesses monitor and influence three small groups that often have the power to build up or destroy an advanced technology concept, product, or company. These groups—industry consultants, security analysts, and top media editors and executives—are widely consulted and quoted. Combined, Hill and Knowlton believes they form a triangle of influence with tremendous impact. Specific programs

Robert G. Strayton, founder and president of Hill and Knowlton's Advanced Technology Practice, is an advocate of strategic communications as a key advantage for organizations of the future.

aim at each of these groups — to analyze current commentary, tailor new messages and materials, and arrange for personal meetings.

In addition, Hill and Knowlton works with top management to use public relations tools to deal effectively with the world's business and trade media, build and maintain credibility with the financial and investment community, prevent or mitigate crises, and establish leadership positions in their areas.

WNEV-TV, CHANNEL 7

WNEV-TV enjoys the advantage of being the only television station located in the heart of downtown Boston. A few blocks away, at the Massachusetts State House, news anchor R.D. Sahl conducts a live interview.

Right in the heart of Boston's Government Center—just blocks away from Old North Church, the Massachusetts State House, and City Hall—stand the studios and offices of WNEV-TV, Channel 7.

Appropriately, WNEV-TV is Boston's only locally owned and operated network-affiliated (CBS) television station. It thrives in the midst of the city it serves, but its signal reaches far beyond into southern Maine and New Hampshire, out west toward Springfield, and south throughout Cape Cod and Rhode Island.

To comprehensively cover the news of this region, president and general manager Sy Yanoff formed the New England News Exchange in 1983.

The News Exchange is an unprecedented association of newspapers, television stations, and radio stations located throughout all six New England states. Its purpose has been to broaden the range and enhance the quality of news coverage in the area. In Boston, this means that Channel 7's "News 7: New England" programs have had an advantage over their competitors in the coverage of regional news. Channel 7 regularly calls upon its reporters stationed at the *Lawrence Eagle-Tribune,* the *Middlesex News* in Framingham, the *Worcester Telegram & Gazette,* and the *Patriot Ledger* in Quincy for live reports on late-breaking news in these areas. In turn, WNEV reporters offer background information or strong leads to their newspaper and radio counterparts.

The New England News Exchange is unique because it represents a cooperative effort among 7 daily and 12 weekly newspapers interacting with 9 television stations and 10 radio stations. It's successful because it has grown larger and stronger in its five-year history; it has benefited each member's community, and it has been used as a model for similar associations. It also has complemented the efforts of Channel 7's 100-person news department, which has been honored with an unprecedented three consecutive New England Emmy Awards for Outstanding News Program.

Innovation is the key to programming a television station to serve, enlighten, and entertain the diverse public that is New England. In 1987 and 1988 a bold new programming lineup was introduced that meant Channel 7 would be the first in the market to offer viewers the earliest local evening newscast, from 5 to 6 p.m., followed by "News 7: New England" at 6 p.m., and the area's earliest national newscast, "The CBS Evening News with Dan Rather" at 6:30 p.m. Such alternative programming was an idea whose time had come.

Others followed: A weekly one-hour news magazine program that captures the times of our lives, "Our Times," debuted on Saturday evenings. Also new on the scene was "Boston Common," a one-hour Sunday-morning public-affairs talk program. "Studio 7," a quarterly, one-hour prime-time program, was developed to showcase creativity in the arts and sciences, and "Talk of the Town," a weekday program was created to add a little sparkle to the morning talk-show lineup.

They are among the newest additions to WNEV-TV's total program-

"Ready to Go!" hosts Scot Reese and Liz Callaway offer young people ages 6 to 12 useful information that helps them get "ready to go" each weekday morning on Channel 7.

WNEV-TV's success is based upon the efforts of 300 talented professionals who work in the areas of news, programming, engineering, marketing, public relations, research, sales, and administration.

news, programming, engineering, public relations, marketing, research, sales, and administration—who by their creative expressions have made Channel 7 a success.

As a broadcaster, WNEV-TV's signal beams to 2 million homes a diversity of words and pictures. Human conflicts, political victories, medical miracles, and the exploration of outer space only begin to suggest the breadth of Channel 7's coverage.

WNEV-TV not only mirrors the times and chronicles events, but it also brings to light issues of importance to the community as ascertained through interviews with social, religious, business, and civic leaders. Channel 7 has mounted stationwide, citywide, and statewide campaigns to reduce crime, offer health care information, raise awareness of constitutional freedoms, and help tackle the difficult problems of hunger at home.

WNEV-TV is owned by New England Television Corporation, a Boston company with approximately 150 New England residents as stockholders. Boston's only locally owned network affiliate is dedicated to reaching the homes of its viewers by providing quality programming that will inform, entertain, and even inspire the citizens of New England. WNEV-TV's challenge is to serve all of the television needs of its diverse viewing audience. Only when that is achieved will Channel 7 be satisfied.

Photos by Lucy Cobos, WNEV-TV

ming picture, which also includes "Urban Update" and "Higher Ground" for the area's black viewers; "Revista" and "Asian Focus" for the Hispanic and Asian communities, respectively; and "Jewish Perspective" and "Sunday Mass" for viewers interested in religious programming.

Editorials prepared by the station's Editorial Committee, rebuttals offered by leading experts in a variety of fields, and public service announcements highlighting areas of concern to the community complete WNEV-TV's daily local programming schedule.

The only thing missing from this lineup was a children's program, and in early 1988 WNEV-TV did something about that, too, by creating "Ready to Go!" the country's only live, one-hour morning program for young people produced by a local television station. The inspiration? To fulfill a need well in advance of appeals made by legislators and child advocates for more quality programming for children.

Developed by a team whose production credits include "Zoom" and "Sesame Street," the show helps young people ages six to 12 get "ready to go"

weekdays by offering news and weather updates, adventure series, challenging contests, dramas about growing up, and interviews with interesting young people.

Behind the scenes at WNEV-TV, there's another story to tell, one that goes beyond program development, state-of-the-art technology, and commitment to the community. It's the story of more than 300 talented employees—professionals in the areas of

Channel 7 offers its viewers a rich diversity of local news, information, entertainment, and public affairs programming. Editorials, commentaries, and public service announcements complete WNEV-TV's daily program schedule.

THE CHRISTIAN SCIENCE PUBLISHING SOCIETY

The Christian Science Center, Boston.

Long known as publisher of the Pulitzer Prize-winning daily newspaper, *The Christian Science Monitor*, The Christian Science Publishing Society took a close look at its objectives in publishing the news and decided to broaden its horizons. That was in 1982 when The *Monitor*, for all its accolades, seemed to have topped out with a combined circulation of approximately 200,000 between its daily domestic and weekly international editions. The Society believed that it could serve more people with its honest and fair reporting on world events by expanding into broadcast media. Today The Christian Science Publishing Society is one of the biggest independent multimedia publishers in the world.

In January 1984 the *Monitor* launched into public radio in the United States with a one-hour weekend program called "MonitoRadio." Today it also produces a daily half-hour edition of "MonitoRadio." Both are heard nationwide.

During 1985 the *Monitor* entered the world of television in the United States and is now producing "World Monitor: A Television Presentation of the Christian Science Monitor," a nightly half-hour program anchored in Boston and using live satellite interconnects with its bureaus in London, Tokyo, and Washington, D.C. Broadcast nationwide on cable by The Discovery Channel, the new show reaches more than 32 million homes. Its affiliate, The Christian Science Monitor Syndicate,

Inc., owns and operates Boston's WQTV Channel 68, purchased in 1986.

News and programming prepared by the Society's 150 staff journalists and 1,000 stringers serve all the *Monitor*'s radio and television programs, including "The World Service of *The Chris-*

Satellite transmitters at the Christian Science Broadcasting Center in Boston help to carry the Society's news and programming throughout the world.

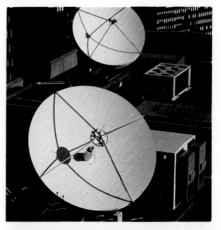

tian Science Monitor," the shortwave broadcast that will cover the globe by 1989. The *Monitor* has joined a select group of the world's major shortwave "publishers," such as the British Broadcasting Corporation, The Voice of America, the Australian Broadcasting Corporation, and Radio Moscow.

In March 1987 the Society began broadcasting this news and information program to Europe, the Soviet Union, the Middle East, and Africa via a powerful new shortwave transmitter in Maine. A second station in the Mariana Islands broadcasts to Japan and Korea and ultimately, to China, Southeast Asia, Australia, and New Zealand. In 1989 a two-transmitter station in South Carolina will broadcast to Canada and Latin America.

Also mindful of its responsibility to keep its news-printing activities abreast of the times, the Society introduced *World Monitor, The Christian Monitor Monthly* magazine in fall 1988. Its goal is to explore significant, sometimes complex issues in an easy-to-understand and enjoyable writing style. It calls on a variety of well-known figures to write on topics in their fields of expertise.

The new magazine, when combined with the Society's new radio, television, and shortwave activities, is amply fulfilling the publishing role that Christian Science founder Mary Baker Eddy first envisioned in 1908, when she directed her church to start a daily newspaper whose objective was to "injure no man, but to bless all mankind."

The shortwave broadcasting facilities for WCSN in Scotts Corners, Maine.

XENERGY

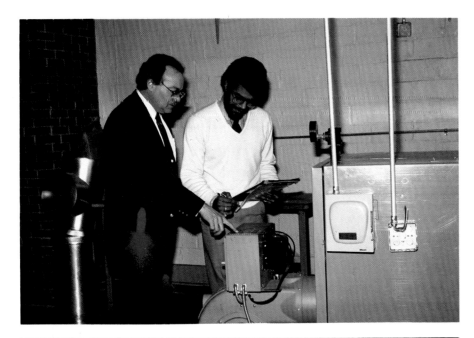

Helping industrial, commercial, and residential clients save energy costs is facilitated by XENERGY's unique combination of engineering, computer software, fuel management, and program operations.

The Empire State Building had a problem that had nothing to do with a giant gorilla. No, the most famous building in the United States was guilty of wasting valuable energy. Along with 200 other buildings in Manhattan, the magnificent skyscraper was the target of a Con Edison survey. A team from Boston-based XENERGY converged on the skyscraper to do an "energy audit" and find out in detail where $6 million in steam and electrical power went in and out throughout the structure. The investigation revealed that while the building was deemed fairly efficient, 15,000 light fixtures could use better ballasts, and replacing antiquated fan motors would cut power used for mov-

An expert in demand management, XENERGY helps utilities best meet the country's future needs for electricity.

ing hot and cold air by 20 percent.

XENERGY, a Boston-based, energy-management company of 110 employees located in six states, has performed 70,000 such energy audits since its inception in 1975, 1.5 years after the OPEC oil embargo created the first nationwide energy crisis. That year the company was formed to help business and government conserve resources. By systematic and scientific study of all forms of energy use in existing buildings, the firm could make recommendations for managing future

energy use. In 1981, with the help of a new software program called XENCAP™, XENERGY was able to reduce the cost of its energy audit by a factor of 10.

The comprehensive data collected and analyzed by XENERGY for large commercial/industrial users has proven to be a boon for utility companies that are seeking detailed information on how their customers use energy. XENERGY's utility planning services group has performed contract research for 100 of the country's largest utilities, which then can make informed business and marketing decisions based on energy usage trends among their commercial, industrial, and residential customers.

Equipment available for saving energy has progressed far beyond the days of simple insulation. Sensors turn off lights, and computers control heating, ventilating, and air conditioning in buildings that are blocks long. XENERGY designs such systems for both new or renovated space, and the company's separate engineering department supervises construction of the designs. For architects, engineers, and developers of new buildings or facility upgrades, XENERGY can run simulations to test various energy system options before commitments are made. Because it believes that most buildings and industrial facilities can benefit from improved energy systems, XENERGY also offers a guaranteed savings program contract through Econoler/USA, enabling building owners to finance system upgrades by borrowing against future energy savings.

Tucked into a hill along Burlington's Mall Road, XENERGY's red-brick building houses 75 employees, their numerous personal computers, and two powerful VAX computers. Management provides a free catered lunch every day at noon for even more energy savings—of the human kind.

MASSACHUSETTS PORT AUTHORITY

Boston has always been the trade and travel gateway to New England. From the city's earliest days as a shipping and fishing center, Boston's transportation facilities have played a central role in the economic development not only of eastern Massachusetts, but of all the New England states.

Since 1959 several of Boston's most important transportation facilities, including Logan International Airport, have been owned and operated by the Massachusetts Port Authority (Massport). Massport is an independent, revenue-bonding authority charged by the state legislature to operate Boston's air and sea terminals, the Tobin Memorial Bridge, and numerous waterfront development properties. It is supported by revenues from the facilities it owns and operates: from landing fees, terminal rents, port tariffs, and tolls. Annual revenues for 1987 totalled nearly $175 million.

In creating Massport, the state legislature instructed the seven-member board not only to take charge of Boston's air and sea terminals, but also to promote the economic development of the entire region. The first course was to get New England moving again. In the early 1960s the age of jet travel was just beginning, and Massport began a vigorous program to modernize and expand the airport. New terminals, longer runways, and new facilities were built to meet the region's growing demand for air transportation.

As Logan expanded, bringing more revenue to Massport, the authority began to make plans for additional airport facilities—but the cost in human terms was high. Because Logan International Airport is located at the heart of a densely populated urban area in East Boston, development and expansion took place at the expense of the residential neighborhoods of East Boston, Revere, and Winthrop. Eventually the environmental cost to surrounding communities became so great that the airport's expansion was brought to a

The Tobin Memorial Bridge is one of several city facilities owned and operated by the Massachusetts Port Authority (Massport) since 1959.

standstill by environmental and political activism.

The authority adopted new policies that would allow Logan to meet the growing demand for aviation services while protecting the airport's surrounding neighborhoods. Fortunately, these events came at a time when new technologies and new programs made it possible to accommodate additional growth in airport traffic without further physical incursions into surrounding neighborhoods. Larger, less noisy planes, advanced noise abatement, and soundproofing mechanisms improved. Better ground traffic management has allowed Logan to more than double its number of passengers between 1975 and 1988—all without further expansion of the airport's physical bound-

The Callahan and Sumner tunnels provide the only direct routes for traffic coming to and from Logan International Airport and the downtown area. To help alleviate congestion, Massport is involved in the planning of a third harbor tunnel scheduled to be built in the 1990s.

aries and with increasingly less noise. In 1987, 23 million passengers flew into or out of Logan.

While adopting an airport development policy sensitive to Boston's residents, Massport also began an ambitious revitalization of Boston's working waterfront. In 1959, when Massport assumed control of Boston's public marine terminals, the harbor was already in trouble. Lack of facilities for modern containerized shipping only accelerated a long, steady decline in shipping activity trade, which had begun in the nineteenth century when the Erie Canal and the growing web of America's railroads bypassed Boston's wharves in favor of those in New York. Since 1978 the authority has invested $120 million to renovate maritime facilities, and the effort has paid off.

Massport's three public marine terminals—Moran Terminal in Charlestown and Conley Terminal and Harbor Gateway Terminal in South Boston—have experienced four consecutive years in which cargo handled exceeded one million tons. The cargo flowing through these terminals each year is

Logan International Airport is the 12th-busiest airport in the world, with an annual passenger volume exceeding 23 million and climbing.

Winding through Boston's downtown, Interstate 93 forms the city's central artery. State officials plan to "depress" the highway by building an underground roadway. Future construction will affect every Massport harbor and Logan International Airport.

valued at $4 billion. In addition, the 23 private terminals in the Port of Boston account for another $4 billion in cargo activity, primarily in bulk products such as fuel oil. Passenger traffic also plays a vital and growing part in the region's maritime economy: the 20,000 cruise vacationers using Massport's Black Falcon Cruise Terminal contribute more than $7 million annually to local hotels, restaurants, and retail stores.

In rehabilitating waterfront parcels that cannot be employed for modern cargo operations, Massport has stimu-

lated the interest and subsequent involvement of the private sector in a wide range of development projects. The development of the World Trade Center, for instance, required the concerted effort of Massport and a team of private developers. This once-dilapidated marine terminal is now a center for international commerce and foreign trade. In 1987, for example, it successfully hosted Digital's DEC

Massport renovated three cargo terminals to accommodate the containerized shipping industry.

World '87 trade show, an event that drew more than 60,000 people to Boston.

At other times Massport has preserved the traditional use of a facility, as in the case of the Boston Fish Pier. This 73-year-old structure houses one of the oldest fishing exchanges in the nation. Today revenues from the rental of prime office space at the pier subsidize the modernized fish-processing operations, thus maintaining a home for one of Boston's most visible and historic industries. Another traditional waterfront occupation may find a new home at the East Boston Piers, where Massport and the state are currently exploring the possibility of combining a lobster pier with a public park project. At Boston Marine Works, site of the

Massport's rehabilitated Fish Pier now boasts a modern structure that houses one of the oldest fishing exchanges in the nation.

former Boston Shipyard, Massport has implemented a careful plan to preserve an industry, generate capital, and save jobs. The once-bankrupt and aging facility has been transformed into a successful center for small-scale ship and boat repair and marine-related activities, with a public marina scheduled for

future development.

In its development and rehabilitation programs, Massport has made substantial efforts to limit the environmental impacts of its facilities on neighboring communities. At the Tobin Memorial Bridge, Massport moved to safeguard its neighbors from problems associated with past use of lead in paint and gasoline. Sections of the bridge over residential neighborhoods have been repainted with non-lead-based paint. Old soil containing lead paint chips has been removed from the backyards of private homes and replaced with fresh loam and sod. On the waterfront, Massport has worked with community leaders to plan truck routes, to help local residents apply for jobs in new developments, and to provide public access to the harbor.

At Logan, Massport has become a nationally recognized leader in noise abatement efforts, instituting tough noise rules and a pioneering soundproofing program for schools and homes. One national aviation expert has referred to Massport as the "Thomas Edison of airport operators."

In 1988 Massport became the first airport to institute a program aimed at cutting down air traffic congestion and delay. By reallocating landing fees and ending subsidies for smaller aircraft, the PACE program (Program for Airport Capacity Efficiency) is scheduled to bring relief to the crowded skies and restore the level of service once enjoyed by air travelers. Massport is also taking steps to encourage air carriers to use larger, more efficient aircraft to move more people with fewer takeoffs and landings, especially during peak hours.

Another problem that will top the Massport agenda through the 1990s is that of ground transportation to and from the airport. Congestion in the Callahan and Sumner tunnels leading from downtown to the airport via Route 1A cause severe delays. Massport hopes to shift 10 percent of airport-bound travelers from private autos to public transit by means of year-round advertising awareness campaigns and other initiatives. Massport's Logan Express park-and-ride services for suburban residents have enjoyed considerable success, but the most imaginative of Massport's alternative transportation service has been the unique Airport Water Shuttle, a joint venture with the Beacon Companies, developer of Rowes Wharf. A 24-hour, toll-free telephone line (1-800-23LOGAN) gives callers information on the various options for getting to the airport without taking a car.

Maintaining efficient ground transportation in and around all the Massport properties, but especially to the airport, will be an even bigger challenge as the city begins one of its largest transportation construction projects to date—the $4-billion Central Artery/ Third Harbor Tunnel project. The project is to replace the existing elevated artery of Interstate 93 with an 8- to 10-lane underground roadway running under the harbor and the downtown area. A four-lane tunnel will run from the industrial section of South Boston

across the harbor and directly on to Logan International Airport. The Third Harbor Tunnel promises, like no other transportation project, to produce significant improvements in traffic flow to the airport.

In cooperation with the state's Executive Office of Transportation and Construction, Massport will be playing a major planning and engineering role as it attempts to ensure that Logan International Airport and Boston's seaport facilities will get full advantage of the new Central Artery and Third Harbor Tunnel. Massport has been developing alternate physical concept plans for the terminal areas, roadways, parking, ground transportation, cargo, maintenance, and support facilities. The Authority is considering alternatives such as over-water transportation and special facilities to improve access, including new terminal areas, platforms, and roadways. As the system to and around Logan is transformed by the roadway construction, Massport will also be compelled to handle the 35 million passengers projected to pass through the airport in the year 2000.

Massport's first assignment, to

"help get New England moving," is a continuing mission. The authority's success is measured by the ability to work with both the users of its facilities and its neighbors as it accommodates the needs of Boston's booming economy. Looking ahead to the next century, Boston's prosperity will depend in large measure on the capacity and efficiency of the region's transportation infrastructure. With the demand for hassle-free transportation rising at a steady rate, Massport is committing all its resources to the creation of a transportation system that will serve the next wave of metropolitan growth.

The "Foster," one of several Logan Water Shuttle boats, transports passengers to and from Rowes Wharf in downtown Boston and Logan International Airport in seven minutes.

Massport's Black Falcon cruise terminal hosted 20 ships and nearly 20,000 passengers in 1988.

THE BOSTON HERALD

At one time the city of Boston was home to 11 newspapers—a situation said to have been wonderful for readers but terrible for those in the newspaper business. Today the competition for readers and advertisers has narrowed to two major players: *The Boston Globe* and the smaller but feistier *Boston Herald.*

While the competition may have narrowed, it seems no less fierce. In general, the *Herald* likes to distinguish itself from the *Globe* as the city's more populist newspaper; the tabloid format is easy to read, emphasis is on local news, and a slew of contests are intended to bring readers back for more.

Just south of downtown, where bridges bring traffic into Chinatown over the Massachusetts Turnpike, *The Boston Herald* is located in a modest low-lying brick building that it has occupied since 1972. Large dramatic photographs for which it is famous line the hallways inside. Outside it's easy to spot the *Herald* just by looking for the bright yellow-and-red delivery trucks parked next to the plant.

Since 1841 the *Herald* name has appeared on the masthead of the newspaper throughout a series of different ownerships. In his 1987 book, *Newspaper Row: Journalism in the Pre-Television Era*, Boston journalist Herbert A. Kenny neatly summed up the *Herald*'s complex family tree in a

until 1958, when the remaining newspaper on the row, the *Globe,* moved to a new plant on Morrissey Boulevard in Dorcester. The row extended from the Old South Meeting House on the corner of Milk Street to the Old State House on the corner of State Street. The concentration of papers along the row was at first a convenience, giving citizens one place to go to exchange news, buy advertising space, and pick up the newspaper of their choice. Soon the street became a general meeting place where newspapermen, intellectuals, politicians, businessmen, and gossips of the day came to mingle with one another at nearby restaurants and saloons. Eventually the growing congestion of the downtown area would force out the surviving newspapers and their cumbersome delivery trucks.

The *Herald* was one of the first to leave. In 1906 the paper sold its plant to the *Post* and moved to 171 Tremont Street. The paper would move again to Mason Street and finally, again to the South End plant where it can be found today. "By moving from downtown Boston to the roomier fringes of the city, the papers were able to build more efficient plants and arrange for more rapid and less expensive delivery of newspapers; but something was sacrificed, something exciting, stimulating, and energizing," Kenny laments.

While the *Herald,* as the Republican voice of the financial elite of State Street, dominated the field in the late nineteenth century, the *Boston Post* took over as circulation leader until its demise in the 1950s. In 1972 the *Herald Traveler,* as it was then known, succumbed to the Hearst chain when the FCC revoked its license to operate the more profitable Channel 5 television channel. William Randolph Hearst had been purchasing papers in Boston since 1904, and he merged the *Herald Traveler* with his *Record-American,* calling the result *The Boston Herald American.* In 1981 the newspaper changed formats from a broadsheet to the tab-

loid that the *Herald* is today.

In 1982 News America Corporation, owned by publisher Rubert Murdoch, purchased the Hearst-operated *Herald* and immediately began a campaign to boost the paper's lagging circulation. In April 1983 the *Herald* introduced Wingo, a contest that has become a *Herald* trademark. In the first six months of Wingo, a number game that requires readers to pick up a paper daily, daily circulation jumped from 236,552 to 317,612. Since Murdoch's purchase, circulation has increased by 100,000 daily copies and 25,000 Sunday editions. Advertising lineage, the final measure of a paper's prosperity, has also increased steadily, although at a slower rate than circulation. According to publisher Patrick J. Purcell, "The Boston area's economic strength has made this a very competitive newspaper market." Also competing for advertising today are numerous suburban newspapers that have sprung up in areas surrounding Boston.

During its colorful history the *Herald* has won nine Pulitzer Prizes. The most recent prize was awarded to the entire photography staff for coverage of the blizzard of 1978. The *Herald* staff of 20 photographers also competes successfully for annual awards from the Boston Press Association and National Press Photographers Association.

Many *Herald* fans in Boston turn to the paper for its extensive coverage of sports, its infamous gossip column, "The Eye"; and the rambunctious political columns of Howie Carr and Peter Lucas. More than 600 employees representing 13 unions work for the *Herald.* In addition to its regular columns, the *Herald* recently added special weekday sections covering business, food, lifestyle trends, and upcoming weekend activities. The Sunday paper contains a separate sports pull-out section, a magazine, and an arts and entertainment section. And as always there are the contests. In addition to the popular Wingo, the paper sponsors trivia contests and random drawings that have sent lucky Bostonians to Walt Disney World, the West Indies, Ireland, and Spain.

single paragraph: "The *Herald* helped establish 'newspaper row' by building a plant there; but early on, it moved away, then absorbed the *Traveler,* moved further away, and later bought the *Journal* and took it out of the row, only to be absorbed itself by the *Record-American* owned by the Hearst Corporation."

Washington Street served as the city's "newspaper row" from 1878, with the construction of the Herald plant,

BOSTON THERMAL ENERGY CORPORATION

Established in 1987, Boston Thermal Energy Corporation is the city's newest utility. The company has quickly proven the economic advantages of steam to the city's energy users, and currently delivers district steam service to heat and cool nearly 500 of Boston's major buildings.

Under the city streets, a 22-mile network of concrete-encased pipe brings steam to customers from three strategically located power plants. The most common use of steam is for heating and air conditioning. Six area hospitals and four universities rely on Boston Thermal's energy service 24 hours a day, 365 days a year. In fact, a majority of Boston's landmark buildings are steam customers, including The John Hancock and Prudential Towers, City Hall, and Faneuil Hall.

The same Boston Thermal steam that provides comfort to millions of square feet of office space also cooks lobsters at the Top of the Hub Restaurant, sterilizes surgical instruments at area hospitals, heats New England Aquarium fish tanks, and presses clothes for local laundries. During the cold winter months, Boston Thermal steam also keeps 1,184 units of low-income housing warm.

Keeping pace with the aggressive urban development of the city, Boston Thermal's team of energy specialists have implemented a capital-improvement program to maximize operating efficiency. This system-wide program is part of a detailed business plan to provide Boston with long-term, high-quality energy service at stable rates. Boston Thermal is committed to the continued growth and prosperity of the downtown area and is determined to do its part. A well-managed district steam system is an important building block of the city's infrastructure and a key ingredient in attracting new business to the downtown area."

Boston Thermal is a subsidiary of the second-largest steam supplier in America, Catalyst Thermal Energy Corporation. A leader in the revitaliza-

Boston Thermal Energy Corporation's Kneeland Street Station supplies 1.1 million pounds of steam per hour to heat and cool the city of Boston.

tion of district steam systems, Catalyst owns and operates a number of other systems, which serve Baltimore, Maryland; Philadelphia, Pennsylvania; St. Louis, Missouri; Cleveland and Youngstown, Ohio. Catalyst has grown rapidly by renovating, and expanding systems acquired from local utilities. Sound energy management, technological refinement, and aggressive marketing have contributed to the operating success of this steam supplier.

Supported by the national expertise of its parent, Boston Thermal Energy Corporation's energy team has opened a new chapter for district heating service in Boston.

CABLEVISION OF BOSTON

Customer service is available at any of the five walk-in cable centers throughout Boston (top), or by calling Cablevision's customer service line in Boston (above).

Cablevision of Boston/Brookline represents one of the best entertainment bargains of any urban cable television system in the nation. Cablevision welcomes nearly 1,000 new homes per month to a varied programming menu that includes popular networks such as CNN, SportsChannel, Home Box Office, and MTV. The system is nearing 100,000 subscribers in Boston and Brookline.

A recent national survey of cable companies indicated that Cablevision provides 67 percent more programming at 33 percent less cost than the nationwide average. In addition, general manager Dick Clark points out that Cablevision's low-cost Metro service compares even more favorably with neighboring systems in the Boston area.

As general manager, Clark supervises a company of 350 employees, including a field force of 115 and more than 90 customer service representatives. These men and women are stationed at the main office and at five customer service centers located throughout Boston's neighborhoods. The firm has committed itself to constantly improving its service, adding customer service representatives and technicians, and upgrading its phone system to better serve Boston's cable TV viewers.

Cablevision of Boston received its initial license from the City of Boston in 1982 and its Brookline operating license a year later. It is part of a nation-wide organization founded by cable pioneer Charles F. Dolan. Dolan is the chairman of the board of Cablevision Systems Corporation, which is one of the 10 largest cable operators in the nation.

In 1961 Dolan established the company that is now Manhattan Cable, the nation's first urban cable system. There he created Home Box Office, the first premium service in the cable industry. In 1973 Dolan began to provide cable television service to a small area of Nassau County. This Long Island system has since expanded to include cable systems nationwide.

In addition to its varied assortment of national networks, Cablevision of Boston/Brookline offers its own local-origination channel, which features 32 hours per week of lively programming produced and directed by its in-house staff.

Included in the local programming lineup are ACE Award winners "The Cable Comedy Show" and "Teen Beat." These shows have been singled out by the National Cable Television Association for excellence in local programming. Cablevision's Channel 23 also features regular public affairs programming focusing on Boston City Hall and Massachusetts State politics. Cablevision also makes an effort to broadcast specials of particular interest to the community, including high school and college sports, political debates, local election-night coverage, and other events. The annual broadcast of the St. Patrick's Day Breakfast from South Boston has become a New England tradition on cable TV.

Cablevision also makes more than $700,000 per year available to the Access Foundation in Boston and $125,000 to Brookline Community Cable to encourage public participation in local television programming. People from every neighborhood of Boston and Brookline have realized their dreams of television production courtesy of Cablevision of Boston/Brookline. In addition, the company has been singled out by the City of Boston for excellence in the area of women and minority hiring.

AT&T

AT&T has a special tie to Boston and Massachusetts. It was in a Court Street laboratory that Alexander Graham Bell invented the telephone in 1876, changing forever the way humans communicate with one another. The entity that put Bell's amazing invention to work, the American Telephone and Telegraph Company, was established in 1885 and became the country's largest private business until the divestiture of the Bell telephone companies at the end of 1983, nearly a century later.

At the dozen AT&T Phone Centers in greater Boston, the latest in telephones, typewriters, facsimile machines, and answering systems for home or office use can be demonstrated, leased, or purchased.

Since then AT&T has been solidifying its historic position as a leader and innovator of advanced networks linking telephones, fiber optics, and computers to help businesses, governments, and individuals manage information

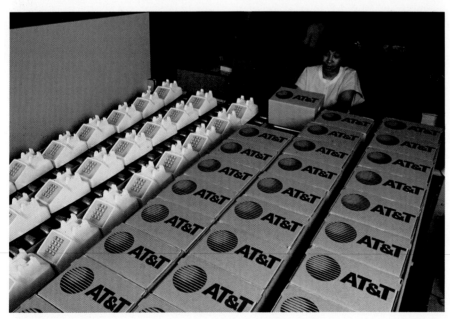

and move it across states, countries, and even oceans. Be it the sound of human voices or the silent flicker of bytes passing between computers, information must be moved more quickly, more accurately, and in greater volume to satisfy the demands of our increasingly high-tech society.

In addition, the company is building on its strength in network design and systems engineering to develop data networks for business customers, integrating their equipment and information sources to give their employees access to the right information at the moment it's needed.

From research and manufacturing in North Andover, to network operations in Chesterfield, to marketing and sales in Boston, to data processing in Fairhaven, AT&T's presence in the greater Boston area is substantial. The company employs more than 13,000 people statewide, making it the Commonwealth's sixth-largest employer.

The way Bay Staters receive telephone service changed on January 1, 1984, when the government-ordered breakup of the Bell System took effect. It was then that New England Telephone, provider of telecommunications services for generations of Massachusetts customers, became a separate company from AT&T, its former parent. AT&T then became a long-distance company and equipment manufacturer, relinquishing its role in routing local calls to the regional "Baby Bells."

AT&T services and products include voice, data, and image telecommunications services, computers for integrated networks and stand-alone uses; telephone products, ranging from voice instruments to complex switching and transmission systems; and components for high-technology products and systems. AT&T customers are residential, government, and business users; telephone companies; and manufacturers of telecommunication,

Repair people such as Delores Squares refurbish business telephones at AT&T's Watertown facility.

data-processing, and other electronic equipment.

International long-distance service is one of the fastest-growing areas of AT&T's business. In 1987 the firm handled more than 964 million international calls, compared to just 90 million in 1970. Satellites and undersea cables link Boston-area callers to western Massachusetts, the other 49 states, and 250 foreign locations.

AT&T also provides products and services to the U.S. government, including telephone switches, computers, private lines, and large special network systems, such as the one used by the General Services Administration in four New England states. In a pilot partnership between AT&T and the GSA, AT&T employees staff a center in Boston's new O'Neill Federal Building and oversee the telecommunications system for GSA offices in Massachusetts, Connecticut, Vermont, and New Hampshire.

Near Boston in the Merrimack Valley, AT&T's largest manufacturing plant produces equipment for transmitting telephone messages, TV programs, and computer data. Installed in local telephone company central offices, in manholes, and on hilltops, this equipment allows large numbers of conversations to be sent simultaneously over one of several transmission modes— wire, cable, microwave radio, or fiber optics.

In North Andover, Andover, and Ward Hill, AT&T Bell Laboratories' engineers and scientists are constantly seeking new ways to ensure that telephone calls are completed quickly and transmitted clearly. Data processing and printing of bills are done in Fairhaven, at one of AT&T's four corporate data-processing centers. Three of the latest digital long-distance switching machines in Cambridge, Springfield, and Framingham route calls near the speed of light.

Marketing offices in Boston, Lexington, Quincy, Burlington, and Springfield bring AT&T's information-age products and services to business customers both large and small that are installed and maintained by a force of 350

systems technicians. At 19 Phone Center stores statewide, sales associates demonstrate, lease, and sell the latest in telephones, answering systems, typewriters, and facsimile machines for the home or small business. In nine offices across Massachusetts, nearly 800 AT&T operators assist customers with their long-distance calling, and at the Customer Service Centers in Springfield and Framingham, technicians perform most of the testing, maintenance, and service functions that used to be done manually by on-site technicians. Telephone communication equipment is manufactured, repaired, and distributed at AT&T's facility in Watertown.

In addition, AT&T is visible through its corporate philanthropy supporting educational, health-care, social-action, and cultural organizations nationwide. In 1987 AT&T donated more than $350,000 in Massachusetts alone. In Boston, AT&T supports the Fund for the Homeless, Massachusetts General Hospital, the United Way of Massachusetts Bay, the Boston Ballet, the Corporate Volunteer Council of Greater Boston, and

Equipment shop operator John Nicolosi checks a robot that moves circuit boards on the D5 Digital Terminal System assembly line at the Merrimack Valley Works, AT&T's largest manufacturing plant in America.

Susan Starmer, a data presenter at the Lexington customer demonstration center, demonstrates AT&T's Image Director document scanner, which reads documents and transmits their contents to a computer's screen and its memory.

Business Volunteers for the Arts. Twenty-three Massachusetts colleges and universities received either grants or computer equipment from the company in 1987.

HOUGHTON MIFFLIN COMPANY

James T. Field (left) and William D. Ticknor, who founded the publishing house, with one of the firm's early writers, Nathaniel Hawthorne.

The abiding sense of tradition evident at the publishing house of Houghton Mifflin Company is only befitting of a firm that includes among its authors Longfellow, Emerson, Hawthorne, Dickens, Thackeray, Tennyson, Browning, and Twain, writers largely responsible for making Boston the nation's literary capital rivaled only by a certain city to the south.

Houghton Mifflin had its origins at the Old Corner Bookstore at Washington and School streets in the Golden Age of literary Boston. Built just after the Great Fire of 1711, the bookstore was the literary center of Boston for more than a half-century. It was head-quarters for the exclusive Temple Club in 1829, the Tremont in 1851, and later the Somerset, the Union, and the Saturday clubs.

In 1832 publishers William D. Ticknor and John Allen bought the store, but their partnership was short-lived, and Ticknor subsequently chose James T. Fields as his partner. Together they assembled one of the most distinguished groups of writers ever to share the same publishing house. They exercised tact and discrimination and provided generous royalties for their American and English authors while the firm took its place as a leading mid-nineteenth-century publisher.

An association beginning during the Civil War, with Henry O. Houghton of the Riverside Press and later with George H. Mifflin, culminated in a merger in 1880 and the birth of the new partnership of Houghton, Mifflin and Company. By 1908 it would be incorporated.

The firm quickly established an education department to publish books for the growing number of public school students. Today the educational-publishing divisions are the backbone of the company. An extensive list of elementary, high school, and college textbooks; software; and other educational and testing materials developed in Boston and by subsidiaries in Chicago and Canada, now accounts for the largest segment of the business. Among the firm's best-selling educational publications are the *Houghton Mifflin Reading,* high school mathematics textbooks, college-level English and accounting programs, and standardized tests, such as the Iowa *Tests of Basic Skills* and the *Stanford-Binet Intelligence Scale.*

Houghton Mifflin's general publishing activities have also remained important. Fine literature for children and adults is published under the Houghton Mifflin, Ticknor & Fields, and Clarion imprints. Through the years Houghton Mifflin authors have received Pulitzer Prizes and American book awards, as well as Caldecott and Newbery medals for children's literature.

For more than 150 years the firm's goal has been to shape information, instruction, and entertainment into forms that provide the features valued by its customers. The company develops and manages ideas and intellectual properties with the help of an extensive network of author relationships, and a staff of experienced editorial talent.

Houghton Mifflin publishes works representing a variety of authors for a broad range of markets. Kate Wiggins' *Rebecca of Sunnybrook Farm,* Edward

The educational-publishing division is the backbone of Houghton Mifflin.

research and be typeset by a computer. Introduced in 1969, *The American Heritage Dictionary* was acclaimed by literary critics, academicians, and the public, and remained on the *New York Times* nonfiction bestseller list for 39 weeks. Other reference publications, including a variety of children's dictionaries, were derived from the extensive word base. In 1976 the publisher began a new venture into business software. Since then Houghton Mifflin has licensed its spelling and verification software in several languages to dozens of computer and word-processing program manufacturers.

The Houghton Mifflin Company of the 1980s is located in two separate facilities on Beacon Hill. The firm's Trade & Reference Division occupies handsome turn-of-the-century buildings overlooking the Boston Common at Two and Three Park Street, where the company has been located for more than a century. Corporate headquarters and the School, College, and Business Software divisions are housed in the contemporary One Beacon Street high rise. Harold T. Miller, chief executive officer since 1973 and chairman since 1979, directs the operations of Houghton Mifflin Company and its professional staff of more than 2,000.

Bellamy's *Looking Backward,* Henry James' *The Portrait of a Lady* and *The Bostonians,* Adolf Hitler's *Mein Kampf,* Winston Churchill's six-volume *The Second World War,* Esther Forbes' *Johnny Tremain,* and Rachel Carson's *Silent Spring,* were all published by the firm as it built a list of distinguished, best-selling twentieth-century authors. This list also included Woodrow Wilson, Margaret Deland, and Brooks Adams, and by mid-century added Henry Cabot Lodge, Theodore Roosevelt, Amy Lowell, Archibald MacLeish, General George Patton, and Field Marshal Bernard Montgomery.

Its contemporary authors include Roger Tory Peterson, who began the popular Field Guide series more than 50 years ago; Stephen Birnbaum; Louis Auchincloss; J.R.R. Tolkien; Howard Fast; John Kenneth Galbraith; Arthur Schlesinger; Tracy Kidder; and Chris Van Allsburg.

Society has moved into the information age, so the firm now publishes materials in electronic as well as print formats. In 1964 Houghton Mifflin began work on a new dictionary, the first to establish a computerized word base derived from extensive word-frequency

Houghton Mifflin has moved into the information age as the firm now publishes in electronic as well as print format.

BOSTON EDISON

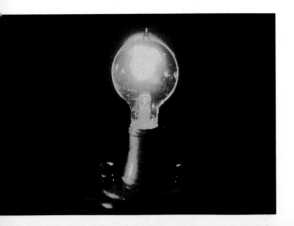

A replica of Thomas Alva Edison's first incandescent lamp. Boston Edison, which served its first customer February 20, 1886, used the inventor's patents. Courtesy, General Electric Company

third-largest utility currently provides electricity to a 600-square-mile area of eastern Massachusetts, including a total population of 1.5 million. Through a combination of programs—plant renovation and long-range resource planning of conservation and outside

Boston Edison recently refurbished the 148-year-old Custom House clock and tower as a gift to the City of Boston. In the early years of electric lighting, Boston was considered "the best-lighted city in America."

In silhouette against the sky, Boston Edison lineworkers mount a bushing atop a transformer.

Day in, day out, 40 cities and towns in greater Boston depend on Boston Edison for more than 3,000 megawatts of electricity. And it is a big responsibility that is only getting bigger. Overall demand for electricity has been growing by leaps and bounds, and promises to increase by an average of 1.7 percent annually through the year 2000. Since 1985 Edison has seen its sales—measured in kilowatt-hours—grow by nearly 5 percent each year from new users alone. At the end of 1987 the city's business leaders began to seriously question whether the region's present energy resources would be able to sustain continued growth.

Boston Edison has concrete plans to meet the demand for electricity through the year 2010. New England's

contracts—Boston Edison hopes to meet the future energy needs of its customers without building new plants, an expensive and unpopular option. Along the way, the firm plans to remake itself into a more efficient service-oriented, and profitable, organization.

In 1987, the year of its 101st anniversary, the company launched a New Directions campaign to mobilize for change. Increasing demand for energy was only one reason to rethink operations. Regulatory decisions by the Massachusetts Department of Public

Utilities; the temporary closing of Pilgrim Station, the firm's nuclear reactor in Plymouth; and the rise of competition—from other utilities, small power producers, and large companies seeking energy sources of their own—all contributed to a pressing situation. Boston Edison would have to find more energy and institute more services without the aid of rate increases to keep its customers. "You have a choice," summed up company chairman and chief executive officer Stephen J. Sweeney. "You either fight regulation, or you adapt to the fact that there's a new ballgame with new rules, and that's what we've done."

To start, Boston Edison initiated a campaign to cut costs in its Prudential Tower offices. Budgets were cut by 5 percent and the work force downsized by more than 300 to approximately 4,000 full-time employees. A new president, Bernard W. Reznicek, took the helm, and other key executives were hired to oversee critical programs. Ralph G. Bird, a retired admiral formerly in charge of the Navy's nuclear submarines, was hired to correct safety problems identified at the Pilgrim reactor and to bring it back on-line.

With its own house in order, Boston Edison formalized plans to meet energy needs through the next decade. Completing a $1.5-million study funded in part by the Electric Power Research In-

"Boston underground" is a way of life for Boston Edison and other utility crews that maintain the maze of services that keep pace with change in the city. This is an underground cable crew working in downtown Boston.

stitute, the company embarked on a 25-year project to extend the life of five of its six fossil fuel stations. These stations contribute the bulk of Edison's own energy resources and are vital to the region. By extending the useful operating life of these plants, the firm expects to save customers more than $200 million in avoided new construction costs through the year 2010.

Boston Edison is also assembling a supply of energy from third-party producers. Currently the company buys energy from neighboring utilities through the New England Power Pool and contracts from independent producers for a total of 750 megawatts of its energy supply. In 1986 Boston Edison became the first utility in Massachusetts to have a plan approved for an auction process involving small power producers and cogeneration facilities. Boston Edison anticipates entering into agreements to purchase between 200 and 350 megawatts of power from these facilities.

Since a megawatt saved is a megawatt earned, the company has also put into place a number of incentive programs designed to encourage customers to conserve energy. Nonresidential consumers, who combined use nearly 70 percent of Edison's resources, are given cash incentives to renovate, change their use patterns, or cut back during peak hours. Conservation materials are supplied free of charge to residential customers who participate in energy survey programs, and rebates are also available to these smaller users. Recently the utility took steps to make its offices more energy efficient. Lighting fixtures on 18 floors of the Prudential Tower were replaced with energy-efficient fluorescent lamps and ballasts. Connected with a sophisticated sensor system, the renovations are expected to cut Edison's own electricity needs in the tower by 66 percent.

The system diagram board—114 feet long, 11 feet high, and marked with 2,500 symbols—is Boston Edison's map of its 600-square-mile territory in 40 cities and towns. This is Boston Edison's System Control and Data Acquisition Center.

Just in case outside supply sources fail to provide the energy needed, Edison has put in place a number of contingency plans. These include the prelicensing of a Combustion Turbine Peaking Unit in Walpole and site banking for other generating units should the construction option prove necessary. The firm is looking at the potential redevelopment of the retired Edgar Generating Station in North Weymouth and studying the feasibility of connecting the region with power sources in Nova Scotia by means of an underseas transmission line.

Since advanced technology has made the energy field more competitive—one can now use trash, methane, peat, wind, and recycled steam to produce electricity—Edison also seeks to build customer loyalty through a number of helpful programs. EdisonCare is a deferred billing plan for residential customers who are hospitalized. Edison customers can smooth out the seasonal peaks and valleys in their monthly bills through a budget billing program. The

Gatekeeper program trained 500 meter readers and customer service employees to watch for signs that an elderly resident could need help. Radio on Alert formalizes a way for field employees to use their two-way radios to report criminal behavior and emergencies. Safe Place offers customers a temporary haven in neighborhood Edison offices.

Capping a busy year of new directions, Boston Edison repaired the famous clock atop the 148-year-old Custom House, and lit the new clock and the tower as a gift to the City of Boston. In addition, the company promised to donate the design costs and half the installation fees of energy-efficient energy systems when the tower undergoes a planned renovation by a developer chosen by the city.

AFFILIATED PUBLICATIONS, INC.

Affiliated Publications, Inc. was born when the third-generation publisher of *The Boston Globe,* William Davis Taylor, made the decision to transform the family-owned newspaper into a public company. Under the leadership of his son, the paper's fourth publisher with the Taylor name, William O. Taylor II, Affiliated has branched out from its successful newspaper operation to include specialty magazines, books, and personal communications, in addition to the *Globe.* The company now has major investments in communications of the future, specifically cellular telephones and paging systems.

The Boston Globe—the largest newspaper in New England—started as a fragile operation that nearly folded a year after it was founded in 1872 by eight Boston merchants. Bailed out by an infusion of capital from department store founder Eben Jordan, the *Globe* started again under the guiding hand of Chas. H. "General" Taylor, an experienced journalist who had worked as a correspondent for the *New York Tribune.* Joint ownership of the *Globe* by Taylor and Jordan continued through the heirs and estates of each until the corporation went public in 1973.

The *Globe*'s dominance in New England can be traced to several landmark decisions on the part of its publishers and editors. By introducing material aimed at women and children, General Taylor immediately broadened the newspaper's audience. During World War II, the *Globe* made an investment for the future when it refused to save rationed advertising space for large customers, giving its "Help Wanted" section unlimited space instead, a policy that resulted in a tremendous lead in classified advertising.

Under the liberal editorship of Thomas Winship, the *Globe* began to feature investigative reporting, tackling local and national issues and solidifying its reputation outside New England. In 1985 the paper won the most prestigious journalism award, the Pulitzer Prize Gold Medal for Public Service, for "the massive and balanced coverage of

Affiliated Publications, Inc., is the parent company of The Boston Globe *and the* Boston Sunday Globe, *New England's largest newspapers.*

the Boston school desegregation conflict." As of this writing, the *Globe* has won 12 Pulitzer prizes.

To be sure, the *Globe* has also benefited from the vigorous Boston economy. In a period when many metropolitan newspapers in other parts of the country showed declines in advertising volume, the paper broke records in every major advertising category in 1987. On September 13, 1987, the *Sunday Globe* set an all-time high for classified advertising with a total of 235 pages. Circulation figures have also climbed. Figures certified by the Audit Bureau of Circulation in 1987 reveal

the *Globe* to be the unchallenged leader in New England with a daily circulation of 502,521 and Sunday circulation of 781,407.

Also in 1987 the *Globe* completed a three-year press replacement program. The newspaper is now printed entirely by high-speed offset presses at both printing facilities in Dorcester and at the paper's satellite plant in Billerica, Massachusetts. Equipped for even further expansion, the *Globe* introduced a 40-page Sunday New Hampshire section that same year, edited out of new offices in Manchester and printed in the Billerica plant. At present more than 90 percent of Affiliated's revenues come from the newspaper operation.

But Affiliated has other irons in the fire, as well. In 1981 Affiliated invested $12,000,000 in McCaw Communications Companies, Inc., a West Coast

company that was primarily involved in cable television at that time. Since then, McCaw has sold its cable TV interests and transformed itself into a major player in the burgeoning communications industry of cellular telephones and paging. By 1988, in fact, McCaw was the largest non-wireline cellular telephone operator in the country. In May of 1988, Affiliated and McCaw completed a major reorganization of their various joint interests in cellular and paging, giving Affiliated approximately 43 percent of McCaw Cellular Communications, Inc. of Kirkland, Washington, McCaw's surviving parent company.

Affiliated's newest acquisition is Billboard Publications, Inc. (BPI), the New York-based publisher of *Billboard Magazine* and nine other specialty magazines on art, theater, music, design,

and photography. With annual revenues of $60 million, BPI also owns Watson-Guptill Publications, a book-publishing subsidiary that brings out about 75 new books each year under four different imprints, and the Billboard Information Network, a data base for the music and home-entertainment industries.

Affiliated also owns The Globe Pequot Press Inc., publisher and retailer of fine books. Headquartered in Chester, Connecticut, Globe Pequot has expanded to include nonfiction books about New England, as well as regional trade, academic, and professional books. Globe Pequot also opened the first bookstore in New England devoted to travel. Located at the corner of School and Washington streets downtown, the Globe Corner Bookstore brings the *Globe* back to its former

home on "newspaper row."

Despite its new and far-flung ventures, Affiliated is still very much a part of its hometown. The Boston Globe Foundation funnels $3 million in grants to the community each year. In recent years it has placed particular emphasis on literacy programs and public school education. In 1986 the foundation announced its single-largest gift to date—a million-dollar grant to the Boston Public Library for branch reading programs and renovation of the main building. The foundation also awards four-year scholarships to the University of Massachusetts for approximately 30 Boston high school graduates annually. Perhaps its best-known program, Globe Santa, distributes toys to more than 50,000 children each Christmas, a Boston tradition going back many years.

MASSACHUSETTS BAY TRANSPORTATION AUTHORITY

The MBTA recently purchased 26 locomotives and 157 coaches for its Commuter Rail Fleet. Ridership has increased nearly 50 percent since 1982.

In 1947, when a new public agency called the Metropolitan Transit Authority was set up to supervise transportation for 14 cities and towns surrounding Boston, the city already had a mass-transit system that was more than 200 years old. In 1630 a three-mile ferry service from Chelsea across Boston Harbor to Charlestown had marked the beginning of public transportation in Boston. The city had seen the coming of private rail systems, electric streetcars, the nation's first underground streetcar tunnel, and the country's first underwater traffic tunnel. South Station basked in the limelight as the nation's foremost railroad terminal, catering to 34 million passengers in 1915.

Before the creation of a state transportation agency, the city of Boston was the first American city to have a unified transit system. Between 1900 and the 1940s this system expanded, opening new subway routes—elevated, at ground level, and underground. The first motor buses and trackless trolleys—buses connected to overhead electrical wires—went into service. The system expanded to serve the growing Boston region.

In 1964 the Metropolitan Transit Authority was renamed the Massachusetts Bay Transportation Authority (MBTA) and its jurisdiction was expanded to include 78 cities and towns. The MBTA, directed by general manager James F. O'Leary, is governed by a seven-member board of directors appointed by the governor to serve co-terminous with him. The secretary of the Executive Office of Transportation and Construction also serves as the chairman of the board. In the face of changing populations, industries, and technologies, the Authority, with nearly 7,000 employees, assumes the responsibility for meeting the daily transportation needs of approximately 650,000 passengers.

The MBTA is best known for its four subway lines and the large round "T" signs that mark each station entrance. Red, Green, Blue, and Orange, these subway lines make a colorful pattern on the subway map of Boston. Each has its own distinct history and personality.

Oldest and most representative of Boston is the Green Line, actually a trolley system of streetcars that must negotiate sharp curves, street and pedestrian traffic, low platforms, and small tunnels along 33 miles and four branches. The total ridership on the Green Line stands at 220,000 on a typical weekday.

The Red Line is the longest and most heavily travelled of the rapid transit lines, carrying 182,000 passengers daily north into Somerville and Cambridge and branching into two southern spurs that continue into Braintree and Ashmont.

The Green Line, seen here on the elevated portion near Boston Garden, runs through downtown Boston in the nation's oldest subway tunnel, completed in 1897.

The renovated Orange Line carries 120,000 passengers daily along a 10.8-mile stretch from Forest Hills through downtown Boston to Malden.

The shortest of the subway lines is the Blue Line, which carries 40,000 passengers each day from Wonderland Station in Revere past Logan International Airport and into downtown Boston.

In addition to those riding the subway, 400,000 passengers use the MBTA's fleet of 1,000 buses. More than 10,000 special-needs and elderly residents take advantage of lift-equipped, door-to-door transportation offered by MBTA's The Ride program. Four lines of trackless trolleys transport approximately 19,000 riders daily, primarily in Cambridge. Nearly 60,000 people ride the 11-branch high-speed commuter rail system. Through subsidy contracts with two commuter boat lines, the MBTA serves 2,000 passengers a day who prefer to travel from the South Shore by sea routes.

The MBTA's commuter rail system is the fastest-growing of all transportation modes, with a 48-percent increase in ridership since 1982. The Authority has met this increased demand in service by purchasing 157 passenger coaches and 26 locomotives, as well as a comprehensive, $200-million program to upgrade track and stations and to increase parking systemwide.

Since 1980 the MBTA has placed a priority on upgrading existing routes and equipment, spending $1.2 billion on major construction projects and another $336 million on new trains, streetcars, and buses. The Authority seeks to transform Boston public transportation from "the oldest subway system in America into one of the nation's newest." MBTA's most recent projects include the rehabilitation of stations and lengthening of platforms of 11 Red and Orange line stations, reconstructing tracks along the Red and Green lines, and relocating a 4.7-mile stretch

System Map—the MBTA serves nearly 650,000 passengers a day on three rapid transit routes, a four-branch streetcar system, 157 bus routes, and 11 commuter rail lines.

of the Orange Line from an aging elevated structure to a below-grade trough that runs parallel to the old line.

While the next decade will see a greater amount of attention directed toward the expansion of commuter lines, the Massachusetts Bay Transportation Authority has, in the meantime, restored an 8.25-mile section of the Needham Branch commuter rail line that operated between 1830 and 1979. Back in operation, the line serves a densely populated community center southwest of downtown Boston. The

One of 58 new rapid transit cars for the Red Line Fleet, which provides service along its 18-mile route to such places as Harvard Square, downtown Boston, and historic Quincy.

renovation of South Station into a $150-million transportation center will continue into the next decade. This center will house Amtrak, MBTA commuter rail lines, an express and intercity bus terminal, an airport bus link, and a connection to the Red Line, and it will also provide substantial public parking facilities.

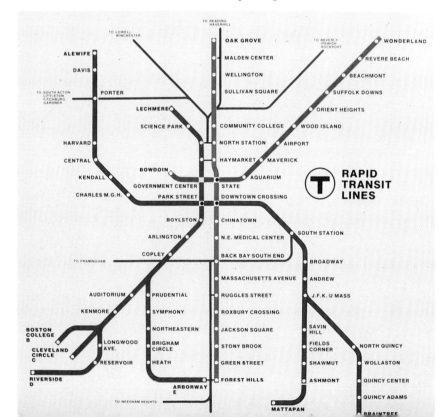

MCI

Every day more than 5,000 Boston businessmen use the services of MCI, the second-largest long-distance telephone company in the United States. High above the city, in the Prudential Tower, more than 200 employees of the Boston office work in four groups—sales, national accounts, telemarketing, and operations—to be sure the 20 million monthly long-distance calls are routed, completed, and billed to their customers' satisfaction, and to hook up new customers with their growing fiber-optic network.

MCI got its start largely by serving commercial customers, then by offering long-distance savings to residential customers to capitalize on unused calling capacity at night. In the past several years, however, while continuing to expand its residential base, the company's emphasis in terms of management focus and resource commitment has returned to the corporate user segment. One example of this is the development of the Corporate Account Service, a customized billing report that allows corporations to receive a consolidated bill detailing all calls made from many different operating sites.

In addition to an emphasis on product development for the commercial segment, MCI has tenaciously pursued opportunities to demonstrate its ability to deliver high-quality service. The company's success in Boston can largely be attributed to the acquisition of some major Boston accounts that switched to MCI, in part due to a trial period during which MCI's transmissions were judged to be of higher quality than other carriers, but also due to its use of other unique business services, such as the customized billing report.

MCI was founded in 1968 by William G. McGowan, who continues to serve as the company's chairman and chief executive officer. In 1972, after four years of federal regulatory battles, MCI began to offer long-distance service between St. Louis and Chicago. It was the first company authorized by the FCC to compete with AT&T in domestic long-distance service and, in 1983, was the first company to offer an alternative international long-distance service.

Following the break-up of the Bell monopoly, local telephone companies were ordered to allow customers to choose a primary long-distance carrier to automatically handle all long-distance calls made by dialing "1," the area code, and phone number. By the end of 1988 about 95 percent of the nation's telephones were signed up under a single long-distance carrier, with MCI winning between 10 and 15 percent of these conversions.

Today MCI offers service to the world. Its international system connects more than 200 countries, and its 15,000 employees serve millions of residential, business, and government cus-

MCI uses its domestic network—the backbone of the company—to connect customers to its worldwide system.

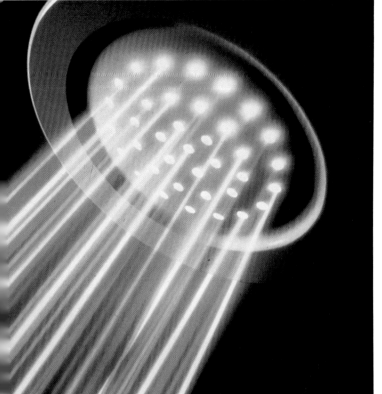

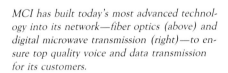

MCI has built today's most advanced technology into its network—fiber optics (above) and digital microwave transmission (right)—to ensure top quality voice and data transmission for its customers.

tomers throughout the United States and abroad.

Calls via MCI are routed through a combination of in-place and rapidly expanding digital microwave and fiberoptic, transmission facilities connected by digital switches. Most of the company's new digital capacity is provided by fiber optic cable and electronics. Since 1981 MCI has spent nearly one billion dollars per year on installing these systems.

The firm does not manufacture these systems, but instead buys these advanced components from competing suppliers worldwide. This policy has, in many instances, hastened—and even forced—the development and deployment of new technologies. For example, MCI recently installed, and now operates, the only 1.3 gigabit fiber optic link in the world. While the future of telecommunications lies in fiber optics

and its superior ability to handle high volumes at high speeds, the company believes it is not always the best technology for all routes and applications. For this reason MCI has built diversity into its system, using digital radio for moderate traffic areas and satellite transmission for point-to-multipoint broadcast applications.

MCI uses its domestic network—the backbone of the company—to connect customers to its worldwide system. The firm has two international gateway

switches in New Jersey and California to route calls overseas, and uses 20 transoceanic cables worldwide. These transmission facilities are, in most cases, owned jointly by MCI and the foreign country being served. MCI also makes use of the international satellite network, owned and operated by 110 nations, to reach virtually anywhere in the world. MCI is presently constructing, with partners, new transoceanic fiber optic cables linking the United States with Europe and the Pacific Rim.

WMJX-FM/WMEX-AM

The colorful posters advertising the continuous soft hits of WMJX-FM are a familiar sight on buses throughout Boston.

With the proliferation of numerous adult contemporary music stations in Boston, the radio battle for the "AC" music listener is tough competition. WMJX is a top player in Boston's adult contemporary arena. Hot on the trail of that affluent, educated audience, age 25 to 54, is the ambitious WMJX outfit based in the Salada Tea Building on

Back Bay's Stuart Street. WMJX-FM, on the air since January 1982, and WMEX-AM, on the air since March 1984, are owned and operated by Greater Media, Inc., owner of 13 other radio stations, 4 newspapers, and 5 cable television systems throughout the United States.

Both Boston GMI stations' combination signal reaches five different markets: Boston and Worcester, Massachusetts; Providence, Rhode Island; Manchester, New Hampshire; and parts of Cape Cod. WMJX' antenna is located at the top of the Prudential

Building, one of Boston's tallest building. The WMJX signal is as strong or stronger than any other Boston FM radio outlet. Utilizing state-of-the-art digital components, the WMJX engineering department has incorporated the most up-to-date concept in antenna design, assuring maximum signal and fidelity to home, in-office, and in-car listeners.

Close to a half-million people listen to WMJX/WMEX in one week. WMJX is a foreground station, which means in addition to playing light and familiar music the AC audience searches out,

WMJX provides listeners with quality, up-to-the-minute news, traffic, and weather reports. The station plays "continuous soft hits" from the past three decades, a diverse selection from artists and groups such as Neil Diamond, Lionel Ritchie, The Beatles, Whitney Houston, James Taylor, Dionne Warwick, Stevie Wonder, Chicago, Billy Joel, and others.

News can be heard at the top and bottom of the hour each morning and once every hour while Bostonians drive home every afternoon. Rounding out the WMJX news schedule are those very necessary all-day weather reports with popular Channel 7 meteorologist Harvey Leonard and frequent traffic reports from the WMJX skywatch helicopter.

WMJX is also becoming well known for its special reports. The station's news reporters covered the 1988 presidential election, traveling out of state to report the primary action and to broadcast exclusive interviews with the contenders. In 1987 the station received a gold medal for Best Special Event from the International Radio Festival of New York for "The Magic of Ireland," a four-hour remote broadcast from Ireland that WMJX believes to be the first extended international broadcast produced by an FM station in Boston.

In 1988, WMJX won top honors in the Massachusetts Associated Press Broadcast Awards in the Public Affairs, Enterprise Reporting and Special Event coverage categories. That same year WMJX won first place in the Radio-Television News Directors Association Awards competition for its continuing coverage of the presidential campaign of Massachusetts Governor Michael Dukakis.

Among the most popular of the station's regular specialty shows are David Allen Boucher's ultramellow "Bedtime Magic" from 8 p.m. to midnight. A consistent market leader, "Bedtime Magic" weaves relaxing, soft, contemporary songs and light jazz with Boucher's whispery commentary. "Bedtime Magic" is the most popular choice of the FM band in its nightly slot.

On Sunday mornings the appropriately entitled "Sunday Morning Jazz Show" can be heard with Jesse Sandidge. A ratings success story, the "Sunday Morning Jazz Show" has been on the air since 1982, featuring traditional mainstream, and fusion-style jazz music. Jesse Sandidge, an accomplished jazz trumpet player himself, can often be seen and heard in and around Boston hosting local jazz club performances and concerts.

The longest continually broadcast public affairs program in the city of Boston, "Bay State Forum" is broadcast on WMJX Sunday mornings, beginning at 8:30 a.m. Guests have included Mayor Raymond Flynn, Lieutenant Governor Evelyn Murphy, State Senator George Keverian, and many others.

The WMJX call letters reflect the life-style of the Boston radio listener, involvement with the arts, entertainment, sports, and history. Each letter in the WMJX logo carries special meaning. The "W" comes from the Wilbur Theater, an historic theater in the heart of Boston's theater district. It represents the entertainment value of the on-air product heard on WMJX. The "M" is from the Museum of Fine Arts, symbolic of the cultural aspect of New England which the station both reflects and supports. The "J" is borrowed from John Hancock's signature. It marks the stability and tradition of WMJX, most especially in terms of its commitment to news, public affairs and other services. And the "X" is from the Boston Red Sox, supporting the station's interest in sports and the great tradition of the city's championship spirit. Together they spell the magic of Boston.

The WMJX logo is unlike any other radio station's logo because WMJX is unlike any other radio station. The entertainment, the culture, the commitment—the magic of Boston—it's all heard on WMJX.

Swinging back in time, sister station WMEX-AM fills a niche in the Boston radio market with 1950s and 1960s rock and roll programming. Boston's original 24-hour-a-day oldies station, WMEX boasts legendary call letters which date back to 1935. WMEX is an upbeat, fun, nostalgic sound geared toward adults ages 25 to 54. The WMEX Radio Road Show complete with a 1957 fire-red Ford Fairlane convertible, is often seen at remote broadcasts at grand openings, anniversary celebrations, and community events.

WMJX/WMEX spends hundreds of thousands of dollars promoting the radio stations in the Boston market, maintaining a high visibility for their advertisers. WMJX/WMEX have a large client base who continue to advertise on both stations successfully.

BAY STATE-SPRAY AND PROVINCETOWN STEAMSHIP INC.

Looking for a way to beat the traffic congestion in downtown Boston? Or perhaps you're searching for a stimulating setting for your next business meeting? How about a new place to go on a romantic date?

The Bay State-Spray and Provincetown Steamship Inc., a passenger boat line headquartered on Long Wharf in downtown Boston, has the solutions to all of these dilemmas. With its fleet of modern vessels, Bay State Provincetown Cruises feature a variety of commuter routes, sightseeing cruises, and charter cruises for pleasure and business functions.

Founded in 1962 by Richard Nakashian, Bay State Provincetown Cruises set sail in the business world with only one vessel, the *Spray*—a replica of the boat that Joshua Sorcum sailed around the world singlehandedly. Today Janet and Joe Pallotta continue with a fleet of vessels complete with the most up-to-date conveniences and facilities, including spacious floor areas for dancing, special amenities for business functions, and accommodations for the handicapped.

Many captains with years of nautical experience operate the boats, and

trained, courteous crews assure the comfort and safety of all passengers. In addition to the cruises, the company employs many other related services, including caterers, musicians, and decorators to provide the food and entertainment for business conferences, reunions, weddings, and other social functions.

The company's regularly scheduled cruises sail to some of the area's most well-known attractions: Nantasket Beach, Boston's most popular bathing spot; Provincetown on Cape Cod; and Boston's numerous Harbor Island State Parks. Bay State also sails express service from Boston to the famous resorts of Martha's Vineyard off of Cape Cod.

Bay State's moonlit Boston Harbor dinner cruises featuring live bands and the finest cuisine cruise around the harbor and waterfront. Whale-watching excursions have become a popular recreational and educational pastime. Every year tourists, school groups, and native Bostonians alike cruise aboard the scenic Inner Harbor-Constitution Cruise, a narrated seagoing version of the Historic Freedom Trail.

Bay State Provincetown Cruises

The Bay State-Spray and Provincetown Steamship Company fleet of eight vessels provides a variety of regularly scheduled and charter cruises.

prove that commuting by water can be both reliable and enjoyable as seen with the year-round commuter operation between Hull, Massachusetts, and Long Wharf in downtown Boston. In addition, Inner Harbor Water Shuttles provide convenient links between the downtown areas.

Lunch break is another time to experience a Bay State voyage. A half-hour lunch cruise gives passengers the opportunity to relax and soak up some sunshine—for less than the price of a hot dog.

With so much to offer, the extension of the city onto the water further distinguishes Boston from other premier cities. The next time you are looking for the latest in recreation, a different environment, or the best way to get from here to there, think water. Bay State-Spray and Provincetown Steamship Inc. may have just the cruise to where you want to go.

BOSTON BUSINESS JOURNAL

In the beginning the *Boston Business Journal* had all the markings of a typical start-up: faith, hope, and short pockets. It was 1980; regional business papers were springing up around the country, the economy was poised for a comeback, and Boston seemed an ideal place to capitalize on those trends. But in a city notorious for its demanding and discerning readers, *BBJ*, as it's often called, had to struggle to prove itself from the very first issue published in March 1981.

Today the *Boston Business Journal* is a leader in its field and a standard of excellence in business reporting. The newspaper has 45,000 readers, and ad-

The Boston Business Journal, *with 45,000 readers, has become a standard of excellence in business reporting. Founder and publisher Bob Bergenheim has added the bimonthly magazine,* Boston Business, *and branched into Providence, Rhode Island, with the* Providence Business News.

vertising revenue has increased by an average of 40 percent each year. To quote a news broadcast on Boston's WGBH-TV: "It's an entrepreneurial wonder . . . a news junkie's dream."

Once the daily was on its feet, publisher Bob Bergenheim launched the glossy feature magazine, *Boston Business,* in the fall of 1985. Beginning as

a quarterly, the magazine soon evolved into a bimonthly in response to advertiser and reader support. In 1986 the company spread further, introducing a weekly to the neighboring business community of Providence, Rhode Island. The *Providence Business News* has a circulation of 23,000 and is as much of a fixture in its area as the *BBJ* is in Boston, where its revenue grew a whopping 68 percent between 1986 and 1987. From the original three employees—Bergenheim, his son Roger, and editor Nancy P. McMillan—the roster swelled to 71.

Founder Bergenheim is a longtime observer of and active member in the Boston business community from his years as a member of the editorial and executive staffs of the *Christian Science Monitor,* as publisher of the *Boston Herald-American,* and later, as a vice-president and trustee of Boston University. His publications have continued those roles as both observers and participants in the cities they cover.

Each year, for instance, *BBJ* singles out business or government leaders who have changed the course of the city and honors them at a gala party attended by hundreds of prominent Bostonians. The paper is also a co-sponsor of the prestigious Seminars on Economic Policy and Presidential Politics organized by the Bank of Boston.

Staff reporters and editors, too, lend their time and expertise as speakers before groups as varied as the Harvard Business School and the New England Association of Metal Platers and Metal Finishers. *BBJ* sponsors a series of off-the-record breakfast meetings where business leaders can meet, chat, and, no doubt, argue with those who report the news.

In late 1987 Bergenheim's publications were purchased by MCP, Inc., a Minneapolis company that owns 15 publications nationwide. "With the added resources of MCP," says Bergenheim, who remains in charge of the New England operation, "we'll be able to work even more diligently to improve the quality of our publications and our contributions to the business communities."

WBZ-AM BOSTON

Radio stations and their on-air talent come and go, but the story of WBZ doesn't fall under that truism. As the city's first radio station, WBZ-Boston has been broadcasting for more than 60 years—and with the same call letters. Dave Maynard, of morning talk-show fame, has been with WBZ for better than half of those years. Bostonians who tune to 1030 AM know what they're getting—and they must like what they hear, because according to Arbitron ratings, WBZ consistently has the most listened-to morning show in the city.

WBZ's presence is felt all over Boston. With fall comes the Farmstand. According to station lore, a caller to the Dave Maynard show happened to mention that he had a garden overflowing with produce but no one with whom to share it. Come to WBZ and we'll sell it and give the proceeds to charity, Maynard told the gardener. And so a stand was set up beside WBZ headquarters on busy Soldiers Field Road. Today the Farmstand is such a large event that it's held on the station's helipad. Two 18-wheelers bring produce from private gardeners and from operations with produce to donate. Funds go to Children's Hospital, the station's favorite cause.

At Christmastime the station conducts a two-week auction of donated items at Downtown Crossing, with proceeds also going to Children's Hospital. In its most fantastic promotion to date, the station is building a house in Holden, Massachusetts, in conjunction with Mr. Build employees, and is auctioning it off to raise additional funds for the hospital. WBZ announcer Bruce Stevens has been soliciting donations of materials and labor over the air. WBZ Radio's commitment to helping the community is also evident with its

40-member, volunteer Call For Action program; the American Red Cross Blood Brotherhood drives; Crime Patrol, a stolen car look-out service; and the Salvation Army food and clothing drives.

WBZ emphasizes news and commentary in its programming. News is broadcast at the top and bottom of each hour all day. A feature called "60-6" broadcasts an hour of news beginning at 5 p.m., which includes traffic updates every 10 minutes and the only Paul Harvey "The Rest of the Story" broadcast in the city. Two call-in programs, between 6 p.m. and 1 a.m., include guest appearances by well-known Bostonians.

Traditionally, WBZ broadcasts the annual Boston Marathon, and blankets the air waves during snow storms with its "Stormcenter" reports of road and traffic conditions, business closings, and school cancellations. WBZ's 1987

reportage of the Boston Marathon won both Associated Press and United Press International's Broadcast Award for Best Sports Reporting. The station also uses a staff of 50 meteorologists tracing the weather for its "Accuweather" forecasts.

WBZ is part of Group W, Westinghouse Broadcasting, a communications company that is actively acquiring AM and FM radio stations nationwide. The firm owns nine other AM stations, including KDKA in Pittsburgh, the first radio station to broadcast in the United States.

A record-breaking $36,000 was raised for Children's Hospital at the sixth annual Farmstand sponsored by WBZ Radio. On hand for the activities in the Incredible Broadcast Machine were all the WBZ personalities. Dave Maynard, who organized the Farmstand, grabbed an apron and sold vegetables while signing autographs for visitors. Photo by Karin Ericson

The four-bedroom colonial House for Children's Hospital, built entirely of donated labor and materials, was auctioned for $225,000 with all proceeds benefiting Boston's Children's Hospital. From ground breaking on October 9, 1987, to the last day of the auction on May 31, 1988, more than 400 people volunteered unselfishly through WBZ Radio's fund-raising efforts. Photo by Walter Doyle

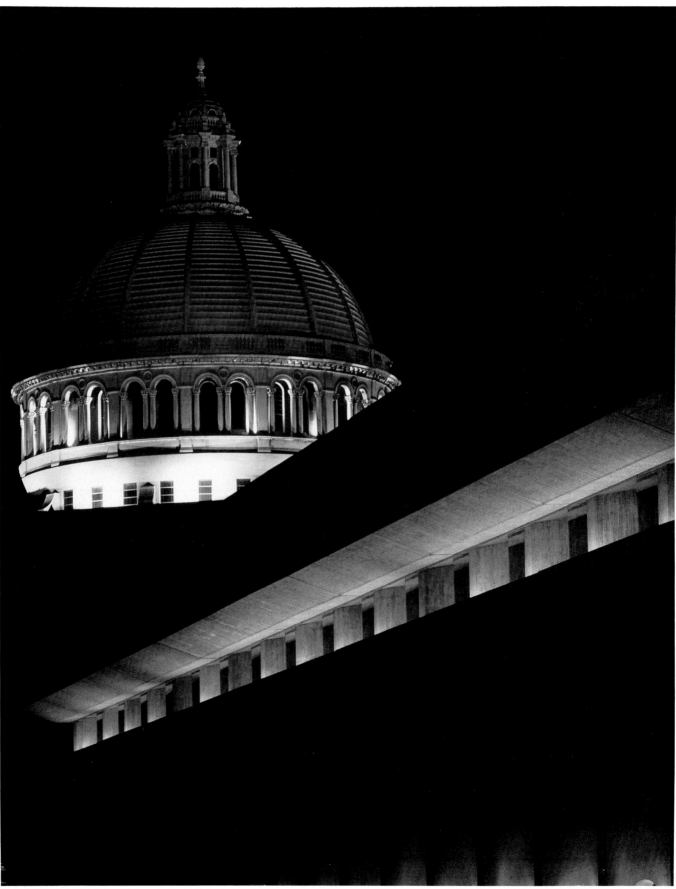

Photo © Paul Corkum

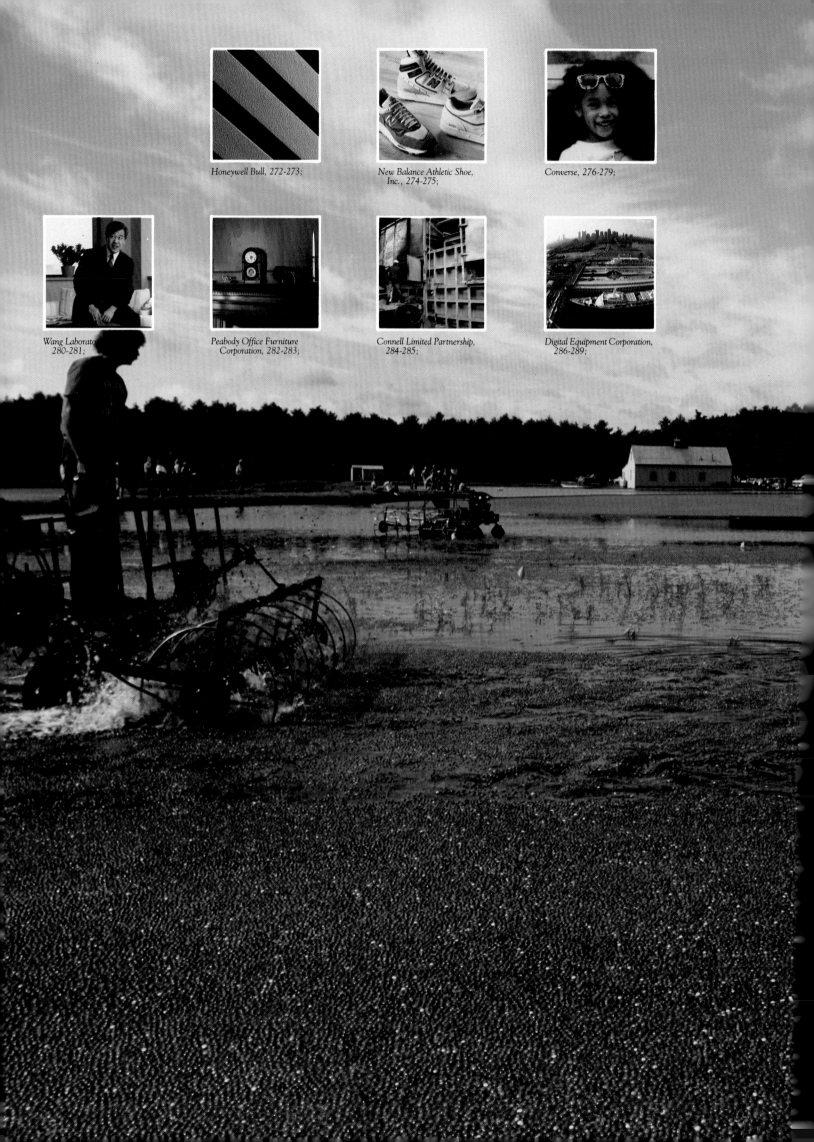

Symmons Industries, Inc.,
290-291;

Ames Safety Envelope
Company, 292

CHAPTER FOURTEEN

Manufacturing

*Producing goods for individuals
and industry, manufacturing
firms provide employment for
many Boston area residents.*

Photo © Stanley Rowin

HONEYWELL BULL

Honeywell Bull Inc. is a new and unusual company created by three partners in three countries in March 1987. The privately held company is owned 42.5 percent by Honeywell Inc. of the United States, 42.5 percent by Compagnie des Machines Bull of France, and 15 percent by NEC of Japan. The creation of the new company represents the renewal of Honeywell Information Systems (HIS), which has been a major player in the computer arena since 1955. Honeywell Bull will continue to support the large and broad customer base established under HIS, which includes such notable companies as Metropolitan Life, General Electric, Coleco, and Ultimate.

The partnership is built on the strength of long-term relationships among Compagnie des Machines Bull, Honeywell Inc., and NEC Corporation. Together the threesome has produced compatible computer architectures, shared product lines, and complemented each company's distribution territories. Compagnie des Machines Bull is an international information systems company founded in Zurich in 1933 to manufacture tabulating machines invented by Frederick R.

An artist's rendition of the new Billerica, Massachusetts, office building scheduled for completion in mid-1989.

The Honeywell Bull facility of 256,800 square feet is used for printed circuit board manufacturing. Approximately 850 employees work in this Brighton, Massachusetts, facility.

Bull. Today it employs 26,800 people and had 1987 revenues of $3.007 billion. NEC Corporation is a $16.8-billion company founded in 1899 and headquartered in Tokyo. NEC is one of the world's largest manufacturers and suppliers of communications systems and equipment. Founded in 1885 Honeywell Inc., a $6.7-billion corporation, is an international electronics corporation that supplies automation and control systems for homes and buildings, industry, aerospace, and defense.

Historically, Honeywell was a computer-age pioneer when it formed the

Datamatic Corporation in Newton, Massachusetts, in 1955, leading to the development of the D-1000, an electronic office automation computer. In 1962 a Honeywell 800 was the first computer to successfully transmit data via earth satellite when information stored in a system at Honeywell's factory was relayed by a Telstar satellite to a computer at Bell Laboratories. Since that time Honeywell's success has centered on advanced, integrated systems that conserve energy, improve productivity, or meet defense needs.

Each of the three partners brings specific expertise to the new venture— Bull in communications, Honeywell in systems integrations, and NEC in large systems technology and semiconductors. The French and American companies have long offered the same product lines and a jointly developed common systems architecture, DSA (Distributed Systems Architecture) to interconnect their equipment. The relationship with NEC goes back 25 years and also reflects the shared resources and long-term perspectives of companies that are in business to effectively serve worldwide markets.

Through extensive research and development efforts, Honeywell Bull will expand on compatibility and connectivity between desk-top PCs to large-scale mainframes, local area connections, and around-the-world networks by using their own equipment or that of others.

Honeywell Bull sees its position as a successful systems integrator. To meet its customers' multinational

needs, Honeywell Bull markets a broad range of compatible systems from micros to minis to mainframes. Since its customers are often large organizations that require communication with systems from different suppliers, its strength lies in networking, data management, transaction processing, and systems integration.

In the greater Boston area Honeywell Bull manufactures small and large systems and employs 5,000 people in a broad range of activities. At its production center in Brighton, printed circuit boards are assembled for the company's small systems. Not too far away in Newton, its customer service operation covers all hardware and software service for United States customers and specific international customers. The division has more than 250 field locations for on-site service and more than a dozen walk-in/mail-in services and support centers. Nearby Waltham is headquarters for the company's United States marketing, sales, and service team. In Billerica, senior engineering and manufacturing personnel develop software for small systems, and in Westwood, the publications and distribution center packages and mails computer manuals and software and produces the company's internal and sales publications.

Further north at facilities in Lawrence, Massachusetts, Honeywell Bull manufactures the DPS 6 and the DPS 6 PLUS microcomputers. First introduced in 1980, the DPS 6 line includes 11 systems that can support from two to 120 users. This family of mini and supermini computers provides key strengths for department, transaction, and distributed-data processing, and includes office automation options. The DPS 6 PLUS, introduced in June 1986 as a follow-on to the mid-range DPS 6 systems, extends the mid-range of the DPS 6 line to support between four and 160 users. The DPS 6 and PLUS are used by state and local gov-

The DPS 6 PLUS is an extension of Honeywell Bull's current DPS 6 computer systems—a family of compatible micros, minis, and superminis.

ernments, large companies such as Metropolitan Life, Blue Cross/Blue Shield, and by hospitals and manufacturers such as General Electric. The 1.3-million-square-foot facility will assume a larger role when the mainframe manufacturing operation moves from Phoenix to Boston in 1988.

Honeywell Bull has received recognition for its efforts in good corporate citizenship in support of the arts, human services, and educational programs. Of particular interest to the company are programs that serve the handicapped. In partnership with the LABB Educational Collaborative

Honeywell Bull DPS 6, DPS 6 PLUS, and DPS 8000 computers are manufactured in Lawrence, Massachusetts. The facility is 1.3 million square feet and sits on 20 acres of land.

(Lexington, Arlington, Bedford, Burlington) for the developmentally disabled, the Horace Mann School for the Deaf, and the Perkins School for the Blind, Honeywell Bull offers in-house training programs that provide competitive work skills for these special-needs people. Out of these programs, Honeywell Bull has gained more than 40 permanent employees.

NEW BALANCE ATHLETIC SHOE, INC.

Just past the Lars Anderson Bridge—that elegant brick enclave leading from Harvard University into Allston—people are at work making New Balance athletic shoes. Four of the country's few remaining domestic shoe-manufacturing facilities belong to New Balance Athletic Shoe, Inc. Two are located in Maine, while the others are in Massachusetts—one in Lawrence and one in Allston, not far from the firm's corporate headquarters.

First incorporated as the New Balance Arch Company in 1906 by William J. Riley of Belmont, Massachusetts, the company spent its first 50 years producing arch supports and orthopedic shoes in a small Watertown, Massachusetts, facility until Riley's

New Balance makes a complete line of running, basketball, and tennis shoes. In addition, New Balance also manufactures walking, hiking, soccer, tennis, aerobics, cross-training, and children's shoes. All New Balance shoes are available in a full range of widths.

death in 1955. Throughout the 1950s and 1960s an increasing number of runners turned to New Balance for custom-made shoes due to the firm's unique expertise in handcrafting specialized footwear. The demand for New Balance athletic shoes grew, and soon the production of custom-made running shoes was the company's primary source of business.

On Boston Marathon Day in 1972 New Balance was purchased by its cur-

rent owner, James S. Davis. At that point in time the entire operation consisted of six people making 30 pairs of Trackster running shoes each day. The Trackster was popular not only because of its technical orientation but also because of its availability in a wide range of sizes and widths. This system of width sizing, New Balance's first innovation, is just as important today. With shoes ranging in widths from 2A to 4E and sizes from 5 to 16, New Balance takes pride in catering to the needs of the individual.

In 1976 New Balance introduced the 320 running shoe, which was quickly singled out as the number-one running shoe on the market by *Runner's World* magazine. According to the magazine, "The 320 earned its first-place rating for . . . the addition of the high-heel pad and the replacement of the leather tongue with nylon." Then, as now, New Balance was an innovative leader in athletic footwear. This rating clinched New Balance's reputation as the premier manufacturer of technically advanced athletic shoes.

While New Balance still enjoys a prominent position in the running shoe market, the company's growth has led to diversification. Today the New Bal-

New Balance manufactures its shoes in two plants in Boston and Lawrence, Massachusetts, as well as in two plants in Maine and one in Workington, England. New Balance handcrafts its shoes with pride in the United States.

New Balance and performance go hand in hand. Two-time Olympic marathon runner Peter Pfitzinger is among a group of athletes retained by New Balance to personify quality and performance.

ance product line is not limited to running shoes alone. The firm manufactures a full line of basketball, tennis, aerobic, walking, cross-training, hiking, soccer, and children's shoes. In each instance New Balance offers the most innovative footwear on the market.

In addition to the company's commitment to quality and innovation, New Balance remains dedicated to domestic manufacturing. Despite intense price competition from foreign shoemakers, approximately 80 percent of all New Balance products are manufactured in the United States. The corporation firmly believes that domestic production leads to better quality control. This standard of quality is the reason behind New Balance's success nationwide and around the world.

World-class athletes have also played an important role in the firm's continued success. New Balance is one of the few companies with its own group of professional athletes who as-

sist in the areas of product research and development. At any company the research and development department drives new product innovation. At New Balance some of the world's finest athletes drive research and development. James Worthy, M.L. Carr, and Red Auerbach have used their expertise in the development of the New Balance basketball line, Olympians Peter Pfitzinger and Francie Larrieu-Smith in the running line, Roy Emerson in tennis, Bryan Robson in soccer, and Lou Whittaker in walking and hiking. With the valuable input of these athletes, the New Balance research and development team works together to meet the ever-changing needs and demands of athletes of all ability levels.

When New Balance introduces a new shoe, it is the end result of months—even years—of extensive research and development. Weekly meetings are held between New Balance's research and development department and the company's marketing specialists to discuss current trends and opportunities. Once a product concept is defined, testing procedures begin with the making of a prototype. A sketch of the product goes to a pattern maker who designs and stitches the shoe's upper and to an industrial designer who handles the technical design of the outsole.

After the shoe's technical compo-

nents have been crafted and combined, the prototype is ready for review by the firm's research and development, marketing, sales, and process engineering departments. Samples are wear-tested by athletes and technical experts who carefully evaluate the shoe's features for performance and longevity. The original shoe concept may be modified or redesigned several times before a final sample is approved for mass production.

Through this integrated process New Balance seeks to uphold its reputation for providing athletes with top-quality, technically advanced shoes that fit as well as they perform. Since its very beginning New Balance has catered to the needs of the individual. With continued dedication to its long-standing principles, this New Balance tradition is a part of the future as well as the past. When a New Balance shoe reaches the market, it is ready to take on the toughest competitors of all—athletes from all walks of life who are constantly looking for both a better performance and a better shoe.

While other athletic shoe companies have their shoes made in the Far East, New Balance is proud of its commitment to domestic manufacturing. This commitment is good for the local economy, as well as ensuring strict quality standards are maintained.

CONVERSE INC.

Gilbert "Gib" Ford, president of Converse Inc.

For as long as athletic shoes have been around, manufacturers have searched for ways to "return" energy to the athlete. Though many embedded midsole and heel substances have been tried—air, gel, EVA—none have been able to provide significantly higher jumps and faster racing times.

But in 1988 Converse announced the Energy Wave, an exclusive superpolymer compound that springs back much like a mini trampoline, resulting in added height to a leap, reduced racing times, and less fatigue during workouts. This revolutionary footwear technology is taking athletes higher than they've ever gone before—and taking Converse along with them.

Based in North Reading, Converse Inc. is the largest U.S. manufacturer of athletic footwear. Converse produces a wide variety of models for performance and casual use, as well as a complete line of Activewear for men and women. With offices in Paris, Brussels, London,

Munich, Tokyo, Toronto, Osaka, San Juan, and Pusan, Converse markets products in more than 90 countries worldwide.

Over its 80-year history Converse has developed a solid reputation for quality, safety, and durability. The company's shoes are consistently rated at or near the top by professional athletes and independent surveys of athletic shoe wearers. As a result, Converse has acquired numerous endorsements from sports stars and fitness organizations. Among the athletes endorsing Converse are basketball stars Larry Bird and Earvin "Magic" Johnson, tennis pros Jimmy Connors and Chris Evert, Cleveland Browns quarterback Bernie Kosar, New York Yankee first baseman Don Mattingly, and Olympic running coach Arthur Lydiard.

Professional leagues and amateur fitness organizations have long recognized the performance and comfort features of Converse shoes. Converse was the first official shoe of the National Basketball Association, and a new agreement, signed in 1988, gives Converse the exclusive right to market, advertise, and promote a full line of basketball shoes featuring NBA and team logos through 1996.

In 1987 Converse was named the official shoe of the Walker's Club of America, the first and foremost walking organization in the United States. With 50,000 members, the 76-year-old club is dedicated to helping people achieve a high level of fitness without the fre-

Models show the Conosaur collection of clothing and footwear.

quent injuries involved with high-impact sports. In conjunction with the endorsement, Converse produced a new comfort and support system called Advanced Motion Enhancement (AME) in its biomechanics laboratory and an educational video titled "Walking for Fitness."

The AME system and the Energy Wave are among many innovations for the shoe manufacturer. Founded by Marcuis Converse in 1908, the company opened its first plant in Malden to produce rubber overshoes and boots. In 1912 Converse began making canvas shoes to be more seasonally independent and to capitalize on a new lawn tennis craze of that era. Five years later Converse introduced the legendary All-Star model—a khaki-color high-top sneaker with leather shoelace eyes and rubber trim.

Throughout the 1920s the firm improved the All-Star to the point where almost every serious basketball player in the world wore Converse All-Stars. Much of the credit for the development of the shoe belongs to Chuck Taylor, the first in a long line of top-flight athletes who have held top-flight management positions at Converse. A former Indiana basketball star and member of the old New York Celtics, Taylor was known as Converse's Ambassador to

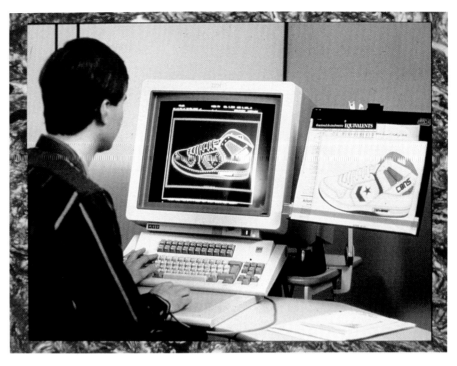

Converse uses a state-of-the-art CAD/CAM system to help with the design and manufacture of new products.

Shoe construction still requires hands-on expertise as shown by a Converse employee.

Basketball and saw his own name added to the All-Star logo patch in 1936.

Over the next 40 years Converse expanded its operations. Under the direction of the Stone family, the company opened stitching plants in New Hampshire, Maine, and Puerto Rico.

In 1972 the Eltra Corporation bought Converse from the Stone family and also acquired the footwear division of BFGoodrich. The merger of BFGoodrich gave Converse an expansive manufacturing facility in Lumberton, North Carolina.

In 1979 Eltra was acquired by the Allied Corporation and in 1981 Allied decided to sell Converse. Through the combined effort of a group of Converse managers, Converse was purchased and privately owned and operated.

In 1982 Converse became a public company with its stock traded on the NASDAQ national market.

Current president Gilbert "Gib" Ford replaced the former president John P. O'Neil, whose family has been with Converse almost since its founding. Ford, a former basketball star at the University of Texas and captain of the 1956 gold-medal U.S. Olympic basketball team, has been with Converse

since 1961.

Today Converse is a subsidiary of St. Louis-based Interco Incorporated, which also owns Florsheim Shoes, London Fog apparel, and Ethan Allen furniture stores. Headquartered in spacious offices built by the firm in North Reading, Converse also has two main North American production plants in Lumberton, North Carolina, and Reynosa, Mexico, as well as several overseas manufacturing facilities.

Longtime tennis endorser, Jimmy Connors.

Recently Converse decreased its dependence on overseas production by expanding its two domestic plants. In 1988 Converse completed the construction of a 20,000-square-foot addition to its Lumberton facility. The additional space will contain cement process machinery for canvas and leather basketball shoe production. The Lumberton factory, employing more than 2,000 workers, now boasts 400,000 square feet of production space.

The firm also recently expanded its Reynosa, Mexico, plant, doubling its size to 48,000 square feet and nearly doubling its personnel to 440 people. The Mexican plant was built in 1985 to provide stitching for leather basketball shoes.

The canvas All-Star, first introduced in 1917, has sold more than 500 million pairs.

Converse's headquarters also houses the company's own state-of-the-art biomechanics laboratory, which features ultrasensitive testing equipment for the most up-to-date scientific study of foot movement. Precise measurements of foot size, shape, and movement are analyzed by the corporation's staff of biomedical engineers to produce the most advanced materials and styles for today's performance-oriented athletes. The laboratory includes three-dimensional digitizers, transducers to measure force loads on different areas of the foot, and even a small basketball court with high-speed cameras to shoot photos of foot movement during competition.

Converse's Energy Wave shoes are flying high and so are the company's sales. In fiscal year 1988 sales broke the $318-million barrier—a 37-percent increase over the previous year.

One major factor in the firm's sales growth has been a resurgence of its Canvas All-Star model. The standard for basketball players for several generations, the All-Star model is now pro-

NBA superstar Magic Johnson (left) competes wearing the most advanced footwear, the CONS ERX basketball shoe (opposite).

duced in more than 60 different colors and styles, enjoying a sudden and nostalgic renaissance among fashion-conscious young people. Sales for "the great American sneaker" jumped 70.3 percent in 1988. More than 13 million pairs of All-Stars were shipped that year—far exceeding all previous company records.

In addition to its flagship line of athletic shoes, Converse also produces children's athletic, canvas, and specialty shoes. The Conosaur collection, introduced in 1987 plays off a dinosaur theme and has become one of the company's most successful product launches, boosted the firm's sales in this area to nearly $30 million.

Converse Activewear, another strong sales area, includes a wide variety of T-shirts, fleece casual suits, and a contemporary collection of garment-dyed articles. The company plans to develop these lines further, as well as expand into theme programs that tie in with new footwear, such as the Conosaur kid's line.

Internationally Converse has traditionally marketed its products through licensed distributors, it is now building direct company operations in key European, Asian, and North American locations. This factor helped increase Converse's international business by more than 60 percent in 1988.

"Converse products have enjoyed good reception in overseas markets over the years," says Converse president Ford. "We have built a reputation

for quality, authenticity, and style, and now we are turning that foundation into significant business."

Sales increases have allowed the company to reinvest substantially in computer enhancements, inventory management, order entry, and customer service improvements in 1988. New enhancements to the corporation's mainframe computer have been installed and will integrate and upgrade all data-processing capabilities. A new state-of-the-art order-entry system is being developed that will dramatically increase the speed of operations.

The company's main distribution center in Charlotte, North Carolina, has been automated with a bar-coding system that provides faster, more accurate order handling, improves inventory management, and provides accounts with their own inventory-control opportunities.

"All these new and improved technologies will assist Converse in better serving our customers from start to finish," says Ford. "We are committed to improving our products, our service, our communications, in short, our business."

Though the firm's wide array of athletic footwear and sportswear has achieved significant success, the Energy Wave is in the forefront of the

Converse Inc., the largest U.S. manufacturer of athletic footwear, is headquartered in North Reading, Massachusetts.

company's future plans. Developed and tested for two years in Converse's biomechanics lab, the Energy Wave sole construction is now included in all of Converse's top line of products. Independent laboratory tests for energy return showed that the Energy Wave far out-performed the competition.

In independent lab tests, the Energy Wave also proved to have superior cushioning properties. While EVA, for example, lost 20 percent of its cushioning value in the first 25 miles of use, the Energy Wave lost only .5 percent.

"Unlike other energy return systems, Converse created a totally new compound that dramatically improves 'rebound' after impact without sacrificing stability or cushioning," says Converse biomechanic laboratory manager Rick Bunch. "Converse has produced in the Energy Wave the optimum combination of shock absorption and maximum energy return."

For many years Converse Inc. has produced high-quality shoes for both professional and amateur athletes. Now the Energy Wave promises to make Converse the wave of the future in athletic footwear.

WANG LABORATORIES, INC.

Dr. An Wang, founder, chairman, and chief executive officer.

Wang Laboratories, Inc., was founded in Boston's South End in 1951 and has grown and prospered along with the Commonwealth's economy. The company began as a builder of specialized digital equipment, pioneered the modern desk-top calculator, gained prominence in small business computing and office automation, and is now among the nation's leading computer and communications companies.

Company founder, chairman, and chief executive officer Dr. An Wang came to the United States from China in 1945 to study applied physics at Harvard University, receiving his M.S. in 1946 and his Ph.D. two years later. After graduation he did postdoctoral work at the Harvard Computational Laboratory. Dr. Wang gained increasing recognition from the scientific community following his invention of the magnetic pulse controlling device, the principle upon which magnetic core memory is based. For more than 20 years core memory was a basic component of the modern computer. Dr. Wang was recently honored for this invention through his election to the National Inventors' Hall of Fame in Arlington, Virginia.

Wang Laboratories and its founder have contributed heavily to the greater Boston community and to its cultural, educational, and health care institutions. The Wang Center for the Performing Arts, the Wang Celebrity Series, and the outpatient care unit of Massachusetts General Hospital are among its many philanthropic achievements. Dr. Wang is a former trustee of Northeastern University and the Museum of Science. He has also served on the board of overseers of Harvard University, the board of directors of the Bank of Boston, and the Massachusetts Board of Regents.

Today Wang Laboratories, with headquarters in Lowell, ranks 146th among the *Fortune* 500. For the fiscal year that ended June 30, 1988, the company reported revenues of $3.07 billion. The firm has 30,000 employees, of whom approximately 10,000 work in Massachusetts. Dr. Wang's son, Frederick A. Wang, became president in 1986 and chief operating officer in 1987.

Wang is a leading worldwide supplier of computer-based information processing systems, including data, text, image, and voice processing, as well as telecommunications and networking products. Wang's products and services are designed to help its customers manage 100 percent of their business information, by providing them with solutions that enable them to manage their operations and communicate information more effectively.

Wang's ongoing objective is to ensure that its systems and services are the industry's easiest to apply to customer business goals. Its product strategy is based on a simple premise: that the unlimited potential of technology is best harnessed by making it easy for people to perform their jobs more productively and effectively. This has been the hallmark of Wang Laboratories for more than three decades.

As a result Wang's products are not only the easiest for office workers to learn and use, but are also the easiest for data processing professionals to program, support, expand, and integrate with each other and with other vendors' products. The company's flagship product offering is the VS minicomputer family. All VS models, from the entry level VS 5E to the VS 7000 series of high end superminicomputers, are easily upgradeable and can run the same software. VS systems offer integration of functions so that one system can support different types of information processing.

In addition to a wide selection of software available from third parties, Wang offers proprietary software designed to perform the most common

Frederick A. Wang, president and chief operating officer.

Wang Laboratories' corporate headquarters in Lowell.

The Wang Integrated Image Systems (WIIS)— information comes in many forms. Imaging can bring them all together.

business information processing functions with maximum ease. These products include Wang OFFICE, an industry-leading integrated office package for electronic mail, messages, and time management; PACE (Professional Application Creation Environment), which provides data base management and application building facilities; and WP Plus, an advanced word processing product. Wang also provides technical support for third party and customer development of industry-specific or customer-specific application programs.

To satisfy customer needs for the integration of information processing with local and wide area communications, Wang offers products that can be linked in interconnected, integrated networks. Wang's networking and communications products, separately or together with compatible equipment of other manufacturers, can network personal computers (including Wang's family of Professional Computers), minicomputers, and mainframes. These products, which conform to major international standards, can tie together different parts of an organization or its separate locations, such as headquarters and branch offices.

Wang Integrated Image Systems (WIIS) allow the integration of paper-based image documents with data and text, and let users incorporate image information into office and data processing systems. By doing so, WIIS helps to manage the 95 percent of information that cannot be handled by conventional data processing methods, and can dramatically cut the costs of information storage and management by reducing or eliminating paper filing systems.

Wang products and services are marketed through hundreds of sales and customer service offices in all 50 states, through 23 overseas subsidiaries, and through independent distributors in more than 100 countries. Executive Briefing Centers, where customers and prospects can see Wang solutions demonstrated, are located throughout the world. The Boston district office on Kneeland Street houses an Executive Briefing Center and customer education center as well as sales offices.

In addition to the Massachusetts facilities, Wang has manufacturing operations in Puerto Rico, Ireland, Scotland, Australia, the Republic of China, and Mexico. The administration, sales, marketing, research and development, and customer engineering operations are located principally in Lowell and neighboring communities.

Every day businesses deal with virtually tons of information. Budget requests, signed contracts, financial reports, insurance claims, news clippings, letters. Corporations need this information to stay competitive and profitable. But the sheer volume of it makes the right information difficult to find at the right place at the right time. That's because about 95 percent of corporate information is on paper.

Now there's a way to put virtually all important business information into a secure, accessible, on-line computer system—a way to capture information, index it to find it quickly, process it fast and efficiently, store it securely, retrieve it instantly, and share it with users throughout an organization. With Wang Integrated Image Systems (WIIS), masses of corporate information can be transformed into clear, crisp images and then electronically accessed from microfilm and/or optical disk quickly and easily.

More important, WIIS integrates information management with other information-processing functions. Users can access and integrate image, data processing, word processing, communications, and spreadsheet applications from one VS workstation.

Paper documents are not going to disappear. But WIIS will make a large contribution to solving the problems of paperwork.

PEABODY OFFICE FURNITURE CORPORATION

Standing at South Station and looking northwest to the financial district, it's not hard to spot Peabody Office Furniture Corporation. Squeezed between new glass high-rise buildings, Peabody's low, brick building looks as solid as a rock—a good analogy when one considers that the business celebrated its 90th anniversary in 1989.

A peek inside Peabody headquarters reveals showrooms of gleaming wood furniture, ergonomic chairs, and original works of art. Upstairs are examples of modern office systems, individual offices that stand on their own with partitions that serve to hold desks, shelves, filing cabinets, and assorted drawers. Though Peabody is credited with the marketing of office systems soon after they were developed, including Westinghouse Furniture Systems and All-

steel Inc., its reputation was originally founded on conventional fine wood furniture. Peabody is still known today as the "wood house," retailing traditional lines of fine woods with modern and period designs from high-quality manufacturers such as Kittinger, Jofco, Dunbar, Harwood House, Cumberland Gunlocke, and Mueller.

Company founder L.J. Peabody started a mail-order business in 1899 on Devonshire Street to sell typewriters and other equipment. Twelve years later Peabody had expanded into the furniture business and moved the company to a first-floor store on Devonshire, where furniture could be displayed. Five moves later, in 1967, the firm settled in its current location at 234 Congress Street. Company warehouses were moved out of the city and into the suburbs in 1972, first to Newtonville and then to the present location: a 90,000-square-foot opera-

tions center in Medford.

Also in the late 1960s the firm began to introduce the open-plan concept of office systems to its Boston business clients. Because these individual offices with changeable walls can save up to 25 percent more office space, they were immediately accepted. But the need to provide more information on just how these offices should fit together prompted Peabody to expand its design department to specialize in this area. Staffed by consultants who have interior design degrees, this department purchased computer-aided-design software to design space quickly and efficiently.

Throughout its history the company has remained a family-owned and -operated business. L.J.'s son, Lester C. Peabody, took over the management of the firm and in time was joined by his

Gannett Welsh & Kotler Incorporated. Richard Mandelkorn Photography

Naumkeag Trust

Peabody Office Furniture Corporation, which celebrates its 90th anniversary in 1989, retails a traditional line of fine wood furniture as well as modern and period designs from high-quality manufacturers.

nent slidebank representing the work of many accomplished artists, and a permanent display of accessories. In gallery fashion, Peabody regularly hosts exhibitions and open houses to introduce artists who have created works of art for corporations. The firm commissions artwork locally and from artists throughout the United States and

son, Jonathan. In 1985 the first non-family member became company president. John B. Halloran, Jr., joined the firm in 1970 as an account manager and rose through the corporate ranks. In 1986 president Halloran was also appointed general manager. Lester Peabody remains chairman of the board of the privately held company and Jonathan Peabody serves as senior vice-president/finance and treasurer.

Under Halloran's management, Peabody has emphasized the service aspect of the business. Halloran continues to build a company that can supply all the office-related products and services that large, modern corporations need. And with new office towers opening in Boston every year, there's plenty to do. Peabody consultants plan moves, design new office layouts, and order, deliver, install, and maintain furniture and office accessories.

To manage all these functions, Halloran reorganized the company structure in September 1987 and created several new management positions to promote smooth communications with both vendors and customers. A new senior vice-president/customer assurance works with the sales, client-services, warehouse, and installation departments to keep an eye on projects in accordance with the Peabody motto: "Promises made, promises kept." With the new vendor-relations department, Peabody plans to promote close working relationships with valued vendors in order to provide clients with the largest and best selection of quality furnishings.

Hasbro, Inc. Richard Mandelkorn Photography

Since the company believes its corporate customers have become more sophisticated consumers, Peabody has taken the initiative to help them make informed choices. The firm has published and distributed "The Peabody Report," a compilation of questions and answers on a number of dilemmas facing businesses that are starting up, refinishing, or moving an office.

Since many corporations today are willing to spend more to create a unique image and an impressive office environment, Peabody added a corporate art and accessories department in 1985. Art consultants work with company representatives, other designers, specifiers, or architects to create customized interiors. Peabody has a large in-house display of art and accessories, including area rugs, sculptures, paintings, clocks, and lamps. The gallery inventory includes a large selection of art, a perma-

abroad. Peabody has been cited by Governor Michael Dukakis for its support of the collection of art in the corporate environment.

Peabody started a new Boston tradition in 1986 when it hosted its own Post-NEOCON trade show in Quincy Market's Great Hall. NEOCON is the national furniture trade show held in Chicago each summer to display the newest in office trends and furnishings. Peabody Office Furniture Corporation invited major manufacturers to extend their showing by shipping their furniture to Boston for Peabody clients and Boston designers and architects to see. Peabody's Post-NEOCON is now an annual event, and more than 45 manufacturers and 800-plus professionals accept the firm's invitation to the Boston show in June.

CONNELL LIMITED PARTNERSHIP

We live in a fantastic age of information, but computers still cannot do everything. There is a need for traditional manufacturing, and a Boston-based company is on the leading edge of a resurgence in metals processing and traditional manufacturing in this country.

Connell Limited Partnership is comprised of six industrial companies that recycle metals and manufacture tools and equipment. Its products are used to make many items, including automobiles, appliances, and even computers. Connell's leading role in recycling ferrous and aluminum scrap and manufacturing earned the company an 11th-place position in a 1987 survey by *New England Business* magazine of the top 250 private companies in New England.

Connell Limited Partnership is the brainchild of chairman and chief executive officer William F. Connell. Born and raised in nearby Lynn, Massachusetts, Connell graduated from Boston College in 1959, served as an officer in the U.S. Army, and went on to earn an MBA from Harvard Business School in 1963. His business career began at Litton Industries, makers of products that range from ships to microwave ovens, where he became assistant treasurer. In 1968 he joined Ogden Corporation as treasurer and rose to executive vice-president. Ogden was then a billion-dollar conglomerate and included most of the companies that Connell acquired in March 1987.

Connell's acquisition of six businesses involved in metals recycling and manufacturing was based on his optimism about the resurgence of basic industries in this country. Once powerful industries, steel, machine tool manufacturers, and metal fabricators has all but succumbed to the foreign competition during the past two decades. Connell believes that heavy industry has made substantial gains in productivity, and, with the assistance of low inflation and a more competitively priced dollar, that there exists an environment in which United States manufacturing industries can again thrive.

Though most of the Connell operations are located in the industrial South

One of 25 reverberatory furnaces at Wabash Alloys, equipped with state-of-the-art burners and pollution control equipment, producing high-quality alloy under constant Statistical Process Control.

and Midwest, company headquarters is in the Massachusetts Technology Center, an office building not a stone's throw away from Logan Airport's Terminal A. The firm employs 3,000 people nationally. The Boston headquarters coordinates six divisions, setting policy and performing the company's centralized planning, legal, finance, human resources, tax, and insurance functions. Though Connell's core staff is small, it does a big job: The partnership did more than $600 million in sales in its first nine months ending December 31, 1987, and sales will be close to one billion dollars in 1988.

Two of the organization's businesses recycle metals. Luria Brothers Division buys, sells, and processes ferrous scrap. Ferrous scrap is generated as an industrial by-product in the manufacture and fabrication of steel and is also recovered from obsolete scrap steel products such as old automobiles, used railroad cars,

and worn-out appliances. Most ferrous scrap is ultimately reused as raw material in the manufacture of iron and steel.

At five plants, in Indiana, Ohio, Wisconsin, Arkansas, and Tennessee, the company's Wabash Alloys Division recycles scrap aluminum for resale in ingot, sow, and liquid form. Wabash's newest facility in Dickson, Tennessee, opened in 1987 near Toyota's and Saturn's auto manufacturing plants—the "new Detroit." Automobile manufacturers are increasingly using aluminum in car engines rather than the heavier cast iron. In late 1986 Wabash signed a joint venture agreement with Teksid, a subsidiary of the FIAT group of Italy, to supply aluminum for cast-aluminum cylinder heads. Wabash has a minority interest in the joint venture and will provide all of the metal required by the venture.

Outside of Connell's metal recycling businesses, four other divisions supply manufactured products to a wide variety of industries. The company's Danly Machine Division in Cicero, Illinois, is the leading independent United States producer of heavy stamping presses. In addition, Danly repairs and retrofits older presses and manufactures automation equipment for presses. Most North American auto producers use Danly presses at their plants for fashioning car doors and other parts. Danly Die Set, another Connell division, has long been the largest United States supplier of die sets and die makers' supplies used in the automotive, appliance, farm equipment, electronic, and jewelry industries.

With facilities in Mayville, Wisconsin, and Casa Grande, Arizona, the Mayville Division is a premier fabricator of high-quality precision metal components, such as tubular and sheet-metal frames, sheet-metal cabinets and panels, and electro/mechanical assemblies used in the making of computer, telecommuciations, photocopying, and medical equipment. Mayville makes extensive use of robotics as well as Computer Aided Design (CAD) and Computer Aided Manufacturing (CAM).

The company's Yuba Heat Transfer Division in Tulsa, Oklahoma, is today one of the leading manufacturers in the field of heat transfer equipment, and it supplies such products as feedwater heaters, condensers, and air reheaters to utility companies throughout the United States and in numerous foreign countries. Yuba products are custom designed and sold to both fossil and nuclear electric utilities. In late 1986 Yuba entered into a license agreement with Asea Brown Boveri Ltd. of Switzerland to significantly broaden Yuba's technology base and products.

These companies have long histories—some close to 100 years—and are leaders in their respective markets. By continuing to look for opportunities to improve productivity, by investing in research and development, and by making strategic acquisitions, Connell Limited Partnership expects to maintain that leadership.

Luria, for example, invented and patented a tool and a process called a CLIPRESS system that is used by auto manufacturers to roll and stack metal left over after the body stamping process, enabling them to get several times

the amount of scrap into the same space—costs decrease and productivity increases dramatically.

Recently Connell began exploring the reuse of plastics and announced its intention to form an alliance with General Electric to recycle thermoplastic automobile parts, including bumpers, fenders, doors, truck lids, etc. These parts can be recycled up to 20 times, preventing the need to put this material

A 3,500-ton two slide quick die change transfer press manufactured by Danly Machine.

into landfills, as well as providing Connell with a steady market and its customers with inexpensive "raw" materials.

Connell Limited Partnership is a leader in the revitalization and the retooling of industrial America.

DIGITAL EQUIPMENT CORPORATION

In Boston the question is not how far does this *Fortune* 50 company's influence extend, but rather, where does it not? With more than 33,000 employees in Massachusetts alone, Digital is one of the state's largest industrial employers. From its corporate headquarters in rural Maynard, Digital can be found in almost every corner of the city—from Roxbury, where inner-city residents build computer keyboards, to Children's Hospital, where Digital's VAX computers help professionals provide cost-effective quality health care services. Digital can even be found on television with its Digital Discovery

Digital's VAX computers help professionals provide cost-effective, quality health care services.

programs such as "Evening at Pops," (whose producing station, WGBH, is the largest single recipient of Digital's employee matching gift program), "The Infinite Voyage," and "The Nightly Business Report."

In 1957 MIT engineer Kenneth Harry Olsen began Digital with three employees, $70,000 in venture capital, and 8,500 square feet of rented space in an old wool mill in Maynard, Massachusetts, 30 miles west of Boston. Thirty years later Olsen is still president, and Digital is the world's leading manufacturer of networked computer systems. The company employs more than 118,000 people worldwide in 64 countries and posts nearly $10 billion in annual revenues. Although its business is truly global by any definition, a

Traditional New England values run deep in the way Digital does business. Headquartered in Maynard, Massachusetts, the company plays an important role in the economy of the region.

full one-third of the firm's employees are based in New England. Traditional New England values run deep in the way Digital does business—that same wool mill is now corporate headquarters—and the company also plays an important role in the economy of the region.

The computer age was still in its infancy when Digital was founded. There were only a few computers in the world back then, and most were owned by universities and large research laboratories. The vacuum tube was the predominant technology, and computer owners spent more time searching for blown tubes than doing useful work. Those early machines, costing one million dollars and more, were housed in air-conditioned, glass-walled sanctuaries, and were attended to by staffs of white-coated specialists. Work had to be brought to the computers, and results were usually not ready until a day later.

Olsen envisioned a computer that was smaller, sturdier, and less expensive: a "minicomputer" that an ordinary engineer might use in his everyday work. After working at MIT's Lincoln labs, he was convinced that he would

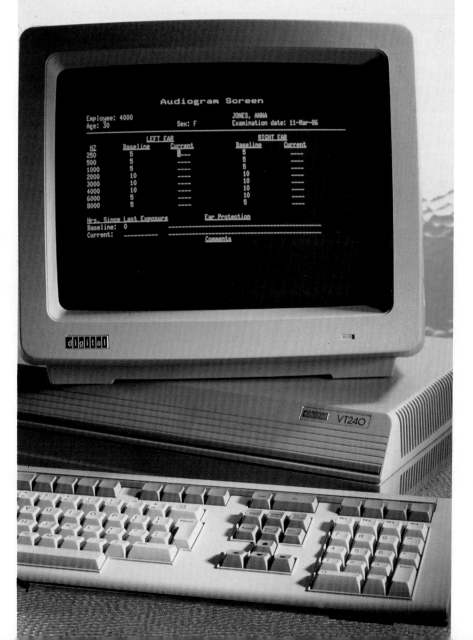

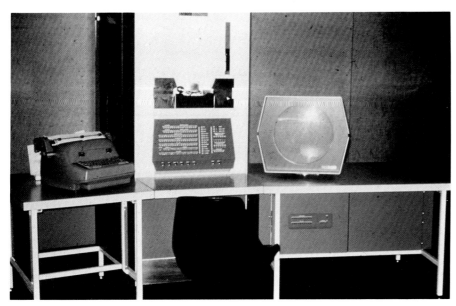

The PDP-1 system introduced in 1960 was the world's first small, interactive computer.

not only construct such a computer, but also make it interactive and easy to use. The company he formed would demystify the computer; it would liberate it from those glass-walled sanctuaries, and put it at the fingertips of anyone who had useful work to do. The results created an entirely new market segment and revolutionized the computer industry.

The PDP-1 System, introduced in 1960, was the world's first small, interactive computer and sold for about $125,000. The PDP-5 System, the first minicomputer, followed in 1963 and lowered the cost of interactive computing even further. The PDP-8 System, the world's first mass-produced minicomputer, costing less than $20,000, was unveiled in 1965. By the time the PDP-11 minicomputer was introduced in 1971, Digital had clearly established an obvious place in the history of the computer industry.

Today that place is secured by the VAX family of 32-bit computers that range in size and performance from the desk-top to the data center, and in function by means of Digital's VMS and UNIX-based operating systems. From the first member of that family— the VAX-11/780, introduced in 1977—to today's newest VAX systems,

every VAX computer uses the same software and can be linked together by Digital's unique networking capabilities, which allow Digital's famous minicomputers to have the speed and memory of larger, more expensive mainframes.

In 1986 Olsen was recognized as America's Most Successful Entrepreneur by *Fortune* magazine. The magazine wrote: "In 29 years he has taken Digital Equipment Corporation from nothing to $7.6 billion in annual revenues. DEC today is bigger, even adjusting for inflation, than Ford Motor Company when death claimed Henry Ford, than U.S. Steel when Andrew Carnegie sold out, than Standard Oil when John D. Rockefeller stepped aside."

A year later, Digital captured the attention of all of Boston when it hosted a nine-day version of its annual trade show, DECworld '87. To demonstrate its computing capabilities and products, Digital brought in two ocean liners, the *Queen Elizabeth II* and the Star Line's *Oceanic,* docked them alongside Boston's World Trade Center, and invited more than 35,000 chief executive officers, board members, and senior executives from around the world to the event. According to the Greater Boston Chamber of Commerce, DECworld '87 filled up 60 Boston area hotels and

To demonstrate its computing capabilities and products, Digital brought in the Star Line's Oceanic and the QEII, docked them alongside Boston's World Trade Center, and invited more than 35,000 chief executive officers, board members, and senior executives from around the world to DECworld '87.

According to the Greater Boston Chamber of Commerce, DECworld '87 filled up to 60 Boston-area hotels and pumped approximately $50 million in the area's economy over a two-week period.

pumped approximately $50 million into the area's economy over a two-week period.

While going about its daily business, Digital's influence on the Boston area is tremendous. As one of the state's largest employers, Digital has been a leader in extending employment opportunities to Boston's inner-city residents at a time in which inner-city unemployment in the country is estimated to be around 25 percent. Between one plant in the Roxbury section of Boston and another in Springfield, Massachusetts, Digital employs a total of 1,125 minority personnel.

In 1987 *Business Week* magazine pointed to Digital's Massachusetts plants as among the most successful of 15 inner-city factories built by major corporations since the mid-1960s. "Digital Equipment has . . . succeeded with an inner-city factory by using methods that most companies cannot or will not employ," concluded the magazine. Specifically, instead of manufacturing a product the firm could, in a pinch, purchase elsewhere, Digital set up the Springfield plant as the company's only supplier of tape-drive memory systems for the popular VAX computer. The Springfield plant expanded to 450,000 square feet while its work force grew to 800.

In the inner-city neighborhood of

Digital has operated a high-volume manufacturing facility in the inner-city neighborhood of Roxbury since 1980.

Roxbury, Digital has operated a high-volume manufacturing facility since 1980. The Boston plant supplies keyboards for most of Digital's products, including the MicroVAX, VAXstation, and VAXmate computers. Product-focused participative management teams divide the plant's 325 employees into self-managed work teams responsible for building a product from beginning to end. By encouraging the participation of all its workers in all aspects of production, Digital has increased its production volume by 100 percent and has built a highly skilled work force.

Digital has not only provided employment opportunities for the disadvantaged, but has also played a large role in implementing the kind of educational and training programs needed to make its inner-city plants work. At Boston's Opportunities Industrialization Center (OIC), Digital grants have been used to develop and implement office automation programs for educationally and economically disadvantaged students in the greater Boston area. Digital employees from the Roxbury plant participate in these programs as well. The Digital/Freedom House Program provides college scholarships to minority students graduating from the Boston public school system

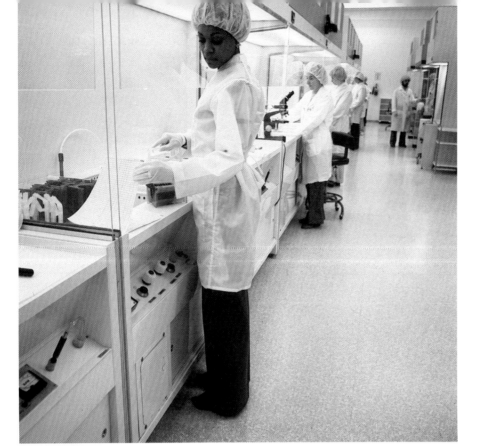

Through its external research programs, Digital invests in university research to augment its own internal research and development efforts.

who wish to pursue courses in science. Digital is also a member of ACCESS, a unique program providing "last-dollar" funds to hundreds of Boston high school seniors hoping to go to college.

Digital provides cash and equipment grants and technical assistance to a variety of other Boston-based organizations through its Corporate Contributions and local Community-Relations programs. In the area of health care, Digital has been an active participant in the drive to reduce costs. Major grants to Massachusetts General Hospital, Shriner's Hospital, and Children's Hospital have been made to help these institutions deliver quality health care more efficiently, by tracking costs through computers. Digital grants have helped Tufts New England Medical Center in its rehabilitative-medicine research and have funded close captioning at WGBH-TV.

Digital is also the largest corporate supporter of the Massachusetts Technology Park Corporation's Microelectronics Center. Through the center, Digital is assisting 11 universities in the Commonwealth with the enhancing of their faculties, labs, curricula, and computing resources to teach and develop Very-Large-Scale-Integration (VLSI)-related programs. Digital believes that these programs are essential to the continued growth of technology-related industries in the state. Some of the schools participating include Tufts University, Northeastern University, Boston University, MIT, and Harvard University.

Through its external research program, Digital invests in university research to augment its own internal research and development efforts. Major local recipients have included Project Athena at MIT, recipient of Digital's largest grant ever, which is studying how to best utilize distributed workstations in undergraduate engineering education. Another grant recipient, Project Pericles at Harvard Law School, is investigating how public defenders can better utilize technology in their legal work.

In 1987 Digital donated more than $22 million in cash and equipment to nonprofit institutions worldwide. Digital matches, dollar for dollar, employee gifts to schools, nonprofit organizations, and United Way programs.

But as in all corporate giving, the amount of the gift is never as important as how it is bestowed. Recognizing this truism, the U.S. Department of Labor honored Digital as a recipient of its 1985 "Exemplary Voluntary Effort Award," based on the company's "exemplary voluntary efforts in establishing and participating in community service programs." Specifically, Digital Equipment Corporation received this award for establishing a dropout-prevention program with the Oxford, Massachusetts, public schools, that centered around technology training.

VAX computers range in size and performance from the desk-top to the data center and can be linked together by Digital's unique networking capabilities.

SYMMONS INDUSTRIES, INC.

For 50 years Symmons Industries, Inc., has produced pressure-balancing shower valves that prevent sudden changes in water temperature. So many homes, hotels, hospitals, and public buildings use the Symmons valve that the firm has become one of the leading shower system manufacturers in the country. The valve has also been successfully introduced in many developing countries overseas.

It all began in the late 1930s, when an idea surfaced in the mind of a young engineer named Paul C. Symmons. Symmons was working in Boston for a small plumbing manufacturer when he began to study the problem of sudden temperature changes in the shower. He believed the basic problem was one of water pressure that caused shower temperature to fluctuate so drastically. In the shower he observed a common phenomenon: The water got suddenly hot when someone elsewhere in the building turned on a cold-water faucet or flushed a toilet. Conversely, turning on a hot-water faucet or other demands on the hot-water supply would cause water in the shower to run cold. While the human hand under a faucet is relatively unaffected by temperature variations, the human body in a shower is very sensitive to these same fluctuations. The temperature changes not only made for an unpleasant bathing experience, but

Symmons corporate officers (left to right): John L. Diohep, vice-president/sales; Kevin V. Symmons, vice-president/general manager; Dennis R. Murphy, vice-president/finance; and Albert G. Fehrm, president.

also caused serious accidents—particularly among the elderly—as people quickly backed away from scalding or freezing water.

In 1938 Symmons started a company to manufacture the first pressure-balancing shower valve. He and a handful of employees set up shop in the vacant Chickering Piano Building on

Tremont Street in downtown Boston. "Paul made the original patterns himself out of wood," recounts company president Albert G. Fehrm. After considerable research and testing, Symmons perfected a valve that was essentially the same as the one produced today. Made of bronze, brass, and stainless steel, the valve uses a hydraulic piston as the prime control unit. As soon as the valve is turned on, both hot and cold water exert pressure on opposite ends of the piston, holding it in a balanced position in the valve. If the hot-water pressure drops, the piston reacts and reduces the cold inlet opening. The piston continually equalizes the pressure of hot and cold water inside the valve even when supply pressures change drastically.

In 1967 mass-production techniques made it possible for Symmons to introduce a competitively priced pressure-balancing valve, much lower in cost than its original heavy-duty product. This new valve made it possible to market a product for all residential applications that had originally been equipped with conventional two-handle shower controls. Symmons attributes its dynamic growth and dominance in the pressure-balancing market

The main office and manufacturing facilities of Symmons Industries, Inc., in Braintree.

to the introduction of this product.

Yet another valve was introduced in 1975 to address the needs of the health care industry. That year Symmons introduced a pressure-balancing valve with a built-in thermometer that allows a nurse in a hospital or attendant in a nursing home to accurately set the water temperature. The federal government now requires that all federally funded housing for the elderly have safety-type shower valves.

Symmons has discovered that architects seek out pressure-balancing valves for some unusual but critically important uses. Symmons valves help workers on the famed King Ranch bathe valuable livestock in Texas. And closer to home, at the Woods Hole Oceanographic Institute, seals are bathed in water controlled by Symmons valves. Symmons valves can also be found in the Moscow Hotel, Mezhdunarodnaya, in the Westin Hotel in Singapore's Rafel City, and in Saudi Arabia's military city of King Khalid.

Since its patent expired in 1960 Symmons is no longer the exclusive manufacturer of pressure-balancing valves, but the firm has maintained its position among the top manufacturers of this product for several reasons. The quality of the metal valve has not been compromised by a switch to cheaper plastic and rubber materials. Recognizing this quality, other plumbing fitting manufacturers contract with Symmons to put valves in their product lines. And its geographic location has given the company a boost: In 1973, when Massachusetts became the first state to mandate the use of safety-type shower valves in all showers, the Massachusetts firm was the first in line for business, say company officials. Symmons has installed its valves in almost every hotel built in the Boston area in the past 10 years, according to these officials.

The company left its Tremont Street home in 1956, moving to larger facilities in South Boston. Eleven years later it expanded to its present 100,000-

Some of the computer-controlled automatic machinery producing Symmons products.

square-foot facility in Braintree. "Our plant is not a pure assembly line," explains Fehrm. "We are automated, using dedicated equipment that can do varied and complex tasks. This unique equipment has not put anyone out of work, however. Increased production and our elaborate quality-control procedures continue to boost our work force annually."

Symmons Industries, Inc., attributes its high degree of quality control to complete in-plant production, right up to the final chrome plating of the trim that enhances the beauty of the installed product. While pressure-balancing products account for a signif-

icant portion of Symmons' business, the firm also produces a wide range of associated products, such as thermostatic controllers, metering valves for both the shower and lavatory, and single-handle kitchen and lavatory fittings. The most recent addition to its product line is a stylish line of polished brass shower systems to answer the current demand for the high-fashion decorator bathroom fittings. This new product is appropriately named Olde Braintree Brass.

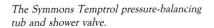

The Symmons Temptrol pressure-balancing tub and shower valve.

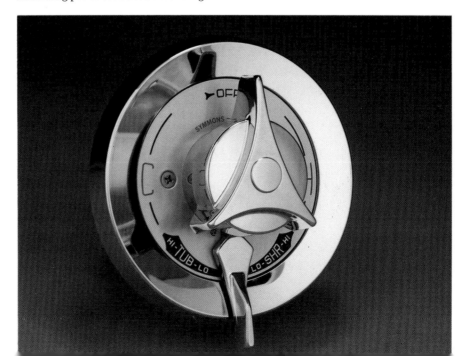

AMES SAFETY ENVELOPE COMPANY

Just off Somerville Avenue, a main thoroughfare through the city of Somerville, Massachusetts, 7,000 tons of paper per year is cut, folded, and glued to produce the host of made-to-order filing, mailing, and packaging products needed to keep offices organized around the country. Ames Safety Envelope also has the dual honors of being the nation's largest supplier of hospital color-coded folders and the largest private employer in Somerville, a city bordering Cambridge to the north.

The firm was begun in 1919 by John W. Fitzgerald, an observant and enterprising postal worker who discovered that people were using flimsy envelopes to send valuable, negotiable notes through the mail. According to his son, Albert, who would later run the business, John Fitzgerald found that many of these envelopes would break as he was stamping them in the registered mail division. Thus was born the notion for a "safety" envelope.

Fitzgerald used $500 of savings to buy supplies and designed an envelope with a sturdy double fold at the top and bottom. As legend has it, he would walk to his job at the post office folding envelopes as he went. Two of his aunts were enlisted for gluing. He served as his own paper cutter, die cutter, and salesman, approaching banks, brokerages, and law firms with his new product.

Soon Fitzgerald left the post office to produce envelopes and expandable mailing envelopes full time. Casting about for a company name, Fitzgerald searched for something "Yankee" sounding that would also appear in the first pages of the phone book. Ames,

also the name of a Boston building, was adopted. In downtown Boston, Ames Safety Envelope moved several times, from Purchase Street, to Sudbury Street, and finally to 610 Atlantic Avenue, where a slow elevator served as transportation to the firm's sixth-floor offices. In 1938 the company purchased a one-level building in Somerville for $12,000.

During the 1960s several important events took place that would change the organization completely. At Ames, John Fitzgerald's son, Albert, became president, and the company began to explore new markets. At the same time, hospitals were gearing up to fulfill new accreditation requirements that assigned unit numbers to patients in order to maintain a single lifetime medical file on each individual. Soon a color-coded folder system evolved to make filing and retrieving information easy and orderly. In 1963 Ames won its

Ames Safety Envelope Company is the largest private employer in Somerville with 460 people producing made-to-order filing, mailing, and packaging products.

first bid—making color-coded files for Massachusetts General Hospital. Under Albert Fitzgerald, Ames geared up to produce color-coded products and files for libraries and government agencies.

While Ames began by making mailing envelopes, this product accounts for no more than 10 percent of the firm's sales today. However, one of the company's newest products is used for mailing. Under contracts with manufacturers, Ames has produced a sturdy envelope with an antistatic lining for mailing computer floppy disks.

Bob Arnold, also a member of the Fitzgerald clan, became president of the company in 1978. His amiable style has guided the employees through some difficult transition years and set the tone for innovative employee benefits. It has been through Arnold's able direction that Ames has become an active, viable member of the Somerville civic community.

Ames Safety Envelope Company has evolved into a modern firm with annual sales of $32 million, eight regional sales offices, and a warehouse in Dallas,

Texas. The Somerville plant, which has been expanded three times, now contains 13 Heidelberg letterpress and off-set printing presses and employs 460 people. Every morning at 10 a.m., in an Ames tradition, the company treats its employees to five-cent coffee—a nod, perhaps, to the good old days of the enterprising John Fitzgerald.

Photo © Kenneth Martin

Bank of Boston, 296-299;

The Greater Boston Chamber of Commerce, 300;

The New England, 301;

International Business Machines, 302-303;

Fidelity Investments, 304-

Peat Marwick Main & Co., 311;

State Street Bank and Trust Company, 312-313;

Wellington Management Company/Thorndike, Doran, Paine & Lewis, 314-315;

Bank of New England, 316-317;

Shawmut Bank, N.A., 318-321;

MerchantsBank of Boston, 326;

Farragut Mortgage Company, 327;

Frank B. Hall & Co. of Massachusetts, 328-329;

Harold Cabot & Company, 330-331;

Olympic International Bank Trust Co., 332-335;

Bear, Stearns & Co. Inc., 339;

Exclusive Temporaries, Inc., 340-341;

Tofias, Fleishman, Shapiro & Co., P.C., 342-343;

The Boston Company, 344-345;

The Forum Corporation,

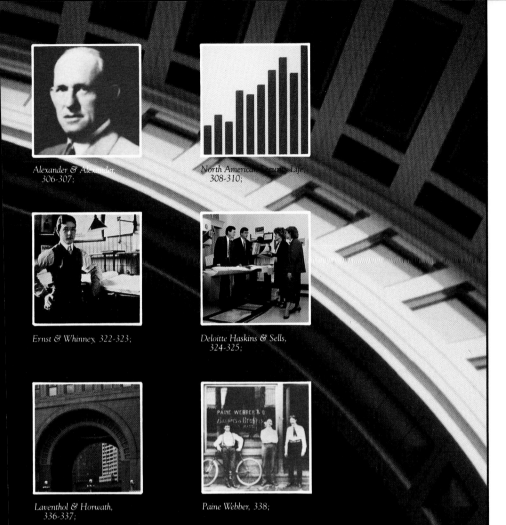

CHAPTER FIFTEEN

Business

*Business and financial
institutions, accounting firms,
and computer technology
combine to put some impressive
numbers on Boston's ledger.*

Photo © Martha Everson

BANK OF BOSTON

Elementary school students from the Josiah Quincy School in Boston's Chinatown district perform at Bank of Boston's headquarters building. The bank established a formal partnership with the school in 1986, and later that year the Josiah Quincy School was named one of the best schools in the country by U.S. Secretary of Education William J. Bennett.

The bank's 100 Federal Street building, with its distinctive waistline bulge, is a unique feature on the Boston skyline. Here, looking east, the bank building stands guard over the Charles River.

Against the bright backdrop of a red, gold, and green dragon boat with streamers, banners, and kites flying, Pam Burke sits on the library floor and reads to seven small children. The branch manager of Bank of Boston's nearby Washington Street office, Burke is one of a group of branch staff who come to the Josiah Quincy School in Chinatown once a week as volunteer readers. Since 1982 Bank of Boston has supported the creation of the dragon boat, a community mural, a school pushcart, a lion dance costume, and the only marching band in a Boston elementary school. More recently the bank has made a major commitment to spearhead creation of a computer lab for the school.

In its 200 years Bank of Boston has been to the ends of the world and back again. It began as a bank to finance trade abroad for Boston merchants trading with the Far East and, later, with Latin America. It helped America

grow, backing projects such as the transcontinental railroad. It also expanded overseas, opening branches and making foreign loans.

While the bank continues to conduct a substantial part of its business in the areas of international and corporate banking, today's priorities lie closer to home: Through mergers and acquisitions Bank of Boston has expanded its banking services throughout its native Massachusetts and into other New England states. The bank now refers to itself as "The Superregional . . . Plus"— regionally dominant throughout economically prosperous New England, plus extending its capabilities nationally and worldwide to meet the global needs of its customers.

Bank of Boston is, in fact, many banks. An international multibank holding company, Bank of Boston Corporation has $34 billion in assets at June 30, 1988, making it the largest banking company in New England and the 13th largest in the United States. While Bank of Boston has offices in 16 states and 30 countries worldwide, its major banking subsidiaries are based in the six-state New England region: The First National Bank of Boston, with offices throughout Massachusetts; Casco Northern Bank in Maine; Bank of Bos-

ton Connecticut; and Rhode Island Hospital Trust National Bank. Together these banking subsidiaries comprise a New England branch network of more than 250 offices.

The flagship subsidiary is The First National Bank of Boston—or more simply, Bank of Boston. Headquartered in the downtown financial district, the bank is housed in a distinctive granite structure often referred to by residents as the "pregnant building" because it bulges out in the middle.

Bank of Boston's organization structure separates its businesses into four groups: World Banking, New England, Real Estate, and Treasury/Banking Services. As part of a strategic reorganization in 1985, each of these groups is an independent, separately managed business with its own direction and with individual control over and accountability for its own costs and profitability. Decentralized, numbers-driven, and strategically focused on the future, the bank provides a broad range of superior financial services to customers throughout New England, and in carefully delineated national and international markets.

In tandem with the company's particular focus on its New England roots, Bank of Boston has put a spotlight on its role in its native city. With a branch network that reaches into virtually every one of Boston's neighborhoods, the bank is looking more closely at the role these offices play in their communities' development—whether through their day-to-day banking operations, innovative finance projects, special fundraising programs, or corporate philanthropy.

Under president and chief executive officer Ira Stepanian, Bank of Boston adopted a formal community mission statement in 1985, and two years later published a booklet outlining the scope and breadth of its efforts in support of its communities.

"When the Josiah Quincy School Marching Band played at the Bank of Boston's head office recently," writes Stepanian in the booklet's introduction, " I had the opportunity to visit with the children. It occurred to me that this vibrant group exemplifies all that is best about our involvement with our communities. What began as support of a single project at the school has blossomed into a full-fledged partnership, one in which the bank contributes dollars, facilities, services, technical assistance, and, most of all, the caring and concern of many members of our staff."

If one area has been the hallmark of the bank's community involvement, it is undeniably education. Beginning in 1974, the bank established a partnership with Boston's Hyde Park High School, a multifaceted relationship that received the Exemplary Partnership Award in 1984 from President Ronald Reagan and became the model for the bank's 1986 partnership with the Josiah Quincy Elementary School, where bank manager Pam Burke goes to read aloud. In 1987 the bank became the first company in Boston

also to enter into a formal partnership with a middle school, the John W. McCormack School in Dorchester's Columbia Point section. Through continuing programs at these schools, bank staff members interact with students, faculty, and parents, and play active and meaningful roles in helping to enrich the educational experiences of Boston's youth.

The single-largest, most innovative community program ever created by Bank of Boston is a point of civic pride for the whole city. In commemorating its 200th birthday in 1984, the bank established a $1.5-million endowment to support public education in the city of Boston. The Boston Plan for Excellence in the Public Schools was designed as an umbrella under which other corporations and foundations would also create education programs. Within three years contributions by

Bank of Boston president and chief executive officer Ira Stepanian wishes amateur athletes well at the opening ceremony of the 1986 Bay State Games. Bank of Boston is the presenting sponsor of this Olympic-style series of athletic competitions.

More than 500 Bank of Boston volunteers were scheduled to join a field of 20,000 in front of the Massachusetts State House to begin the Walk for Hunger. Walkers solicit pledges for each mile completed along the 20-mile course, and the proceeds are donated to Project Bread, which funds more than 200 local agencies providing food for the hungry. Bank of Boston matches dollar for dollar its staff members' pledges.

more than 60 donors brought the Boston Plan endowment to $13 million—the nation's largest for education—sustaining seven individual programs, including a middle school athletics and basic skills program, a financial aid advice and last-dollar college scholarship program, and Bank of Boston's own initial program, which funds grassroots, imaginative programs in individual schools.

An award-winning initiative in the area of drug education has been one of the key elements in Bank of Boston's outreach into the community since 1986. With former Boston Celtic basketball player M.L. Carr as spokesman, the bank has taken the M.L. Carr Challenge: "Stand Tall Against Drugs" to students from more than 70 middle schools in 40 Massachusetts communities.

Other programs for young people include such locally sponsored activities as the bank's Shoot Straight basketball clinics, which bring the lessons of teamwork to boys and girls in grades three through six in many communities. Bank of Boston is the presenting sponsor of the Bay State Games, a series of Olympic-style competitions in which 12,000 amateur athletes from 314 Massachusetts communities take part. In 1987 the bank created and funded a college scholarship program for outstanding student-athlete participants of the Bay State Games.

Each spring Bank of Boston fields a team of volunteers who join the Boston Walk for Hunger to raise money for Project Bread. The bank is also a major contributor to the Associated Grantmakers' Summer Funding Process, a program that allows thousands of inner-city children from the Boston area to go to summer camps.

Of course, the biggest impact any bank might have on the communities surrounding it is not through community programs, but through its fundamental activity—the delivery of financial services to individuals, businesses of all sizes, municipalities and public agencies, nonprofit organizations, and the Commonwealth itself.

Through the most creative and competitive products and services that can be devised, the bank enables individual consumers to buy and improve homes, finance their children's college educations, and enjoy their retirement. Working within its communities, the bank finances housing and helps provide not only the capital, but in some cases the technical assistance needed to make possible economic development. Economic development is the very lifeblood of a community's wellbeing and, as New England's largest banking institution, Bank of Boston recognizes a special obligation to act as a catalyst for that development. In addition to its very substantial commercial lending, the bank has formed partnerships with many public and nonprofit agencies, often developing special loan programs to stimulate small business development.

Two recent examples are programs developed by the bank for communities south of Boston. Under the terms of one program, a city foregoes interest on its own deposits with the bank in return for reduced interest rates on loans to small businesses in targeted areas. Under this program a hardware store was able to add a second story, a manufacturer of automotive equipment more than doubled its space, and a family business purchased new equipment and added employees for its thriving pasta factory. Small improvements in critical areas can provide the momentum to produce widespread revitalization of a community.

In another example, in 1987 Bank of Boston established a $2.5-million loan pool at below-market rates of interest to foster economic development and employment in five communities in the southeastern region of Massachusetts.

The bank also offers both financing and technical assistance to nonprofit organizations that serve a host of community needs—housing in particular. While Bank of Boston is one of the largest construction lenders in the country, it also provides special loan programs to help expand the supply of decent, affordable housing, a persistent problem in the country's urban areas, and assists nonprofit organizations in structuring proposals and projects that qualify them for financing.

For example, when the Boston-based women's shelter Casa Myrna Vasquez lost its building in a fire, it sought to build a replacement in a new, confidential location. Bank of Boston provided a construction loan to enable the agency to transform its former shelter into transitional housing, a community resource center, and administrative offices. The former shelter now provides critically needed second-stage housing for eight families and helps them bridge the gap between emergency services and self-sufficiency.

As society's needs have changed, so,

Six-foot-six-inch M.L. Carr, a former member of the Boston Celtics, has traveled to 40 Massachusetts communities, encouraging middle school students from more than 70 schools to accept the Bank of Boston/M.L. Carr Challenge to "Stand Tall Against Drugs."

too, have the world and Bank of Boston changed over the past two centuries. And still more change is certain to come. The original bank was small, capitalized at slightly more than a quarter-million dollars. Today's Bank of Boston is one of the nation's most strongly capitalized banks, with total capital of more that $1.8 billion. That fledgling institution of 1784, the second bank chartered in a new and growing America, has kept pace with the times and firmly established itself as New England's leading superregional bank— a sophisticated provider of financial services to commercial and individual customers, an international bank serving existing customers abroad, and a community member that reinvests in the companies and people of greater Boston.

THE GREATER BOSTON CHAMBER OF COMMERCE

A financial center, a leader in education and health care, a high-technology mecca, a world-renowned arts and cultural community, a transportation hub, an international trade center, a sports and entertainment capital, a city of historic landmarks—Boston is distinctive for its diversity, energy, and charm. The Greater Boston Chamber of Commerce serves its business community with pride and vigor. Courtesy, Aerial Photos International, Inc.

The official voice of Boston's business community is the Greater Boston Chamber of Commerce. Now in new offices at the Federal Reserve building at 600 Atlantic Avenue, today's chamber is the fourth-generation descendant of the Grain Exchange, a 1,000-member organization that represented grain and produce merchants in the years between 1793 and 1804, before Boston was a city.

For its 3,000 contemporary members, the chamber plays a number of important roles. In the political arena, the chamber monitors pending state and city legislation and policies to assure that business interests are well considered in the public decision-making process. According to James L. Sullivan, current president, the chamber's most important legislative victories include the repeal in 1982 of the state's Sunday blue law restrictions. Sullivan estimates that 4,000 jobs have been created in the city since the repeal. The chamber also lobbied successfully in 1987 for passage of a bill requiring prompt payment by the Commonwealth to private contractors with whom the state does business.

Through its network of working committees, clubs, and councils, the chamber is a forum for communication and cooperation among the various segments of the greater Boston community. The chamber has developed productive working relationships with the city and state administrations, and, as the leading advocate for business, is an active participant in debates on current local and state issues. The 1980s have witnessed intense chamber efforts on universal health care in Massachusetts, construction of the third harbor tunnel/depressed central artery, the cleanup of Boston Harbor, the region's energy supply, planned growth within the city, solid and hazardous waste disposal, AIDS in the work place, the special needs of minority businesses and small businesses, and fiscal issues affecting the state's business climate.

The chamber has long been an advocate for improved public education and is at the heart of the greater Boston business community's nationally acclaimed efforts to work in partnership with the Boston Public Schools.

The chamber also sponsors the Greater Boston Business-to-Business Expo and Conference each October. The three-day event is a showcase for some 400 Boston businesses and is attended by company presidents, chief executive officers, purchasing agents, and general managers in search of local services and products. The organization publishes annually a directory of members, issues a monthly newsletter, and produces a variety of special reports, bulletins, and informational pamphlets for both members and the general public.

As the story of Boston's surging economy spreads, the telephone at the Greater Boston Chamber of Commerce rings nonstop with questions about the city—and the chamber continues its efforts to market Boston as a world-class city in which to live, to work, and to conduct business.

THE NEW ENGLAND

Since just before World War II Bostonians and visitors in Copley Square have been able to find the time by looking up at the clock atop The New England building on Boylston Street. The building is headquarters for the first chartered mutual life insurance company in the United States, and one of the nation's top 25 money managers.

In 1835 the Massachusetts Legislature granted to Judge Willard Phillips and four associates the first charter for a mutual life insurance company. Judge Phillips entered the life insurance business with the somewhat unusual conviction for his time that life insurance should incorporate a savings function, allowing policyholders access to their money, if needed, during their lifetime.

Founded as New England Mutual Life Insurance Company, the firm has been known as New England Mutual and New England Life. Today known as The New England, it is a broad-based family of financial services companies providing security and financial independence for its clients.

New England Mutual Life Insurance Company and New England Variable Life Insurance Company are sources for insurance products and services,

Judge Willard Phillips, founder.

including whole, ordinary, interest-sensitive Universal and Variable life, as well as term and disability insurance, annuities, and pension planning.

Employee benefits are offered through The New England Employee Benefits Group, which can help clients select products such as 401(k) plans, long-term disability insurance, investment options, and Section 125/flexible compensation plans.

New England Financial Advisors offers educational programs and customized financial planning programs to individuals and corporations as part of their benefits program.

The New England also has an investment group. New England Securities is a registered broker/dealer. Loomis, Sayles & Company ranks among the nation's oldest and largest investment counseling firms. Back Bay Advisors offers fixed-income investment management; Copley Real Estate Advisors is one of the top five U.S. real estate investment management firms. The Private Placements Group provides custom financing for a broad

The home office of The New England at 501 Boylston Street prior to the 1962 addition, and (inset) the home office today.

range of borrowers, while the Mortgages Group is a financier for developers and owners of commercial and industrial properties. Marlborough Capital Advisors supplies financing for growing companies through equity and debt investments.

While The New England has grown and diversified to meet the changing needs of clients in the twentieth century, it has consistently contributed to the needs of the Boston community at large. The New England has a long history of participation in the Red Cross Blood Drive and United Way. In 1964 The New England established a fund for advancing medical science at Harvard Medical School, and more recently contributed one million dollars toward a $6-million endowment for ACCESS, a unique program that helps finance college costs for graduates of Boston high schools.

INTERNATIONAL BUSINESS MACHINES

Hidden behind the trees lining Route 128, Boston's high-tech corridor, is the northeastern area headquarters for one of the country's high-tech leaders—IBM. The company occupies two major office sites where Route 128 winds through the suburb of Waltham, and has several other Boston-area locations as well, including marketing operations at Copley Place in Boston's Back Bay, the Cambridge Scientific Center in Kendall Square, and the IBM ROLM Division in Lexington.

IBM first came to Boston in 1914 as the Computing-Tabulating-Recording Company. CTR had begun only three years earlier in New York as a corporation that manufactured tabulating machines, scales, and time recorders. In 1924 the company changed its name to something more general and all-encompassing—International Business Machines. A year later the firm paid its first dividend as a public enterprise.

During the Depression IBM expanded, adding more sales representatives and developing new machines that performed accounting operations with punched cards. And rather than turn to factory layoffs during slow selling periods, the company produced parts for inventory and stored them. This strategy was rewarded in 1936, when the

U.S. government selected IBM to provide machines and services for the massive bookkeeping operation created by the new Social Security Act. The inventory was ready for immediate service.

IBM's well-known full-employment practice originates from this time. For more than 50 years IBM has not laid

IBM's new sales and service offices at 404 Wyman Street, Waltham.

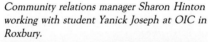

Community relations manager Sharon Hinton working with student Yanick Joseph at OIC in Roxbury.

off a regular employee for economic reasons. Instead, the company retrains its work force when necessary to meet changing business conditions. Today IBM's hiring activities are closely watched as an indicator of the health of the computer industry.

But before computers there was the IBM typewriter. IBM purchased Electromatic Typewriters, Inc., of Rochester, New York, in 1933. The first IBM electric typewriter was put on the market two years later. And, in 1944, after six years of development in cooperation with Harvard University, IBM completed development of the Automatic Sequence Controlled Calculator, the first operating machine that could execute long computations automatically.

In 1952 the company introduced its first large vacuum-tube computer, the IBM 701, which executed 17,000 instructions per second. Although the nineteen 701s shipped were used primarily for government and scientific research work, vacuum-tube technology rapidly moved computers into business applications such as billing, payroll, and inventory control.

All of IBM's many innovations in

computer technology since then have been designed to make information handling quicker and more economical. And technological advances have enabled IBM customers to connect computers in vast networks in order to share information more efficiently within their organizations.

Today, in the Boston area, six marketing branches—as well as the northeast office of the National Service Division—supply large, medium, and small computers to business, government, and scientific laboratories; specialized systems to retail stores, supermarkets, and restaurants; and personal computers, copiers, peripherals, displays, and software programs to a variety of customers. The IBM ROLM Division markets and services telephone communication systems throughout New England.

In Cambridge's Kendall Square, amidst the growing complex of buildings around the Massachusetts Institute of Technology, 45 IBM computer scientists conduct advanced technology work in systems and programming for commercial development. The IBM Scientific Center in Cambridge was established in 1964 as a result of a close association with MIT in the development of computer time sharing, the means by which a computer system

supports multiple users. Subsequently the center developed the Virtual Machine 370, IBM's most widely used time-sharing system. The center also developed IBM's internal communications network, V-NET, through which IBM technologists worldwide communicate with each other.

Computer operator specialist Douglas M. Richter, Jr., working at PS2 M50 attached to the Token-Ring.

Operations specialist systems engineer Bruce Haimowitz is shown working in the Customer Center at Copley Place.

In the Boston community, IBM is known for several substantial educational and civic programs. The company has provided Boston's Opportunities Industrialization Center with both equipment and instructors. Located in Roxbury, one of the city's most depressed neighborhoods, the center trains the unemployed to type, enter data, and work with word-processing programs. On the average, 80 percent of the center's graduates find jobs using skills acquired after 12 to 22 weeks of training.

IBM employees active in community programs can request cash from the company's Fund for Community Service to support worthwhile projects. IBM also grants sabbaticals to professional employees who wish to teach at area colleges and universities with a high enrollent of minority, disadvantaged, or disabled students, or with programs geared to those students. Over the past five years IBM has also donated more than $23 million to Boston-area schools, colleges, and universities to fund professorships, graduate fellowships, and advanced educational projects.

FIDELITY INVESTMENTS

Though mutual funds have been in existence for some time, many investors didn't discover them until the 1980s. Leading the pack of mutual funds companies is Fidelity Investments, which began the 1980s with $9.7 billion in assets under management. Today, just seven years later, that figure has increased nearly eightfold to more than $75 billion. Boston, synonymous with baked beans and seafood, has now become the industry focal point of the mutual fund through the efforts of Fidelity Investments.

The Fidelity block of office buildings in the heart of downtown is well known to area workers, who can glimpse the price of their favorite stock as it flashes across the Congress Street stock ticker. The most visible of the company's services is its 51 Investor Centers nationwide. These centers have been designed to provide easy access for customers who want to make transactions in person, and for those who need investment information. Behind the scenes, 3,800 Fidelity employees work in 21 Boston locations.

This financial services company has been making investment history since 1946, when Edward C. Johnson II, a Harvard-educated lawyer, created Fidelity and began to manage its $3-

The Fidelity Building, Boston—Fidelity Investments' world headquarters.

million Fidelity fund. Johnson's success in buying little-known stocks with growth potential won Fidelity a mention in Adam Smith's *The Money Game* as "The Green Bay Packers of the bond league." When his son, Edward C. Johnson III, became company president in 1972, Fidelity's only products were stock funds and the stock market was down. So the new president, who became chairman in 1976, began searching for a new idea and found one—check writing for money market funds. Thus Ned Johnson, as he's known, started Fidelity down the road to the tremendous diversification for which it's known today.

Several historical and political events spurred sales of the rapidly growing number of Fidelity mutual funds. IRA legislation, with its tax-deferred returns, spurred investments in mutual funds. Equally important was the unprecedented rise in stock values. The year 1982 ushered in the greatest bull market in United States history, and, as headlines heralded the rise of the Dow, the public looked for ways to par-

ticipate again in stocks.

Fidelity made their participation easy and convenient. No small amount of the company's success has been attributed to the company's user-friendly strategies. Fidelity was the first to offer investors check-writing privileges drawn on money market funds. It has also expanded the variety of investment services available while making it easier for investors to participate. A toll-free, 24-hour telephone service allows customers to check their balances, make exchanges, or simply obtain information regarding Fidelity's funds and services. Believing that some investors would rather talk face-to-face with company representatives, Fidelity has increased the number of street level Investor Centers.

The firm manages more than 125 stock, fixed-income, and money market funds. The best performers have well-

Bruce Johnstone (standing), portfolio manager and head of Fidelity's growth and income group, in the company's equity trading room.

recognized names such as Magellan, Destiny I, and Puritan. Fidelity's innovative sector funds, each composed of stocks from a single industry, have also drawn considerable attention. The company offers, in addition to its retail funds, funds to institutional investors such as company pension funds, banks, and insurance companies. Investors can make use of an in-house brokerage service and the Ultra Service Account (USA), which features discount brokerage service, automatic bill paying, the Fidelity Visa and Mastercard, and an all-in-one statement of financial transactions.

Such a service-intensive business depends heavily on technology. At the receiving end of Fidelity's 800 number, well trained professional representatives field a steady stream of calls from customers. At computers in Boston, Dallas, Salt Lake City, and Cincinnati, service personnel answer questions and execute orders. For handling transactions, Fidelity has almost as many computer terminals as employees. The system is so important that Fidelity's Boston and Dallas offices are backed up with electrical generators and a battery pack that would keep the current running to computers nationwide during any blackout or power interruption

until the generators can kick in.

As a part of the never-ending search for attractive securities to add to their funds, Fidelity's managers and security analysts visit more than 10,000 companies, agencies, and municipalities annually. To assist the researchers, the Fidelity library maintains a wide variety of annual reports and trade publications.

After investment decisions are made, portfolio managers issue orders to buy or sell. Stationed behind Quotrons, Portfolio managers and traders execute the orders at the appropriate stock, fixed-income, money market, municipal, or tax-exempt trading desks. Fidelity portfolio managers buy and sell more than 2 billion shares of stock annually.

As the company moves into the next decade, more funds will be offered through banks, insurance companies, and brokerages. Fidelity Investments will continue to develop innovative ways to help investors participate in the financial markets and pursue their investment goals.

Fidelity's fixed-income trading desk, where its fixed-income group portfolio managers trade treasury securities, corporate bonds, and money market instruments.

ALEXANDER & ALEXANDER

William F. Alexander

Located in modern office space at One Constitution Plaza in Charlestown, Alexander & Alexander Boston, a retail insurance broker, is represented by 200 individuals working to meet the many diverse insurance needs of business and industry. A&A provides insurance brokerage, risk analysis and management, human resource management, and other financial services to companies that typically employ more than 100 people.

Two Alexander brothers, William and Charles, founded the insurance firm in 1898 in Clarksburg, West Virginia. The brokers gained their first large account in 1905 with a natural gas company by developing the Inherent Explosion Clause. A major railroad account, The Baltimore & Ohio (B&O), was obtained in 1914, and the firm grew with the expansion of steam railroads and the petroleum industry.

New offices opened in succession: Baltimore, New York, Tulsa, and St. Louis. In 1922 A&A was incorporated in Maryland. In 1969 the firm went public, and in 1982 was listed on the New York Stock Exchange. In modern times A&A has grown as a result of 220 acquisitions of insurance brokers, agencies, and consulting concerns.

A&A came to Boston in 1968, but its presence in the city was heightened by the 1983 acquisition of the Boston-based brokerage firm OBrion, Russell & Co.—a merger that effectively doubled the size of A&A Boston. The merger spurred the large retail broker to search for larger quarters where the staffs could be combined, and in 1985 A&A left its State Street offices for Constitution Plaza and its wide, panoramic view of Boston Harbor and the North End.

Today A&A is considered to be one of the largest brokers of property/casualty insurance in the Northeast. The firm also handles a variety of specialized coverages. In addition to traditional services, A&A has gained a reputation for developing innovative funding me-

Charles B. Alexander

chanisms for large companies seeking to minimize fixed insurance costs.

Casualty specialists assist clients in the development of cost-effective risk management programs to protect their financial assets from liability and worker compensation exposures. The specialists' knowledge extends from insurance, self-insured programs, and retrospective rating plans to the latest techniques of risk transfer and alternative funding such as rent-a-captive, pure fronting, and captive arrangements.

The firm maintains a staff of property engineers and account managers that specializes in property conservation and loss prevention. Marine specialists with field underwriting and claims adjusting experience are also on staff.

A team approach pairs an account executive to each client. Depending on the situation, an A&A account executive can call upon resources in property engineering, safety, risk analysis and information systems, loss control, insurance placement, claims administration, and financial analysis.

The claims department monitors claim activities as soon as coverages begin. This important A&A service coordinates the efforts of its clients and underwriters in order to expedite claim payments.

The A&A Northeast Region International Office is also headquartered at One Constitution Plaza. The international office helps coordinate A&A's global network of international insurance professionals. A&A's global network enables it to keep pace with currency fluctuations and political change. Each affiliated A&A office has its own staff of professionals knowledgeable about insurance practices of their respective countries.

A&A operates in 158 cities throughout the United States, Canada, and the United Kingdom, and in more than 70 other countries and territories through subsidiaries, joint ventures, and correspondent relationships.

NORTH AMERICAN SECURITY LIFE

William Atherton, president.

by portfolios of mutual funds. Customers can participate in a number of mutual fund portfolios and, at the same time, benefit from the favorable taxation rules applicable to insurance products. Unlike returns from mutual funds offered by noninsurers, accumulated gains from insurance products are tax-deferred. While the Tax Reform Act of 1986 eliminated many deductions for investors, the tax break on accumulative earnings from variable annuities was retained, enhancing the demand for these products.

In addition, the special benefits of an annuity provide a guaranteed death benefit and monthly income guaranteed payable for life, with no initial sales charge deducted from the investment. People who are in their late fifties and who are approaching retirement are said to be the average mutual fund customer and form the target audience of this company. NASL believes its investment product is the answer to two of the most pressing questions asked by today's investor: "How do I keep more of my earnings?" And "How do I retire?"

In its first year of sales, NASL sold $150 million in annuity products. Tillinghast, a national actuarial consulting firm, listed it among the top 20 in the country in its first year of business. Ambitious goals outline $.5 billion in sales in 1988 and $2 billion by 1991.

This is only a small example of the panache with which the company has established itself in Boston. A wholly owned subsidiary of one of Canada's leading mutual life insurance firms, NASL was set up by its parent to re-establish its waning position in the United States. More than 100 years old, the parent was represented by agents in the United States until 1983, when it was decided that the system of sales through commissioned agents was becoming prohibitively expensive to continue in this country. Within six months the company had scrapped its

When president William Atherton talks about the beginning of one of Boston's newest life insurance companies, he likes to call upon an analogy, likening his new organization to those "small acorns from which big oaks will grow." Certainly sales for the firm's variable insurance products have been sprouting since sales officially began in 1987.

The acorn itself was planted in 1984,

when operations of this Canadian-owned company opened in a Boston warehouse with a modern marketing plan and three executives borrowed from parent company North American Life. Upon completion of several carefully crafted co-ventures with independent brokers and money managers, the firm was ready to do business.

North American Security Life (NASL) sells variable annuities funded

U.S. operations and had begun looking at other ways to do business with its large neighbor to the south.

For the new venture the officers looked at the possibility of marketing their variable annuity products to the largest distribution network of financial instruments in the United States: stockbrokers. The new firm was begun with the belief that once stockbrokers and mutual fund salesmen recognize the full value of investment-type insurance products and are provided with access to them, variable annuity and variable life products will take a progressively greater share of the mutual fund market. When this anticipated trend takes hold, NASL plans to be a prominent supplier.

In 1986 the company played a fundamental role in helping to create a

One of Boston's newest insurance companies, North American Security Life occupies offices in the refurbished Essex Hotel on Atlantic Avenue.

new marketing venture in Greenwich, Connecticut, to help it work with stockbrokers in 10 regions throughout the United States. This entity, Wood-Logan Associates, was begun by two experienced variable annuity marketers. Scott Logan previously participated in the development of a variable annuity prior to joining Massachusetts Financial Services in Boston, where he was a critical force in helping that organization become the first to successfully wholesale variable annuities through stockbrokers. In 1982 MFS was acquired by Sun Life, and its domination of the market has continued.

H. Douglas Wood was the top MFS wholesaler in 1981. When MFS was acquired by Sun Life, Wood was recruited by Integrated Resources of New York to create a variable annuity subsidiary patterned after the MFS model. As a result of Wood's efforts, Integrated Resources ranks second in variable annuity sales behind MFS. Logan and Wood were so convinced of the potential market for variable annuities that they left their employers to begin a new marketing organization. NASL has teamed with these two industry leaders in a joint venture.

For NASL, Wood-Logan Associates pitches NASL products and solicits selling agreements between stockbrokers and NASL. Contracts with A.G. Edwards, Shearson Lehman Hutton, Inc., and PaineWebber currently account for 60 percent of NASL sales. Since the company began to sell its products in late 1986, Wood-Logan has arranged selling agreements with more than 105 brokerage firms.

Watching over the portfolios maintained by NASL are three independent money managers: M.D. Sass Investors Services, Inc., Oechsle International Advisors, L.P., and Criterion Funds, Inc. M.D. Sass manages the stock, bond, and money market portfolios for NASL's most popular product: the Venture Variable Account. M.D. Sass also provides brokers with recommendations for automatic asset allocation to help the investor control risk and remove indecision from the process of apportioning investments among in-

struments with varying degrees of risk. Based in New York, M.D. Sass has $2.8 billion under management and relies on the judgement and experience of 12 portfolio managers and analysts.

As stipulated by the Securities and Exchange Commission (SEC), a group of five directors are charged with fiduciary responsibility over the NASL Series funds. Among these directors is Robert Myers, formerly the enrolled actuary for the U.S. Social Security System.

In addition to the Venture Variable

Impressive sales have been recorded in North American Security Life's first two years in Boston.

Account, NASL offers a Venture Fixed Account. A Venture Life Plan with additional life insurance benefits that will allow investors to borrow against their assets is in the making. Soon NASL will offer two families of mutual funds.

From offices in the refurbished Essex Hotel across Atlantic Avenue from where Amtrak parks its trains, NASL's Boston operations employs an ever-growing work force. There the staff takes the baton from NASL's wholesalers to administer the policies, issuing contracts and statements, handling customer inquiries, processing funds, and executing portfolio transfers. With 56 employees as of summer 1988, the company's total assets exceeded $200 million.

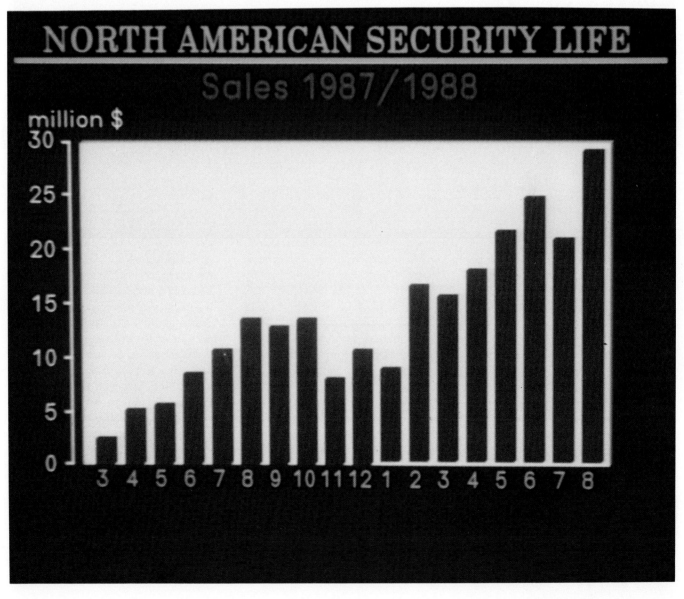

PEAT MARWICK MAIN & CO.

Senior consultant Mary E. Reno with Robert D. Happ, Boston Business Unit managing partner (left), and John T. Murray, Jr., partner in charge of Software Testing Services (right), in Peat Marwick's Software Test Center.

"The secret of success is constancy of purpose." —Benjamin Disraeli

Peat Marwick Main & Co. is the United States member-firm of KPMG, the worldwide certified public accounting firm. Through the KPMG network of more than 600 offices in 114 countries, Peat Marwick provides audit, tax, management consulting, and business advisory services to companies of all sizes.

KPMG was formed in 1987 with the merger of Peat, Marwick, Mitchell & Co. and KMG/Main Hurdman, two firms rich in tradition and history. The result is a unique professional services organization with geographical balance and a global delivery system that are coupled with an intimate understanding of the international marketplace.

The Boston office of Peat Marwick was founded in 1910 on Congress Street with a staff of two. Today the office at One Boston Place serves as headquarters for the Boston Business Unit, which comprises five New England offices and employs more than 750 professionals. Enormous growth and technological advances have taken place during the firm's 78-year Boston history, but its basic mission and guiding philosophy remain unchanged. As a partnership serving the area's business community, Peat Marwick continues its commitment to render outstanding service to clients, foster economic development and growth, maintain a leadership role in civic and community affairs, and fund research and continuing-education programs.

According to Boston managing partner Robert D. Happ, the strength of the firm depends on its people and its available resources. "In today's ac-

Peat Marwick strives to recruit the best students from area colleges and universities. Catherine Hudson, Boston College class of 1987, joined the firm through its internship program, was promoted to staff technician, and is now a consultant in the Route 128 office. Partner John T. Murray, Jr., is at left.

counting and consulting profession," says Happ, "these two factors are what distinguishes one firm from another, and form the basis for future success.

"Our clients range from start-ups to multinationals across nearly every industry. Obviously, the needs of the entrepreneur and the needs of a *Fortune* 1000 company differ dramatically." To ensure that services are tailored to fit each company's requirements, professionals participate in extensive internal training programs and specialize along industry lines such as health care, government, financial services, education, real estate, banking, and commercial entities.

To maximize the resources available to clients, the firm recently entered into a strategic alliance with Regis McKenna, Inc., in Cambridge, and Pittiglio Rabin Todd & McGrath in Wellesley Hills, two firms that specialize in providing consulting services to the high-technology and related industries. In 1983 Peat Marwick established an office off Route 128 in Burlington to serve high-tech clients. A merger with Nolan, Norton & Co., in Lexington, an information-technology planning and management firm, expanded Peat Marwick's consulting services and enabled the firm to access a wealth of additional research materials and database information.

Across the city Peat Marwick professionals are actively involved in civic and community affairs. Partners sit on the boards of Boston hospitals, symphonies, museums, and libraries. The firm takes an active role in fund raising and volunteering for nonprofit organizations. In addition, the Peat Marwick Foundation offers grants to universities for research.

Peat Marwick is also working closely with city and state government to stimulate economic growth in the future. Recently the Boston office formed an International Division to provide guidance and services to overseas companies that are investing in Massachusetts and to assist local businesses doing business overseas. Peat Marwick Main & Co. is poised to move ahead with Boston into the twenty-first century.

STATE STREET BANK AND TRUST COMPANY

Once used as a sign for a naval instrument maker's shop, this eighteenth-century wooden figure now stands at the entrance to State Street's executive offices. It serves as a symbol of the bank's commitment to continued growth through a focused strategy.

While other banks have looked across state boundaries for opportunities to grow, State Street Bank and Trust is looking across oceans. In today's financial scene, "Users of capital are put in touch with suppliers of capital with increasing disregard for where either is located," noted chairman William S. Edgerly in 1986. Accordingly, State Street has adopted a global orientation in its securities processing, investment management, and banking services.

State Street's banking and capital markets products and services include corporate banking, specialized lending, corporate finance, international banking, securities trading, money market operations, and foreign exchange. A head office banking approach distinguishes the bank from others that address this market through subsidiaries or loan production offices. The head office approach allows corporate cus-

tomers to work directly with banking professionals who have access to top-level management and product specialists. Headquartered in Boston, State Street maintains offices in New York, Los Angeles, London, Brussels, Munich, Zurich, Sydney, Tokyo, and Hong Kong.

In addition to its banking services, State Street provides securities processing, recordkeeping, and investment management services, and it is currently one of the world's leading securities custodians. At year-end 1987 total assets under custody were $529 billion.

It was 1924 when State Street was selected by the first mutual fund in the United States to provide fund accounting and recordkeeping services. Today, with 40 percent of the U.S. mutual fund industry's assets in its custody, State Street has become the nation's largest supplier of custody services to the mutual fund industry. State Street provides services to all participants in the mutual fund industry, including independent investment companies, broker/dealers, insurance companies, and banks collaborating with fund managers and distributors. Custody services include portfolio accounting, general ledger accounting, and securities custody.

Building on its capabilities as a custodian for the mutual fund industry, State Street has become a leading supplier of custody, recordkeeping, investment management, and benefit plan services to institutional investors such as pensions, endowments, and foundations. During 1987 the bank was ranked as the nation's largest master trust custodian bank. In line with the trend toward increased global securities trading, State Street has established a global custody service to support its customers' needs.

Closer to home, in its operations in Quincy, Massachusetts, a large contingent of the bank's 7,000 employees is equipped with computer workstations to perform recordkeeping, processing, and monitoring services. Company officials believe that State Street's success can be directly linked to both the consistent quality of these services and the

bank's commitment to work with its customers to develop new products that meet the customers' diverse, and often changing, recordkeeping and reporting requirements.

Building on its experience as a sophisticated recordkeeper, State Street also provides trustee services for asset-backed securities such as collateralized mortgage obligations and automobile loan bond issues. In 1986 State Street was selected trustee for the securitization of $4 billion of GMAC automobile loans, the largest private debt offering in U.S. history.

For individuals, State Street offers trust, investment management, estate planning, and advisory services. State Street was the first issuer of credit cards in New England, more than 20 years ago, and continues to be an innovator in card services today—the most recent

The State Street Bank Building was the first high rise constructed in downtown Boston. Completed in 1966, it serves as the bank's head office, and its rooftop letters signal the center of Boston's financial district.

example being its affinity card programs.

State Street traces its institutional beginnings to the Union Bank, a small trust company that obtained its charter in 1792. Union Bank was founded by Boston sea captains and merchants who wanted a bank that would finance their trading activities and manage their profits. Under a renewed charter, the Union Bank became the National Bank of Boston in 1865. In 1925 National Union Bank of Boston merged with State Street Trust Company and, after five other mergers, evolved into today's State Street Bank. Headquar-

ters are in the downtown high-rise building that carries the State Street name at its top. The building, distinctive for its honeycombed look, was one of the first such high-rise buildings.

Formed in 1973 the State Street Foundation makes substantial contributions each year to the Boston community from funds made available by the parent company, State Street Boston Corporation. The majority of these funds go to the disadvantaged of Suffolk County, and to those in the Quincy area, where State Street is one of the largest employers. In recent years Boston has become a model for other U.S. cities in the formation of public/private partnerships. State Street Bank and Trust Company is a leader in this movement, particularly in the areas of low-income housing and educational programs for Boston's inner-city youth.

WELLINGTON MANAGEMENT COMPANY/THORNDIKE, DORAN, PAINE & LEWIS

In offices above State Street, Wellington Management Company/Thorndike, Doran, Paine & Lewis starts every day with their morning meeting. Each morning at 8:50 a.m., all 75 investment professionals can be found in a large, three-tier conference room seated in front of microphones and computer monitors, conversing with their colleagues in Atlanta, Georgia; Washington, D.C., and Valley Forge, Pennsylvania.

These meetings have been held every morning for the past 27 years. They reinforce an environment cultivated by the founders of the company that today acts as manager or adviser for investments totaling more than $67 billion, from clients including corporate and public retirement trusts, mutual funds, educational endowments and foundations, and individuals. An early brochure about the company explains the importance of the meeting. "It's made necessary because nobody knows every-

thing." The meeting is strictly informational. The investment professionals "challenge, debate with, enlighten, and otherwise teach each other." There is a lot of give and take in the meetings, and everyone is expected to speak his or her mind. For Wellington/TDP&L these priorities have paid off time and again.

The firm traces its Boston origins back to the winter of 1958, when four Boston security analysts decided to pool $2,000 each to start their own private investment fund. Meeting over breakfast and dinner, Nicholas Thorndike, Robert Doran, Stephen Paine, and George Lewis planned which stocks to acquire for their "Professional Investors" portfolio. They agreed that their investment policy would remain flexible: No investment was so sacred that it couldn't be sold; no investment so unconventional that it couldn't be included. Before 1960 was finished the four men faced

a happy dilemma: The assets they managed had grown to $150,000, the minimum account at the companies that employed them. It was time to start their own business.

Thorndike, Doran, Paine & Lewis (TDP&L) was the first investment counseling firm to open in Boston since the Depression. But in 1960 the presidential campaign of another young Bostonian, John F. Kennedy, made anything seem possible. The original Professional Investors mutual fund was renamed the Ivest Fund, and shares were sold to the public. In addition, the four began counseling institutions and other individuals.

In 1966 Wellington Management Company of Philadelphia approached TDP&L with the idea of merging. Founded in 1933, Wellington Management managed the first balanced mutual fund in the country, which was also one of the most conservative, Wellington Fund. The subsequent merger in 1967 placed the five-year-old TDP&L in the spotlight, inspiring *Business Week* to suggest that "the moves they (TDP&L) make [in financial services] may shake the entire industry."

Indeed, Wellington/TDP&L began to add specialized products and services in the 1970s and 1980s. Today the firm is organized as a private Massachusetts partnership and demonstrates its continuing commitment to serve the needs of its clients through five investment divisions and a wholly owned subsidiary:

Wellington Management Company acts, under contract, as investment adviser to mutual funds. It provides a wide range of investment products to more than 50 mutual fund portfolios for 10 mutual fund-sponsoring organizations worldwide.

Thorndike, Doran, Paine & Lewis is recognized as a diversified, growth-style investment counselor to institutional and individual accounts.

Wellington Investment Advisers provides a value-yield investment approach to a limited number of institutional accounts.

Wellington International Investors is the international investing unit for the firm, providing global management to institutions and mutual funds.

Wellington Real Estate provides real estate investment management services to corporate and public pension plans and other institutional clients.

The firm's subsidiary, Wellington Trust Company of Boston, N.A., offers specialized investment products to institutional investors. The trust company provides a variety of specialty products and services to employee benefit funds and eleemosynary institutions.

Locally based institutions are an important part of Wellington/TDP&L's client base. Those clients include Charette Corporation, the City of Boston Retirement System, the Commonwealth of Massachusetts, Digital Equipment Corporation, Massachusetts Audubon Society, Massachusetts Institute of Technology, Neworld Savings Bank, and the Stop & Shop Corporation.

While the firm keeps a low profile within the investment community, the best-kept secret about Wellington/TDP&L may be its art collection. The company's offices serve as a living museum of contemporary art; the collection represents a continuous reminder of the firm's interest in fostering creative solutions to client needs.

BANK OF NEW ENGLAND

Walter J. Connolly, Jr., chairman.

When asked one day to sum up his firm's corporate culture, an employee at Bank of New England smiled and paraphrased his chief executive officer, Walter J. Connolly, Jr. "We take our name seriously," said the employee.

Bank of New England's headquarters is located in Boston, a city that is alive with historical attractions, culture, and education. Boston blends the best of the old and the new into one of the most exciting cities in the country today.

In addition to the history and culture, business has been thriving in Boston and throughout New England. For three years Bank of New England has been aggressively merging and acquiring banks throughout the region. The institution's latest merger with eight Massachusetts banks owned by The Conifer Group means this banking giant has a grand total of 482 branches and nearly 500 automatic teller machines (ATMs) spread throughout Massachusetts and three other New England states.

To become the super-regional bank that it is today, Bank of New England went all the way to the U.S. Supreme Court. It was the merger with Connecticut Bank and Trust Company in 1985 that set legal sparks flying over whether the Massachusetts-chartered bank, with roots extending back to 1834, could merge across the state's borders with a Connecticut bank.

On June 10, 1985, the CBT merger was validated by the high court, and interstate banking was born, with some regional restrictions. Bank of New England went on to combine with the Old Colony banks in Rhode Island, Maine National Bank, and, most recently, the Conifer Group of Worcester, Massachusetts. Today Bank of New England Corporation has assets of more than $30 billion, making it one of the top 20 bank holding companies in the United States.

Since the Conifer merger, priority has been placed on consolidating. While reaping the benefits of a large regional bank with great lending power, Bank of New England has sought to preserve the individuality, local orientation, and personal service of the corporation's separate banks. Community banking, private banking, and commercial lending units have been maintained in each bank, but the goal is to gradually offer standardized products throughout the system. Meanwhile, support functions such as systems and marketing have been consolidated, and areas of specialization such as asset-based financing and treasury services have been centralized.

Throughout New England, the bank's goal has been to enhance service and improve convenience as cost effectively as possible. Bank of New England expanded its 24-hour ATM banking services through its affiliation with the YANKEE 24 and New York Cash Exchange networks. Bank of New England customers now have access to their money at more than 2,600 ATMs in New England as well as at 18,600 cash machines throughout the United States.

Bank of New England is aggressively expanding its product line. The bank has been granted approval from the Federal Reserve Board to offer investment advice to its customers. The bank is also looking for new market opportunities, especially in securities, real estate, and insurance—areas where current regulations prohibit banks from entering.

Gordon I. Ulmer, president.

Bank of New England is broadly organized by nine lines of business—community banking, private banking, commercial banking, asset-based financing, multinational banking, international banking, treasury, processing services, and support services. In the community banking area, the institution received significant attention for several new and innovative consumer banking products. A discount brokerage subsidiary, New England Discount Brokerage, Inc., complements the bank's private banking business. Through specialized lending groups, the bank offers commercial real estate loans and loans for businesses as diverse as communications, project finance, and high technology.

One of the fastest-growing and most successful lines of business for the bank has been asset-based financing, including commercial financing, leasing, and equipment finance. This is also an area that has benefited greatly from the increased size and lending capabilities of the new and larger Bank of New England Corporation. With a national network exceeding 20 offices and a portfolio surpassing $2 billion, Bank of New England is one of the nation's

largest asset-based lenders.

Sixteen commercial finance offices

Bank of New England is a name taken seriously by its employees, respected throughout the area, and recognized worldwide.

lend expertise in leveraged-buyout financing. In equipment finance, the bank now provides more than $200 million to dealers, distributors, and lessors of capital equipment in New England and beyond. The bank's leasing business, centralized in Banc-NewEngland Leasing Group, has 14 offices nationwide and is ranked among the 10 bank-affiliated lessors in the country.

Multinational customers, primarily large corporate and select middle-market companies, are served through offices in Boston and seven other cities. Financial packages with cash management, foreign exchange, letter of credit, and other services are available to multinational commercial customers. As a result of the bank's growing capital base, it has expanded its capacity to underwrite and syndicate credits and to place debt or equity through its investment banking subsidiary, BNE Associates, Inc.

Bank of New England, while recognized in cities worldwide, is proud to be rooted in the New England landscape.

SHAWMUT BANK, N.A.

Shawmut Bank, N.A., is headquartered in the 38-story One Federal Street building, which also serves as co-headquarters for the $26-billion Shawmut National Corporation. Shawmut Bank, N.A., is one of the two lead banks, with Connecticut National Bank, of Shawmut National, the super-regional bank holding company that came into existence in February 1988 upon the merger of Shawmut Corporation and Hartford National Corporation. One of the top 25 bank holding companies in the nation, Shawmut National focuses on the consumer market, the small- to middle-size business market, and has a special niche providing service to the insurance industry.

The decade of the 1980s brought much change to the 152-year-old Shawmut Bank. First under the leadership of John P. LaWare, and now John P. Hamill, the bank has grown from approximately $2 billion in assets to more than $8 billion in the third quarter of 1988. Shawmut Bank, N.A., provided management and services to Shawmut Corporation with $3 billion in assets in 1980, and in 1988 supported a Massachusetts franchise of more than $15 billion.

This growth has been carefully managed to assure that service to Shawmut's customers has been enhanced. Shawmut's Mission Statement includes, "Our most important constituency is our customers. Without them, we have no business. We must assure that our customers: receive quality service, have a full range of service options, and are charged competitively for value received.

"A bank thrives and grows only to the extent that its community thrives and grows," is another point from the Mission Statement. Shawmut is a leader in community involvement, actively participating in a search for solutions to community problems.

The same philosophies were true in April 1836, when banking was simpler and 43 Boston citizens petitioned the Massachusetts legislature for a bank charter declaring that, "The mercantile community in this city require a considerable increase of Bank Capital therein

. . ." In those days, if a merchant wanted to borrow money to build a ship or start a business, he went to a bank, discussed it with the cashier, and took out notes printed by the bank for the amount needed. These notes were backed by specie—gold. It is a different way of doing business but just as today, meeting customers' needs.

The citizens got their charter, and in May the shareholders met to elect the first 12 directors at the Exchange Coffee House. The bank, organized on May 6, 1836, was called the Warren Bank in honor of the Revolutionary War hero Dr. Joseph Warren, who was killed at the Battle of Bunker Hill. Less than one year later, to avoid confusion with other institutions called Warren, the name was changed to Shawmut, an anglicized version of Mushauwomeog, the Indian name for Boston. In 1912 the bank would adopt the likeness of the sachem of the Mushauwomeog Tribe, Obbatinewat, as its registered trademark.

By October of its first year the new bank had offices in rented rooms at 16 State Street near the Merchants Exchange. In May 1837, one year after the founding of the bank, financial panic hit the country, and over the next six years every third bank went out of operation. Shawmut prevailed and has paid a dividend to its shareholders every year since its founding. In 1864 the National Bank Act was passed to help stabilize the currency and pay for the Civil War. Shawmut became a national bank under federal charter, changed its name to Shawmut National Bank, and began to issue national bank notes.

In 1871 Shawmut moved from State Street for the first time, occupying new headquarters at 50 Congress. But in November 1872 fire ravaged downtown Boston burning 776 buildings, including 50 Congress. On the ashes of the old building, Shawmut erected a new structure, moving into 60 Congress in the fall of 1873. With the coming of the Industrial Age at the end of the Civil War, Shawmut began investing in businesses such as gas and electric utilities and AT&T.

At the end of the nineteenth century Shawmut began a series of mergers. In

The Shawmut Bank, N.A., headquarters—One Federal Street, Boston.

1898 nine banks merged with Shawmut, capitalization became $3 million, and the name was changed to National Shawmut Bank. Over the next three decades six more banks would merge with Shawmut. In 1907 Shawmut moved from its 60 Congress Street headquarters to 40 Water Street, a facility that boasted truly elegant accommodations, including a marble and bronze banking floor inlaid with bronze medallions of the Shawmut Indian. In 1914, following the passage of the Federal Reserve Act, Shawmut became a member of the Federal Reserve System.

The bank's structure and products began to change rapidly to meet customer needs. Shawmut had already added one of the first credit departments in the country, and it established the first installment loan program for the purchase of automobiles in 1916. Following the end of World War I Shawmut again expanded services, adding a business extension department, a foreign department, and a time sales department. In 1926 the bank established the Devonshire Financial Service Corporation to encourage installment sales of autos by granting loans through automobile dealers. In 1928 the Shawmut Association was created to make investments in other banks.

The first branch office opened in the fast-developing area around Copley Square. The facility included a women's department to serve a population that had often been overlooked. By 1931 the number of branches had grown to 12 to accommodate a spreading population. As automobiles became more accessible, more and more people moved to the suburbs—a typical house in Newton cost $9,000—and in 1926 Shawmut made its first mortgage. Shawmut began opening branches again in 1941 after the decade of the Great Depression. Following World War II the pent-up demand for consumer goods saw Shawmut expand its consumer lending for the purchase of

John P. Hamill, president and chief executive officer, Shawmut Bank, N.A.

consumer goods. It also saw the expansion of the commercial loan portfolio.

Some of the most exciting and expansive years prior to the 1980s in Shawmut's history were 1960 through 1972. During that period Shawmut began to computerize its operations and introduce many new services. Among the most important steps taken was the transformation of Shawmut Association into a corporation called Shawmut Association, Inc. In 1975 the name was changed to Shawmut Corporation, and

a new corporate identification program stipulated that all Shawmut banks would have the common trademark of a blue Indian and would bear the name Shawmut. Also in 1975, Shawmut's new headquarters opened at One Federal Street.

Shawmut has structured itself as two banks—a consumer bank to meet the needs of the individual, and a commercial bank to serve the business community. Shawmut has segmented its market in Massachusetts to provide optimum service to its customers. Shawmut Bank, N.A., serves the market east of Route 495 with more than 100 offices. The bank is geared toward

serving small and medium-size businesses. Loans to these businesses represent 40 percent of the total commercial loans of the bank, and more than 50 percent of the demand deposits.

In order to provide home-office-type decision making at the local level, the bank has established business banking centers near concentrations of small businesses. These centers provide a full range of services for small business, and are staffed by commercial lenders and other specialists who bring the expertise of the home office closer to the customer. In 1985 Shawmut instituted a Corporate Finance Division, and two years later added venture capital subsidiaries to meet the needs of expanding businesses for capital and merger and acquisition expertise.

The consumer market remains as important today as when Shawmut made the first installment loan in the early 1900s. In a business where convenience is paramount, Shawmut has an extensive branch and electronic banking machine network covering the marketplace. Through its Private Banking Division, Shawmut has targeted the affluent market. These customers often have more complex and varied financial needs than the average consumer. Shawmut's approach is to put an account officer together with a customer so that he or she comes to fully understand that customer's needs. When the need arises, appropriate specialists are brought in to provide the best alternatives to fulfill that customer's financial plan.

Fee-producing services have shown strong growth in recent years. Shawmut was among the first to offer discount brokerage services to the market. More than $10 billion in trust assets are under management by Shawmut National Corporation, making it a major player in the trust arena. Corporate services provide sophisticated financial services to businesses throughout the region. Shawmut Bank's sister bank in Connecticut, Connecticut National Bank, is among the top five providers of service to the insurance industry. Similar services are offered to the insurance, health, education, and general business communities through Shawmut Bank, N.A.

As a member of Shawmut National Corporation, Shawmut Bank, N.A., is backed with $1.6 billion in capital and a presence in the three southern New England states that represent 85 percent of the economic activity in the region. Over the past several years an increased capital base has positioned Shawmut National to be able to take advantage of opportunities for geographic and product expansion. During the first year of the new Shawmut National Corporation particular attention is being spent effecting cost savings on an intrastate basis, merging operations

and building efficiencies. The following year interstate operations will be the prime focus of attention.

Shawmut Bank, N.A., looks to the future with great optimism. The region's economy is strong and diversified, and shows promise for continued growth. The greater Boston market continues to be one of the strongest in the nation with its strong base in the

Obbatinewat, the Shawmut Indian whose likeness has become Shawmut Bank's registered trademark. The sculpture was created by Adelbert Ames, Jr., in 1910.

service, health care, educational, financial services, and high-technology industries providing opportunities for Shawmut to continue to grow and prosper.

ERNST & WHINNEY

Managing partner Thomas Lankford operates the Boston office from high above the Hub in the John Hancock Tower.

A.C. Ernst, founder.

In a city full of high-rise offices with exquisite views, Thomas M. Lankford just might have the best of them all. Looking out not one, but two, floor-to-ceiling plate-glass walls of the Hancock Tower's 46th floor, Ernst & Whinney's managing partner can spot many buildings belonging to Boston clients. On a clear day, he can even see New Hampshire's White Mountains. Of course, it has taken a few years for the accounting firm to get to this vantage spot.

The firm actually got its start in Cleveland in 1903. A general accounting practice run by two brothers, Alwin C. "A.C." and Theodore, Ernst & Ernst was begun in an era when the scope of accounting in this country was, by and large, no more than the scope of bookkeeping. For most companies at the turn of the century, a condensed balance sheet and summarized income statement sufficed. But, as the nation's business entered a period of unparalleled vigor spawning the industrial mergers of the early 1900s, it was clear that the discipline would change accounting techniques and company accounts came under greater examination.

In 1906 Theodore asked for a return

of his investment to take advantage of other business interests. Less reserved about the future of the profession than his brother, A.C. continued to build his practice with determined interest in auditing and in the practical application of accounting theory. Soon enough his patience would be rewarded. In 1913 the 16th Amendment to the Constitution allowed Congress to impose taxes on an individual's income. The demands of World War I created additional need for consistent accounting in business. In 1917 Ernst & Ernst's annual revenues surpassed one million dollars, and the firm opened its Boston

Thomas Flannery and Sarah Madaus avail themselves of one of the desk-top computers in use throughout the office.

office, its ninth.

Hard work was the not-so-secret secret of A.C.'s success in modern accounting. Boston's staff of accountants worked long hours—10 hours a day, six, sometimes seven, days a week, 52 weeks a year. As its local reputation grew, Ernst & Ernst's client roster expanded to include tax work and a large number of bank examinations. In the 1930s businesses would be asked to keep even better transaction records. The 1933 Securities Act stipulated that annual statements by public corporations must be certified by independent accountants. The 1934 Securities Exchange Act further regulated stock trades, and the 1935 Social Security

Regular meetings keep partners Eric Wolf, John McCafferty, and Hans Meyer attuned to the firm's ever-changing role in the business world.

Act placed additional responsibilities on the collective shoulders of accountants and auditors.

Following World War II, Ernst & Ernst/Boston began to tailor tax planning for the business or personal needs of owners and managers, to assist with inventory management, and to prepare business plans for such diverse industries as banking, insurance, sporting goods, health care, and printing and publishing. In the 1950s small, privately held high-technology companies began springing up on the outskirts of Boston, and Ernst & Ernst was called upon by many emerging ventures engaged in the invention of new devices for defense, aerospace, communications, manufacturing, and medical use.

By the 1970s the Boston office was part of Ernst & Ernst's worldwide organization. In 1979 a name change derived from Ernst & Ernst and Whinney, Murray & Co., one of the United Kingdom's leading accounting firms, would produce the name by which the firm is known today. In 1987 Ernst & Whinney employed 30,000 people in more than 400 offices in 76 countries. Demand for audit professionals has continued since the 1970s. Proliferating financial service companies, the formation of bank holding corporations, and the move toward cost-containment by hospitals and other health-care organizations have all contributed to increased business for Ernst & Whinney in Boston.

The Boston office is divided into four contemporary divisions: audit, tax, emerging business, and management consulting. Though the audit department is still considered the firm's bread and butter, future expansion will focus on management consulting activities, Lankford says. Since cutting costs is key to becoming more competitive, the firm hopes to use its accounting expertise to help clients plan better and improve the productivity of their operations. For manufacturers, for example, informa-

Partners Peter Nurczynski, Stephen Bassett, and Robert Elam meet in the firm's library.

tion can be used in such a way to plan just-in-time production, eliminating costly inventory surpluses. Ernst & Whinney expects its consulting practice to be a more significant part of its service in the future as more and more businesses turn to auditors for help in improving their productivity. Such services mean the firm works with a company year round, not just on a quarterly basis. As a result of continued demand for the services of all four of its departments, the firm has stepped up its hiring in Boston.

In 1981 the firm began to use computers extensively, and today desk-top and portable computers are in use throughout the office. Ernst & Whinney maintains two offices in Boston, a

practice office on two floors of the Hancock Tower in Back Bay and an office in the Exchange Place tower downtown. Ernst & Whinney has additional offices in New England business centers: in Manchester, New Hampshire; Portland, Maine; Burlington, Vermont; Providence, Rhode Island; and Hartford, Connecticut. On the whole the firm has made it a point to avoid centralizing, opening small offices instead in areas close to major clients. According to Lankford, the idea is to have an office "within an hour's drive for the client who needs our services."

DELOITTE HASKINS & SELLS

The managing partner, audit partners, and a consultant to management partner hold an engagement planning meeting in the office.

This engagement team, analyzing manufacturing operations at a high-technology client location, includes partners from emerging business services and tax.

Founded in 1892, Deloitte Haskins & Sells is today one of the fastest-growing accounting and consulting firms in the world. A network of more than 450 offices extends through 65 countries, employing more than 26,000 people. DH&S prides itself on providing high-quality professional services that add significant value to the business performance of its clients.

The Boston office of DH&S opened in 1918 in the old chamber of commerce building downtown. It was the thirteenth domestic office of the firm that was then known as Haskins & Sells. In 1969 DH&S moved its Boston office to 28 State Street. In 1986 DH&S moved to its present quarters at One Financial Center.

DH&S Boston professionals offer four primary services to clients: audit services, tax consulting, management consulting, and emerging and mid-size business services. Company philosophy dictates that each client receive the assistance of an engagement team that includes an auditor, a tax professional, and a management consultant and is

headed by a client service partner.

Areas of specialization in the Boston office include services for some of Boston's largest and most vibrant industries: high technology, broadcasting/communications, and health care. The DH&S high-technology specialists assist computer software companies, bio-

technology firms, and many types of manufacturers. They possess expertise in corporate finance, tax, operations management, information systems, human resources, strategic business planning, accounting, and auditing. As clients grow, DH&S professionals tailor services to their changing needs.

Broadcasting and communications are dynamic businesses in Boston, and DH&S specialists work with radio stations, television networks, and cable TV networks in strategic business and tax planning, capital formation, and corporate finance. They also provide specialized assistance in mergers and acquisitions.

Health care specialists at DH&S's

Boston office serve hospitals, multi-hospital systems, alternative delivery systems, and elderly care facilities. They combine skills in accounting, auditing, management consulting, and third-party reimbursement with an understanding of health care business gained through years of experience. They also

consult with clients on issues such as information systems, strategic financial planning, and accounts receivable management.

DH&S audit professionals nationwide have earned a reputation as technical leaders in the development and use of advanced auditing techniques for more cost-effective audit services. They use microcomputer-based audit systems in order to enhance audit quality and help clients strengthen their financial management processes. Tax professionals assist clients in developing long-term strategies designed to take maximum advantage of existing tax laws. The Executive Financial Counseling Group provides personal tax and financial planning services to individuals with high incomes. Tax specialists monitor tax legislation and conduct seminars on emerging tax issues. They also assist clients in presenting critical tax issues to various federal and state taxing authorities.

The Consultants to Management department provides focused and specialized financial management, information technology, productivity, computer assurance, and specific industry related services to its clients in finance, manufacturing, high technology, state and local government, health care, utilities, real estate, and retailing. By applying a methodology called DH&S Concept/90, consultants help companies to collect the information necessary to meet their business needs and to analyze that information in order to respond quickly to competition.

Emerging business professionals help their clients raise capital and forecast revenues, expenses, and production to ensure orderly growth and development. They also provide accounting, auditing, and tax services to these clients, as well as assistance in budgeting.

Deloitte Haskins & Sells professionals make a point of sharing their knowledge and expertise in industry issues with members of industry-specific associations and other industry-related organizations. Boston office high-technology specialists, for instance, participate in the Massachusetts High Tech Council, the MIT Enterprise Forum, EMERGE, the 128 Venture Group, and the Computer Museum. Health care specialists are actively involved in the Healthcare Financial Management Association and the Massachusetts Hospital Association. Broadcast/communications specialists take an active role in the National Association for Cable Television and Broadcasters. Acknowledging the importance of working for those in need, the Boston DH&S staff also supports the United Way of Massachusetts Bay and the Greater Boston Business for Charity Program.

The growth of Deloitte Haskins & Sells in Boston may be attributed to the quality services its employees render to clients, their responsiveness to the needs of the community in which they operate, and the advanced and specialized services they provide to Boston's fastest-growing industries.

MERCHANTSBANK OF BOSTON

MerchantsBank of Boston is a $500-million bank headquartered on Tremont Street just across from the Boston Common and the subway entrance to Park Street Station. A state-chartered institution, MerchantsBank is also a cooperative bank. Its services, though, are virtually identical to those of commercial banks and include interest-bearing NOW checking accounts, overdraft protection, direct deposit, combined monthly statements, retirement accounts, and access to nationwide automatic teller machines. In addition to its downtown office, Merchants has seven branches in the Boston area.

With seven branches in the Boston area, MerchantsBank is headquartered on Tremont Street and blends with the historic locale across from the Boston Common.

Like other commercial banks, MerchantsBank has also made moves to diversify into activities that earn steady fee income for the bank. In one of its most important moves, the institution shifted its residential mortgages operations to a new subsidiary, Farragut Mortgage Company, a highly successful venture that earns the bulk of its revenues administering mortgages for other investors on a fee basis.

Founded as Merchants Co-operative Savings Fund and Loan Association in December 1881, the bank opened only four years after cooperative banking started in Massachusetts. The concept, imported from England and Germany to Philadelphia by Benjamin Franklin, was based on the idea that a bank owned and operated by savers could help those same savers to buy a house.

In Boston, Josiah Quincy hoped to help the working class of Boston move out of crowded tenements, and he became president of the first cooperative bank in the state. At that time cooperative banks had only one type of account, called serial shares. These shares were supposed to be purchased monthly with the funds going to help other savers purchase homes. Interest charged on home loans was then divided among the shareholders for profit. The idea caught on, and by 1900 there were 124 cooperative banks in Massachusetts.

MerchantsBank's contemporary investment focus is also on construction and commercial real estate loans, particularly for the development of single-family and multifamily housing units. In certain instances the bank participates with developers and shares in the profits when properties are sold. In 1986 total volume generated by construction and commercial real estate lending was $155 million, compared to $101 million for the previous year. Recently MerchantsBank of Boston arranged $7.3 million financing for a development of 128 single-family homes in Hudson, Massachusetts; $2.5 million for two hotels in Virginia; $3.7 million for apartments in Indiana; and $4.2 million for apartments in Texas.

FARRAGUT MORTGAGE COMPANY

A significant step in MerchantsBank's continuing effort to expand its traditional residential lending services was taken in December 1984 through the acquisition of Farragut Mortgage Company. Begun in 1982 by South Boston real estate broker David Bernotas, Farragut was an idea whose time had come.

Historically people looked for mortgages at those same commercial banks that had given them consumer loans. But because some banks were losing deposits to other investment outlets in the 1980s, supply of credit was not keeping up with the demand for mortgages in Boston's booming neighborhoods. Farragut and others have solved the problem with the help of quasi-government agencies such as the Federal Home Loan Mortgage Corporation ("Freddie Mac"), and the Federal National Mortgage Association ("Fannie Mae").

In brief, the company borrows capital from a bank at a certain interest rate, sells mortgages to home buyers at a higher rate, and then sells it to a secondary market, such as Freddie Mac, Fannie Mae, and other institutional investors. Farragut receives fees for continuing to service the loans by collecting monthly payments and remitting them to investors. In late 1986 the company raised more than $6 million by selling more than one million shares of common stock. This offering has made Farragut one of only a handful of publicly held mortgage banking companies in the country.

There is perhaps no better indicator of the explosive growth of Farragut than its mortgage loan servicing portfolio, which increased from $9 million in December 1984 to $880 million in December 1986. During that year net income increased more than 270 percent and the work force grew from 60 to 200, prompting the company to move its headquarters from Belmont to Waltham. In March 1987 the portfolio surpassed the billion-dollar mark.

Today there are more than 793 mortgage lenders in the state. With a 1.08-percent market share, Farragut weighed in as the 14th-largest lender in Massachusetts in 1987. An ever-changing menu of loans and an aggressive marketing program, however, promises to upgrade that ranking. The company is one of the first lenders in the nation to offer single-digit mortgage rates with the introduction of a 9.95-percent, 30-year fixed-rate mortgage in February 1986—an offer that brought news cameras into Farragut's offices and tied up the phones for days. In early 1987 Farragut introduced a guaranteed five-week closing program targeted to new home buyers and a no-points, no-closing-costs package for those wishing to refinance. Farragut also successfully introduced an adjustable-rate mortgage acceptable for sale to the secondary market. These and other new products have been marketed by 25 full-time telemarketers and advertised by a $1.8-million blitz of print and radio ads. Farragut also set up a national WATS line.

But the effort won't stop here. Farragut Mortgage Company is also spreading the word by expanding geographically, adding offices in New England for loan origination and processing. In 1987 Farragut acquired the Standard Mortgage Company of Exton, Pennsylvania, which will serve as base for further expansion in the Mid-Atlantic region.

A subsidiary of MerchantsBank of Boston, Farragut Mortgage Company in Waltham was founded to expand the bank's residential lending services.

FRANK B. HALL & CO. OF MASSACHUSETTS

In 1933 Frederic C. Church and Charles Colby Hewitt consolidated several local insurance agencies and established the firm of Boit, Dalton & Church. They sought to build a large insurance agency, and by 1971, when it merged with and became the Northeast regional headquarters of the worldwide broker, Frank B. Hall & Co., Inc., the firm had become the largest broker in New England. In all probability they would never have guessed that by the 1980s their sons would be insuring such

things as multimillion-dollar satellites, makers of space shuttles, or managers of mutual funds, a product that was invented in their own neighborhood.

While the name of the business changed, other names have remained the same at Hall of Massachusetts. The sons of the two founders, Colby Hewitt, Jr., and Frederic C. Church, Jr., con-

The historic New Bedford waterfront area. Photography by James Blank

tinue to run the business. Company headquarters are even in the same historic Batterymarch Building, where their fathers had hung their shingle. With the help of 250 employees, the large property and liability broker provides insurance brokerage and risk management for nearly 600 commercial clients.

Since its founding in the 1930s Hall of Massachusetts has prospered by responding to dramatic changes in business insurance needs with a variety of new coverages and services. An expanded postwar society and global economy changed the nature of the industry. A more vigorous marketplace, an increasingly litigious society, new knowledge of hazardous substances, and a myriad of government regulations gave new meaning to the term "liability." Hall and other brokers began to concentrate on risk analysis, loss control, claims management, self-insurance, and other specialized efforts to help forecast and head off potential future losses for their clients.

In particular, Hall has pioneered liability coverages for certain professionals. Programs to insure architects,

Site of the first skirmish of the Revolutionary War on April 19, 1775, Lexington epitomizes the quiet New England village though just 12 miles northwest of Boston. Photography by Stuart Cohen

engineers, and investment managers of mutual funds against potential errors and omissions claims are among its specialities. The company also specializes in facilitating municipal insurance pools, whereby a number of municipal governments may collectively purchase insurance against potential property loss and liability claims. Other significant industry niches include liability and property insurance for hotels and high-tech, aviation, and space technology industries. Hall of Massachusetts also facilitates and manages programs of self-insurance for hospitals and other institutions with high-dollar insurance needs.

A subsidiary, Frank B. Hall Risk Management, Inc., offers a comprehensive risk-management program for busi-

nesses lacking a risk manager on staff. A full-time information center manager is available to help clients design programs to organize their insurance data.

Hall of Massachusetts operates autonomously from its parent and is structured to meet the specific needs of New England. As a part of the Frank B. Hall group, however, its Boston professionals have access to a global network of facilities and the resources of experts on six continents in serving a growing number of multinational clients in the United States and abroad.

In the Boston community, Hall of Massachusetts' personnel participate in civic, educational, and charitable endeavors, serving as directors and trustees at the New England Deaconess

Since its founding in 1933, Frank B. Hall & Co. of Massachusetts has expanded its insurance brokerage and risk-management coverage to nearly 600 commercial clients. Photo of communication satellites (inset) by Peter Meazel. The photo of the control panel at the natural gas plant in Dorchester is by Edith G. Haun

Hospital, the New England Conservatory of Music, Wheelock College, Hampshire College, and the Archdiocese of Boston Catholic Charities.

Frederic C. Church, Jr., currently serves as president of the Boys and Girls Clubs of Boston, following in the footsteps of his father. Colby Hewitt, Jr., is chairman of the Greater Boston Forum for Health Action, Inc., a group searching for creative responses to the need for cost-effective health care.

HAROLD CABOT & COMPANY

You never know what you might see in the halls of Cabot Advertising in Charlestown's Constitution Plaza. Giant cacti sprout from corners of one office; a red couch in the shape of human lips adorns yet another. Inflated dinosaurs, Samauri swords. Is this Boston?

Blame it on those crazy "creatives"—nearly one-third of Cabot employees are so defined—for such a smattering of decors. Cabot, the agency of choice for such clients as New England Telephone, Anderson-Little, the Harvard Community Health Plan, and Prime Computer, is proud of its creative work force—and it shows. It is even more proud of changes made in recent years to upgrade that force.

In 1986 Cabot president and chief executive officer Bill Monaghan steered the agency into a period of renewal. A Boston agency founded in 1930, Cabot began the transition with a physical move from cramped quarters at 10 High Street to One Constitution Plaza. Inflated dinosaurs are now flanked by exquisite plate-glass window views of Boston Harbor and the North End.

In the summer of 1986 the agency began to invest in new talent, hiring four new account supervisors, director of public relations, media director, and general manager for direct marketing. In addition, the agency became one of only two Boston shops to hire an account planner who represents the uninitiated view of the consumer in the development of all creative projects.

Reborn, Cabot sees itself as the quintessential mid-size agency—big enough to deliver the full range of integrated marketing and creative advertising business demands, yet small enough so that every account, regardless of its size, is reviewed by agency owners. With 146 employees, the agency does approximately $80 million in business each year for 25 clients. As an independent, privately held agency, Cabot officials promise not to join the rash of merger activity seen in the

"The Place We Call Home," an ad for New England Telephone Company (NET), emphasizes to New Englanders that NET, not AT&T or any other phone company, is their company.

advertising community in recent years.

Instead the agency is focused on what it does best: broadcast and print advertising for packaged-foods and service industries. Although the agency's historic strength is service industry advertising, Cabot believes it is one of the premier packaged goods agencies in

New England. All together, the agency's senior vice-presidents, vice-presidents, and account executives have worked on advertising campaigns for a total of 59 different foods, 48 health and beauty aids, 22 beverages, 22 household products, and 15 pet foods. Cabot people have worked behind the scenes for some of the most highly visible and memorable products in recent advertising history, products such as Pepsi, Budweiser, Jell-O, Charmin, and Chuck Wagon dog food.

While most of Cabot's clients are headquartered in New England, they operate in a wide variety of local, regional, national, and international marketing arenas. Cabot has active working relationships with advertising agencies in Great Britain, France, and Australia to allow the agency to handle marketing programs for its U.S. clients in Europe and the Asia/Pacific region. Global campaigns for Prime Computer, one of the agency's largest accounts, are managed within this system.

The advertising process at Cabot begins with research and the production of a "fact book" concerning the product or business. After an advertising strategy is determined, creative takes over. Each project gets direct super-

"Or Call Prime Computer" conveys to businesses concerned about selection of a computer system that they can make the complicated decision themselves or *"Call Prime."*

The Harvard Health Plan, an HMO in Massachusetts, communicates with this "St. Everywhere" ad campaign that the health plan has offices throughout Massachusetts.

vision by Cabot's 50-person creative department of writers, art directors, broadcast producers, print production specialists, mechanical artists, and typographers. While an account is assigned a "core" copy/art team, other teams are brought in to keep the creative juices flowing. Marketing, communications, media, public relations, and/or direct-mail plans are developed.

The media department develops the most impactful and efficient media plan for the brand or service, then negotiates for radio and television time and for premium positioning within print publications. Each buyer at Cabot has a minimum of four years and as many as 20 years of solid negotiating background. Print and broadcast departments produce the final product in the form of art, copy, and audio or videotapes. For quick turn-around a 55-font Mergenthaler Digital Typesetter enables the agency to produce camera-ready materials in-house for clients, particularly for retail clients who require ads overnight for placement in daily newspapers.

Apart from advertising Cabot has three other in-house divisions. Cabot Public Relations develops and executes strategic, corporate, and product mar-

keting programs. Public relations personnel also assist clients by providing media spokespersons, presentation training, assistance with investor/financial relations, new product introductions, special events, and organizational development programs.

Cabot Direct Marketing uses broadcast, print, mail, telemarketing, electronic media, trade show contacts, and other outlets to solicit orders from consumers. Software created by the agency helps businesses to build databases of potential customers for a product. Other software applications evaluate results of direct-marketing efforts.

Cabot Design has handled a variety of assignments for the agency's clients.

Cabot has designed New England Telephone's annual report, as well as its employee magazine. When Polaroid brought out its "convertibles" glasses, Cabot designed the posters, banners, counter-cards, sales presentation piece, and display box. The group is also responsible for in-store signage and promotional materials for all Ground Round restaurants and Anderson-Little/Richman Brothers clothing stores.

"Obviously Your Dog . . . " is an ad for Superior Brands, Inc., manufacturer of dog treats and other products. It communicates the high palatability of one of the brand's dog bones, Master's Choice.

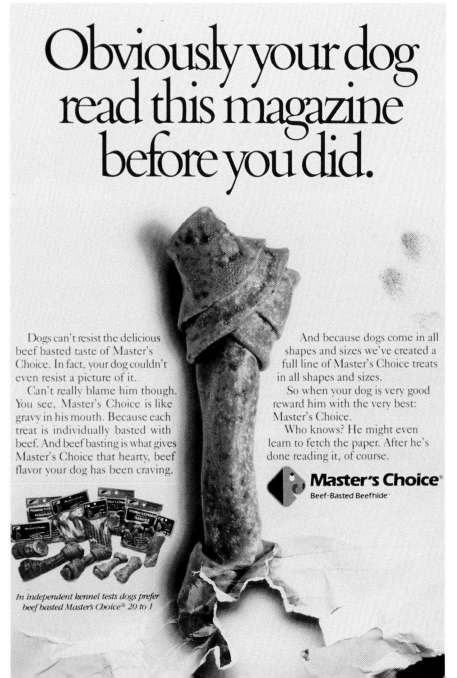

OLYMPIC INTERNATIONAL BANK & TRUST COMPANY

Olympic International Bank & Trust Co. was established in 1985 with the clear and simple commitment of providing quality banking with the resources of the larger banks and the personalized attention of the smaller banks. It was the first commercial bank to open in the City of Boston in 15 years.

In the midst of mega-mergers by other banks in Boston and the New England region, Olympic Bank dared to "swim against the tide" in an attempt to return to the days of neighborhood banking. Other banks are burdened with portfolios containing old, long-term investments that bear fixed interest rates substantially below current market rates. Olympic Bank has no such encumbrances as it started fresh, strong, and energetic, and is keeping current with the times.

It was Boston banker Bill O'Brien who saw a developing market niche and

Olympic Bank's president, William J. O'Brien, and chairman of the board, Victor A. Nicolazzo, Jr.

decided to satisfy it. O'Brien, also known as "the dean of de novo banks," exemplifies a new breed of banker. He has developed a managerial style that mixes skill, experience, and egalitarianism, along with an aggressive determination to form a distinctive bank in the Boston business community.

Originally from Dorchester, Massachusetts, O'Brien now resides in Quincy. He graduated from Bentley College, Boston, where he majored in finance and accounting. While working as a manager for Rapids Furniture Company in Boston, he realized his interest in banking and took the examiner's test. He worked as a Massachusetts Bank Examiner from 1966 to 1968, before accepting a position with Charlesbank Trust Company in Cambridge. Four years later, at 29 years of age, he was elected chief executive officer—one of the youngest ever to attain such a position in Massachusetts. It was a sign of things to come.

O'Brien experienced the displacements of fellow officers and employees that follow bank mergers when Charlesbank Trust merged with a large Boston bank in 1983. During this period of time O'Brien was approached by a business acquaintance who represented an elite group of athletes. The athletes, along with their agents, contemplated the idea of forming their own bank that would offer them the specialized attention they required. They selected O'Brien, because of his banking expertise and background, to be the president and chief executive officer of the new bank and to aid them in realizing their dream. Their idea was truly reminiscent of the 1800s, when groups of merchants banded together in Boston to organize their own banks. The banks they formed, at that time, continually merged to become today's regional giants.

O'Brien attended a developmental meeting with this group to discuss their ideas. While athletes would become an important component in the initial membership of the bank, O'Brien believed the bank should reach out to embrace all commercial ventures and entrepreneurs. A representative for K.C. Jones, Victor A. Nicolazzo, Jr., president of Bigelow Oil Co., also attended the meeting. Nicolazzo became "enthusiastically committed" with the Olympic strategy from the beginning and serves as chairman of the board.

The name "Olympic" was selected because it symbolizes strength and the pursuit of superior attainments. The pyramid structure of the logo represents upward growth of small, medium, and large businesses. The inner triangle depicts the small businessperson in the banking marketplace with room to expand; the middle triangle represents the medium-size businessperson with gradual growth in the marketplace, and the large, outer triangle indicates the

bank's outlook to the future and ability to grow with its customers.

Olympic Bank, the oldest of the newest breed of local, de novo banks, is a full-service commercial bank offering a broad range of financial products. The bank successfully caters to disenchanted mid-size companies and high-salaried individuals who have been left "sitting on the bench" by the merger fever infecting older banking institutions. These companies and individuals need more services than those offered by small banks, but are often overlooked by large commercial banks. "High interest rates and the movement toward consolidation in the banking industry have made it increasingly difficult for small businesses to obtain capital," says Bill O'Brien. "On one hand, large banks can secure their profits much quicker by lending to large corporations and foreign governments; on the other hand, the small banks, which are eager to lend to small businesses, must charge higher rates than they do their larger, more established custom-

Despite the diversity of its clients, all Olympic Bank customers are serviced in the same fashion. The bank's president believes in an open-door policy and will personally meet with customers in his comfortable, harbor-view office.

ers. So those who can afford it least . . . pay the most. Olympic Bank will devote its efforts to changing that situation."

The bank was named "Olympic Bank" not only for the obvious athletic connotation, but also to bring the general concept of excellence to mind. On May 6, 1985, the bank opened its doors with $5 million in assets. At that time this was the highest initial capitalization in Massachusetts history. In less than nine months total assets had grown to $70 million. At the end of its first year the bank finished in the black—a feat not usually accomplished by new banks until their third year. In an unusual move for a new bank, Olympic went public in July 1986 with stock subscribed for at $10 per share. By year-

end 1986 the bank could claim $166 million in assets.

Olympic's 18-member board has drawn special attention because of some well-known sports figures, such as K.C. Jones, former head coach of the Boston Celtics; John McKenzie, former right wing hockey player with the Boston Bruins; and Dave Cowens, former Boston Celtic. It came as no surprise that Olympic Bank came to be known as "the athletes' bank." "While that identification was helpful at first," says Bill O'Brien, "Olympic Bank would prefer to be known as 'the bank for business.'"

O'Brien, Nicolazzo, and the other board members are determined to make their bank prosper. What's behind the prosperity? It's the bank's philosophy of quality over quantity and the enormous dedication of the bank's staff and board of directors who provide a personal approach to banking. Each of the 18 board members has a mind for business. Each is a person who is familiar with corporate intricacies and has suc-

cessfully developed his or her company into the distinctive business it is today. There are 16 different industries and professions represented by Olympic Bank's board of directors. From transportation and real estate, to basketball and the restaurant business, customers know they can depend on the board for expert advice and guidance when making investment decisions or business expansions.

Olympic Bank is not a traditional bank. Tellers are obsolete; they have been replaced by customer service representatives. These individuals have in-

One of the many customer advantages at Olympic Bank is the availability of the bank's conference rooms.

stant access to account information by way of desk-top computer terminals. The bank's computer system was designed with the future in mind—in other words, the day when businesses and individuals conduct their banking via personal computers at their home or office location.

A state-chartered bank and member of the FDIC, Olympic specializes in the

services that medium-size companies need: term certificates, checking, savings, money market accounts, IRA/ Keogh plans. "We have twenty-first century technology with a seventeenth century attitude," says O'Brien. The bank can expedite wire transfers in the fastest, most efficient manner as it is a member of the on-line program with the Federal Reserve Bank of Boston. The bank also offers a discount brokerage service, FAX capabilities, a night depository, safe deposit boxes, Mastercard, VISA, and American Express. In addition, the bank's conference rooms

are available for customers to use for their own business meetings.

Twenty-four hour service! Olympic Bank offers its customers around-the-clock access to their accounts. All business and individual customers can conveniently deposit or withdraw at hundreds of XPRESS 24-hour automatic teller machines throughout Massachusetts and make cash withdrawals at a number of CIRRUS machines throughout the United States and Canada.

The bank generates new business, as the saying goes, "the old-fashioned way" by word of mouth, an active call

Walking into the bank's spacious lobby at 303 Congress Street in Boston, customers are greeted by customer service representatives who provide the personalized attention they deserve and require.

officer program, and the aggressiveness of the board of directors who actively market the bank. Cognizant of the fact that Boston's economic future depends on the growth prospects of the high-technology, professional, educational, and cultural-service industries, Olympic Bank intends to offer innovative financial services with far-reaching

community benefits. Special attention will be devoted to implementing more customer-oriented technology.

Olympic Bank has made an impression on the banking industry. Its management has blended theories of relationship banking together with the experiences of real-life banking. The bank was able to join the two together to form a professional, full-service bank. The result has been remarkable. With increased technology and futuristic ideas, Olympic Bank is fully prepared for the next generation of customers—clearly Olympic Bank is "the Bank for Business."

LAVENTHOL & HORWATH

A visitor to the offices of the nation's ninth-largest accounting firm, Laventhol & Horwath, located in Government Center across from the New City Hall at 2 Center Plaza, will find a very pleasant environment.

With a panoramic view of the harbor, Faneuil Hall, and the ever-expanding skyline of Boston, the office appears comfortable, attractive, and warm, with a roll-up-your-sleeves, user-friendly atmosphere.

Indeed, since 1915 Laventhol & Horwath auditors and accountants have helped small to medium-size privately owned companies grow into large privately owned companies. In so doing, L&H has grown along the way. Today Laventhol & Horwath has offices in 50 U.S. cities and more than 220 affiliated offices in 70 countries through Horwath & Horwath International.

Since it was started in the 1960s, the Boston office of Laventhol & Horwath has become one of the firm's major offices and one of the largest business, financial counseling, tax, and ac-

counting practices in the city. It serves organizations in manufacturing, real estate, retailing, services, and high technology as well as nonprofit organizations, colleges, hotels, and restaurants. In addition to general audit and tax services, the Boston practice also offers services in connection with SEC filings, advice on corporate mergers and acquisitions, bankruptcy and insurance claims services, real estate consulting, business advisory services to family-owned or closely held companies, litigation assistance to attorneys, and a host of specialized services to the real estate, leisure, entertainment, hospitality, and health care industries.

Laventhol & Horwath is organized into four areas—auditing, accounting, tax services, and management advisory services. The firm's initial contact with a client usually begins with a discussion of the client's business and the examination of the client's financial statements and the rendering of an independent opinion of those statements. L&H also provides compilation and review services to fit a client's particular needs. Often problems are identified along the way, and other L&H professionals are called upon to assist the client.

Many of these additional advisory services have been added by the Boston office of Laventhol & Horwath over the

past decade as tax reform, increasing competition, computer technology, and development of new management techniques have all made running a business more and more complex. Taxes in particular are such a major part of a company's ability to grow that since 1970 L&H's Tax Department has grown tenfold.

What began as a small department for handling individual and corporate taxes has evolved into a department of 35 professionals with a variety of specialties in pension and estate taxes, personal financial planning, and tax planning for developers and their corporate and individual partnerships. L&H also maintains a national tax office in Washington, D.C., to monitor current developments in Congress, the Treasury, and the courts, and forward that information via computer to other L&H offices.

Laventhol & Horwath formalized its advisory services for emerging businesses in Boston in 1984 with the creation of the Accounting and Business

Front row, from left: partners Nicholas L. Iacuzio, Burton R. Gesserman, and William H. Miller. Back row, from left: Stanley J. Miller, Mark J. Feingold, and B. Burton Schneider. The Real Estate Advisory Services group has performed market feasibility studies for mixed-use development such as the Boston Harbor Hotel on Rowes Wharf.

Front row, from left: partners Timothy S. Egan, Richard J. Eckstein, David Love, and Richard W. Talkov. Back row, from left: Michael D. Cunningham, David I. Shactman, and Robert D. Bernson. L&H has played a fundamental role in the market and financial analysis underlying the development of many of Boston's new buildings.

Advisory Services group (ABAS) to service smaller and start-up businesses. With 23 staffers and three partners, ABAS is one of the firm's fastest-growing departments. Staffers are trained to assist in the many financial decisions a growing company faces, including plant expansion, lease/buy agreements, personnel increases, banking relations, and strategic planning. Periodic monitoring by ABAS partners and staff gives the client the opportunity to discuss tax planning prior to the firm's year-end. The idea is to catch problems at important phases of growth, when young companies often go under.

To serve the diverse needs of the continually expanding Northeast real estate industry, the Boston office of L&H offers a wide range of real estate, accounting, tax, and consulting services to assist in evaluating, financing, and managing real estate projects. Twenty-five consulting professionals have performed numerous assignments, including market feasibility studies for real estate and hotel development projects throughout metropolitan Boston and all of New England.

The Boston Real Estate Advisory Services Group is particularly knowledgeable in the market feasibility of

Front row, from left: partners Douglas J. McGregor, Donald A. Greenhalgh, Alan Jay Rosenstein, and Paul D. Schneider. Back row, from left: Donald Lasden, Gerald R. Schneider, Sidney L. Ostroff, and Allen G. Sneider. L&H real estate advisers have worked with developers on the initial planning of several highly visible ventures such as the Bostonian Hotel.

mixed-use real estate development, where residential, retail, office, and other kinds of space are combined in one building project. In the downtown area alone, L&H real estate advisers have worked with developers on the initial planning of several highly visible ventures such as the Boston Harbor Hotel on Rowes Wharf, Heritage on the Common, the Bostonian Hotel, and

the Lafayette Hotel.

Another important and recent advisory service of L&H is its family-owned business program. L&H conducts presentations, workshops, seminars, and individual family consultations to help family businesses redefine strategy, eliminate conflict, and reach business goals.

One of the newest and most creative services offered by L&H has been designed to assist the legal profession. It consists of litigation support consulting and expert testimony available to attorneys who are dealing with legal matters involving financially related issues.

Laventhol & Horwath, as a public service, has also extended its accounting expertise to the Massachusetts cultural community. For more than 15 years L&H has provided accounting and other related services to a wide variety of nonprofit cultural organizations. In addition, during the past 10 years L&H has worked in a partnership relationship with the Massachusetts Cultural Alliance, a service organization comprised of more than 200 members of the Massachusetts cultural community. This relationship has taken the form of sponsorship of its Annual Issues Conferences, assistance with its long-range planning efforts, as well as many other undertakings.

From left: managers Eric R. Wille, Deborah B. Haskell, Charles I. Frey, Charles E. Preus, Anthony Timiraos, and Sari A. Rapkin. L&H professionals provide financial, tax, and business consulting services to entrepreneurial companies of all sizes.

PAINE WEBBER

On a gray and rainy day not too long after the Crash of 1987, PaineWebber senior vice-president Lewis H. Milkey was handing out bright blue-and-white stickers to the staff coming and going from his corner office. "Set Your Goal, Meet Your Goal," read one of the tags sticking to the vice-president's own shirt. It was the first of the month, Milkey pointed out, and a good time for a small morale booster. "Were the goals realistic?" a visitor asked. "I believe so," Milkey replied.

Indeed, there is more at stake for PaineWebber now that it is one of the nation's largest independent investment firms, with a capital base of more than one billion dollars. Since its earliest days as a local Boston brokerage firm, PaineWebber has provided investment products and services to retail, corporate, institutional clients, and public agencies. Though the firm has 300 offices worldwide, PaineWebber's busiest and most important office is still in Boston, where the firm got its start in 1879.

It was in that year that two clerks at the Blackstone Bank in Haymarket Square decided to improve their for-

PaineWebber got its start in Boston in 1879.

tunes by quitting the bank to form a brokerage firm. William A. Paine and Wallace G. Webber had seen the coming of copper mining, an industry that had received loans from their bank. Their idea was to broker copper mining stocks. In 1897 the fledgling firm branched out into other stocks.

A wartime merger in 1942 with another Boston brokerage firm, Jackson & Curtis, brought additional capital and manpower to the firm, renamed Paine, Webber, Jackson & Curtis. As Boston became a center for investment banking and corporate finance, the firm expanded from the first small office on 48 Congress into the Prudential Center and two other offices on Federal Street. Departments for venture capital, tax-advantaged investments, institutional sales, and municipal committing were opened in Boston.

Under the expert management of Nelson Darling, George Gardner, Jr., and Albert Pratt, the firm solidified its national reputation. Control of the firm remained in the hands of the

With 300 offices worldwide, PaineWebber's busiest office is still its flagship office at 265 Franklin Street in Boston.

partners of Paine, Webber, Jackson & Curtis until 1970, when the firm incorporated. Ten years later it institutionalized its original name of PaineWebber, but without the comma between names.

In 1985 the firm and a local developer built Boston's PaineWebber Building, a 20-story modern brick office building at 265 Franklin Street. Three separate downtown offices were consolidated on five floors of the new structure. The Boston operation remains the company's flagship office. Working among this cadre is the founder's son, Stephen Paine, who at the age of 90 still brokers for his clients.

The Boston office of PaineWebber contributes to the United Way, several religious charities, and the New England Aquarium's Harbor Clean-Up Fund. The F. Ward Paine Foundation, founded in 1942, gives financial aid to those PaineWebber employees and their dependents who have suffered misfortune. Each year the foundation awards moneys to the City of Boston to distribute to families in need.

BEAR, STEARNS & CO. INC.

In a spare moment, when not doing business with high-net-worth clients around New England, stockbrokers at Bear, Stearns & Co. Inc. can take in a panoramic view of Boston from their offices high up in the city's financial district. There, on two skyscraper floors of One Federal Street, more than $15 million per year is paid out in salaries to top investment industry talent who together in 1987 produced $40 million in office revenues. "We're building a firm based on reputation, relationships, and opportunities. We are not a sales office," states senior managing director Keith Kretschmer.

Bear Stearns first made a name for itself in New England during the late

Bear Stearns brokers at work.

1950s, when it pioneered common stock block trading with its institutional clients in Boston. By the 1970s growth in institutional business had increased dramatically and necessitated opening a Boston office of this New York-based investment bank. At that time managing director Thomas Hughes was brought on to head up the Institutional Fixed Income Department, whose trading volume today exceeds $100 billion, much of this for money management firms and mutual fund companies such as Fidelity and Putman, and for major New England banks and insurance companies such as Shawmut and John Hancock. "What we strive for in continuing our success," says Institutional Equity Department associate director Robert Littlehale, "is a constant flow of investment ideas and research recommendations that work for our clients."

In a time when not only institutions but also corporations, governments, municipalities, and individual investors have come to depend on an investment bank's ability to seize opportunities in the market and, in doing so, offer investments that suit their particular needs, Bear Stearns Boston has expanded its business into institutional debt trading and sales, public finance, municipal bond market-making, corporate finance services, and individual investor brokerage services.

Notably, an innovative lease/pur-

chase program for state and local governments put a national spotlight on associate director Anita Molino and the firm's Public Finance Department. Some years back Molino found that governments were acquiring vast amounts of equipment through leasing arrangements. At Bear Stearns, she came up with a way to refinance these leases as a package, selling certificates of participation on the bond market. One program participant, the State of New York, saved millions with such financing.

Under the leadership of associate director Thomas Shields, the Corporate Finance Department provides a wide variety of investment banking services to New England-based businesses, such as securities underwriting, financial advisory for mergers and acquisitions, and leveraged buyouts. Bear Stearns Boston has played an integral role in the development of its major clients. For example, in providing financial advisory on 15 transactions totaling in excess of one billion dollars for Home Owners Federal Savings & Loan Association, Bear Stearns Boston assisted Home Owners in growing from assets of $450 million to assets of $3 billion since 1984.

As for Bear, Stearns & Co. Inc. Boston's future, managing director Howel Evans asserts: "Our goal is to be the most innovative investment banking firm in New England."

EXCLUSIVE TEMPORARIES, INC.

In a small 950-square-foot office at 10 Post Office Square, four full-time employees work to keep 200 others working. From this downtown office and two suburban locations along Route 128 in Framingham and Burlington, Exclusive Temporaries puts individuals in touch with Boston employers who have a need for some extra hands. The New England, Digital Equipment Corporation, Blue Cross-Blue Shield, and Polaroid are just some of the big companies in the area that are using temporaries extensively.

Earl Tate, executive vice-president.

While the increasing use of temporaries in the business community has been well documented, the rapid growth of Exclusive Temporaries, a private, nonfranchise, minority-owned company, shows just how popular temporary employment has become for employers and employees.

It was in 1979 in New Orleans that Bobby D. Higginbotham, senior vice-president in charge of personnel and resources at the Hibernia National Bank, took a long look at the large bill from a temporary agency the bank had contracted with over a two-week period. He began to track the number of temporaries the bank hired in a month and was again surprised. Looking around at other businesses, he found it was not unusual for large corporations to budget a half-million dollars for temporary help.

Two months later Higginbotham left the bank and opened his own temporary service in New Orleans. The office grossed nearly $200,000 in the first year. Higginbotham, however, wanted to go national, and soon he had formed a partnership with Leonard Jenkins, Jr., the man who had coincidently succeeded him at the bank, and Jenkins went to Atlanta to open an office. Other offices in Houston and Dallas came next.

In 1983 Higginbotham contacted Earl Tate, a friend from Southern University in Baton Rouge, Louisiana. He needed someone to open an office in thriving Boston. Today Exclusive Temporaries has a total of 14 offices in eight states, primarily in the South. Another eight offices are planned to expand the firm's presence on the East and West coasts. The company believes it is the largest minority-owned temporary service in the country.

Under Tate's leadership, the busy Boston office grossed more than one million dollars in its first year of operation and then doubled that figure in 1986 and 1987. Tate currently has more than 150 clients in the greater Boston area with repeat business of 91 percent. A majority of Exclusive Temporaries' workers are clerical, but the company also fills light industrial and some technical positions. At one time Digital Equipment Corporation had more than 190 Exclusive Temporaries employees working for almost a year as assembly workers. The Digital contract was a turning point in the growth of Exclusive Temporaries in Boston, according to Tate.

Exclusive Temporaries hires individuals of all ages, and its present work force ranges in age from 18 to 72. While the company is minority owned, 64 percent of its work force is nonminority and covers a diverse cross section of the population. According to Tate, the typical Exclusive Temporary worker in Boston is a female between the ages of 23 and 40. She is a former housewife with three years of college who wants to take a look at different career opportunities and work environments before going back to work full time. During an average week Exclusive Temporaries finds work assignments for between 20 and 50 temps.

Tate believes the firm's success in Boston is a direct result of its policies that are aimed at ensuring good performance by its temps. Outside of a little radio advertising, the company

Denise Carino, operations manager, and Earl Tate.

Forrest Ward, sales manager; Denise Carino, operations manager; Earl Tate, executive vice-president; Terry Winston, marketing representative; and Kenneth Smith, placement manager. (Not pictured: Billie Brown, marketing representative, and Sonia Satchell, receptionist.)

forgoes mass-media advertising, and instead recruits its work force from referrals and recruiting trips to technical and other schools. Each new employee is given an orientation that includes a battery of tests in general and technical skills, including grammar, composition, spelling, word processing, mathematics, ten-key, and warehouse inventory. The organization also asks for two business references as well as one character reference, completing the background check with follow-up calls. Once an employee is on the job, Exclusive Temporaries unit managers call the client to ascertain that the temp's supervisor is satisfied. The company promises to respond to any placement problem within an hour, and dissatisfied clients don't pay.

While Exclusive Temporaries goes to extra lengths to make sure employers are happy with their workers, the firm also helps train individuals to move into more productive, more rewarding work—a politically popular endeavor in Boston today. In addition to periodic in-house training sessions on topics such as business etiquette and grooming, the company contracts with outside organizations to train temps in word processing. Every four to six weeks the Freedom House in Roxbury trains 10 general secretaries in word processing for Exclusive Temporaries. In addition, the firm plans to set up an in-house facility to train 10 to 30 people a month. The company also plans to train between 10 and 20 general clerks to type every six weeks.

Although it is growing more popular, the business of placing temporaries is also becoming more competitive. This situation promises to benefit individual workers all the more. To keep their good workers, Exclusive Temporaries offers free vacations to Hawaii and other exotic destinations as a bonus. The longer an individual works for the company, the more benefits he or she receives. After six months of work, a temporary receives one week's paid vacation. After one year Exclusive Temporaries pays 50 percent of the employee's health insurance. After 18 months an Exclusive temp can take the 11 federal holidays off with pay. The robust demand for reliable temporary workers has even led the company to offer cash bonuses to temps who persuade their friends and acquaintances to work as temps for 80 hours.

TOFIAS, FLEISHMAN, SHAPIRO & CO., P.C.

It is not surprising to find a busy accounting firm of more than 150 CPAs and other professionals at the heart of newly fashionable Kendall Square in Cambridge. Neighbor to the Massachusetts Institute of Technology, this area has seen an explosion of new office space that now serves as home to high-technology businesses and the services they have, in turn, attracted to the area.

At 205 Broadway, the offices of Tofias, Fleishman, Shapiro & Co., P.C., have a rather high-technology look about them, too. This firm is located in a 38,000-square-foot, single-story brick building with bright, white casement windows. Like many businesses that surround it, TFS has only been at the location since 1986.

The history of the firm actually goes back to 1925, when the first of the three professional firms that would ultimately merge and become TFS was founded in Boston. In 1980 the firm was still small, with fewer than 50 em-

The offices of Tofias, Fleishman, Shapiro & Co., P.C., are located in the booming high-technology area of Cambridge, Massachusetts, and the revitalized port area of Portland, Maine.

ployees. That year, however, the operation moved to more upscale and roomy office space on the busy thoroughfare of Soldiers Field Road. The growth since that time has been dramatic, as the firm has expanded, both geographically and service-wise. An office in Portland, Maine, assists clients who, like TFS, are doing business across New England. As part of an industrywide trend, TFS has diversified its services so it can assist clients in a multitude of areas that impact their financial situations.

Most TFS clients are closely held businesses with sales volume ranging from fewer than one million dollars to in excess of $50 million. While the company has grown substantially and is large enough to employ legal, tax, computer, human resource, and other specialists, it is still small enough, corporate officials say, to maintain the kind of close personal attention that results in long-term relationships with clients.

TFS is member of the SEC practice section and the private companies practice section of the American Institute of CPAs. That means TFS has sub-

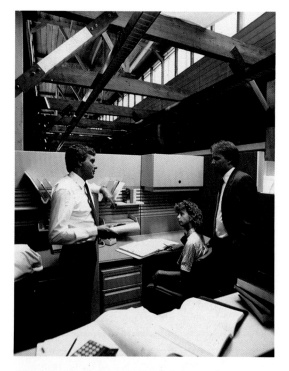

TFS, as one of the New England's largest and fastest growing accounting and management services firms, is a contemporary firm with a reputation for service.

jected its practice to a peer review performed by specially trained CPAs from other firms. These reviews have always resulted in an "unqualified opinion," which means TFS has met the highest professional standards.

Since 1974 TFS has been a member of the National CPA Group (NCPAG), a national and international association of established and respected independent CPA firms and chartered accountants. As a member of this group, the firm maintains its autonomy but can also provide reliable expertise nationally and internationally for those clients whose operations and interests extend beyond the firm's immediate geographic area. Membership also provides access to resources only available to international accounting firms. Member firms are selected by their peers in the NCPAG on the basis of reputation, clientele, performance, and professionalism. Each member firm is reviewed periodically to ensure that its practice is being conducted according to NCPAG's standards.

TFS hires business graduates at the top of their class, individuals with

advanced degrees, and many with experience in working for national firms. TFS encourages its employees to seek advanced degrees with the help of a tuition reimbursement plan and supplements their educations with in-house training programs. TFS believes a critical factor in its success is the fact that it is locally owned. This instills in its employees a greater sense of pride in their work.

Approximately 50 percent of the work of TFS remains in the traditional auditing and accounting area. In producing financial statements for clients, TFS analyzes and projects future budget and financing needs. TFS's long history of quality performance in auditing is well known in the Boston financial community. With today's new and more complex tax laws, the services provided by the Tax Department of TFS have become even more important. The department works with clients to reduce their future potential tax liabilities. And, as another service TFS will evaluate its clients' computer systems and suggest methods for more efficient management using today's technology.

In addition, TFS has moved into other specialty areas. Many problems identified through periodic financial or

Knowledge in all areas of business management distinguishes TFS and allows for a comprehensive approach for meeting its clients' needs.

The quality of its staff is the greatest selling point TFS has in obtaining and keeping satisfied clients.

tax review can be referred to these other TFS specialists for consultation on a fee basis. For real estate investors, developers, syndicators, builders, property managers, and brokers, TFS real estate services track market conditions and pinpoint opportunities for acquisition and development.

One of its newest services is consultation on human resource problems. TFS has helped clients to attract, hire, and retain key executives; to structure compensation and benefit packages; to set up training programs; and to comply with the modern maze of personnel policies, many of which are now legally mandated. In a related area, TFS consults on issues surrounding employment benefits. TFS consultants advise both individuals and businesses on the design and implementation of the proper retirement plan. They can also assist in the maintenance of the plan on an ongoing basis.

TFS is also involved in personal financial planning, including income tax analysis, estate planning, sheltering income, investing for growth, and planning for college funds or retirement.

TFS tailors a financial plan for each individual and then follows through with stockbrokers, attorneys, and insurance agents to make sure decisions are implemented.

Through a rather unique department, TFS can help clients to document losses of all kinds—fidelity, surety, business interruption—to speed the processing of claims. The Litigation Services Department specialists, who are often CPAs as well as members of the bar, work with attorneys to provide investigative accounting, analysis of financial reports, and loss statements.

Other management advisory services are available through Tofias, Fleishman, Shapiro & Co., P.C. Specialists will consult with management about its analysis, organizing, operating, or controlling functions. They can also help choose the most appropriate business structure, and help find additional financing and suggest possible mergers and acquisitions.

THE BOSTON COMPANY

One Boston Place, The Boston Company's headquarters, rises majestically behind the Old State House building in Boston's financial district.

was the first such charter in the Commonwealth. Under the charter, the firm was granted safe deposit privileges only, to do no more than trust services, receiving "on deposit for safekeeping" money, securities, jewelry, and similar items of value. The depression following the Civil War delayed the company's beginning, but in June 1875 the bank opened its doors with a staff of eight.

As its reputation grew, many of Boston's most prominent and influential families came to rely on the firm's skill and prudence to safeguard their fortunes. Within 25 years Boston Safe Deposit and Trust Company had become the largest trust company in New England. In 1964 The Boston Company, Inc., was formed to be the parent company for Boston Safe Deposit and Trust Company. This change provided the legal means for expansion into other geographical markets as well as other services such as real estate investments and mutual funds.

As a limited-service bank Boston Safe Deposit and Trust Company can take deposits and make consumer

The individual financial needs of The Boston Company's "Privileged Clients" are catered to in the private banking offices at One Boston Place.

While the traditions of The Boston Company reach back more than 100 years, a dynamic new era began in 1981 when the company was acquired by Shearson Lehman Hutton Inc., which is a subsidiary of the American Express Company. In Boston, the firm is most visible through its subsidiary, Boston Safe Deposit and Trust Company, an organization that preceded its parent.

Today The Boston Company can be found at One Boston Place, often called "The Boston Company building," and in the nearby Exchange Place office tower, the Park Square building, the Riverview Business Park in Malden, Massachusetts, and the Wel-lington Business Center in Medford, Massachusetts. The Boston Company is also well known to magazine readers through its recent "Privileged Client" ad campaign in magazines such as The New Yorker, Forbes, and Town and Country.

The Boston Safe Deposit and Trust Company officially began in 1867, when the Massachusetts legislature passed a bill "to incorporate Boston Safe Deposit and Trust Company." It

loans. Many of its customers are wealthy individuals with annual net incomes in excess of $250,000. Since the acquisition by Shearson, Boston Safe has become one of the nation's fastest-growing banks with deposits increasing eighteenfold between 1981 and 1986. In 1986 mortgage and personal loans grew by 132 percent. In 1988 *Forbes* magazine called Boston Safe, "the nation's fastest-growing lender to the rich and near-rich." In 1988 *American Banker* rated Boston Safe as the 20th-largest bank in the country in terms of total deposits. Company officials attribute The Boston Company's success to its ability to focus on providing products in only three markets: individual financial services, institutional fund management, and mutual fund administration.

Organizationally, The Boston Company is divided into seven groups. The Individual Client Group provides financial services to wealthy individuals, including asset management, mortgages, personal loans, deposits, and trust services. The Institutional Markets Group offers a wide range of financial products and services for tax-exempt pension plans of the nation's largest institutional clients and endowments. Primary services include master trust and custody of assets, defined contribution services, active and passive investment management, and real estate investments. In 1986 The Boston Company was chosen as custodian for the more than $40-billion California Public Employees Retirement Fund, the largest retirement fund in the country.

The firm's Mutual Funds Group provides advisory, administrative, custodial, and transfer agent services to registered investment companies. Through The Boston Company Advisors, Inc., the group offers a family of funds under The Boston Company name. The Mutual Funds Group also provides automated investment and account-processing capabilities to many banks nationwide.

The Treasury Group provides investment services and pursues funding opportunities in the global capital

markets. Treasury manages Boston Safe Deposit and Trust Company's balance sheet and offers a broad range of investment-related services to institutional clients. These services include cash management, foreign exchange, economic research, and discount brokerage through Boston Institutional Services, Inc. The Financial Management Group is responsible for the financial, accounting, audit, and controllership activities of the firm and its subsidiaries, as well as the company's banking activities in the United Kingdom.

Two other corporate groups are the company's backbone. The Corporate Operations Group oversees all data-processing, custody, and banking operations. The firm's computer facilities run around the clock. The Corporate Administration Group manages all the legal, marketing, personnel, facilities, finance, and audit duties for the company.

Through its principal subsidiary, Boston Safe, The Boston Company has

Managers within The Boston Company's Institutional Markets Group exercise their professional judgment and market expertise to effectively serve institutional clients throughout the world.

The Boston Company has become a recognized leader in investment technology, and maintains state-of-the-art equipment, extensive data bases, and corresponding software systems.

long been involved with philanthropy. In 1917 it organized the Permanent Charities Fund of Boston, now the Boston Foundation. Among the recipients of corporate grants are Saturday-morning free admission at the Museum of Fine Arts, the Freedom Trail, and Boston's public television station, WBGH-TV.

THE FORUM CORPORATION

A large, international airline experienced one of its worst years on record and was forced to lay off tens of thousands of employees, immediately affecting daily operations and employee morale.

A large, industrial equipment company was losing customers to cut-throat foreign competition. The chief executive officer determined that a total reorientation of the company's sales efforts was required, but there was tremendous resistance on the part of most players, who viewed the change as a threat.

Instances of major companies facing enormous human resource challenges are not hard to find in daily newspapers. Surviving in a business environment made chaotic by increasing competition, rapid technological developments, and a changing work force is the popular theme of recent books, magazine articles, and even movies. How do you mobilize thousands of employees to make necessary changes?

The Forum Corporation thinks it knows how. In fact, Forum has proved it in 20 years of consulting for *Fortune* 1,000 companies. Working with top management and human resources departments, Forum first helps companies get to the source of their problems, and then, armed with this knowledge, Forum creates a customized program of action. Special areas of expertise are in helping businesses create customer focus, fostering innovation, increasing sales productivity, improving leadership and managerial effectiveness, and shaping corporate culture.

In the airline's case, for example, the client experienced the best summer in its history only 18 months after its poor performance period. With the help of customer focus and leadership projects designed with Forum, it smoothly handled a 15-percent increase in customer traffic with no staff increase. Unsolicited positive comments increased by 35 percent, and complaints decreased by 25 percent. At the equipment company, sales training and a new reward system helped to foster a new set of skills and incentives for the sales force and resulted in a 12-percent increase in

John W. Humphrey, chairman and chief executive officer, in the lobby of One Exchange Place, the headquarters of The Forum Corporation in Boston. Photo by Lou Jones

sales after six months.

Chairman John Humphrey, who is widely known as "the manager's manager," founded The Forum Corporation with four partners in 1971. Eleven years later Forum had grown fast enough to make *Inc.* magazine's annual list of fastest-growing companies. Forum is known among its clients for the extremely high quality of its programs and services, the professionalism of its nearly 300 people, and the substantive research it conducts into how to create competitive advantage through people.

Typically a Forum account executive serves as the liaison between the client organization and the Forum staff of design and program specialists, customer service representatives, instructors, consultants, researchers, writers, and editors. The Forum Corporation has offices in Boston's Exchange Place and in 10 other cities worldwide.

Photo © Gene Peach

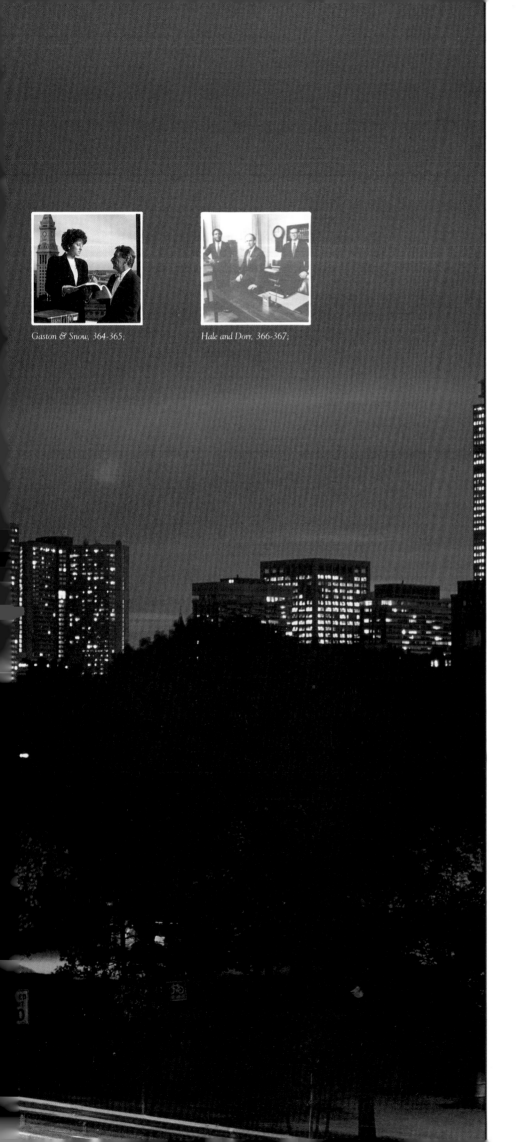

Gaston & Snow, 364-365;

Hale and Dorr, 366-367;

CHAPTER SIXTEEN

Professions

Greater Boston's professional community brings a wealth of service, ability, and insight to the area.

Photo © Paul Corkum

349

PALMER & DODGE

On four floors of historic Beacon Hill's only high rise, One Beacon Street, lawyers at Palmer & Dodge handle complex legal matters, something the firm has done for more than 100 years. The firm contains one of the largest litigation departments in New England—approximately one-third of its 150 lawyers are trial lawyers—and includes a thriving business law department that has more than doubled in size over the past five years.

Although Palmer & Dodge is organized into seven departments—litigation, real estate, tax, public law, probate, labor, and business law—clients are also served by interdepartmental teams in areas such as environmental law, higher education, publishing and entertainment, health care, public finance, international law, and government relations and public affairs. Palmer & Dodge has been nationally prominent in the financing of state and local governments for nearly all of its 100 years.

Founded by Storey, Thorndike & Hoar in 1887, the firm has taken on

A cross section of lawyers within the firm includes (from left) Neil P. Arkuss, Tax Department; John Taylor Williams, Business Law Department; Cathy M. Judd-Stein, Real Estate Department; Marie-Armide L. Ellis, Public Law Department; and John G. Casagrande, Jr., Real Estate Department.

the names of various senior partners, including those of Palmer & Dodge, whose names replaced those of the original founders in 1931. At one time the firm's name expanded to include five partners, one of whom was Robert F. Bradford, a governor of Massachusetts. The firm broke with legal tradition and is now called Palmer & Dodge.

Today the firm is known for its diverse and high-profile clientele. Litigation clients, for example, include *Fortune* 500 companies, high-tech growth companies, state agencies, municipal governments, colleges and uni-

versities, closely held corporations, public utilities, insurers, hospitals, architects, engineers, and a host of medium and small corporations, both publicly and privately held. The firm also has a long history of serving as general counsel to schools and colleges. Among its clients in this area is the Massachusetts Institute of Technology.

The large litigation department at Palmer & Dodge is best known for its First Amendment, products-liability, and insurance-rate work. Trial attorneys and legal assistants are supported by a network of microcomputers, which are used to electronically file, manage, and retrieve documents and transcripts of testimony.

The expanding business law department represents a full range of clients from closely held private enterprises to companies listed on the New York Stock Exchange. The firm's high-tech group works with emerging companies such as Genzyme Corporation and Galileo Electro-Optics Corporation, and providers of venture capital such as the Massachusetts Technology Development Corporation and Zero Stage Capital Company. The private business group handles the concerns of more traditional closely held businesses. The energy group lawyers represent such clients as the Tampa Electric Company and Colonial Gas, while the banking lawyers serve many of the major banking institutions in the state. In the firm's publishing and entertainment group, lawyers represent publishers, production companies, lenders, and broadcasters as well as individual creators.

The managing partner meets with members of the Executive Committee (from left) Scott P. Lewis, Litigation Department; Jackson W. Wright, Jr., Probate Department; James W. Perkins, Public Law Department (center seated); Ronald H. Kessel, Business Law Department; and Jeffrey Swope, Litigation Department.

Partners of the Litigation Department photographed in the Massachusetts Supreme Judicial courtroom (from left): Laurie S. Gill, Francis C. Lynch, and Michael J. Lacek.

In its environmental practice, Palmer & Dodge advises those seeking to protect the environment as well as those parties who are subject to compliance rules. The firm participated in the organization of the Massachusetts Water Resources Authority and has assisted other public bodies in drafting and implementing environmental cleanup legislation. The firm is assisting the Commonwealth of Puerto Rico in structuring and financing its cleanup efforts and in responding to EPA enforcement initiatives.

The firm's international group represents domestic companies and individual businessmen in investment and operations activity abroad. It also represents foreign companies entering or operating in the U.S. market. Among its clients in this area are banks and financial institutions and corporations doing business in a variety of technologies, including computer software, telecommunications, and genetic engineering.

The government relations and public affairs group offers a full range of legal and professional services to clients on legislative, regulatory, community and public affairs issues at all levels of government. Through its frequent involvement in and monitoring of governmental activity and its practical knowledge of public policy-making processes, the group can help clients incorporate governmental and regulatory factors into their business strategies. In addition, the group can also assist

clients in their efforts to participate in the processes of government in connection with legislation, regulations, on a specific transaction.

Real estate lawyers advise clients on all aspects of commercial real estate transactions, from acquisitions and financing through construction, development, and management. The firm has acted as real estate counsel on such developments as the proposed Pier 4 project on the South Boston waterfront, the Unicorn Park office development in Wobum, and other projects ranging from waterfront condominiums to a downtown hotel and retail complex. Palmer & Dodge also represents investors, architects, contractors, and real estate lenders, including New England's largest construction lender, and services the real estate needs of the firm's business clients.

While the firm recruits first-year associates from national law schools and judicial clerkships, it has also been aggressive in welcoming lawyers from other firms, often from other major Boston firms. An early example was the addition of Robert G. Dodge, who brought his preeminent advocacy skills to the firm as partner in 1910. More recent additions include Robert W. Meserve, former president of the American Bar Association, who joined Palmer & Dodge as a litigation partner in 1978. Since that year a total of 18 lawyers from other law firms, businesses, and government have joined the firm as partners.

No doubt the progressive working environment at Palmer & Dodge plays a role in attracting talent. Recognizing that there are now many dual-career couples, part-time positions and parental leaves are made available to both male and female partners and associates seeking flexible work arrangements in order to raise their children. The firm also helps associates and staff to finance dependent-care expense with pretax salary deductions. It is one of Boston's only major firms with a sabbatical-leave program for partners. The firm also seeks to hire minority staff at all levels.

Palmer & Dodge has constantly

demonstrated a commitment to the community, not just of Boston, but in the larger sense. Moorfield Storey, a founder of the firm, served as president of the NAACP for 19 years before that organization's transition to black leadership. In contemporary times Palmer & Dodge lawyers continue to have a substantial involvement in pro bono activities, contributing especially to civil rights and civil liberties law-reform efforts. The firm lends three attorneys each year for four-month stints as full-time staff lawyers to the Greater Boston Elderly Legal Services and also provides staff rotation at other governmental and nonprofit agencies when their

Two members of the Labor and Employment Law Department (from left): Henry G. Stewart, partner, and Judith A. Malone, senior associate.

needs fit the aspirations and qualifications of individual attorneys at Palmer & Dodge.

Palmer & Dodge is looking forward to meeting the challenges of the coming years by continuing to grow and adapt its capabilities to the changing business environment, while maintaining its tradition of excellence and its commitment to service to the community.

BURNS & LEVINSON

One of the city's most experienced trial lawyers, Thomas D. Burns on February 1, 1960, was a co-founder with Lawrence M. Levinson, a noted business lawyer, of Boston's fastest-growing firm. Specializing in civil litigation, corporate, business, real estate, family, environmental, and health law, the firm's major clients are banks, insurance companies, real estate entrepreneurs, hospitals, large and small businesses—publicly and privately held.

What has become a firm of more than 100 lawyers 28 years later started as a partnership between Burns and Levinson, two lawyers with complementary experience. A native of Andover, Massachusetts, Burns earned his law degree at Boston University Law School. A graduate of Harvard Law School, Levinson had come to Boston from Atlanta. Both had seen combat in World War II; Levinson, as a major in the Army, Burns, as a Navy lieutenant. Burns handled litigation and Levinson, after a clerkship with a federal judge, served clients in business

matters. Two secretaries formed the support staff. Mrs. Levinson kept what books the firm had.

Two additional lawyers joined the new firm at its inception. Robert Weinstein founded and developed the real estate department, and a trial lawyer, William Clancy, joined Burns in the courts. It was a division of labor that continues in the firm today.

The business section, headed by Levinson, includes the real estate, corporate, tax, estates and trusts, finance, and labor law departments. The real estate group, headed by Weinstein, counsels developers of industrial parks, large commercial and residential properties, and handles low- and moderate-income housing projects. Lawyers specializing in securities, mergers, and acquisitions advise and guide the firm's clients under the leadership of Samuel P. Sears, Jr. Howard D. Medwed heads the sophisticated and

The lawyers of Burns & Levinson.

growing tax department. Steven C. Goodwin heads the estate and trust department with its trust and estate lawyers, investment managers, and trust accounting staff. Norman C. Spector heads the finance division in the representation of many of the leading area banks as well as borrowers. The business litigation department under the leadership of James F. Kavanaugh, Jr., operates closely with the business section with a view to continuous cross-fertilization of ideas and attainment of business-oriented litigation results.

The trial department has 14 partners and 40 associates and is divided into general and business litigation representing corporate and individual clients, railroads, insurance companies, and other law firms. Business matters include antitrust, stockholders' suits, and product liability cases. While Burns & Levinson is still half the size of the city's largest firm, it enjoys one of the largest presences in the state and federal courts. The firm is a leader in the field of litigation involving toxic and hazardous substances, and has

a toxic tort department of 13 lawyers, and has represented clients in more than 4,000 cases. The head of the toxic tort department is Lawrence G. Cetrulo, who serves as liaison counsel in the Massachusetts and federal courts for all asbestos litigation. George M. Ford has established at the firm one of the largest family law departments among the city's law firms.

The chairman of the management committee is 44-year-old Samuel P. Sears, Jr. He is assisted by a non-lawyer chief operating officer, Mitchell Adams, a Harvard Business School

Department heads at Burns & Levinson. Front row (from left): George M. Ford, family law; Lawrence M. Levinson, corporate and business; Thomas D. Burns, general litigation; and Robert W. Weinstein, real estate. In the rear (from left): Lawrence G. Cetrulo, toxic torts; Howard D. Medwed, tax; Steven C. Goodwin, probate; James F. Kavanaugh, Jr., business litigation.

graduate.

Burns & Levinson is heavily engaged in pro bono appointments from both the state and federal courts, and encourages its people to be active in bar

association work and community organizations.

The firm operates on a well-cultivated philosophy—give as much encouragement and responsibility as possible to young lawyers in developing their own contacts, individual skills, and practice. This philosophy has resulted in the firm's rapid growth from four lawyers to a major firm in one generation.

Burns & Levinson looks forward to its continued growth into the next century as a leader in the Boston legal community.

HUTCHINS & WHEELER

When the Boston Beer Company, brewer of Samuel Adams Boston Lager™ and Boston Lightship™ beers, decided to construct its own brewery, its officials went downtown to tell the news to its lawyers at Hutchins & Wheeler, an old-line law firm with a modern clientele. In 1987 Hutchins & Wheeler represented the company in connection with the venture-capital equity financing and industrial revenue bond financing that will enable the company to construct a brewery in the Jamaica Plain section of the city.

As the economy of greater Boston has grown and diversified, Hutchins & Wheeler's practice has reached out into emerging growth areas. The firm now represents a variety of entrepreneurs and established major companies in the computer, electronics, biotechnology, and health care fields. The growing needs of such a diversified clientele has required the firm to significantly expand its size in recent years. Its projections call for the addition of 40 lawyers to its 1987 staff of 65 attorneys over the next few years. The strong New England economy promises to send more companies such as the Boston Beer Company to firms that specialize in emerging and growth businesses.

In addition, Boston's investment banking and venture capital community has for many years turned to Hutchins & Wheeler for advice in connection with the many corporate financings that originate in Boston.

Hutchins & Wheeler is a general practice firm that has been continuously engaged in the practice of law under the same name since 1844. While work on behalf of corporate entities, generally called business law, now accounts for the majority of its workload, the firm also maintains its traditional practice areas in tax, real estate, and trust and estate law.

Like many of the established firms in Boston, Hutchins & Wheeler began as a firm that specialized in the trust services required by the mercantile and shipping families who dominated New England's economy prior to the Civil War. At that time lawyers were often called upon to take custody of the family savings. Twenty-five years ago, however, the firm made the decision to expand into the modern business economy. Its practice now includes corporate, securities, and banking law; tax and employee benefits law; personal tax planning; estate and trust planning and administration; foundation and not-for-profit corporation law; health-care law; litigation; creditors' rights; municipal and government law; and real estate law.

The firm has a diversity of clients and is not dependent upon any single client for a major portion of its work. Most of the partners and associates specialize in one or more areas of the firm's practice. To exchange knowledge, facilitate associate training, and manage their collective workload, lawyers in each major specialty area work together through the firm's four major departments: business, trusts and estates, litigation, and real estate. Flexible practice

Hutchins & Wheeler attorneys at Unitrode Corporation's facilities.

groups also exist to include partners and associates who have concentrated in a particular field of law. These groups and departments combine efforts to solve problems that involve issues from diverse fields of law such as the business, estate planning, creditors' rights, and tax issues inherent in the transfer of control of a privately held business from one generation to the next.

Hutchins & Wheeler clients vary from start-up companies to those whose securities are traded on national exchanges and also include numerous banks, venture-capital and leveraged buy-out sponsors, and other financial institutions. Transactions are handled by the firm nationwide and abroad.

Throughout its history the firm has been engaged as general and special counsel to New England hospitals and health care professionals. Today the firm also assists medical corporations, health care management companies, hospices, home health agencies, and rehabilitation and social service agencies. The firm also represents Massachusetts municipalities on a regular basis and various state and local boards on an appointive basis.

The firm's real estate practice encompasses the needs of real estate developers, syndicators, contractors, brokers, architects, and banks, and of those whose need for real estate law are occasional, such as corporate clients seeking new space. Representation of not-for-profit clients, including grant-making foundations, mirror business client needs for advice in planning, organization, reorganization, merger, and dissolution.

In the estate practice, Hutchins & Wheeler serves as fiduciary for more

Hutchins & Wheeler's new quarters under construction at 101 Federal Street.

than 300 private trusts and continues its long-standing practice of providing comprehensive estate planning advice. For those clients such as hospitals, which require immediate access to attorneys at all times, the firm offers access to its lawyers 24 hours a day, in the belief that an early preventive call for legal advice can often minimize the subsequent need for more expensive services.

With new offices at 101 Federal Street, Hutchins & Wheeler is prepared for a period of continued growth to meet the needs of its clients. By echoing its clients' entrepreneurial approach, the firm will be prepared to serve the growth areas in the New England economy in the coming years.

SHAPIRO, ISRAEL & WEINER

Shapiro, Israel & Weiner, P.C., a professional legal corporation, is an integral part of the Boston area's recent unprecedented commercial growth. This rapid expansion has presented new legal problems for the region's businesses and industries, and Shapiro, Israel & Weiner continues to be committed to finding creative and effective solutions to these problems.

Founded in 1969 by two Boston University instructors, the firm has grown gradually in order to offer personalized service often unavailable in larger law firms. Today Shapiro, Israel & Weiner, with 14 lawyers licensed in the states of Massachusetts, Rhode Island, Connecticut, New York, Virginia, and Missouri, and a staff exceeding 30, represents major corporations, financial institutions, and real estate developers in Boston, New England, and throughout the United States.

"What distinguishes us from other law firms in the Boston area is our people-oriented approach," says founding partner Edward A. Shapiro. "As professionals, we care about our clients. We are counselors and advocates in the true sense of those words."

Long known for its ability in corporate law, the firm has built a strong reputation in such specialized areas as business formation, acquisition, and reorganization. Tax planning, corporate financing, and real property law are also areas in which the firm is committed.

Carl B. Israel, the co-founding and managing partner, is an honors graduate of Boston University School of Law. His expertise lies in the areas of corporate acquisitions, buy-outs, minority stockholder rights, and partnership divorces. In addition, he has an extensive commercial real estate practice. Edward A. Shapiro received a Master of Jurisprudence from Boston University Graduate School of Tax after obtaining his Juris Doctorate Degree from Boston University School of Law. Shapiro's expertise also concentrates on international and domestic corporate areas of practice with a heavy emphasis on the legal aspects involved in corporate transactions of closely held companies.

The firm has a strong reputation as business litigators. The litigation department is headed by Barry Y. Weiner, another graduate of Boston University School of Law, who joined the firm in the early 1970s. A noted litigator, Weiner has specialties in the areas of corporate securities, real estate, municipal law, construction, personal injury, and probate. He has litigated in state and federal courts throughout the northeast.

The firm's expertise in zoning and land use is well known throughout Massachusetts, where centuries of complex cases, statutes, and land-use restrictions have made this legal field particularly complex. The firm's specialist in zoning and land use, William E. Ryckman, Jr., served as principal draftsman for the 1975 Comprehensive Revi-

The firm's team approach and personal commitment to its clients' business matters is a key factor to Shapiro, Israel & Weiner's success story. The partners (from left to right) are Joel B. Rosenthal, Barry Y. Weiner, Edward A. Shapiro, and Carl B. Israel.

sion of Massachusetts General Laws Chapter 40A (The Zoning Act). A professor of law at Boston University since 1962, Ryckman has performed comprehensive reviews of zoning ordinances for numerous cities and towns, including Cambridge, Brookline, Lynn, Medford, and Sandwich.

As Shapiro, Israel & Weiner has grown and expanded, it has taken on new partners to meet the specialized needs of its clients. Joel B. Rosenthal is a recognized expert in the areas of corporate finance reorganization, and

Left: The firm's commitment to full-service representation provides the opportunity for Carl B. Israel and Edward A. Shapiro to consult on leading-edge technology with Eli M. Zukovsky, vice-president of Engineering for CAPE Systems, a corporation specializing in computer-aided production engineering systems.

Below left: Shapiro, Israel & Weiner's experience in corporate acquisitions and international trade brings Barry Y. Weiner to Fishery Products, Inc., to discuss the merger of Canadian and Alaskan fish-processing plants with its president, Donald Short.

Above: The firm's extensive commercial real estate practice often brings Joel B. Rosenthal and Edward A. Shapiro to a hands-on construction site with developer Fred J. Greatorex of W&G Development Corporation.

loan workouts. He counsels banks and other financial institutions on structuring of complex financing transactions including leveraged buyouts and real estate transactions. An honors graduate of the National Law Center of the George Washington University, Rosenthal has served as a Special Assistant Attorney General for the Commonwealth of Massachusetts in various bankruptcy proceedings, and has represented major creditors, both secured and unsecured, in many of the region's significant bankruptcy cases.

The attorneys at Shapiro, Israel & Weiner believe in certain common tenets for success: a proactive rather than reactive stance to business issues and problems, and a commitment to results. Whether the client is a major corporation or a small, local business, the firm always provides full service, from initial case research to closing, settlement, or trial.

"When a client retains us, they are retaining our entire firm, not just a single attorney within the office," says Israel. "Our team approach allows the input of valuable knowledge from several related perspectives."

Over the years the firm's involvement with local business has carried over to many important community projects. The partners serve on the boards of several health, educational, and philanthropic institutions and provide pro bono legal services for a number of Boston charitable foundations and civic organizations. In addition, they serve in leadership roles in bar as-

sociations and for state and national political parties and candidates.

Shapiro, Israel & Weiner, strongly committed to the city of Boston, is located at 100 North Washington Street in a nineteenth-century structure owned by the firm in limited partnership with three other professional firms. In 1985 the firm considered moving outside Boston but chose to remain downtown and renovate a building in Boston's historic North End, with a modern addition. Weiner emphasizes, "We want to continue to be a part of Boston's prospering industry and help enhance the city's position as the hub of this region."

BRIGGS ASSOCIATES INC.
CONSULTING ENGINEERS

Winston C. Perry (left), chief executive officer, and David S. Campbell, president and treasurer, purchased Briggs Associates in 1983 and reorganized it into the multimillion-dollar consulting engineering corporation of today.

Briggs Associates is a professional consulting engineering firm headquartered in Rockland, Massachusetts, with five offices throughout New England, as well as offices in Columbia, Maryland, and Orlando, Florida. The company provides developers, construction companies, real estate investors, lending institutions, and building owners with the multiple types of engineering investigations they need to make informed decisions about the purchase, use, and reuse of land and buildings.

The firm was started in 1959 by Robert Briggs, a designer of airfields, who decided to get into the soil-testing business. Realizing the potential for a wide variety of interrelated engineering services, two Briggs employees, Winston C. Perry and David S. Campbell, P.E., purchased the company in 1983 and immediately began to reorganize and expand its services along functional lines under divisions headed by vice-presidents. Today Perry, the chief executive officer, and Campbell, the firm's president and treasurer, credit the reorganization as a primary factor in enabling the company to grow into a multimillion-dollar corporation employing more than 200 full-time professionals.

Their intent is to make Briggs a one-stop engineering firm that will supply clients with all the civil, geotechnical, hydrogeological, environmental, and quality-assurance/quality-control engineering services they need to operate their businesses in a safe, efficient, and cost-effective manner.

To implement a host of consulting engineering, scientific testing, and planning services covering land, water, air, industrial environmental safety, and hazardous waste issues, Briggs con-

Winston Perry (left), David Campbell, and the company's helicopter, which is used with video cameras and infrared scanning technology to search for water damage to roofs.

sists of four divisions. The Land Use Division, the Earth Sciences Division, the Building Construction Services Division, and the Commercial and Industrial Services Division offer specialized services that are designed to provide clients with a wide range of consulting engineering services coupled with technical expertise using the most sophisticated, state-of-the-art technology to the highest professional standards.

Inside Briggs' Rockland headquarters, just 20 minutes south of downtown Boston, it's easy to see that engineering consulting and testing can often be a dirty business. Although one wing of the operation is filled with busily humming Macintosh computers, an opposite wing holds boxes of dirt samples and "cores" taken from deep inside the earth. Briggs owns many pieces of specialized testing machinery, including a specially built compression machine that tests a sample of concrete building material up to one million pounds. A special X-ray laboratory room and mobile X-ray labs bombard welded or cast metals with X rays to search for cracks or other weak spots. Briggs has been approved for similar nondestructive testing for the Trident nuclear submarine fleet, also X rays of airplane parts for the Federal Aviation Administration (FAA), and in-service

inspections of nuclear and fossil fuel power plants.

To date, the company has completed more than 50,000 projects for clients. On a recent project Briggs assisted the city of East Providence, Rhode Island, in designing a master plan that will direct the development of some very sensitive coastal land along the East Providence waterfront. In Boston, Briggs has acted as quality-assurance/quality-control consultant for the developers of many of the city's largest downtown office towers. On one recent project the firm tested the reinforced concrete, structural steel, fireproofing, masonry, windows, and roof construction that went into the building of the 46-story International Place office tower complex.

Briggs assists building owners and managers with roofing failure investigations. With the help of the company's helicopter, videotape camera, and infrared scanning technology, Briggs engineers search for roof damage caused by water. Since wet subsurface roofing materials allow more heat transfer than dry materials, the monitor clearly reveals these hot spots. Briggs then provides a videotape of roof damage and a roof replacement plan that can save clients a great deal of money on partial versus full reroofing costs.

An increasing amount of legislation and a corresponding number of moves by insurers, banks, and law firms have created a great need for the services that Briggs offers. In 1983, for instance, the state of Massachusetts passed Massachusetts General Law 21E, which stipulates that any parcel of land purchased for commercial/industrial use must be inspected for the presence of hazardous waste. While the law offers some protection from the unknown, the accepted practice for 21E inspections combines a visual inspection of the site with historic research. Believing this procedure to be incomplete, Briggs offers environmental site assessments with supplemental subsurface-soil and water testing, and is working to make this practice widespread. The company believes that the cost of complete environmental assessments are negligible

Briggs Associates is a one-stop engineering firm that will supply clients with all the civil, geotechnical, hydrogeological, environmental, and quality-assurance/quality-control engineering services they need to operate their businesses safely and efficiently.

when compared to costly litigation and cleanup programs.

Briggs keeps up with all local, state, and federal environmental statutes in order to assist clients with the planning and implementation involved in removing asbestos and improving indoor air quality. With respect to hazardous waste, Briggs provides law firms and title insurance firms with expertise in the permit applications, waste analysis, and compliance services necessary for site certification. Briggs acts as liaison between clients and governmental regulatory agencies, such as the Massachusetts Department of Environmental Quality Engineering (DEQE) and the federal Environmental Protection Agency (EPA).

In addition to the corporate headquarters in Rockland, Massachusetts, Briggs Associates other offices are located in Portsmouth, New Hampshire; Cumberland, Rhode Island; Enfield, Connecticut; Columbia, Maryland; and Orlando, Florida.

SCHNEIDER, REILLY, ZABIN & COSTELLO

Joseph Schneider, founder of Schneider, Reilly, Zabin & Costello.

Standing behind his desk in One Center Plaza, Albert P. Zabin recalls the words of Babe Ruth, who, when told he would be offered a contract with the Boston Red Sox, reportedly replied: "You mean they're really going to pay me to play baseball?" "That's how I feel sometimes," says Zabin about the small law firm for which he has worked since 1962.

In a startling contrast to many Boston firms that now seek to employ in excess of 100 lawyers, Schneider, Reilly, Zabin & Costello consists of only seven trial lawyers. "We try very hard to stay small," says Zabin, managing partner. "We turn a lot of prospective business away to stay small." Instead, the firm sees itself as an elite group that will litigate only claims that are "substantial," involving $250,000 or more, or those that interest the lawyers personally.

While the firm's early reputation was built on its success in winning record awards in personal injury cases, the firm has gradually moved into the area of business litigation, trying complex cases involving patents, products liability, and trade secrets that often involve issues of advanced technology and complex legal issues.

Having a general trial practice in all courts, Schneider, Reilly, Zabin & Costello litigates cases in the areas of admiralty, personal injury, antitrust, railroad, products liability, medical malpractice, and aviation law. The firm also handles commercial, zoning, toxic tort, insurance, intellectual property, and appeals cases.

Partners Joseph Schneider and Joseph E. Reilly started the firm in the 1930s. It was Schneider who would determine much of the firm's tenor and direction—not only because of his irrepressible character, but because the firm lost Reilly in 1956, when he was

killed in an accident on the Southeast Expressway. A Russian immigrant, Schneider was a varsity boxer at Boston Latin High School prior to attending Harvard and Boston University Law School for two years. He read for the bar, in the days when one could, and eventually became the first Jewish president of the Massachusetts Bar Association. His wife, Esther L. Schneider, practiced law alongside him, an unusual practice even today. He was also one of the founders of an organization that preceded the Association of Trial Lawyers of America.

Apart from his leadership roles within the profession, Schneider was considered an expert personal injury lawyer. He won what was, at the time, the largest award in Massachusetts in a personal injury case—$300,000—against Peretti Brothers Construction Company for a client who suffered brain damage while on the job. Schneider continued to practice law in the firm he founded until his death in 1985.

It was Schneider's reputation as a skillful and exacting trial lawyer that brought Zabin to the firm upon graduation from Harvard University Law School. With the addition of two young lawyers, Zabin and, in 1973, Robert V. Costello, the firm entered a new period. "Schneider always appreciated aggressive boxer types and lawyers with broad interests," says Zabin of the new team.

In 1971 Zabin won the largest products liability case in Massachusetts up to that time. In this case a scuba diving vest manufactured in Massachusetts by New England Divers had failed and caused the death of an Alabama dentist. The case was further complicated by the fact that the accident occurred in Okinawa, Japan. Massachusetts law required that although the case was tried in the state, Japanese law would govern the outcome. Zabin had to educate himself on points of Japanese law and enlist the assistance of several Japanese as expert witnesses and translators.

In the spring of 1974 the whole firm was brought to the test. The federal court in Boston decided to catch up on

Robert N. Costello and Albert P. Zabin.

its civil docket and clear a pool of back-logged cases. Over a period of eight weeks Costello and Zabin won 10 of its 11 cases. This frantic time was a turning point for the firm, sealing its reputation in the world of litigation.

Some of the firm's notable cases in commercial litigation have involved damages resulting from stolen trade secrets. In 1983 the firm represented Irving Willis, an inventor who charged American Permac and its German parent corporation dry cleaners with breach of contract in failing to exploit an automated garment retrieval system Willis had devised. The case drew on testimony from a robotics expert at the Massachusetts Institute of Technology.

At the trial's conclusion, Willis was awarded $2.85 million in damages.

Zabin, a frequent contributor and former associate editor of the *Massachusetts Law Quarterly*, also authored "The New Wrongful Death Act in Massachusetts," an article often cited as an authority by the Massachusetts Appeals Court and the Massachusetts Supreme Judicial Court. Costello was a founder of the Massachusetts Bar Association's Computer College and is a frequent lecturer for continuing legal education programs for the Massachusetts Bar Association and the Massachusetts Academy of Trial Lawyers.

Most of the cases the firm litigates for corporate clients touch on other disciplines besides law, says Zabin. He and his colleagues find much satisfaction in the constant learning process these cases demand. Lawyers with Schneider, Reilly, Zabin & Costello have been trained as engineers, pilots, and nurses. A registered nurse, associate Marcia J. Allar has had many articles published in medical literature and is a member of the American Association of Nurse Attorneys. Zabin himself never misses the science section of *The New York Times*, and Costello is an avid reader of computer literature. The firm's technical library, he says, is nearly as large as its law library.

RIEMER & BRAUNSTEIN, ESQ.

Serigraphs by Israeli artist Yaacov Agam line the walls of the slate-blue-and-maroon reception area of Riemer & Braunstein in Government Center's Three Center Plaza. Brightly colored, the kaleidoscopic images are meant to reflect what managing partner, and sometime art collector, Stanley Riemer likes to call the "modern, young, and forward-looking" atmosphere of the firm co-founded by his father more than 50 years ago.

Modern not only because of its outlook but also because it is larger and dif-

during the Depression represented businesses primarily in collection and bankruptcy, recalls the younger Riemer. In 1943 the firm became Cohn, Riemer & Pollack, and gained prominence in legal and business circles by representing creditors in their attempts to retrieve assets. A prolific writer, Bernard Riemer wrote articles on this specialty that were often cited in court decisions. Each of Bernard Riemer and Joe Braunstein, who became a partner during the 1960s, served separately as president of the Commer-

ners, the firm changed its name in 1979 to Riemer & Braunstein.

Despite the hard-earned reputation the firm gained as one of Boston's major bankruptcy firms, the younger partners of the firm saw an opportunity to expand the firm's focus. Very early in his career, Stanley Riemer discovered that his father's name and reputation gave him and the firm access to a wider area of business concerns. He also discovered that banks, in particular, were interested in bankruptcy representation and other services of a small, atten-

ferent from the family firm that it was for its early decades; 54 lawyers handle the business of the firm, a number that qualified it to appear on a recent list of Boston's 25 largest firms. Young because the median age of the 14 partners is 37. And finally, forward-looking because the firm has already proved it is capable of major metamorphosis, breaking out from a well-established niche in bankruptcy law to become a well-rounded business practice.

In 1933, when two Jewish residents of Boston, Bernard A. Riemer and Ralph Cohn, established the firm of Cohn & Riemer, many Jewish firms

Left: (From left) Founder Bernard A. Riemer (seated), Joseph Braunstein, chairman of the firm's bankruptcy and commercial departments, and Stanley J. Riemer, managing partner, in the firm's reception area in front of a tapestry by Agam entitled "Form Color Relief."

Right: Harold C. DuLong (left), managing partner of the firm's Route 128 branch office, and Richard B. Jacobs, with historic Suffolk County Courthouse in the background.

cial Law League of America, a national bar group. Bernard Riemer remains a senior partner of the firm and has been actively engaged in the practice of law since 1929. After the retirement and death of two of its three named part-

tive, and aggressive firm. In four short years the younger Riemer, together with other partners who today still form the nucleus of the firm, had established a thriving banking department in the firm. Today Riemer & Braunstein regularly represents such banking giants as BayBank, Shawmut Bank, and Bank of Boston in lending, work-out, litigation, and many other types of matters. Only 30 years old at the time, a tender age he often tried to disguise from clients, Stanley Riemer became managing partner in 1977.

As an extension of its specialty in banking, the firm recently created the

Reimer & Braunstein Scholar in Banking Law faculty position at the Boston University Law School. A faculty member, selected annually by the dean, conducts educational programs and research relating to the financial-services industry in the city's only graduate banking law program.

Although the firm maintains a general practice, activity at Riemer & Braunstein is principally oriented toward the representation of business. The firm has a diversified client base that comprises numerous financial in-

real estate practice.

Riemer & Braunstein was the first Boston law firm to open a branch office on Route 128, offering services to suburban banking operations as well as to clients involved in the myriad of real estate ventures along the burgeoning strip since 1973. Fully staffed and located in Burlington, Massachusetts, the branch office is approximately 15 miles from the firm's downtown office in Government Center.

Riemer & Braunstein also enjoys a nationally recognized expertise in cor-

loan situations.

The firm has a diversified litigation practice, both trial and appellate, with particular expertise in the Massachusetts unfair competition and business practices law, the developing areas of lender liability and hazardous waste law, and real estate litigation. The firm has also acquired a significant local reputation and expertise in the area of equitable remedies.

The semicircular Center Plaza offices across Cambridge Street from the new City Hall are popular with many

stitutions, large and small corporations and businesses, as well as individuals. There are six general areas of practice within the firm: corporate finance, real estate, general business and tax, litigation, bankruptcy, and commercial.

While the firm's banking practice remains the single-largest activity, Riemer & Braunstein has been involved in real estate practice for more than 10 years, representing clients in leasing, lending, environmental matters, structuring of joint ventures, and all aspects of development projects. The firm represents developers and financial institutions in its commercial

Left: Steven J. Weinstein, chairman of the firm's corporate finance and real estate departments, and David S. Berman (from left), with Steven T. Greene (standing).

Right: Stanley J. Riemer, Peter H. Sutton, chairman of the firm's litigation department, and Joseph Braunstein (left to right), in front of Agam's "Plus Minus, Times, Nine" serigraph.

porate finance and represents financial institutions in a variety of transactions, including commercial loans of all types, leveraged buy-outs and other types of asset-based financing, letter-of-credit-based financing, tax-advantaged financing, and resolution of problem

law firms because behind the Plaza offices, hidden from the street, stands the Suffolk County Court House. Only a little farther up Beacon Hill stands the State House. But Celtics season-ticket holders at Riemer & Braunstein have found yet another reason to revel in the location: The offices are also conveniently located at the end of the parade route for the Boston Celtics basketball team as they celebrate their latest NBA World Championship victories. With a conference room that overlooks Cambridge Street, the law firm traditionally hosts a victory party to coincide with the lunchtime parade.

GASTON & SNOW

Gaston & Snow lawyers have been an integral part of the fabric of the city since the 1800s.

Gaston & Snow, a national law firm of more than 250 lawyers, 800 employees total, is headquartered at One Federal Street in Boston and has offices in New York City, San Francisco, and Phoenix. The firm was established when the Boston firm of Gaston, Snow, Motley & Holt, begun in 1844, merged with the Boston firm of Ely, Bartlett, Brown & Proctor in 1974. Considered the second-largest in Boston, the firm was known as Gaston Snow & Ely Bartlett until the name was shortened in January 1988.

The direction of the firm for the balance of the 1980s and beyond is toward continuous growth in all of its five major departments: corporate, litigation, probate, real estate, and tax. The firm has more than 15,000 clients nationwide, and longtime Boston clients include Shawmut Bank, Liberty Mutual Insurance, Apollo Computer, Paine-Webber, Dean Witter, John Hancock Insurance, and Greylock Management.

Gaston & Snow believes it is one of the few Boston-based firms to adopt a national strategy that utilizes the latest in information-processing technology to link together all of the firm's offices. A document prepared in San Francisco, for example, can be on a client's desk in Boston within hours. The firm also has a centralized word-processing facility that is staffed 24 hours a day to serve both lawyers and clients. A 26,000-volume library is attended by two full-time librarians and includes access to computerized data bases.

The base of the practice consists of corporate law, including finance, banking, real estate, taxation, litigation, and estate planning. Thus, the firm's clients include publicly held national and multinational industrial corporations, public utilities, banks and bank holding companies, major investment banking houses, more than 120 registered investment companies, securities and commodity brokers, insurance companies, other financial intermediaries, large retail chains, estates, and individuals. Such a clientele involves legal work in a variety of specialties that include mergers and acquisitions, real estate and equipment lease financings and syndications, real estate development and financing, proxy contests, public offerings, and public finance.

Practice groups have emerged as clients' needs have been impacted by changing regulatory, sociological, and economic climates. The High Technology and Venture Capital Group, for example, provides advice involving the development, financing, and protection of technology, particularly as related to computers and biotechnology. In addition, the group has attained national prominence in venture financing, representing both the investor and the entrepreneur. According to a 1988 survey by the *IPO Reporter*, the firm placed first in a ranking of the leading law firms representing issuers of initial public offerings in the United States.

In some cases, the development of new specialties has simply been a com-

mon sense response to changes in the competitive marketplace. The Banking Group, for example, has developed a significant expertise and clientele in the regulatory area as nonfinancial institutions have entered into financial markets, and interstate banking relationships have increased. The Environmental Law Group has rapidly expanded to deal with the increasingly complex issues revolving around natural resources, environmental regulations, and hazardous wastes, and the Public Finance Group has created new financing alternatives to stimulate the small-business economy.

Other specialties are based on expertise gained early in the firm's history. Gaston & Snow's mutual fund practice has been one of the firm's major strengths, dating from the time a partner of the firm served as a principal drafter of the Investment Company Act of 1940. The firm has served as counsel for more new mutual fund registration statement filings (17) than any other law firm in the country, according to the 1986 *Mutual Fund Review*, a yearly tabulation published by

a Washington-based information broker specializing in research in the SEC. All of the practice areas are supported by a litigation team with expertise in commercial, securities, employment discrimination, creditors' rights, technology licensing, and admiralty litigation.

The Tax Department supports both corporate and individual clients of the firm in structuring their transactions in a way that minimizes tax costs. The Estates and Trusts Group works closely with the Tax Department in analyzing a client's current situation: their assets, their plans for the future, and their business and family needs.

As is expected of a firm of this size and quality, all of its lawyers participate in varying degrees in local and national professional activities outside their normal practice. These activities are not only useful to the profession but keep the firm informed on emerging trends in the law. Many firm lawyers have been in public service on a full- or part-time basis. Past partners include three governors of Massachusetts and a governor of Maine.

The firm's lawyers serve a national clientele including some of Boston and New England's leading institutions.

Among the present partners are a former attorney general of the Commonwealth, a former under secretary of the United States Department of Commerce, general counsel of the Air Force, vice-president of the Federal Reserve Bank of Boston, chief assistant United States attorney, and chairman of a Massachusetts regulatory agency.

Historically, Gaston & Snow partners have been active in the American Bar Association, chairing various sections and committees. Two partners have been elected president of the Boston Bar Association, and of course, firm lawyers have served on the staffs of such agencies as the Treasury Department, the Department of Justice, the Securities and Exchange Commission, the Federal Reserve Board, the Commodity Futures Trading Commission, and as clerks to justices of the United States Supreme Court and other federal and state court judges.

HALE AND DORR

With a total of 278 attorneys, Hale and Dorr is Boston's largest law firm. Specializing in corporate, litigation, real estate, commercial, tax, and personal law, the firm has offices in the high rise at 60 State Street. Partners at the firm have included such notables as Reginald Heber Smith, a pioneer of Legal Aid; Joseph N. Welch, special counsel to the Army during the Army-McCarthy Senate hearings; and James D. St. Clair, best known for his representation of President Richard M. Nixon during Watergate.

In the heart of the downtown financial district near Faneuil Hall, the firm occupies eight floors of modern office space built on the same site that had been occupied by Hale and Dorr from 1919 to 1969. In 1981 the firm opened a branch office in Washington, D.C. The combined staffs of 800 are linked by an internal computer network.

Hale and Dorr traces its beginning back to the early nineteenth century, when Josiah Parsons Cooke opened a

Hale and Dorr's managing partner John D. Hamilton, Jr. (center), with Harry T. Daniels (left) and John M. Westott, Jr. (right), assistant managing partners. Absent from photo is John A. Burgess, assistant managing partner.

law practice in the Old State House on Boston's State Street. After a succession of partnerships, the firm commenced business under its present name on July 1, 1918, when Dudley Dorr, a respected member of the Boston Bar, became a partner of Richard Hale, Frank Grinnell, Roger Swaim, and John Maguire. Both Hale and Dorr served as partners in the firm until their deaths in 1943 and 1961, respectively.

In 1919 Reginald Heber Smith joined the firm as a partner, bringing with him six legal aid lawyers. During more than 36 years as managing partner of the firm, Smith was active in furthering legal services for the poor. He became the first recipient of the American Bar Association Gold Medal in 1951, and six years later was honored with an

award that bears his name. Today the Reginald Heber Smith Medal is awarded annually to a lawyer with a distinguished record in legal aid. Continuing the tradition, Hale and Dorr is one of the most active Boston firms in pro bono work, maintaining between 50 and 70 open pro bono cases at all times and logging 7,500 hours of donated time a year.

This man of public service, Reginald Heber Smith, also became an early expert in law office management. The Smith System formula for measuring attorney productivity and determining partner compensation has served as a model for numerous law firms and professional service firms in this country and abroad. A series of articles written by Smith describing the system were published in the *American Bar Association Journal* in 1940 and have been reprinted many times in booklet form, most recently in 1984.

In 1954 Smith brought national fame to the firm by recommending

Reginald Heber Smith, partner from 1919 to 1966 and managing partner from 1919 to 1955.

to his partners that the firm assume the fees and expenses on behalf of a new client, the United States Army, in its protest against Senator Joseph McCarthy's investigations at Fort Monmouth, New Jersey. The firm's leading litigator, Joseph N. Welch, became the Army's special counsel in Senate hearings over the dispute. The courtly and scholarly Welch, a deft and erudite courtroom attorney, captured national attention when, in televised Senate committee proceedings, he succeeded in silencing the powerful anti-Communist. McCarthy was censured by his Senate colleagues for his conduct during the hearings, and his four-year campaign against U.S. liberals came to an end. Welch, on the other hand, received national respect for his determination in the face of an aggressive and intimidating adversary.

In 1956 Paul F. Hellmuth succeeded Smith as managing partner and served until his retirement in 1976. Hellmuth earned great distinction for his efforts in Boston on behalf of a variety of important cultural, educational, and community resources.

Today, under the leadership of managing partner John D. Hamilton, Jr., Hale and Dorr is continuing to expand. The firm's litigation practice is the largest in New England and one of the country's most active courtroom practices. In recent years the firm has been involved in a variety of significant cases. Hale and Dorr represented John Hancock Mutual Life Insurance Company in claims arising from a problem with the design and construction of Hancock's glass skyscraper in Copley Square. Recent successes include the firm's defense of Mashpee, Massachusetts, against Indian land claims, Southern Pacific Co. against antitrust claims, and Beatrice Companies, Inc., in environmental litigation.

The firm successfully argued a case before the U.S. Supreme Court that confirmed that the sale of stock of a small business was governed by federal securities laws. In 1985, again in the U.S. Supreme Court, Hale and Dorr successfully represented the State of South Carolina in an Indian land claim case.

In addition to its renowned litigation department, Hale and Dorr's corporate department, under the chairmanship of Paul P. Brountas, is growing in size and reputation. Today the practice group represents a number of large, public, computer-related corporations. The firm also continues to specialize in the representation of small, start-up enterprises and the venture capital investors who often finance these businesses. More recently the firm has developed a strong practice in syndication, representing public and private partnerships in real estate, research and development, and the oil and gas industries. The firm also represents U.S. and foreign clients in international transactions.

Hale and Dorr has developed a significant real estate department, which is head by Philip D. Stevenson. The firm represents syndicators, developers, lenders, and investors nationwide. The firm's real estate expertise has also been instrumental in the growth of its corporate and securities practice in the real estate syndication area. As part of the multifaceted nature of this specialized work, members of the real estate department have also become experts in zoning, environmental requirements, and permit regulations.

Joseph N. Welch and James D. St. Clair, counsel and assistant counsel to the United States Army during the Army-McCarthy hearings, relax on the Capitol lawn during a break in the proceedings.

ROPES & GRAY

John Codman Ropes

Carrying forward a tradition of excellence in the practice of law, Ropes & Gray celebrates its 125th anniversary in 1990. The firm's long and distinguished history parallels the growth of other New England institutions—business, governmental, educational, and charitable—in the period since its founding. As this milestone approached, the firm confirmed its commitment to continued growth by moving its Boston offices to 12 floors in International Place. This new high-rise office complex stands in historic Fort Hill Square, the doorway to the city's financial district, overlooking Boston Harbor.

The firm was established in 1865 by John Codman Ropes and John Chipman Gray, Jr. Both were descendants of Salem merchants and graduates of Harvard College and the Law School. Gray was an officer in the Union Army when Ropes began his law practice in Boston, and they corresponded throughout the Civil War. Both were in their twenties when they set up a partnership at 20 State Street. Ropes served as Assistant United States District Attorney and became a

prolific historian of the Civil War. Gray, a professor at Harvard Law School, became widely known for his treatises on jurisprudence and the rule against perpetuities.

In 1878 William Caleb Loring, who had been a student of Gray's at the Law School, joined the firm. Loring had served as Assistant Attorney General of the Commonwealth and had considerable trial experience. He took special interest in the affairs of business and served as counsel for the New York and New England Railroad. In 1899 he became a justice of the Supreme Judicial Court where he would serve for 20 years.

In the firm's early years most clients were individuals seeking advice with respect to such matters as conveyancing, wills, estates, and trusts. Only 16 of 381 client accounts were of corporations in the years 1872 to 1878. That was to change. In 1899, the year of Ropes' death, the firm had developed a "corporation file," kept in the office of Robert S. Gorham, who pioneered the firm's public finance practice. Gorham, with two other young partners, Roland Boyden and Thomas Nelson Perkins, would carry on the work of the firm with Gray until his death in 1915.

Gray's death ended the era of the founders, but the firm's close relationship with Harvard and the Law School continued. Ropes & Gray lawyers have become professors at the Law School (including Dean James Vorenberg) and have served as members of the Harvard Corporation and the Board of Overseers. For many years Ropes & Gray has been the University's principal law firm.

In the first three decades of this century the firm grew rapidly, primarily under the leadership of Boyden and Perkins. "Business and financial interests were expanding. Public and private financing was on the increase," wrote partner (now of counsel) Edward B.

John Chipman Gray, Jr.

Hanify in a short history of the firm. "There were journeys by Ropes & Gray lawyers on business to Canada, South America, and all parts of the country." The firm opened an office in Paris and engaged the services of an affiliated office in New York. Boyden and Perkins took on international assignments from the United States government at the close of World War I, assuming responsibilities for issues related to the reparations provisions of the Versailles Treaty and the Dawes and Young plans.

In 1927 the firm invited Joseph B. Ely to strengthen its trial practice. He was with the firm only three years before leaving to run successfully for governor. Then, under the leadership of Charles B. Rugg, a former assistant attorney general of the United States, the firm's trial practice grew and flourished. Litigation is now the firm's second-largest practice area, after corporate and banking law.

An enduring tradition for Ropes & Gray lawyers has been public service, whether elected or appointed and at every level of government, as well as in extensive and diverse charitable, educational, and community endeavors. A number of firm lawyers have

gone on to distinguished service as judges. Three have become governors. Charles A. Coolidge served as assistant secretary of defense and returned to become a leader in the renaissance of the city. Archibald Cox and Elliot Richardson have served the nation in several capacities, most memorably together in the Watergate crisis. Henry L. Shattuck, Boston's extraordinary public citizen, devoted a lifetime to the welfare of the city, including service in the city council and the general court. Francis H. Burr and Edward B. Hanify, both still with the firm, have been exemplars of unstinting service to charitable and educational institutions.

Although the firm is large—it has doubled in size over the past 10 years—its practice is managed through practice groups that concentrate in particular areas of the law: corporate and banking, creditors' rights, litigation, taxation, real estate, labor and employment, employee benefits, public law, health care, and trusts and estates. The firm has for many years maintained a substantial trust department through which its lawyers, with advice from investment professionals, manage hundreds of individual trusts. In 1985 Ropes & Gray became the first major law firm in the United States to offer its clients actuarial and benefits consulting services. This Benefits Consulting Group, which has grown to include seven professionals, works closely with firm lawyers to assist clients with respect to employee benefit plans.

The firm's clients include individuals, business corporations, financial institutions, investment companies, utilities, colleges and universities, other charitable institutions, and health care organizations. The firm represents many high-technology companies, and several years ago established an emerging companies group to serve start-up and growing enterprises.

Ropes & Gray established offices in Washington, D.C., in 1981 and in Providence, Rhode Island, four years later. A conference center in New York City was opened in 1987. A computer system as advanced as any in an American law firm serves all the firm's loca-

International Place

tions.

Although the firm has grown and prospered to a degree that no doubt would have astonished Mr. Ropes and Mr. Gray, its standards and ideals have remained close to theirs. In his history of the firm published in 1942, partner Albert Boyden noted that in the first 11 years of the century, the number of people working in the office had grown from 13 to 31. He observed:

"It has been stated, in a tone of voice that sounded authoritative, that these 31 represented the largest law office in the city, and that this giddy numerical eminence has continued from that day to this. It is very likely true, but it is also true that if Ropes-Gray had no claim to distinction except its numbers, no one would bother to write its history. The occasion for this history is not numbers nor length of years. It arises from pride in an organization founded and long maintained in strength, integrity, and independence."

As the firm approaches its 125th birthday, these values still animate the more than 800 men and women who

now make up Ropes & Gray. They are nourished by a heritage of inspiration from an illustrious succession of lawyers who, by their industry and character, established and maintained the firm. Ropes & Gray now renews its commitment to the profession and the community, sharing Edward Hanify's hope that "the firm would endure as long as lawyers practice under our Constitution and legal tradition with excellence and with integrity."

The firm's library at 225 Franklin Street.

SULLIVAN & WORCESTER

A panoramic scene of Boston and the harbor area as viewed from the Sullivan & Worcester offices in One Post Office Square.

The vigorous Boston economy has inspired many an old Yankee law firm to update its image to fit more modern client lists. Sullivan & Worcester is doing just this. Illustrative of Sullivan & Worcester's new entrepreneurial image is its recent role in a precedent-setting real estate deal in which a well-known businessman flew to Boston from Russia in the middle of the night to sign the 15,000 documents necessary to close a real estate transaction involving 17 shopping centers. Thirty-six of the firm's 135 attorneys worked on the deal on behalf of a pension fund manager making a $600-million investment.

Other cases also illustrate the firm's penchant for complex business cases. Sullivan & Worcester has represented foreign investors led by Elkem A/S, the largest publicly owned company in Norway, in its acquisition of Union Carbide Corporation's worldwide ferro-alloy business; has served as counsel to the largest public offering of a mutual fund, the Manhattan Fund; and has represented a large number of railroad systems, including the New York, New Haven, and Hartford Railroad Company in a bankruptcy reorganization that lasted 19 years.

Though it is a general practice firm with the four traditional departments, Sullivan & Worcester prides itself on a tax department that is one of the largest on the East Coast. While all other young associates rotate among the departments for two years, tax associates are routinely sent to Boston University Law School to get a master's degree in taxation. The firm offers full litigation services and also specializes in banking practice, pension compensation and benefits, health care, high technology, securities law, real estate, employment law, and sophisticated communications systems.

Through its Washington, D.C., and New York City offices, Sullivan & Worcester specializes in SEC matters and foreign banking and has expertise in transportation, banking, energy, international trade, and communications law. "We believe we represent as many foreign banks as any other law firm in the United States," says senior partner Michael Davis. "In addition, we have for some time been considered a lawyer's law firm, one that other lawyers bring their business to for certain areas of expertise."

In 1986 the firm celebrated the 75th anniversary of its founding and the 45th under its current name. Sullivan & Worcester was formed in 1941 when John Worcester, then a sole practitioner, merged his practice with the firm of Alger, Dean and Sullivan. The founders would probably not recognize their firm as it looks today, spread out in modern offices on five floors of The One Post Office Square building. As a corporate history notes, "The practice of Sullivan & Worcester during the first decade of its existence was conducted in a somewhat more relaxed manner than is true today . . . The offices were rather plush and quite pleasant in a sort of Victorian style . . . The elevators in the building were quite small; when Mr. Sullivan and John Worcester were both passengers, there was little room for anyone else."

Robert Buchanan and Cindy Clarke prepare a case in the boardroom of Sullivan & Worcester. A general practice firm, it prides itself on a tax department considered to be one of the largest on the East Coast.

George B.H. Macomber
Company, 374-375;

Vappi & Company, Inc.,
376-377;

Rose Associates, Inc.,
378-379;

Trammell Crow Company,
380-381;

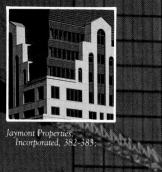

Jaymont Properties,
Incorporated, 382-383;

The Flatley Company,
384-385;

Jung/Brannen Associates, Inc.,
386-387;

Olympia & York Develop
Limited, 388-389;

Cushman & Wakefield of
Massachusetts, Inc., 390;

Meredith & Grew,
Incorporated, 391

CHAPTER SEVENTEEN

Building Greater Boston

*From concept to completion,
Boston's building industry shapes
tomorrow's skyline.*

Photo © Kenneth Martin

GEORGE B.H. MACOMBER COMPANY

The BioSciences Research Building, built for the Harvard Medical School, Brigham & Women's Hospital, and the Howard Hughes Medical Institute, is in the Longwood Medical Area of Boston. Architect: Goldberg Associates. Photo by Peter Lewitt, Architectural Photography

Surrounded by ocean and marsh, Boston has never been an easy city to build in. But somehow this fact has never deterred its citizens from building more, or from creating more land upon which to build. Seven landfills make up the Boston landscape seen today.

For the past 84 years the George B.H. Macomber Company has helped shape the cityscape and its environs, in some cases returning to renovate buildings it put there in the first place.

A family-owned company for three generations, Macomber has managed the construction and renovation of some of the city's most visible structures, including Faneuil Hall Marketplace, Harvard's Weld Boathouse, and, most recently, the new Four Seasons Hotel and Condominiums facing the Public Gardens. With such a backlog of construction experience in the Boston area, Macomber prides itself on its ability to complete complex projects and its adherence to the corporate motto: Build it Right.

The founder of the firm that bears his name began his lifelong career at the age of 11 as a water boy. His superintendent was Charles Clark, whose daughter, Grace, he would later marry. By 1904, at age 36, George Borden Harrington Macomber branched off on

his own. The first project for the young entrepreneur was an ambitious one: the 11-story Post Office Square Building at 79 Milk Street, one of the first structural steel buildings in the United States.

George's son, C. Clark Macomber, assumed the reins of the organization upon the death of his father in 1927. The former Harvard football All-American remained president for 32 years and implemented Construction Management, the system of overseeing a project's planning, design, and construction in an integrated way. During his tenure, Macomber built the nation's first regional shopping mall—Shopper's World in the suburb of Framingham.

In 1959 George Macomber, an MIT graduate and two-time U.S. Olympic skier, became president. Under his leadership the firm has continued to refine its staff of specialists and its project team approach—a necessity in today's highly technical building trade.

The BU Bookstore, a renovation of Peerless Automobile Building, which was originally built by Macomber in 1910. It is located in Kenmore Square, Boston. Architect: John Carl Warnecke. Photo by Ralph Hutchins, Hutchins Photography, Inc.

In 1987 George Macomber appointed the company's first nonfamily president, Richard Collari, a manager and civil engineer with 18 years of experience at Macomber. A family business through and through, George remains active as chairman of the board; his son, John, is a Macomber vice-president; and his daughter, Gay, is the marketing coordinator.

Today Macomber works with private institutions and developers on projects that range from $5 million to $50 million. Internally, a construction executive, project manager, cost estimator, and construction superintendent and other building specialists are assigned to a project for its duration. The project team communicates with the project architect, the owner's representative, community leaders, and trade unions as work progresses. Many satisfied cus-

tomers have returned to Macomber for multiple projects such as the Harvard Community Health Plan, which has turned to Macomber 10 times to expand its facilities.

At any one time a dozen major projects are in the works, and the firm directly employs up to 350 Boston craftsmen and subcontracts with 135 or more subcontractors. Macomber also employs an Equal Opportunity Administrator to monitor company compliance with governmental and Macomber's own affirmative action regulations.

Macomber specialists are equally at home renovating the old as well as constructing the new. Indeed, Macomber chose Russia Wharf, one of the firm's renovation projects, for the location of its corporate headquarters. Macomber has worked successfully within strict regulations from state and federal historical commissions on many renovation projects.

In a recent renovation, for example, Macomber tackled the 150-year-old Building 34 in the Charlestown Navy Yard, transforming what was once a warehouse and chemical laboratory into first-class office space with two new wings. Because the building is located within a national park, strict regulations applied to exterior preservation. Macomber paid special attention to the cleaning of granite blocks on the original building, and clad the additions with individually precast concrete stones matching the original blocks.

In a 350-year-old city the construction of new structures can seldom be accomplished without regard for the old. While at work on the Four Seasons Hotel, built atop a landfill in Back Bay, Macomber engineers monitored soil conditions hourly along Boylston Street to make sure the earth-retention system would hold within design tolerances as they replaced the old pilings with new.

The recent addition of several glit-

Riverfront Office Park, located at the Longfellow Bridge, serves as the Gateway to Kendall Square, Cambridge. Architect: Cambridge Seven Associates. Photo by Alan Lee, "Skyviews"

tering office structures in downtown Boston will only create a demand for more renovation work as older buildings struggle to compete, says the leadership at Macomber. The firm also plans to play a role in the construction of facilities that will serve a necessary social role in the future: outpatient medical facilities and adult living facilities.

The company has already played a role in ushering in the future. In 1985 Macomber managed construction of the Wang "smart building," a $12-million training center in nearby Lowell, Massachusetts. To help train Wang customers, the center was fitted with a $5-million electrical system that in-

The Parris Building, one of four buildings renovated by Macomber at Navy Yard Plaza. This building was originally designed by Alexander Parris, the architect for Faneuil Hall Marketplace, which was also renovated by Macomber. Architect: Boston Architectural Team. Photo by Bruce T. Martin

cluded miles of the latest transmission materials made of fiber optics.

Meanwhile, there's tradition to uphold. George B.H. Macomber Company is returning to transform projects originally built by earlier Macombers such as the Peerless Motor Car Company Building in Kenmore Square. The 1910 structure underwent a $5.5-million renovation to become the Boston University Bookstore.

VAPPI & COMPANY, INC.

Reservoir Place, Waltham. Architect: Symmes Maini & McKee Associates, Inc., Cambridge

nology Highway. The company built offices, manufacturing plants, and distribution centers for Honeywell, Gillette, and Polaroid, along with stores and shopping malls in the developing suburbs. A continuing good relationship with the Massachusetts high-tech community has resulted in numerous recent projects for Digital Equipment Corporation, the Raytheon Company, Draper Laboratories, Biogen, and Lotus.

"The key events were getting the next big job to show we could handle bigger and more complex buildings or do jobs in a hurry . . . ," Vappi said of his growth strategy when interviewed by *U.S. News and World Report* in 1969.

The Vappi office building on a quiet street off Memorial Drive in Cambridge gives no indication of a company performing $80 million to $100 million of construction work annually. This low-key building contractor/construction manager has built or renovated the physical plants of many of the high-profile institutions and companies in and around Boston.

The new South Terminal at Logan Airport, the addition to the Boston Public Library, the Theatre of Electricity at the Museum of Science, and the familiar outpatient building spanning Massachusetts Avenue at Boston City Hospital are recognizable Vappi-built landmarks. Driving west out of the city, Vappi's projects line both sides of the Charles River—the Boston University Law and Education Building, the Cambridge Hyatt Regency Hotel, Harvard's married student dormitories, and Mount Auburn Hospital.

For half of its 61 years, under the direction of founder Cesare Vappi, the company built close to home, renovating warehouses and industrial plants in and around Cambridge and Boston. It was "Caesar's" son, then managing

vice-president, C. Vincent Vappi, who foresaw the postwar university building boom as a way for the company to move up to larger projects. In 1958 Vincent took the reins as president, and two years later had completed his first large-scale university job, a $2.5-million women's residence hall for Boston University.

During the 1950s and 1960s Vincent Vappi also turned the firm's attention to the industrial and research facilities springing up along the newly completed Route 128, America's Tech-

Milton Medical Center, Milton. Architect: FTK Architects, Reading

A civil engineering graduate of Massachusetts Institute of Technology—a client for more than 20 years—Vappi reorganized his company's internal structure, hiring college-educated supervisors and managers, offering them challenging responsibilities, and developing the kind of flexibility needed to take on a wide range of projects.

In the 1960s the firm grew at a

The 17-story, 187-apartment 2000 Commonwealth Avenue, Boston. Architect: Larkin, Glassman & Prager Associates, Inc.

million-dollar renovation jobs performed by a company division specializing in smaller projects to $30-million buildings. In 1987 the firm completed 11 projects as diverse as a logistics facility for Digital Equipment Corporation in Andover, a restoration of a six-story historic building in downtown Boston, and the Omni Theatre at the Boston Museum of Science. The company's staff of 60 administrators and field supervisors prides itself on being with one of the last general contractors capable of performing major work functions with its own forces as project needs may dictate.

The Mugar Omni Theatre at the Museum of Science, Boston. Architect: The Stubbins Associates, Inc., Cambridge

steady pace, branching out to perform work in more distant locations—Clark University in Worcester; Rensselaer Polytechnic Institute in Troy, New York; a shopping center in Springfield; a medical center in Maine; and manufacturing facilities for IBM in two Upstate New York locations.

In the early 1970s Vappi began to concentrate on the large hospital expansions coming on line. Multiple additions to Mount Auburn Hospital, South Shore Hospital, Faulkner Hospital, the Massachusetts Eye and Ear Infirmary, and a $48-million teaching hospital at the University of Massachusetts Medical School in Worcester were completed successfully, along with a number of other hospital projects.

During the same period the firm began to bid work in the public sector—

an $11-million office building for the Division of Employment Security and a similar size project for the Massachusetts Department of Mental Health. In 1975 Vappi completed one of the most visible of its four projects in Boston's Government Center, the John W. McCormack Office Building, which rises above Cambridge Street atop Beacon Hill.

Despite years of experience on projects in such diverse locations as the Rocky Mountain area and the Middle East, Vappi continues to build for its familiar client companies around New England and for greater Boston's education, medical, and government communities. Its projects range from

Vappi & Company, Inc., sees its future in the greater Boston and New England area. The firm believes its strength is in its homegrown key personnel and specialists, and in its long relationships with New England trade unions and subcontractors. "Our key personnel are here; our experts are here," says vice-president for estimating and marketing J. Kevin Hurton. "Boston has been an excellent construction market, and we intend to be part of its continuing growth."

ROSE ASSOCIATES, INC.

In the nearly two decades since it first appeared on the Boston scene, Rose Associates, Inc., has continued to demonstrate those characteristics that have been its guides since its establishment in New York in the 1920s. Professional competence and personal integrity, a style of understated good taste, a continuing commitment to thoughtful planning, firm quality control, and good design—all are the "informing principles" of Rose activities, along with a long-term perspective that prefers relationships to deals and long-range programs to short-term expedients.

For several reasons Boston was a logical destination when Rose began to seek development opportunities beyond the area of metropolitan New York in the 1960s. Easy access to and from the home base in New York, a climate hospitable to development, and, above all, a sense that Boston was poised for a period of dynamic activity were all factors in the decision to invest in the city.

The Keystone Building, a new 32-story office structure at 99 High Street, was the firm's first Boston project. Rose codeveloped the 728,000-square-foot building with the same British partners who had recently completed the State Street Bank Building.

One Financial Center, which houses the company's Boston headquarters, is Rose's most recent and noteworthy contribution to the skyline. With 46 stories, One Financial Center towers over the constant hub of activity surrounding South Station and the eastern edge of the city's downtown district. In One Financial Center, Rose Associates, Inc., achieved what few developers have the opportunity to do: create a building with true landmark value, a building that actually defines an area and becomes a destination point in itself.

Architecturally, the 1.1-million-square-foot office center embodies a synthesis of traditional quality and contemporary spirit. The high rise has six sides that provide an abundance of corner offices, and its continuous bands of windows offer panoramic views of Boston's exciting, ever-changing cityscape.

Today Rose Associates, Inc., continues to act as a major force in Boston's thriving real estate market with a variety of residential, commercial, and mixed-use properties on the drawing boards. One current project that illustrates Rose's long-term commitment to the city is the firm's purchase and rehabilitation of the Boston Wharf properties—78 buildings located in the old leather district along Summer Street, just across Four Point Channel from South Station. Rose has already renovated many of the buildings in the 33-acre tract for residential, office, retail, and light-industrial use.

Rose Associates, Inc., is not only concerned with the design and development of its buildings, but continues to play a role in managing properties in order to maintain the initial quality of the structures.

The company also carries its involvement in the city entirely beyond the real estate area. In Boston, as in the other regions where Rose Associates, Inc., is active, firm members work hard at being good neighbors—contributing to local causes, joining the boards of local charities, teaching, and lecturing at local educational institutions and professional organizations.

In addition to supporting the renovation of Dewey Square Park in front of One Financial Center and the Lite-a-Lite Program of Christmas lights on the Boston Commons, the company provides ongoing financial support for various activities and programs at Boston's Josiah Quincy School in South Cove. In an effort to promote the arts in public education, for instance, Rose Associates, Inc., has for three years supported a program with the Boston Ballet in which approximately 1,000 children from the school participate in dance and movement classes and attended the ballet's annual "Nutcracker" performance.

Daniel Rose, president of Rose Associates, Inc., says: "Boston has been good to us and we try to return the compliment. It was a happy day when our British friends suggested we join them in their proposed next Boston project, which eventually turned out to be the Keystone Building. The years since then have been happy and productive. We look forward in high spirits to a future of active involvement in Boston's efforts to maintain and enhance its position as one of the world's truly great cities."

TRAMMELL CROW COMPANY

Trammell Crow developed the 10-story copper-roofed 745 Atlantic Avenue office building to blend with its low-rise historic neighbors.

Trammell Crow Company has the reputation for building the finest and most flexible office space in the downtown and greater Boston area. Trammell Crow has selected prime locations convenient to the highway networks and business centers in each area. Beginning with the copper-roofed 745 Atlantic Avenue office building at the southern edge of Boston's financial district, Trammell Crow Company has branched out and developed six separate office parks in the suburban communities of Andover, Bedford, Billerica, Burlington, Natick, and Westboro.

With assets in excess of $10 billion and more than 200 million square feet of space under management, Trammell Crow Company is the nation's largest real estate developer. Founded in Dallas more than 40 years ago by the firm's namesake, Trammell Crow, the Dallas-based company transformed itself from a local developer to a giant nationwide operation.

At 745 Atlantic Avenue, Trammell Crow Company developed an office building near South Station and the Federal Reserve Building. The new 10-story brick, granite, precast concrete-and-glass structure complements its low-rise historic surroundings. Details of corbeled brick, stone sills, recessed windows, and arches continue the architectural vocabulary, scale, and texture of the neighboring buildings and echo the historic facing material of nearby South Station. Interior materials including granite and wood add elegance to the lobby and the retail areas.

To accommodate the needs of both small and large high-technology companies for which the Boston suburbs have become known, Trammell Crow Company also is developing a number of office and research parks in greater Boston.

In Andover, Trammell Crow Company developed a two-story office and research park. The buildings are nestled

among 32 wooded acres bordering the Merrimack River. A 25-minute drive from Boston and Logan International Airport, the park is near facilities occupied by several major high-technology corporations, including Digital, Hewlett-Packard, and Wang. Designed for office, manufacturing, and research and development, the four-building park totals 267,000 square feet of space. Each brick-and-glass building is easily devisable and incorporates the latest in mechanical systems for heating and air conditioning.

In Metro West Business Park, Trammell Crow Company is providing the

This suburban mixed-use park at Burlington Center bears the Trammell Crow people-oriented business environment.

region with highly accessible and flexible service center, office, and research and development space. The two- and three-story buildings are located on 63 acres of rolling farmland where more than 60 percent of the park remains open space. Metro West Business Park was built for small growing companies that need all their business functions located under one roof and for larger, more established firms requiring additional space for specific uses.

On Route 128, America's technology highway, Trammell Crow Company is building the finest suburban mixed-used environment in New England. The 635,000-square-foot office, retail, and residential development is built on 74 acres of rolling terrain and combines efficient design with spectacular architecture.

These developments characterize Trammell Crow Company's commitment to people oriented business environments that contribute to employee productivity by offering the finest facilities in locations convenient to other business services and personal amenities.

JAYMONT PROPERTIES, INCORPORATED

Jaymont Properties' senior vice-president Richard Eichhorn echoes many other national developers when he explains why his New York-based company started doing business in Boston in the 1980s. "We couldn't afford not to," Eichhorn says. He continues citing all the activities—education, medicine, high technology, and financial services—that have made Boston's economy vigorous, diverse, and ripe for new office space.

Jaymont Properties differs from

Facing each other, the companion office buildings at 20 (left) and 21 (below) Custom House Street were developed by Jaymont and designed by Cambridge architects Bruner/Cott & Associates.

other developers, and has come primarily to execute from beginning to end what it hopes will be well-planned and well-received structures. Although Jaymont has already initiated three new office buildings in Boston, the company got its start in real estate by doing what it has done nationally in Atlanta, Orlando, Miami, Los Angeles, San Francisco, Chicago, Houston, and New York: save development projects in trouble. With a network of five regional offices, the firm currently owns, manages, and develops a total of 5 million square feet of commercial property nationwide and has 2 million square feet in the planning stages.

In Boston, the company set to work lining up tenants for a pink granite, high-rise office building at 260 Franklin Street. Though the structure was not yet completed, preconstruction leasing was slow. Jaymont bought the property from the original developer, leased out the building, and sold it to JMB Realty Corporation. At the request of the new owners, however, Jaymont continued to manage it, formally opening its own regional office in 260 Franklin in 1985. The company's staff of 18 works closely with a local brokerage, Peter Elliot & Co., to lease its Boston properties.

The story of Two Oliver Street is similar to that of 260 Franklin, its backyard neighbor. The 11-story renovation project was completed in 1986 by Jaymont, and when leasing was complete, the company sold it to Merrill Lynch, Hubbard, Inc. In 1987 Jaymont purchased a second "troubled" property, at 99 Summer Street, and promptly leased an additional 122,000 square feet in five months.

Those who follow Boston real estate attribute Jaymont's success with investment properties to the company's reputation as an aggressive marketer and deal-maker. Because preconstruction leases help secure financing, many developers will offer better deals to tenants who sign leases before ground is broken. Still, no one else advertises its openness to a deal more than Jaymont does. Eichhorn says the family orientation of the company, privately owned

by the Jameel family of Saudi Arabia, makes it easier for Jaymont to respond to offers and make decisions more quickly. The Jameels invest their regional offices with substantial authority to act when they need to, according to Eichhorn. "We absolutely don't believe in vacancies," Eichhorn told *The Boston Globe.* "I'd rather go out and do a deal today than carry the space for another six months and get a marginally higher rent."

In the role of developer, Jaymont has initiated three mid-rise office buildings, at 20 and 21 Custom House Street and at 125 Summer Street—the latter in a joint venture with the Boston development company, A.W. Perry, Inc. As companion buildings facing each other across Custom House Street, the 12- and 10-story buildings were designed by Cambridge architects Bruner/Cott to accommodate retail space at street level, an on-site restaurant, and underground parking.

Jaymont's largest development is a project that marks the firm's presence in the financial district as no other has done before. Scheduled for completion in 1989, 125 Summer is a 22-story office tower that will incorporate the facades of four nineteenth-century buildings on the site. A design by architects Kohn Pedersen Fox Associates of New York promises to make this project Jaymont's most handsome. Classical design elements such as bay windows, cornices, arches, and columns grace a

The facades of four nineteenth-century buildings will be incorporated into the 22-story office tower at 125 Summer Street. The most handsome project to date, it establishes A.W. Perry and Jaymont's presence in Boston's financial district.

granite exterior dominated by a large rounded facade. Interior elements of marble, cherry wood, and brass continue the company's identification with the finest materials. The building will provide a surplus of amenities—another trademark of Jaymont buildings. Underneath 125 Summer, a five-level garage will take orders for car washes, and a concierge service will be available to arrange for in-office catering, valet dry cleaning, theater tickets, and even a visit from the roving shoeshine boy.

A linkage law in the city mandates that developers of new buildings contribute a fixed percentage to a fund that goes toward building low-income housing in Boston. With the 125 Summer project, A.W. Perry and Jaymont have gone beyond city stipulations and have contributed their required sum of $1.29 million not to the general fund but to a specific project in Chinatown.

To address the shortage of entry-level skilled workers in the city, Jaymont has gone into partnership with others in the real estate community and with the Mayor's Office of Jobs and Community Services to set up Boston for Boston, a recruitment and training program. Funded by linkage, the neighborhood outreach program hopes to train and place qualified Boston residents in local businesses. The program attempts to serve as a critical link between the increasing number of city businesses that have a heightened demand for skilled labor and those Boston residents who have training and are looking for employment downtown. Jaymont publicizes the free placement services of the program at 20/21 Custom House Street, 125 Summer Street, and West 99 Summer Street. Jaymont is also doing its duty to promote the use of mass transit: In several of its buildings MBTA passes are sold and van pools are given reserved parking spaces.

In four short years Jaymont Proper-

ties, Incorporated, has earned high marks in Boston for the orderly manner in which it has helped tenants find suitable space to work in its investment properties, for the high quality of its development properties, and for its ability to foresee and help alleviate problems often associated with a growing metropolis.

The troubled property at 99 Summer Street was acquired and renovated by Jaymont and was 65-percent committed within five months.

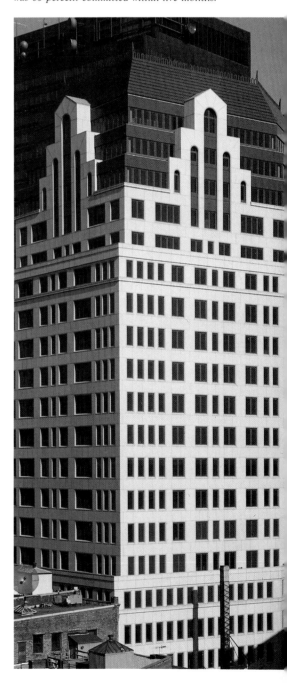

THE FLATLEY COMPANY

The Flatley Company headquarters in Braintree Hill Office Park reflects the meticulous attention to details, such as landscaping and maintenance, which is an integral part of every Flatley project.

Within the carefully landscaped headquarters of The Flatley Company in Braintree Hill Office Park, shuttle vans with passengers going to and from the subway quietly wind their way around waterfalls and flower beds, stopping at each building. Even in late fall the grass is green in the complex; no stray leaf goes unnoticed, no bush goes untrimmed. Developer/builder Thomas J. Flatley has brought new meaning to the idea of planned living, whether his facility is an office park such as Braintree, a hotel, shopping center, nursing home, or apartment complex.

The Flatley Company's Tara Hotel Division is easily recognized by its castles, which can be found throughout New England and New Jersey. Shown is the Sheraton Tara Hotel in Nashua, New Hampshire.

The Flatley Company's Tara Hotel Division is easily recognized by its castles. These luxury hotels resembling medieval castles can be found throughout New England and New Jersey. As the story goes, a Texas hotel with European flavor caught the imagination of the developer while he was on a business trip. An immigrant who came to the United States from Ireland at the age of 18, Flatley named the hotel chain "Tara" after Tara Castle in County Meath, Ireland, which served as seat of the country's High Kings for more than 1,000 years.

Flatley started in the real estate business in 1959, when he completed a Quincy apartment complex. Since then The Flatley Company has become an employer of more than 6,000, serving tens of thousands of people each day in facilities located throughout New England, New Jersey, and Florida. Privately owned, The Flatley Company develops, acquires, and manages residential communities, health care facilities, shopping centers, hotels, and office and industrial parks.

Beginning with a series of multifamily housing communities, Flatley next built several first-class nursing care facilities in Massachusetts. Later came the Sheraton Tara Hotel group. The company has also built or restored more than 7 million square feet of commercial and industrial property, including what is considered to be one of the largest private restorations in the Boston area at the former William F. Schrafft Candy Factory in Charlestown. The

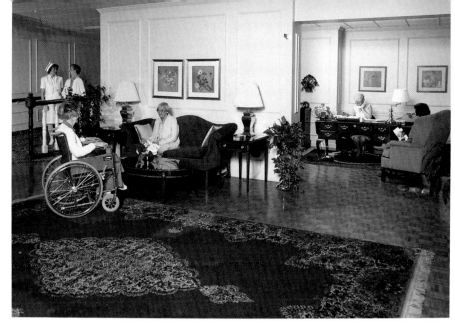

None of the company's projects exemplify the Flatley motto, "We Care," so much as the nursing care and health facilities. The Milton Health Care Facility (shown here) is unique for its day care program for adults with Alzheimer's disease.

Flatley Company purchased the Schrafft Center in 1984 and has spent $20 million restoring the structure and transforming it into one of Boston's finest real estate developments. The restoration effort even extends to the red-neon Schrafft sign that can be seen shining brightly above Charlestown from I-93. Flatley pays the firm $50,000 per year to keep the Schrafft name on the historic building.

Despite the variety of its developments, all Flatley facilities have some similar characteristics. In accordance with the company motto, "We Care," all facilities are heavily staffed with maintenance and service personnel. The firm has its own architectural, construction, and development divisions whose employees, according to corporate legend, must endure periodic unannounced on-site inspections from Thomas Flatley. Even the landscapers working on-site are Flatley employees.

As an extension of its commitment not just to build, but to serve those people who live and work in Flatley facilities, the company operates day care centers and health clubs in several of its parks.

The firm is organized into six divisions grouped according to function. Each division is staffed by an experienced team of professionals in the areas of accounting, marketing, operations, sales, and service. Flatley oversees and interacts with each division on a daily basis.

The residential division, the oldest division, manages 13 luxury apartment complexes that are communities in themselves. The apartment units at each complex are grouped around clubhouses and fitness centers staffed by instructors. Maintenance and security is provided by Flatley and, of course, the grounds are impeccable. The idea is to provide carefree living for busy professionals or empty nesters no longer interested in caring for a large house.

In conjunction with Tufts University Medical School, The Flatley Company operates six Mayo Health Facilities. The division recently celebrated its 25th anniversary. These Massachusetts facilities provide all services associated with long-term care for the elderly. More than 900 nursing, dietary, housekeeping, and other service personnel work in these facilities. The Milton Health Care facility, in particular, is unique for its day care program for adults with Alzheimer's disease.

The Commercial/Industrial/Shopping Center Division was formed in 1970 and manages in excess of 7 million square feet of property that consists of office and industrial parks and shopping centers. These industrial and commercial office parks provide a full array of amenities: jogging trails, dry cleaning services, restaurants, banking facilities, and free shuttle service to public transportation. These properties are meticulously landscaped and are all situated in locations with excellent accessibility to all major routes.

Since the Tara Hotels opened their doors in 1972, the hotel division has grown to include hotels located from Maine to New Jersey.

The media division of The Flatley Company includes WNHT-TV Channel 21 in Concord, New Hampshire, and WSYT-TV Channel 68 in Syracuse, New York, both full broadcasting licensed television stations. WNHT-TV was recently granted CBS affiliation.

The Flatley Company's Braintree headquarters employs more than 400 support personnel providing the glue for this vastly diverse organization. The Flatley Company's commitment to excellence is directed towards the people they serve, whether as residents of health care facilities or residential communities, as guests of the firm's hotels or as tenants in its office and industrial parks and shopping centers. The company has experienced growth and change over the past decades, but throughout this development the underlying philosophy has remained the same, "We Care."

Granada Highlands, Malden.

JUNG/BRANNEN ASSOCIATES, INC.

The award-winning, 46-story One Financial Center serves as a vital southern gateway to Boston's thriving business district.

The first project ever undertaken by Jung/Brannen Associates of Boston was the carefully wrought design of the firm itself, an eminently successful endeavor. Like the buildings the firm designs, Jung/Brannen Associates was conceived in response to strongly held aesthetic convictions and a firm grasp of reality. In 1968 co-founders Yu Sing Jung and Robert Brannen began to shape a practice that would address the problems of modern building projects, including overriding economic pressures, without abandoning the challenge of content—bringing to each project a rich aesthetic language steeped in the craft of modern architecture.

Brannen describes the company's approach as one rooted in "the quality of inevitability," a process by which the right solution emerges and "can only be the way it is." Jung/Brannen, he says, designs buildings from the inside out, analyzing function first and, during the process of design, bringing the artistic resources of the architect to bear on the design solution.

Now one of the 50 largest architectural practices in the United States, Jung/Brannen has grown dramatically over the past 10 years. In response, the firm's founders created a corporate setting in 1982 within which to control quality and promote creativity. As Jung notes, the corporate practice of architecture is one in which there is "a collective standard of the complex issues of architecture." This is the best environment, he says, in which to encourage an architect's individual expression while measuring it against practical constraints and functional issues.

At the core of Jung/Brannen's corporate structure is a matrix system by which "masters" or project directors provide expertise in design, finance, civil engineering, space planning, codes, working drawings, specifications, graphics, marketing, and com-

puters. In conjunction with this system, Jung/Brannen established an in-house school that provides courses in all of the technical and aesthetic areas of modern practice and theory. The courses are both taught and attended by alternating members of the Jung/ Brannen staff depending upon the area of expertise required. With the aim of offering the best environment for talent to thrive, an Employee Stock Owner-

Part of the revitalization of Boston's Fort Hill, 125 High Street includes two new high-rise of- fice towers, the renovation of three intercon- nected nineteenth century brick buildings, and the creation of lively public spaces.

ship Plan was also established, which in 1988 transferred ownership of the company from its founders to the collective staff of the firm.

The tangible results of this reorganization are considerable. The firm has won more than 40 design awards, in the areas of architecture, interior design, preservation, renovation, lighting, materials, and technical achievements. With its innovative use of multichromatic, richly patterned marble, in particular, Jung/Brannen has demonstrated a commitment to decoration in architecture as well as a willingness to discover new methods to achieve the most lasting and affordable results.

From 1982 to 1988 Jung/Brannen Associates of Boston grew from 110 to 190 people. This growth allowed the firm to offer comprehensive interior and space-planning services, which resulted in the largest interior design department in New England. The firm also began marketing a special software package, called Archibus, to other architectural firms, which allows architects to make use of computer-aided design and gives management a new method for monitoring the progress and cost of projects.

With new regional offices, and subsidiaries including Jung/Brannen International, the firm's ability to influence the practice of architecture has expanded significantly in this country and abroad. Notable downtown Boston projects include One Post Office Square, the Meridien Hotel, the John Hancock Clarendon Building, One Exeter Plaza near the Boston Public Library, One Financial Center in Dewey Square, the World Trade Center on Commonwealth Pier, and 125 High Street near South Station.

Scheduled for completion in 1991, 125 High Street exemplifies Jung/Brannen's design attitude. A complex in Boston's Financial District, the solution places a high priority on the interaction of each component with the surrounding community, optimization of benefits to the public, and the creation of a sense of continuity with the existing character of this historic neighborhood. Working closely with the

city's redevelopment authority, the architects analyzed the district's historical development since the early 1800s and proposed a design approach that responsibly addresses issues of context, massing, streetscape, aesthetics, public and private use, traffic, and parking.

In addition, the firm is well known for its early influence on suburban office design. As Brannen notes, the strength of Jung/Brannen's approach is that design solutions emerge from the firm's understanding of the specific practical considerations of multitenanted office buildings, but at the same time, "it is important that we not build a monument to flexibility." Thus, Jung/Brannen Associates developed an ability to impart character to a building in keeping with its practical constraints. Through the use of natural materials, attention to the siting of buildings, and an understanding of the human need for light and positive views, the firm created working environments that serve clients' and users' needs, and

Careful detailing and intricate two-tone brick patterning combine to impart beauty and distinction to 80 William Street at Wellesley Office Park.

also represent achievements in architecture. Among the landmarks in suburban office design are Jung/Brannen's Wellesley Office Park, Andover Tech Center, Computervision Customer Center, Westborough Office Park, and Unicorn Park in Woburn.

A major urban-redevelopment project. One Post Office Square links a 40-story office tower with the luxury Hotel Meridien, enlivening the streetscape of the financial district while respecting the traditional mix of existing buildings.

OLYMPIA & YORK DEVELOPMENTS LIMITED

World Financial Center, New York City. Photo by Wolfgang Hoyt/ESTO

One measure of Boston's economic success is not hard to read. All one has to do is scan the horizon of downtown to find physical proof of the city's boom. In 1987-1988, according to the *Boston Globe,* the city experienced the largest wave in new office space ever to hit its financial district—more than 4.3 million square feet opened for occupancy, most of it to be found in new high-rise buildings. Yet another sign of good times is the large number of high-profile developers who have assembled in Boston to orchestrate the blossoming of downtown.

Among the first to arrive was North America's largest developer, Olympia & York Developments Ltd. A Canadian company renowned for big and beautiful Class A office buildings across the United States, Olympia & York has so far been involved in the development of three Boston projects. The largest and most visible is 53 State Street, also called Exchange Place. Rising 40 stories above the Old State House, Exchange Place is actually two buildings joined together: the refurbished facade of the Boston Exchange building connected to a brand-new tower of green glass.

Before Olympia & York Developments Limited arrived in Boston, it was already the largest developer and owner of major office space in the United States and Canada. This privately held company, run by the Reichmann family of Toronto, directly owns and operates more than 40 million square feet of prime office buildings in a dozen cities in the United States and Canada, including 24 million square feet in New York City. In London, the company has begun to construct 12 million square feet of office, retail, and public space at Canary Wharf.

Olympia & York began its development activity in Toronto in 1955. Among other properties, it developed Canada's tallest and most significant commercial property—First Canadian Place.

Olympia & York entered the U.S. real estate market in 1976 with the ac-

Exchange Place exterior (right) and interior (opposite), 53 State Street, Boston. Photo by Wolfgang Hoyt/ESTO

quisition of eight buildings totaling 11 million square feet in prominent downtown and midtown locations in New York City. In New York, Olympia & York is completing construction of the World Financial Center in lower Manhattan. With more than 8 million square feet of office, retail, and public space in four towers, the office complex houses the corporate headquarters of the American Express Company, Merrill Lynch and Co., Inc., Dow Jones & Co., Inc., and Oppenheimer & Co., Inc., as well as Daiwa Securities and Nikko Securities Inc.

Inevitably Olympia & York eyed Boston's active central business district, whose main occupants—law firms and financial services—were ready to break out of old space and into space more suitable to their new position as the hub of New England's economic renaissance. The first project for O&Y in

Boston was the revival of the Liberty Square Building near the Post Office Square. The firm took the existing structure, restored the old-world elegance of the interior, and upgraded the physical workings of the structure to modern standards of efficiency.

Along Boston's busy State Street, a visitor might be surprised to turn the corner of the Old Stock Exchange and find himself at the foot of an impressive seven-story glass atrium, the entrance to Olympia & York's Exchange Place. Olympia & York kept the old Exchange facade but rebuilt the interior, integrating it into a modern glass office tower. The whole structure provides 1.1 million square feet of prime office space.

Center stage in the atrium lobby is the grand white marble staircase that once graced the original stock exchange. At the top of the stairs presides the original stock exchange clock. Pedestrians cross the atrium on the way to shops, restaurants, and banking facilities on the street and concourse levels. A coherent link between the old and new is the broad plaza, paved in granite, where trees and benches create areas for people to gather. Beyond the atrium's four shiny metallic columns are two banks of high-speed elevators. Separate freight elevators are kept out of sight, as is the modern computer

center that controls all heating, air-conditioning, and ventilation systems.

Olympia & York's current Boston project will be located at a site across from the Boston Commons and Park Street Station, and face the Park Street Church and the city's second-oldest cemetery, Granary Burial Ground.

Understanding the historic importance of the site, the partners have engaged architect Adrian Smith, architect of the stunning Rowes Wharf complex and 75 State Street, to design a building that will "address the Common" in a way the existing structures do not. The present design for the proposed mid-rise building will face the commons with a curved facade and portico entryway. The developers believe the design is "a pure example of a building that

First Canadian Place, Toronto, Ontario. Photo by Wolfgang Hoyt/ESTO

could only be built on this site," which, they contend, is an example of an emerging trend in architecture. This trend is especially true for Boston, a city whose public wants to see small, special-situation projects that are sensitive to the environment.

According to the firm's project partner, Cohen Properties, Inc., Olympia & York has been a trendsetter, as the Tremont Street project demonstrates. Smaller projects custom-built to fit in a specific environment will be on the Boston horizon, which also bodes well for the future of Olympia & York Developments Limited.

CUSHMAN & WAKEFIELD OF MASSACHUSETTS, INC.

In 1917, in New York City, the founders of Cushman & Wakefield, Inc., established a local real estate firm rooted in very strong values: integrity, client service, and entrepreneurial initiative. By 1984, when the Boston office was opened, Cushman & Wakefield had become a key company in the Rockefeller Group and had grown to become the largest firm exclusively serving the needs of business in real estate. The challenge of Cushman & Wakefield of Massachusetts was to become a major player in one of the most competitive markets in the country.

Cushman & Wakefield has met the New England challenge in a substantial way. In so doing, it has already earned an excellent reputation for its professionalism, service, and track record. But what's so striking is that Cushman & Wakefield has accomplished so much in such a short time. Indeed, its achievements in tenant representation, major leases, and multimillion-dollar sales have distinguished the Boston office locally and nationally.

Examples of Cushman & Wakefield's success are many and varied, but several early accomplishments stand out. First, Cushman & Wakefield was named by Lincoln Property Company, one of the nation's leading developers, to be the exclusive leasing agent for 101 Arch Street—a 21-story, 420,000-square-foot office tower in Boston's financial district. In other Massachusetts transactions, Cushman & Wakefield sold the Apple Hill Office Park in Natick and the GTE Building in Westboro, each for approximately $30 mil-

The first outstanding achievement of Cushman & Wakefield in New England was being named the exclusive agent of the 101 Arch Street office tower in Boston.

lion. Cushman & Wakefield also served as the leasing agent for One Memorial Drive in Cambridge, Massachusetts—a 19-story, 350,000-square-foot building developed by Congress Group Ventures, Inc. Finally, Cushman & Wakefield handled all tenant representations for Lotus Development Corp., the Cambridge-based software publisher, locating office space for Lotus nationwide through one central contact point.

Firms such as Lotus benefit from Cushman & Wakefield's national network of more than 60 offices, each providing consistently high service. Access to national and local research is another important benefit that Cushman & Wakefield offers its clients. Using a computerized data bank, in-house researchers track invaluable information on rental and vacancy rates, construction activity, and absorption in downtown and suburban Boston. A compilation of this statistical information is published in *The Boston Trend,* a quarterly survey focusing on Boston's real estate activity.

Another distinctive feature of Cushman & Wakefield is that it never owns or develops property. Rather, it operates as a third party to avoid conflicts of interest, and it approaches each brokerage assignment as if it were the marketing team inside each client's company.

Cushman & Wakefield is further distinguished by its full range of services in six service lines. In addition to commercial and industrial brokerage, the firm is a regional and national leader in investment sales/financial services, property management services, development consulting, and appraisal services. Cushman & Wakefield customizes these services to meet the specific needs of large or small companies

Cushman & Wakefield was responsible for the leasing of One Memorial Drive in Cambridge, a 19-story, 350,000-square-foot structure.

in suburban or downtown markets.

Likewise, Cushman & Wakefield matches the right professionals to each real estate assignment. These professionals always work as a team, and the day-to-day involvement by senior management is another Cushman & Wakefield trademark. Together, the people behind Cushman & Wakefield are the main reason for the firm's success story—local people with the experience and market savvy that translate into results.

Cushman & Wakefield has also expanded its presence in the international market. An example is a unique, long-term agreement with Mitsubishi Trust and Banking Corp. to counsel Japanese investors seeking opportunities in American real estate. Under the agreement, Mitsubishi will seek corporate, private, and pension fund investors among its clientele in Japan, and Cushman & Wakefield will find suitable properties for their investments.

Locally, nationally, and internationally, the Cushman & Wakefield success story—and its reputation for excellence—continues to grow. In New England, the business community respects Cushman & Wakefield as a well-established local firm that derives added strength from its national network. Business New England needs a full-service firm it can count on—and in commercial real estate, Cushman & Wakefield leads the way.

MEREDITH & GREW, INCORPORATED

Much like Boston Meredith & Grew, Incorporated, has grown and developed since its establishment in 1875 far beyond the vision of its founders. The original three-person firm dealt in a market of several hundred thousand square feet, while the company's two hundred people today serve a regional market in excess of 100 million square feet in Boston proper and in suburbs to the north, west, and south. What was originally primarily an office leasing practice now encompasses industrial, research, and development property. Services include income property brokerage, appraisal and counseling, development and project supervision, mortgage finance, and property management.

What is constant despite great growth and the passage of time is Meredith & Grew's commitment to excellence. The firm continues to assemble the brightest young minds to be focused and developed by seasoned professionals of judgment and probity. The fundamentals of the industry are

the cornerstone of success, and the numerous and varied professional designations held by members of the firm—CRE, CPM, CSM, MAI, SIOR, and SREA—are indicative of the recognition, rigorous training, and continuing education in the various disciplines. This enables the firm to tackle virtually any assignment with great confidence.

As transactions have become increasingly complicated and markets increasingly fast-changing, the firm has responded with investments in research, to provide to-the-moment market information to staff and clients, and in technology, to provide faster and more detailed analysis of projected deal structures. As markets have become more global, and to provide services to Boston-based clients with needs in other markets nationwide and internationally, the firm's National Division has for more than a decade been an owner-member of The Office Network, a consortium of firms such as Meredith & Grew with offices in more than 125 markets worldwide.

Meredith & Grew's headquarters offices in The Landmark characterize the organization in many ways. The graceful elegance of a lobby in bronze, marble, and gilt reflects enormous attention to detail, the work of craftsmen

that stands the test of time. The upper-floor offices are organized and efficient. Aside from the physical elements of The Landmark, the entire Federal Center complex is testimony to a company's team approach to meeting the needs of its clients over a long period of time.

Hired in 1975 by offshore interests to manage two parcels of property and study their reuse potential, Meredith & Grew ultimately recommended rehabilitation of the existing art-deco structure and construction of a complementary new building on the underutilized portion of the site. The firm's development services group secured all governmental approvals and undertook the renovation and new construction projects; the finance staff arranged construction and permanent financing; the brokerage staff marketed the existing building as office condominiums and the new structure as rental space; the appraisal and counseling department advised on a host of tax and rehabilitation credit issues; and the property management division is currently overseeing all aspects of day-to-day operations.

Today's Meredith & Grew, Incorporated: The team that's creating history every day!

The award-winning Federal Center serves as headquarters for Meredith & Grew, Incorporated.

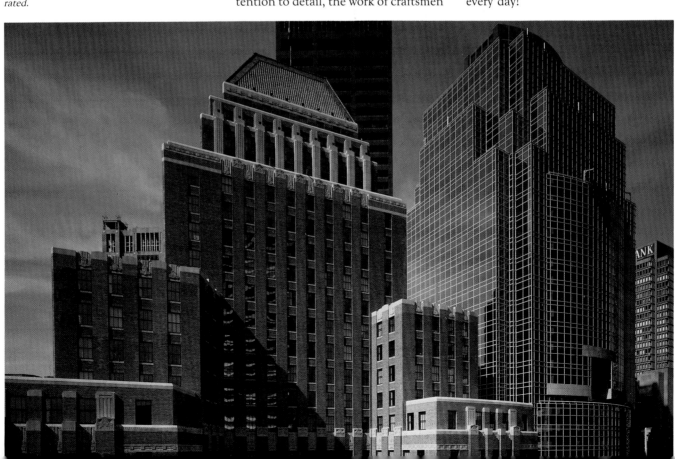

Beth Israel Hospital, 394-395;

Massachusetts Higher
Education Assistance
Corporation and The
Education Resources
Institute, 396;

New England Medical Center,
397;

Lahey Clinic Medical Center,
398-399;

Bentley College, 400-401;

Babson College, 402-403;

Suffolk University, 404-405;

Brandeis University, 406

Massachusetts Eye and Ear
Infirmary, 412;

University of Massachusetts at
Boston, 413

Jewish Memorial Hospital,
408-409;

The University Hospital,
410-411;

CHAPTER EIGHTEEN

Quality of Life

Medical and educational institutions contribute to the quality of life of Boston area residents.

Photo © Paul Corkum

BETH ISRAEL HOSPITAL

All patients checking into Boston's Beth Israel Hospital receive a "welcome envelope" containing several colored pamphlets introducing the medical institution. One pamphlet explains the primary nursing system for which the hospital is famous; another contains the "Statement on the Rights of Patients," first published by the hospital in 1972 and widely adopted by other hospitals, health centers, and government bodies nationwide; a third booklet contains the program schedule for the hospital's closed-circuit patient television station. Also included in the welcome packet is a card inviting patients to critique the hospital.

To heal the sick humanely was the aim of Boston's Jewish community, which sought a hospital of its own in the early 1900s. The community raised $50,000 to move the Mt. Sinai Dispensary, begun in 1902, from Chambers

The main entrance to one of the nation's leading medical centers, Beth Israel Hospital on Brookline Avenue, Boston.

Street in the West End to new hospital quarters—reorganized as the Beth Israel Hospital—at the Dennison Estate in Roxbury. With renovations completed in 1917, Beth Israel Hospital opened with 45 beds. Space soon became precious, and the hospital moved to its present location in Brookline in 1928, opening with 180 beds.

From the beginning Beth Israel put emphasis on teaching and education. One year after the hospital opened in Roxbury, a nursing school was established. The hospital became a teaching affiliate of the Harvard Medical School the same year it moved to Brookline Avenue in the developing Longwood medical area. The area today includes not only Beth Israel itself, but also the Harvard Medical School Campus and such other renowned institutions as The Children's Hospital, Brigham and Women's Hospital, New England Deaconess Hospital, Sidney Farber Cancer Institute, Joslin Diabetes Foundation, and the Harvard School of Public Health. Most of Beth Israel's physi-

cians hold faculty appointments at the school, and more than 1,200 medical students, residents, and fellows train there each year. There also are extensive training programs for nurses, medical technicians, social workers, and dieticians.

Beth Israel's reputation as one of the nation's leading general medical centers was founded on its combination of the latest medical research and technology and sensitivity to patients' concerns. It is a leader in the diagnosis and treatment of heart disease, cancer, infectious diseases, and gastrointestinal and neurological problems. In the division of cardiovascular medicine, staff members have pioneered developments in the treatment of diseased coronary arteries and valves, and in the application of artificial-heart technology.

Its department of obstetrics and gynecology delivers more than 4,600 babies per year and has become one of the leading services of its kind, particularly in the treatment of infertility and difficult pregnancies. The first in-vitro

fertilization baby in New England was conceived and born at Beth Israel, and 53 others have followed.

The department of surgery is a leader in kidney transplants and will soon perform pancreas transplants to try to prevent juvenile diabetes in some patients. In the division of infectious diseases, victims of AIDS are treated with experimental drugs that may ease their suffering and prolong life. Nearly 25,000 inpatients received treatment at the 460-bed hospital in 1986.

Beth Israel was selected as one of the nation's top medical centers by a comprehensive new guide to health care called *The Best Hospitals in America.* The directory, published in 1987 by Henry Holt and Company of New York, cites the hospital's pioneering program of primary nursing, developed in 1975 and replicated in hospitals nationwide, as one of its strongest attractions.

Unlike traditional team nursing, the primary-nursing system assigns each patient an R.N., who has 24-hour responsibility for the care of three or four patients from their admission to discharge. Primary nursing has not only proven instrumental in attracting highly

trained professional nurses to Beth Israel at a time when many hospitals are experiencing severe labor shortages, but it has also enabled nurses to provide patients with more personalized care.

Beth Israel believes that in order to attract top-notch medical personnel, a hospital must also be committed to conducting significant research. With funding from foundations, private donations, and commercial sponsors, the hospital has tripled the amount it spends on research since 1979. In 1986 Beth Israel ranked sixth among the nation's independent hospitals in the amount of grant funding received from the National Institutes of Health, the major federal funding source of medical research.

Beth Israel is particularly active in the fields of cardiology, neurology, radiology, aging, metabolism, nephrology, infectious diseases, orthopedic biomechanics, hematology and oncology, gastroenterology, pulmonary medicine, and dermatology. Among the hospital's most promising research is a highly sensitive blood test that has proven 90 percent accurate in detecting many kinds of cancer. Other projects that have

Beth Israel Hospital is located in the developing Longwood Medical Area of Boston.

gained widespread attention include the use of lasers and balloon catheters to treat blocked arteries. It was at Beth Israel that the cardiac pacemaker was first developed and tested. Today diabetes specialists are testing a nasal inhaler developed at the hospital that will allow patients to administer insulin without frequent injections.

To help meet cost controls imposed by stringent government regulations, Beth Israel has joined other hospitals in emphasizing outpatient care. Outpatient visits reached a record high of more than 181,000 in 1986. The hospital's outpatient surgery program, one of the oldest and most comprehensive in a major teaching hospital, is now responsible for more than 60 percent of all elective surgical procedures performed at Beth Israel. The 24-hour Berenson Emergency Unit, part of the Longwood Area Trauma Center, treated nearly 36,000 patients, and the hospital's home care program provided more than 14,000 visits to chronically ill patients.

MASSACHUSETTS HIGHER EDUCATION ASSISTANCE CORPORATION AND THE EDUCATION RESOURCES INSTITUTE

Ernest T. Freeman, president, The Education Resources Institute.

The question for a graduating high school student these days is not so much whether he or she should go to college as it is whether he or she has the means to go to college. In a city renowned for its wealth of colleges and universities—39 at last count—it's fitting that Boston is also the home of two sister organizations that are working to see that people of all ages and economic backgrounds aren't deprived of a college education simply because of its cost.

As a private, nonprofit corporation, the Massachusetts Higher Education Assistance Corporation (MHEAC) administers federally guaranteed student loans. The Education Resources Institute (TERI), also a private, nonprofit corporation, administers a private loan program with participating banks to keep supplemental loan rates low for students, parents, and educational institutions.

In 1956 MHEAC was founded to administer the Higher Education Loan Plan (HELP) created by bankers, college presidents, and Senator Philip A. Graham. Initially funded by corpora-

tions and foundations, HELP became part of the federal loan program established by the Higher Education Act of 1965. The federal program created federal guarantees to support states willing to expand programs for students. Today MHEAC administers three different kinds of loans: the Guaranteed Student Loan (GSL), the PLUS pro-

gram for parents, and Supplemental Loans for Students (SLS).

TERI picks up where MHEAC leaves off, administering private education loans in conjunction with participating banks. Created in 1985, TERI makes it possible for parents and students to borrow between $2,000 and $20,000 annually. Payments can be limited to interest only during the time the student is attending school, and borrowers can take up to 20 years to repay the loans. Before applying for a TERI loan, students and families are encouraged to apply for government-sponsored financial assistance as well as campus-based aid.

MHEAC and TERI have developed information and counseling services to inform students and their parents of all options now available for financing college costs. Both organizations are committed to informing parents and students about the importance of managing debt and repaying loans. Information about both organizations and their loan programs is available at the Boston Public Library, where TERI operates the Higher Education Information Center. College catalogs, computer programs on career and college options, and resource books on higher education are available at the center. Trained counselors can answer questions about financial aid and career options.

Joseph M. Cronin, president, Massachusetts Higher Education Assistance Corporation.

NEW ENGLAND MEDICAL CENTER

High-quality, compassionate care has been the hallmark of New England Medical Center since it opened as the Boston Dispensary in 1796, making it the oldest health care facility in New England. The Dispensary was founded by Samuel Adams and other prominent Bostonians to ensure good medical care for the poor people of the community.

In the late 1800s the Dispensary was joined by the Floating Hospital for Infants and Children, which started as a hospital ship and grew into a center for the treatment of childhood diseases. The Floating Hospital was the first children's hospital in the country to recognize the importance of family participation in patient care.

Two other centers—the Pratt Clinic, specializing in the diagnosis of complex illnesses, and the Rehabilitation Institute, treating the severely disabled—joined the Dispensary and the Floating Hospital to create New England Medical Center as it is now known.

Today New England Medical Center is a specialized research and referral center, providing comprehensive inpatient and outpatient care to adults and children from Boston's neighborhoods and from around the world. Its position

The latest surgical techniques are a daily routine at the medical center. Photography by Michael Lutch

in the city may be old, but the medical center continues to play a vital role in leading Boston's medical community in state-of-the-art patient care: There are 16,000 inpatient admissions and 260,000 outpatient visits annually to the 480-bed hospital, which is also the primary teaching affiliate of Tufts University School of Medicine.

New England Medical Center physicians provide expertise in all levels of medical care—from the most basic to the most complex. The medical center was a founding member of both the Boston Center for Liver Transplantation and the Boston Center for Heart Transplantation, and was instrumental in the creation of MedFlight, an emergency helicopter service, and the Affiliated Children's Arthritis Centers of New England, a health consortium for the care of children with rheumatic diseases.

Named as one of the best hospitals in America in the 1987 book by Linda Sunshine and John A. Wright, the medical center is a leader in the diagnosis of complex diseases, the treatment of high-risk premature infants, the replacement of artificial joints and ligaments, computer-aided clinical decision-making, and the study and treatment of infectious diseases. The medical center is known for its cardiac program, which includes a full range of high-tech diagnostic services (cardiac catheterization, echocardiography), and expertise in the latest surgical treatments for heart defects and diseases. Coordinated cancer treatment is another area in which the medical center excels, with the institution having been named a national testing facility for the new cancer treatment interleukin-2.

As the New England Medical Center approaches its 200th anniversary, there is every reason to believe it will continue to be a major force in clinical care and research, and will continue its tradition of innovative and compassionate care.

LAHEY CLINIC MEDICAL CENTER

The Lahey Clinic Medical Center, Burlington.

Each day as many as 2,000 outpatients make their way to the Lahey Clinic Medical Center on Burlington's Mall Road, a beltway of landscaped lawns and low-lying buildings located just off Boston's Route 128. At the Lahey Clinic more than 200 physicians and 1,800 nurses, therapists, technologists, and other personnel attend to health concerns ranging from allergies to heart disease.

As a multispecialty center with full-time staff physicians, the Lahey Clinic maintains an environment in which consultation and coordination among specialists is routine. While a patient's care is managed by his or her primary Lahey physician, the patient also has access to the resources of nearly every other area of medicine.

Nationally, the Lahey Clinic is known for its skills in areas as diverse as diagnostic imaging, management of inflammatory bowel disease, and urinary, colon, and rectal surgery. The clinic's multispecialty approach enhances its skills at difficult diagnosis—

the diagnosis of challenging medical problems that benefit from the availability of specialists representing many areas.

The Lahey Clinic is a national or regional center for renal artery bypass, techniques of laser surgery, treatment of kidney stones, and cochlear implantation for the deaf.

Some of medicine's most advanced equipment helps Lahey doctors to help others. The magnetic resonance imaging system uses magnetism combined with radio waves to obtain finely detailed images of internal organs without radiation. The Doppler Color Echocardiographic System uses the latest generation of ultrasound to obtain real-time images of blood flow in the heart, without the need for invasive tests. In the clinic's Center for Renal Stone Disease, an Extracorporeal Shock Wave Lithotripter uses acoustic shock waves to pulverize kidney stones from outside

the body, eliminating the need for surgery.

This center epitomizes the clinic's comprehensive orientation, bringing together the expertise of urologists, ra-

The Lithotripter pulverizes kidney stones with acoustic shock waves.

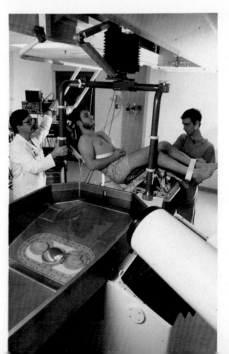

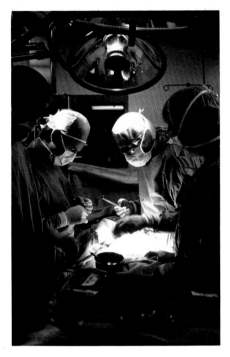

diologists, and internists from several subspecialties, not only to eliminate a patient's existing kidney stones, but also to prevent stone recurrence.

With this approach, staff members have the opportunity to concentrate on the latest advances in their areas of interest while remaining in close contact with specialists in other fields.

At the Lahey Clinic, emphasis is also placed on developing and using techniques of outpatient care whenever possible as part of an effort to eliminate unnecessary hospitalization.

Throughout its history the clinic has been committed to the development of new instrumentation and refinement of medical and surgical techniques. Two research units at the clinic are presently evaluating new techniques for microsurgery and applications for laser technology. The Medical Technology Development Committee seeks to foster collaborative research and development between clinic staff members and the high-technology industry. Participating companies include Mitre Corporation and Arthur D. Little Enterprises, Inc.

The Lahey Clinic first made a name for itself while located in cramped quarters in the heart of Boston. Dr. Frank H. Lahey was a prominent surgeon when he left the Harvard and

In surgery at the Lahey Clinic.

Tufts medical faculties to open a small, private clinic in the Back Bay in 1923.

The new clinic represented a break from medical convention of the time. While most physicians worked solo, referring difficult cases to the medical schools, Lahey brought physicians of different specialties together to pool their knowledge and work as a team to solve health problems.

Lahey himself was a pioneer in thyroid and gall bladder surgery and, under his leadership, the clinic also gained a reputation for surgery of the liver, pancreas, and biliary tract. Dr. Sara M. Jordan, one of the original staff members, became one of the world's preeminent gastroenterologists during her lifelong association with the clinic.

Lahey physicians pioneered techniques in high-voltage radiation therapy for cancer, the safe use of frozen blood in surgery, the development of one of the first heart-lung machines, and arterial infusion chemotherapy. The first feasible portable chemotherapy pump was also invented at the clinic.

After Lahey's death in 1953, the clinic was reorganized into the not-for-profit Lahey Clinic Foundation. Although the city facilities had been

expanded, the staff of nearly 100 physicians was hard pressed for space by 1970. The foundation began a search for a new home in which all activities could be centralized in one large, modern complex.

The resulting seven-story Lahey Clinic Medical Center in Burlington opened its doors in 1980. The building accommodates its large outpatient population in the Charles A. Dana Ambulatory Care Center. The Mary and Arthur R. Clapham Hospital, located within the medical center, contains 200 beds for inpatients.

A Walk-In Center, adjacent to the main lobby, provides care without an appointment on a first-come, first-serve basis for minor or routine health problems. For life-threatening or other urgent problems, the Emergency Department on the medical center's second floor is open 24 hours a day.

The Lahey Clinic Medical Center continues to expand its services and facilities. A new wing is planned for construction on the medical center's east side to add 72 beds, four operating rooms, and office and examining room space for 40 additional physicians. Completion is expected in 1990.

Hand surgery is one of more than 30 subspecialties represented on the Lahey medical staff.

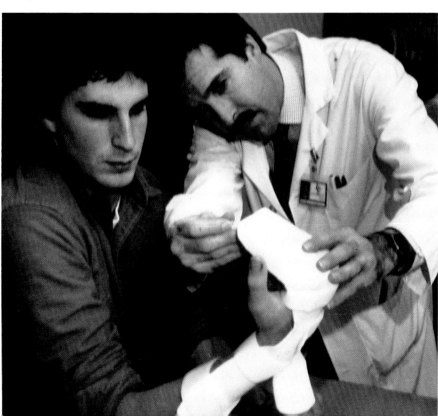

BENTLEY COLLEGE

On a clear day, from the crest of Cedar Hill in suburban Waltham, students at Bentley College can look across to the Prudential Tower and the skyline of New England's cultural capital. It's an appropriate view for the 7,300 students attending Bentley because the corporate district is where many graduates want to be. An oft-repeated and carefully watched statistic at the college reflects these ambitions: More than 90 percent of its undergraduates find employment within six months of graduation.

What started as a two-year program in accounting has become New England's largest institution of higher learning that specializes in business. The college has been authorized to grant undergraduate degrees since 1961. It all began in 1917, when the students of Harry Clark Bentley, chairman of the Accounting Department at Boston University, suggested that he

Bentley College is New England's largest institution of higher learning that specializes in business.

start a school of his own. He began teaching a class of 30 at night in a room on Huntington Avenue. The school moved to three other locations, on Tremont and Boylston streets, until it moved to a 110-acre home in Waltham in 1968.

A turning point for the small business college came when Law Professor Gregory H. Adamian took over as president. Born in Somerville, Massachusetts, to Armenian-American parents, Adamian received a bachelor of arts degree from Harvard, a law degree from Boston University, and a master's degree in public administration from Harvard. Beginning the practice of law in Cambridge in 1950, Adamian soon joined Bentley College as a part-time lecturer in economics and law. In 1955 he became a full-time Bentley faculty member while continuing his law practice. He was promoted to professor of law and chairman of the Law Department in 1968, and college president two years later.

Since his election, Adamian and his staff have transformed Bentley from a single-program institution to a broad

business college that educates graduates and professionals as well as undergraduates in a variety of fields. Also during Adamian's presidency, the faculty has grown from 84 to 364; the physical plant has increased from 16 to 43 buildings; and its endowment has risen from $350,000 in 1970 to $39.3 million in 1987. Gifts and grants have increased by a factor of 12 during the Adamian years.

The curriculum at Bentley, taught by 216 full-time and 148 part-time faculty members, is distinguished by its flexibility and its ties with what college students usually refer to as the "real world." Undergraduates can earn degrees by taking full-time day, part-time evening, and summer courses. While students can earn a B.S. degree in nine fields, from accountancy to marketing, they can also earn a B.A. degree by working with faculty advisers to design a liberal arts program that meets their interests. All freshmen are awarded portable microcomputers to start them on the road to computer literacy in their chosen fields. To help undergraduates get off to a smooth start, the col-

The Bentley College Solomon R. Baker Library is at the center of the Upper Campus.

lege offers housing to all incoming freshmen who request it.

At the graduate level, the stress is on technical expertise for highly specialized business careers, including accountancy, computer information systems, human resource management, and international management. Bentley offers a master of business administration (MBA) in eight concentrations, as well as five M.S. degrees and an advanced professional certificate in taxation. Sixty percent of Bentley undergraduates are from Massachusetts, and nearly all graduate students are state residents.

In the summer of 1986 Bentley consolidated its evening and continuing-education divisions into one School of Continuing and Professional Studies (SCPS). An Adult Information and Referral Center assists part-time students in selecting the appropriate courses, certificate programs, or degree programs offered at Bentley to meet their individual professional goals. SCPS offers nine certificate programs, including microcomputer applications,

paralegal studies, and real property administration. Six other programs concentrate on real estate, tax, accounting, and general professional development. In 1986, 6,000 people were enrolled in SCPS programs, almost equal to the number of students attending degree programs at Bentley.

In addition to the academic programs at Bentley, several new centers link the campus to the corporate world,

providing important forums for professionals and students. Bentley's Center for Business Ethics, one of the first of its kind in the country, holds national conferences every 18 months. Robert E. Mercer, chairman of the board and chief executive officer of The Goodyear Tire & Rubber Company, delivered the keynote address for the 1987 conference, with its theme of "Ethics of Organizational Transformation: Mergers, Takeovers, and Corporate Restructuring." Bentley's Center for Tax Studies sponsors an annual tax forum attended by representatives of the Internal Revenue Service and others who come from around the country to discuss tax laws as they apply to business.

As Bentley has added students, faculty, buildings, and programs, it has begun to consider limiting enrollment. There are geographical limits as to how much it can grow, say college officials. However, Bentley's building program has resulted in expanded facilities, including a new Graduate Center wing to complement a newly expanded student center, a new administration building, a 195-bed apartment complex, and a multimillion-dollar physical education center featuring an Olympic-size pool.

More than 90 percent of Bentley's seniors find employment within six months of graduation.

BABSON COLLEGE

When Babson College was founded in 1919, Roger Ward Babson set out to prepare tomorrow's managers and entrepreneurs for leadership in business, industry, government, and nonprofit organizations. Emphasizing innovation, initiative, and creativity, Babson urged students to "pull the cart, instead of riding it."

For 70 years Babson College has carried on his philosophy. The institution's alumni hold leadership positions in the Boston business community, across the United States, and in 75 countries worldwide. Babson Alumni are accomplished entrepreneurs, lawyers, bankers, and executives in both the public and private sectors.

Whether in business, accounting, or law, Babson educates students to assume managerial responsibilities. The school aggressively encourages the entrepreneurial spirit and teaches students how to become leaders in both business and life. Students learn that management is not a new "pop" science but one of the most complex and challenging of the arts.

At Babson, students earn a business education through liberal arts training and management instruction. The management and liberal arts faculties, working together, provide courses that interrelate across fields. As a result of this interdisciplinary approach, students understand business and the world in which it operates. They learn the workings of human organizations, economic systems, and the dynamics of

Experienced faculty teach practical courses that focus on real-world solutions to business problems. Students are challenged by a faculty who are successful professionals as well as skilled teachers and scholars.

leadership. Liberal arts courses are mastered with insights gained from management action and decision making, and business acumen is developed from the breadth of the liberal arts program.

In both classroom and campus activities, students are challenged by faculty who are successful professionals as well as skilled teachers and scholars. Of the 102 full-time faculty members, 96 percent hold doctoral degrees and many have significant experience as practitioners and consultants in both national and international corporations. Many Babson professors teach abroad, providing foreign students and universities the opportunity to learn "the American way" of business.

Babson offers Bachelor of Science and Master of Business Administration degrees. A coeducational institution, the college has about 1,500 undergraduates who represent more than 40 states and 50 nations. Undergraduates belong to business groups and international organizations. Many run small businesses on campus, applying classroom skills to profitable on-campus ventures.

About 150 full-time and 1,300 part-time graduate students are enrolled at Babson. These M.B.A. candidates represent 350 American colleges and universities, as well as 20 international institutions. Part-time students are em-

Located just 15 miles west of Boston, the Babson College campus spreads across 450 acres of beautiful woodlands in Wellesley, Massachusetts.

ployed in virtually every major corporation and financial institution in the Boston area and throughout New England.

The college's MBA program offers specialized concentration in International Business, as well as specialized programs such as the Management Consulting Field Experience Internship, and the International Management Internship Program (IMIP)—a program in which students earn academic credit while working in the international business arena. The IMIP has placed more than 190 students in leading corporations located in 14 countries worldwide.

Located just 15 miles west of Boston, the Babson campus spreads across 450 acres of beautiful woodlands in Wellesley, Massachusetts. The campus facilities are continually growing to keep pace with technological advancement. The Horn Library houses more than 100,000 volumes, 1,000 periodicals, and an extensive collection of materials on microfilm and microfische. The Horn Computer Center, which maintains Babson's reputation for leadership in computerized fa-

For 70 years Babson College has been preparing tomorrow's managers and entrepreneurs for leadership in business, industry, government, and nonprofit organizations.

cilities for business students, houses two VAX 11/780s, a PDP 11/70, labs with 150 work stations, IBM PCs, Digital Rainbows, VAX terminals, and more than 2,000 software programs. Babson also has networking capabilities to and from all on-campus offices, residence hall rooms, and many classrooms.

The new Center for Executive Education includes a two-story educational wing, complete with interactive tiered lecture rooms and state-of-the-art audiovisual equipment, and a three-story, 130-room residential wing. The School for Executive Education, located in the new center, is one of the leading providers of executive education in the nation. Experienced faculty teach practical courses that focus on real-world solutions to business problems. The companies involved in the Executive Education programs, including Hewlett-Packard, Polaroid, Shawmut Bank, and New England Telephone, help to further Babson's dedication to lifelong learning and high-quality management education at all stages.

In spring 1988 construction began on Babson's new field house, which will hold a gymnasium, indoor track, squash and racketball courts, and a complete fitness facility. Athletics, an integral part of Babson's educational program, include a wide range of varsity sports and intramural teams. The college is a member of the National Collegiate Athletic Association (NCAA), the Eastern College Athletic Conference, and the Massachusetts Association of Intercollegiate Athletics for Women. Over the years Babson's sports teams have won several championships, including three national titles in soccer and one in ice hockey.

In 1978 Babson created the Acad-

emy of Distinguished Entrepreneurs. Every spring, the college honors internationally recognized entrepreneurs at its Founder's Day celebration. Members of the academy include such innovators as the late Ray Kroc of McDonald's Corporation; Diane Von Furstenburg, DVF, Inc.; An Wang, Wang Laboratories; Kenneth Olsen, president of Digital Equipment Corporation; and Royal Little, founder and former chairman of Textron, Inc.

Babson is accredited by the New England Association of Schools and Colleges and is the only college of business administration not affiliated with a university system to receive accreditation by the American Assembly of Collegiate Schools of Business (AACSB).

Over the years Babson College and the Boston area have developed a dynamic partnership that has proved highly beneficial to both: the college's proximity to the stimulating Boston business and financial community has enriched the education of Babson College students. In turn, the college has tuned out graduates offering the kind of capable leadership qualities and strong sense of community and social responsibility that is the foundation of the area's best organizations.

Athletics are an integral part of Babson's educational program and include a wide range of varsity sports and intramural teams. The men's soccer team has won three national titles.

SUFFOLK UNIVERSITY

Suffolk University on historic Beacon Hill. Photo by Richard Pasley

Suffolk University is a dynamic urban university with 5,500 students of diverse backgrounds and ages enrolled in day and evening programs in its College of Liberal Arts and Sciences, School of Management, and Law School. Strategically located on Beacon Hill in the heart of Boston, the university is accessible from all parts of the metropolitan area. It is adjacent to the State House, the Suffolk County Courthouse, and other government buildings, where tomorrow's leaders meet today's.

Founded as a law school in 1906, the university developed by adding a College of Liberal Arts and Sciences in 1934 and a School of Management in 1937. On April 29, 1937, the Law School, the College of Liberal Arts, and the School of Management were chartered as Suffolk University by the Massachusetts General Court. The university is accredited by the New England Association of Schools and Colleges.

The fundamental mission of Suffolk University is to provide higher education of excellent quality at a reasonable cost in a supportive yet challenging environment. President Daniel H. Perlman is particularly proud of "the unique educational opportunities provided by a wide variety of experiential learning activities that utilize our exceptional location to good advantage, including cooperative education, internships, practicums, clinical legal education, work-study assignments, and field experiences . . . "

The Law School, which confers the Juris Doctor degree, provides high-quality instruction in legal theory, as well as process and practice, taking advantage of the urban setting to educate students from throughout the United States. The law school is accredited by the American Bar Association and is a member of the Association of American Law Schools. Suffolk presently has one of the largest Juris Doctor programs in the nation.

The Stephen P. Mugar Law Library is housed on four floors of the Donahue Building. Its spacious reading rooms are open seven days a week with professional assistance available days, evenings, and weekends. The growing collection—presently at 250,000 volumes—is part of a network of state, bar, and private law libraries that provides Suffolk law students with one of the largest collections of legal, business, and government document material in the nation.

The Law School's Center for Continuing Professional Development offers practitioners the opportunity to attend professional seminars presented by outstanding national authorities. The Law School is the new home of the National Board of Trial Advocacy, which certifies attorneys throughout the nation as trial specialists in civil and criminal trial advocacy. In announcing the move of NBTA from Washington, D.C., Law School Dean David J.

Sargent noted that an above average number of the Law School's 15,000 graduates "are actively involved in trial practice. Thus, our affiliation with the National Board of Trial Advocacy is not only fitting but will further enhance our reputation as a trial practice-oriented law school."

The School of Management at Suffolk University emphasizes pragmatic management education for working and preprofessional people. Most students have ongoing commitments that complement their educational experiences. The school offers full-time and part-time programs in accounting, finance, computer information systems, management, and marketing that develop ability in problem solving and decision making.

The undergraduate program combines a strong background in the liberal arts with intensive study in the selected area of business administration. All students are provided a strong foundation in accounting, business law, computer information systems, marketing management, finance, and economics.

At the graduate level, the school offers the MBA, MPA, MPA in Health Administration, and Saturday executive MPA and MBA programs designed for men and women with five years of managerial experience. The Executive

Suffolk University law students in Moot Court competition. Photo by Frank Siteman

MBA program includes an overseas component. The MPA program is accredited by the National Association of Schools of Public Affairs and Administration, one of only four in New England. Suffolk University's School of Management and Law School offer a combined JD/MPA program integrating professional education in law and public management.

The School of Management celebrated its 50th anniversary in September 1987. In his remarks Richard L. McDowell, dean of the School of Management, pointed to "significant new dimensions for the School of Management since its founding as a part-time undergraduate business college in 1937 . . . The school has a strong international dimension and broad computer applications. Virtually all of the faculty are engaged in significant research. In short, the school is part of the mainstream of management education."

The College of Liberal Arts and Sciences awards the bachelor's degree in 15 traditional liberal arts majors, and career-oriented programs in education and human resource development, communications and journalism, medical technology, social work, crime and delinquency, and clinical chemistry. There are preprofessional programs for students planning careers in dentistry, optometry, medicine, veterinary science, and law. Technical programs include biology, chemistry, marine biology, physics, electronic engineering, computer engineering, airway computer science, and airway electronic

Physics engineering students working with a laser. Photo by Richard Pasley

systems. The aviation-related programs include student internships in the control tower at Logan Airport. Other state-of-the-art programs include international economics with a language component, a lawyer's assistant program, and continuing and professional studies (CAPS) program. In addition to its on-campus offerings, the biology department offers courses at its Robert S. Friedman Field Station at Edmunds, Maine.

Graduate programs are offered in education and human resources, including business education, counseling, and human resource development for aviation systems.

The College of Liberal Arts and Sciences and the School of Management

Management school students in the microcomputer laboratory. Photo by Richard Pasley

share the Mildred F. Sawyer Library on Ashburton Place, which contains 98,000 volumes and is a member of the Fenway Consortium with 700,000 volumes.

Michael R. Ronayne, dean of the College of Liberal Arts and Sciences emphasizes, "The purpose of the College of Liberal Arts and Sciences is to provide a dynamic liberal arts education with a professional component, one which is comprehensive and thorough, and prepares students to live enlightened and productive lives and to earn a living."

Suffolk University is a metropolitan and, to a growing extent, a regional, national, and international institution, with students from more than 30 foreign countries. Since 1906, when Gleason L. Archer established a law school for working adults, Suffolk University has graduated more than 32,000 students who have taken their places in the professional world. Among the university's alumni are some of New England's outstanding jurists, attorneys, businessmen and -women, teachers, writers, scientists, and two former mayors of Boston. As it develops new programs to meet emerging needs, Suffolk University continues to be guided by Gleason Archer's commitment to the community and to its people.

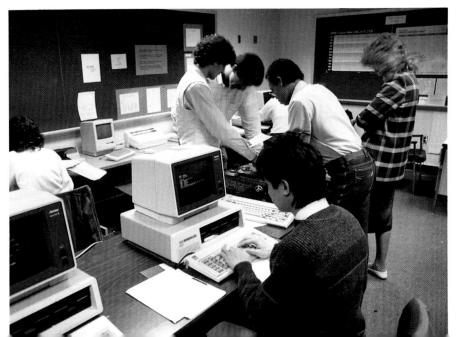

BRANDEIS UNIVERSITY

Brandeis University, which celebrated its 40th anniversary in 1988, is described by its president, Evelyn E. Handler, as "a research university which puts great emphasis upon the liberal arts and undergraduate education." From its inception in 1948, the university has attracted undergraduates on the strength of its unique approach to higher education—to provide opportunities for students to study with senior faculty and pursue advanced research at the undergraduate level.

A nonsectarian institution, Brandeis is the youngest major research university in the United States. Open to all, the university reflects the ideals and principles of the man it was named for—Supreme Court Justice Louis Dembitz Brandeis. A lawyer and social activist, Justice Brandeis symbolized the educated man in action.

Brandeis' current president espouses a strong commitment to the liberal arts. During her lengthy career in higher education, Evelyn Handler also has been a research biologist, a dean, as well as a university president in the public system. She is currently the chairperson of a national committee on high school

Brandeis combines the best of both worlds—a secluded campus just minutes away from a major urban center.

Historic Usen Castle forms the backdrop for students celebrating the conclusion of spring semester.

biology curricula, and has received honorary degrees from the University of Pittsburgh and Hunter College.

President Handler contends that two important traditions in higher education continue at Brandeis: the dedication to teaching that is characteristic of a small, selective college and the facilities and renowned faculty usually associated with a large research university. The school's strong commitment to the liberal arts is described as "a matrix for development" by president Handler. "Through the liberal arts we see into the past, learn the lessons and ideas of previous ages. We see into human character, into our political and social systems, as well as the development of science and technology. Through the liberal arts we also discover our capacity for disciplined inquiry and for defining and solving problems."

Known for its distinguished faculty of researchers and scholars, Brandeis is one of three research universities in the Boston area to be elected to the prestigious Association of American Universities. Although faculty members are involved in significant research, they also instruct all students, from freshmen to those in advanced programs. Ninety percent of the 357 full-time and 102 part-time faculty at Brandeis have doctorates. Eight faculty members have been elected to the National Academy of Sciences, seven to the American Association for the Advancement of

Sciences, and 21 to the American Academy of Arts and Sciences.

With an undergraduate enrollment of 2,775, Brandeis prides itself on a low faculty-to-student ratio of 9 to one, and awards the Bachelor of Arts degree in 32 fields of concentration, from African and Afro-American Studies to Theater Arts. Nearly 600 students are enrolled in the Graduate School of Arts and Sciences, and more than 100 students attend the university's professional school, the Florence Heller Graduate School for Advanced Studies in Social Welfare. Brandeis students have the option of designing their own independent concentration or pursuing a double major. A number of preprofessional programs are also available for students in architecture, business and management, dentistry, law, medicine, education, and several interdisciplinary fields. There are also several combined B.A./M.A. programs for exceptional students.

Located 10 miles west of Boston, Brandeis was founded as the gift of the American Jewish community to higher education. Today the university boasts a modern campus of 96 buildings on 250 acres. Brandeis contains up-to-

The view from the Brandeis Chapels offers a panoramic sweep of the campus.

date facilities and resources for undergraduates and scholars alike.

The science complex houses the Rosenstiel Basic Medical Science Research Center, nationally known for research in molecular and cell biology, structural biology, and immunology. Two VAX 11/780 computers are available to computer science majors. Computer clusters offer students the use of personal computers with software and printers. Dormitory rooms also are wired to access the university's mainframe computer.

In the cultural arena Brandeis is home to the Spingold Theater Arts Center, a professional repertory company, and the Rose Art Museum. The theater arts center provides space for

every facet of the performing arts. And the museum houses a permanent collection of post-World War II art considered among the finest at any American university. Most recently the university received a $3.5-million gift that, when matched, will help fund the construction of a new field house.

As the newest member of the University Athletic Association, Brandeis joins eight other private research universities, such as the University of Chicago, Johns Hopkins University, and New York University in intercollegiate competition. Student athletes compete in 22 varsity sports from cross country to tennis and swimming, and qualify regionally and nationally in individual and team events.

The feeling at Brandeis University today is one of promise. Dedicated to the liberal arts and the pursuit of advanced research, Brandeis has established itself as a center for excellence in higher education. Again, in president Handler's words, "The quality of mind developed and honed through a liberal education will prove to be a key ingredient in regaining American competitiveness. It has been shown that our colleges and universities enable young people to become creative rather than merely technically proficient. And I contend that it is the liberal arts—well-taught—that will make the critical difference."

Between classes, students often gather to compare notes and catch up with friends.

JEWISH MEMORIAL HOSPITAL

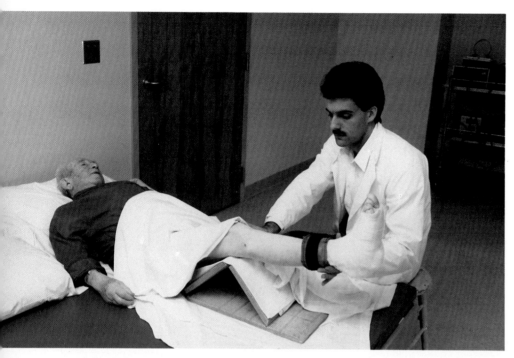

A patient is given physical therapy in the new Murray Fertel Rehabilitation Wing at Jewish Memorial Hospital.

Jewish Memorial Hospital is a 207-bed rehabilitation and chronic care facility providing active medical treatment to inpatients and outpatients of all ages. A teaching hospital affiliated with the Boston University Medical Center, JMH is also a recognized leader in the field of geriatric medicine (diseases of the aged) and has treated significant numbers of the elderly throughout Massachusetts. JMH's relationship with Boston University's Gerontology Center Long-Term Care Program allows the hospital to promote education and research in aging and chronic illnesses while providing high-quality patient care.

The nonprofit teaching hospital is located less than two miles from the Boston University School of Medicine and University Hospital. JMH is supported by an active corps of volunteers whose six auxiliaries raise funds year round. It is also a constituent agency of Combined Jewish Philanthropies.

Patients come to JMH from their homes, acute care hospitals, and nursing homes. All suffer from multiple chronic diseases or the lasting effects of injuries. They require continued hospital level treatment, with an average length of stay of 42 days. Team conferences are held weekly on each of the eight patient care units to share infor-

mation related to each patient's needs and to provide a unified approach to his or her care. The multidisciplinary team consists of the patient's physician, nurse, social worker, physical therapist, occupational therapist, speech/language pathologist, therapeutic recreation specialist, respiratory therapist, and clinical dietician.

Attending and resident physicians and nursing and social work students from Boston University come to JMH to learn the specialties of geriatric medicine and long-term care. Social workers on staff follow patients from

The multidisciplinary team on the Comprehensive Assessment and Rehabilitation Environment (CARE) Unit, a neuropsychiatric program.

admission to discharge, ensuring that their continuity of care needs are met with timely discharges either to home or a nursing home. JMH often refers elderly patients who are returning home with deteriorating health to the Home Medical Service of University Hospital for continued medical and nursing care.

Rehabilitation is a specialty at JMH. It teaches patients how to live with permanent or chronic symptoms arising from old age, disease, or injury. The rehabilitation unit is headed by a physiatrist who works with the departments of physical therapy, occupational therapy, communication disorders, and therapeutic recreation to help determine the most effective treatment program for a patient. An experienced multidisciplinary health care team treats patients suffering from stroke, head trauma, arthritis, spinal cord injury, amputation, and other disabling illnesses. Using modern equipment, patients work with their therapists to become as self-sufficient as possible. In many cases, rehabilitation can allow the individual to return to his community.

Because rehabilitation is considered vital to a patient's successful recovery, the hospital, in 1988, completed a new wing dedicated to furnishing these services. Rehabilitation services—physical therapy, occupational therapy, communication disorders, and therapeutic recreation services—are centralized there. A new podiatry clinic has

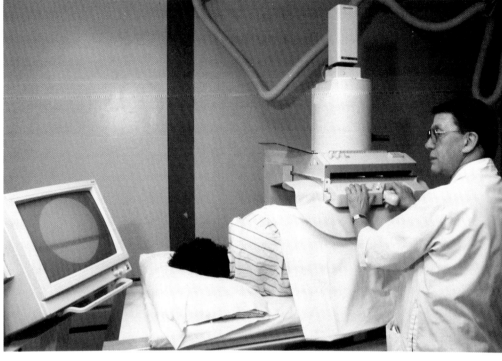

opened as well. All services in the Rehabilitation Wing are designed to provide outpatient as well as inpatient care. The building project has given the hospital a new look, too. On the third level is a new entrance with a covered walkway leading directly from the new lobby to the parking lot.

The new Rehabilitation Wing replaced the 1880 wood-frame structure that served as the original Beth Israel Hospital before it was sold to the Ladies Bikur Cholim Association in 1929. That year the association realized a 15-year-old dream to provide a haven for the chronically ill, and dedicated a 42-bed facility called the Greater Boston Bikur Cholim Hospital. In 1937 it was renamed Jewish Memorial Hospital.

The hospital grew continuously. A wing, an annex, an annex extension, additional patient care units, and a nurses' residence were added, until the hospital reached its current level of 207 beds. In 1971 JMH became affiliated with Boston University Medical Center.

Growth at JMH has taken place through the addition of highly sophisticated services, including a total paren-

teral nutrition program, a long-term solution for patients who are unable to absorb adequate nutrients from their intestinal tracts. A behavioral neuropsychiatric program called the CARE (Comprehensive Assessment and Rehabilitation Environment) Unit evaluates and treats individuals with a wide range of behavioral and functional disorders. It is the only program of its kind

at a chronic care/rehabilitation hospital in greater Boston. The pulmonary care service at JMH expanded to address the backlog in service for many chronically ventilated patients at acute care hospitals across the Commonwealth. The Ventilator Unit provides mechanical support and portable ventilation for patients who cannot breathe on their own. The most recently implemented new service at JMH is outpatient Pediatric Rehabilitation. Up to 30 developmentally delayed children, ages three months to three years, are participating in this ambulatory care service. They receive services in physical therapy, occupational therapy, communication disorders, and rehabilitation psychology. Pediatric Rehabilitation is part of the hospital's growing rehabilitation and ambulatory care services.

Through multidisciplinary treatment, complete rehabilitation services, and coordinated discharge planning, Jewish Memorial Hospital helps the chronically ill recover and return to their homes as quickly as possible and live as independently as their conditions allow.

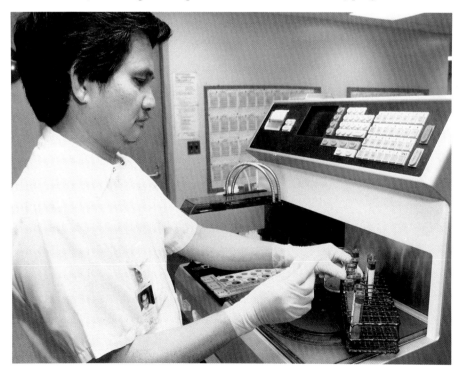

THE UNIVERSITY HOSPITAL

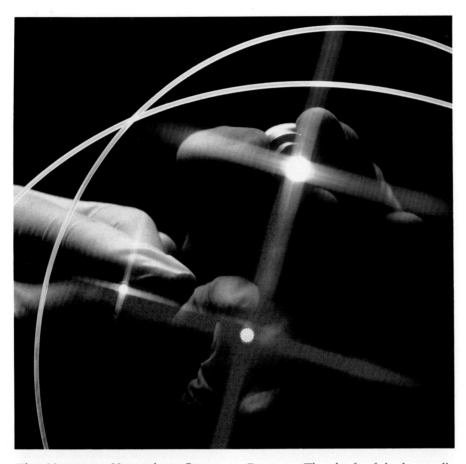

The University Hospital at Boston University Medical Center began as a dispensary and 16-bed facility chartered by the Commonwealth of Massachusetts in 1855. Today the private, nonprofit hospital is a major referral center for the Northeast, focusing strongly on several of the medical areas in which it has become preeminent: cardiovascular and circulatory medicine, the neurosciences, critical care/trauma, and geriatric medicine. With 379 beds, the hospital offers care in all of the adult medical specialties except obstetrics, and plays a leading role in advancing medical knowledge and training future generations of health professionals.

Located in Boston's South End, the University Hospital, together with Boston University School of Medicine and the Goldman School of Graduate Dentistry, comprise Boston University Medical Center. As part of the Medical Center, members of the University Hospital's medical-dental staff also are on the faculty of either the School of Medicine or the School of Graduate Dentistry. The chiefs of the hospital's clinical departments also are chairpersons of the corresponding academic departments for their specialties.

The hospital got its start in Room 17 of the Tremont Temple in downtown Boston, where its rotating staff of 16 physicians gave free medical care to the needy. In 1871 the hospital opened on 14 Burroughs Place (behind the present Wang Center) with 16 beds. Five years later a new hospital was constructed at the present-day location off of Albany Street. In 1962 the hospital and Boston University formally coordinated their resources and activities to more effectively meet the basic objectives of teaching, research, and patient care.

The close relationship between UH and the School of Medicine has pro-

vided fertile ground for medical advancement, accounting for an unusual record of achievements. Among many firsts, the hospital was the site of the earliest and most extensive clinical trials of penicillin; the first to use diuretics for the treatment of patients with hypertension, and the first to develop the research techniques that demonstrated that gallstones could be chemically dissolved as an alternative to surgery. In 1971 UH physicians were the first in the world to use a laser as a scalpel.

The hospital's Evans Memorial Department of Clinical Research and Preventive Medicine was one of the few departments of its kind in the world in 1912, when Bostonian Maria

An intricate glass-and-metal spaceframe caps the lobby of the University Hospital's new Atrium Pavilion. This new building is a symbol of the hospital's commitment to continue providing quality health care to the New England area.

The University Hospital is conveniently located in Boston's historic South End, just minutes from the crossroads of the Massachusetts Turnpike and the Southeast Expressway/Central Artery. The hospital has been an important part of the Boston community for more than a century, and has close ties with neighboring Boston City Hospital.

Antoinette Evans donated a building and an endowment in her late husband's memory to create a hospital department exclusively for clinical research. The hospital also has the oldest continuous Home Medical Service in the nation. Beginning in 1875, UH nurses and doctors, accompanied by medical students, made rounds to deliver home care in nearby neighborhoods, and they are still doing so today. Today's Home Medical Service focuses on the needs of frail, elderly patients.

A number of new programs and services have added to the hospital's areas of strength. One such program is the new Women's Health Group, the nation's only university-based women's health unit with an all-women staff that concentrates on comprehensive coordinated health care for women patients. Other recent innovations include a Laser Center, for clinical care and research in the development of lasers in medicine, and the Northeast Regional Center for Brain Injury, a full-scale, multidisciplinary program for head-injured patients and their families. The center, which is the only one of its kind in the Northeast, offers a coordinated plan of care that encompasses evacua-

tion from the site of injury through any long-term care provisions that must accompany rehabilitation.

The University Hospital employs more than 2,200 people, including physicians, medical residents, nurses, allied health professionals, and service and support personnel. The hospital's skilled staff handles approximately 11,000 inpatient admissions and 80,000 outpatients and emergency visits a year. Working in conjunction with nearby Boston City Hospital, UH forms one of Boston's three level I trauma centers. The hospital developed Boston Med Flight, an emergency medical helicopter service that transports critically ill and injured patients between hospitals and from the scenes of accidents, and operates this service as a consortium with other trauma centers.

In 1984 the Commonwealth of Massachusetts Public Health Council granted approval to UH for the replacement of all the inpatient units in its oldest buildings. The centerpiece of the renovation effort is the Atrium Pavilion, a startling new piece of modern glass-and-steel architecture, and a structure that houses nearly two-thirds of all the hospital's inpatient beds plus all of the surgical support facilities, including a 16-bed Surgical Intensive Care Unit. An unusual feature of the Atrium Pavilion is the extensive use of skylights and windows, which bring natural light to traditionally cloistered hospital areas.

Opened in 1987, the Atrium Pavilion serves as the hospital's new core clinical facility and main entrance. The building is designed to accommodate future space needs of the hospital, and its design will allow for the addition of two patient-care levels to the existing structure. The Atrium Pavilion eventually will have a total of 10 floors.

The University Hospital is working actively with neighbors and community organizations to address health problems that arise from the socioeconomic condition of the South End. While it recognizes that construction of a new facility will not necessarily make problems disappear, UH's advanced facility, innovative programs, trained health-care teams, and productive relationships with community groups will help the hospital to meet the challenges of the next century.

As an academic medical center, the University Hospital trains physicians from all over the world.

MASSACHUSETTS EYE AND EAR INFIRMARY

The Massachusetts Eye and Ear Infirmary is one of a small number of facilities in the world that provide a hospital-based setting for specialty care in ophthalmology, which deals with the medical and surgical treatment of the eye, and otolaryngology, which deals with the medical and surgical treatment of the head and neck, including the ear, nose, and throat.

As the primary teaching hospital in its specialties for Harvard Medical School, the Infirmary's education and research programs attract physicians and scientists from around the world. As a result, a unique blend of clinical care and medical and scientific research exists at the Infirmary.

As a unique specialty care institution, the Infirmary provides a host of one-of-a-kind patient services, including the only eye and ENT emergency room in New England, the region's only ophthalmic laser center, the region's only facility for the testing and treatment of balance disorders, and the region's only center specializing in vision, hearing, and speech rehabilitation. In addition, the Infirmary houses three renowned research laboratories as well as an extensive medical library and archival collection, constituting New En-

Massachusetts Eye and Ear Infirmary

gland's largest center for basic and clinical studies in ophthalmology and otolaryngology.

While more than 90 percent of patients who receive care at the Infirmary each year are Massachusetts residents, others come from around New England and the rest of the United States, as well as from a host of foreign countries. In keeping with the hospital's history of charitable care, no patient is ever turned away because of inability to pay.

More than 300 physicians comprise the Infirmary's medical staff. Infirmary physicians care for the full range of conditions that affect the eye, ear, nose, throat, head, and neck—from a routine

examination of healthy eyes to surgical repair of a detached retina, from the treatment of "swimmer's ear" to surgical implantation of a sophisticated electronic device that can help the profoundly deaf to hear. In addition, a staff of more than 1,400 men and women are employed by the Infirmary, including nurses, dieticians, audiologists, technicians, social workers, secretarial staff, orderlies, and many others.

From its modest beginning more than 160 years ago, the Massachusetts Eye and Ear Infirmary has grown to be a major medical resource that is truly one of a kind in Massachusetts, in New England, and in the world.

In the Pediatric Unit Playroom

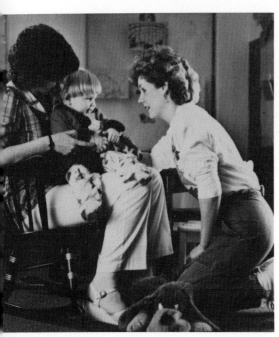

Mastoidectomy in Operating Suite 5

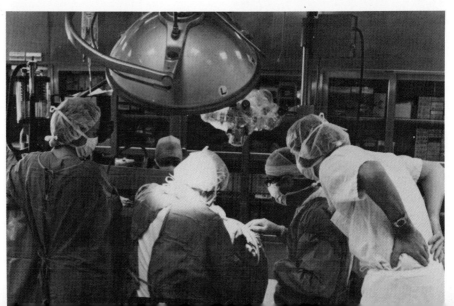

UNIVERSITY OF MASSACHUSETTS AT BOSTON

In only 25 years the University of Massachusetts at Boston has established itself as a nationally known public, urban institution—a component of the University of Massachusetts system with a particular focus on the needs of greater Boston. Also in that short span of time, the quality of its programs and faculty have earned the university special notice: In 1986 *Time* magazine singled out UMass/Boston as one of "nine hot colleges" to watch.

The student body at UMass/Boston is unique among the 39 colleges and universities located in the greater Boston area. The average age of the undergraduate student body is approximately 27 years, while nearly one-quarter of those students are older than 30. More than 56 percent are women and nearly 20 percent are minorities—higher than any other public four-year institution in New England. UMass/Boston draws most of its students from the metropolitan area: 40 percent live in Boston and nearly two-thirds live within the Route 128/I-95 belt. Approximately 2,000 graduate and 11,000 undergraduate students were enrolled during 1987.

The University of Massachusetts at Boston is the urban campus of the

The Harbor Campus of the University of Massachusetts at Boston, looking north and west from Dorchester Bay toward the downtown Boston skyline.

Commonwealth's land-grant university. The University of Massachusetts itself was founded in 1863 and the Boston campus was created in 1964 to bring the benefits of public higher education to the largest metropolitan area in New England. In the beginning the university was housed in a collection of rehabilitated office buildings in and around Park Square. In 1974 the major portion of the university moved to a new facility called the Harbor Campus at Columbia Point on the shoreline near Dorchester and South Boston. The institution's Downtown Center remains at the original location on the corner of Arlington and Stuart streets.

UMass/Boston is made up of six instructional units: the College of Arts and Sciences, the College of Management, the College of Public and Community Service, the College of Education, the College of Nursing, and the Program in Physical Education. The university is authorized to grant bachelor's, master's, and doctoral degrees, as well as certificates of advanced graduate study.

Approximately 578 faculty teach at UMass/Boston. Given the large number of nontraditional students, a conscious decision was made at UMass/Boston to emphasize teaching as well as scholarship. To this end, all faculty,

both senior and junior, are obliged to teach undergraduate courses at all levels. Research is not ignored, however, and the dollar figure for sponsored research has tripled since 1982. Faculty members have been honored with numerous grants and fellowships from the National Science Foundation, the Fulbright Fellowships, the National Endowment for the Humanities, the Ford Foundation, and the Guggenheim Fellowships.

Following the land-grant tradition, the University of Massachusetts at Boston strives to share with the area the results of its cumulative knowledge. For example, the Environmental Sciences Program offers research and policy advice to groups striving to clean up the Boston Harbor. Such UMass/Boston entities as the McCormack Institute of Public Affairs, the Institute for Learning and Teaching, the Trotter Institute for the Study of Black Culture, and the Gerontology Institute seek to share the results of their studies with the decision makers in Boston and its surrounding towns and cities.

Professor James Ryan, a longtime faculty member, conferring with students on the Harbor Campus of UMass/Boston.

Boston Celtics, 432;

Boston Harbor Hotel, 433

CHAPTER NINETEEN

The Marketplace

Boston's retail establishments, service industries, products, and sporting events are enjoyed by residents and visitors to the area.

Photo © Judith Canty

ZAYRE CORPORATION

It was 1956 when Zayre opened the nation's first neighborhood, self-service, general merchandise, discount department store, launching a new concept in retailing. The Max and Morris Feldberg family, owner of a chain of ladies' apparel stores, had then predicted that discounting would be the growth direction of the future.

More than 30 years later the $8-billion, 80,000-employee Zayre Corporation is one of the largest discount and specialty retailers in the United States, operating more than 1,500 stores in suburbs and inner cities coast to coast.

Massachusetts-based and nationally headquartered in Framingham, Zayre Corporation represents six separate retail operations, which include Zayre Stores, T.J. Maxx, Hit or Miss, Chadwick's of Boston, BJ's Wholesale Club, and HomeClub. All of these divisions offer customers genuine value at competitive prices, each with their own distinctive marketing strategy and target consumer.

The corporation's largest division, Zayre Stores, is the nation's fourth-largest discount department store retailer, operating 425 discount department stores in 26 states and featuring more than 100 merchandise categories at competitively low prices.

Maintaining its stronghold as the nation's second-largest off-price retailer, T.J. Maxx operates 300 stores from Portland, Maine, to Portland, Oregon. These apparel "supermarts" offer brand-name, off-price, family apparel, domestics, and giftware.

Hit or Miss, established in the mid-1960s, offers current, high-fashion, brand-name women's apparel at low retail prices in 550 stores.

Chadwick's of Boston, founded in 1983, sells off-price women's apparel through a mail-order catalog.

BJ's Wholesale Club, introduced in 1984, is a warehouse merchandising concept targeting small business institutions and defined groups with thousands of brand-name items at wholesale prices on a membership basis.

HomeClub, the corporation's newest West Coast-based division, is a unique wholesale cash-and-carry home-improvement products club offering more than 25,000 items for the home.

The Zayre Office of Consumer and Community Affairs assists with employee and financial support for the March of Dimes, United Way, Save the Children, Toys for Tots, the Easter Seal Society, Muscular Dystrophy, and many other worthy organizations and charities in the communities that Zayre serves. One of several $100,000 Zayre-Cares grants was awarded locally to Boston City Hospital for the expansion of its Neonatal Intensive Care Unit.

Zayre Corporation is and plans to be a major contender in the highly competitive retail environment well into the next decade.

A major operator of discount department stores, off-price apparel specialty stores, and membership warehouse clubs, Zayre Corporation represents six separate retail businesses. Clockwise (from top): Zayre Stores, Home-Club, Chadwick's of Boston, T.J. Maxx, BJ's Wholesale, and Hit or Miss.

BOSTON ATHLETIC ASSOCIATION

On the third Monday of every April an annual "rite of spring" consumes the city of Boston. Thousands of people line the sidewalks, sit on porches, and lean out windows along a 26.2-mile route that begins at the Hopkinton Town Green, winds its way through a total of eight cities and towns, and finishes at Copley Square in Boston. Though a casual tourist might assume that these people are about to watch a Patriots' Day parade, what they are really doing is scrambling for space to witness one of the major athletic events of our time—the Boston Marathon.

As the legendary granddaddy of all marathons, Boston attracts the best distance runners in the world. Past Boston winners include such Olympians as Johnny A. Kelley, Bill Rodgers, Joan Benoit Samuelson, Alberto Salazar, Geoff Smith, Ibrahim Hussein, and Rosa Mota. Boston is the Kentucky Derby of distance running: Except for the Olympic Marathon, Boston is the only marathon that requires qualifying times to enter, and many runners consider "running Boston" a major milestone.

The prime responsibility for organizing the marathon rests on the shoulders of the Boston Athletic Association, a nonprofit organization founded in 1887. Staffed by several dedicated employees, the marathon is headed by a full-time director who assumes the year-round task of organizing the race. Present director Guy Morse follows a

The 1987 Boston Marathon Men's Open Division was won by Toshihiko Seko from Japan in 2:11:50. Courtesy, Fay Foto Service.

tradition of strong, colorful leadership exemplified by past director Will Cloney and by the late Jock Semple.

The Boston Marathon is a major co-operative effort, involving the support of more than 4,000 volunteers, numerous community groups, officials representing the Commonwealth of Massachusetts and the two cities and six towns along the route, and a strong team of local, national, and international corporate sponsors. All the effort is well worth it: The oldest annual marathon pumps an estimated $60 million in tourist and other revenue into the city of Boston.

Though the race itself is the focus of activities, it is only one of many events held over marathon week. A Sports & Fitness Expo, athletic seminars, a week-long series of press conferences, VIP receptions, dinners, and parties all are part of the week-long festivities.

Preparations for the Boston Marathon begin almost immediately after each year's race at the BAA offices in Boston and Hopkinton. Race applications are prepared, mailed, and later evaluated and processed; meetings are held with officials from local government and with the many volunteer groups; corporate sponsors are arranged and marathon week activities planned and coordinated; and media

credentials are issued to press representatives from all over the world. By the third week in April the city of Boston buzzes with anticipation. In 1988—the 92nd running of the marathon—more than 6,700 runners lined up in Hopkinton, and one million spectators lined the route to watch the race, displaying the support and enthusiasm that has made Boston sports fans renowned all over the world.

The Boston Marathon, with its rich history and sense of tradition, has seen many changes over the years. Strictly a men's race until 1972, the number of women participants in 1988 topped 1,000 for the first time. And after 89 years without prize money, the race now offers one of the richest purses in the sport and boasts being the world's first major marathon to award equal prize money to men and women. Today, more than ever, the love and enthusiasm of athletes and spectators, the officials, press, and volunteers remain undaunted, and leaves no doubt that "Boston is Boston," and will forever be of special significance among all the great athletic events of the world.

Andre Viger clocked in at the winning time of 1:55:42 in the 1987 Men's Wheelchair Division. Courtesy, Fay Foto Service

Crowds turn out along the route of the annual Boston Athletic Association's Boston Marathon to cheer for the runners. Courtesy, Fay Foto Service

CLEAN HARBORS, INC.

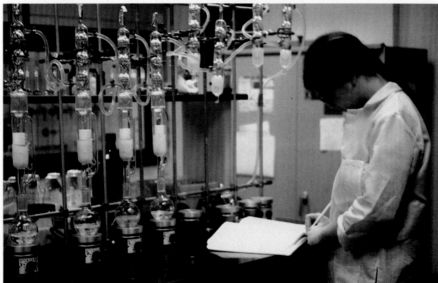

Clean Harbors provides home owners the opportunity to dispose of common chemical products safely.

McKim left Dee's organization and began Clean Harbors. Working out of a trailer in Bridgewater, Massachusetts, McKim's fledgling company posted revenues that grew from $1.5 million in 1982 to more than $70 million in 1987. The firm now operates in eight states and employs more than 850 dedicated professionals.

With the passage of the Federal Resource Conservation and Recovery Act of 1976, the Superfund Act in 1980, and the subsequent Massachusetts laws governing hazardous materials, an entire new concept of waste management has come into existence. Industries take responsibility for the management of chemical wastes in a much more stringent system than in the past. Most of what Clean Harbors handles for these clients is used gasoline, oil, cleansers, dyes, paints, or solvents, all of which must be disposed of carefully and in a manner that is also highly regulated.

Ground water is tested by Clean Harbors' Engineering Division to determine pollution levels and design correct treatment methods.

No one likes to think about hazardous waste; however, the issue is one that touches us all every day. There are more than 61,000 chemical products on the market today that enhance our lives but also produce wastes that can seriously pollute our environment if not properly disposed of.

Clean Harbors, Inc., is a public company in the business of controlling pollution. With locations throughout the Northeast and with the equipment and resources to test, analyze, clean up, transport, and dispose of hazardous materials, Clean Harbors operates a booming business in the region.

The Analytical Services Division at Clean Harbors tests a wide variety of chemicals that may cause harm to the environment.

Founded in 1980 by Alan McKim, Clean Harbors has grown to meet the needs of the public and private sectors in an increasingly complex and highly regulated business.

McKim began his career in 1973 when, at 19 years of age, he was asked by former Patriot football star Bob Dee to join Dee's oil pollution-control business. McKim became chief operating officer in 1979. At the age of 25,

In one of its most important roles, the company maintains an Emergency Response Unit ready to react in minutes to any chemical, petroleum, or other environmentally threatening accident. Like an EMT for the environment, a team of experts is on call 24 hours a day every day of the week. The unit includes a sophisticated communications system that fields calls from emergency numbers in six states. A mobile testing lab, 200 ground vehicles, boats, planes, and a custom-designed Emergency Response Van are positioned to respond within two hours or less to accidents in a six-state area.

More than 3,000 emergencies have been safely handled by Clean Harbors since 1982. Response teams often work with utility companies to clean up spills of PCBs, one of the most frequent emergencies handled by the company. Once commonly used as insulators in electrical transformers until they were banned by the federal government, PCBs pose a serious threat to ground water. In one of the company's most dramatic emergency calls, a team worked in raging seas to pump 200,000 gallons of fuel off the oil tanker *Eldia* when it went aground off Cape Cod in 1983. Recently Clean Harbors was awarded a two-year contract for statewide chemical incident response by the state's Department of Environmental Quality Engineering.

Clean Harbors of Braintree owns and operates several facilities for solvent and petroleum product reclamation, medical waste incineration, and the collection, classification, temporary storage, consolidation, and transportation of hazardous materials for ultimate disposal out of state. The facilities serve laboratories, hospitals, manufacturers, utility companies, and others. Purchased in 1985, the Clean Harbors of Braintree facility has been renovated with state-of-the-art safety and processing equipment.

The company maintains a fleet of more than 200 fully licensed vehicles to transport all forms of solid, semi-solid, and liquid waste. Clean Harbors is licensed to transport in 23 U.S. states and Canada. Also in Braintree, Clean

Comprehensive waste-management services are provided to Clean Harbors' clients throughout the Northeast.

Harbors Analytical Services Division provides testing backup for all Clean Harbors operations, as well as a wide range of testing and monitoring services for clients. With three mainframe computer data systems, the lab runs around the clock for timely analysis.

Clean Harbors' facility in Natick, Massachusetts, specializes in the analysis and consolidation of lab-pack chemicals and household hazardous wastes. Lab-packs are discarded, used, or outdated laboratory chemicals that are packed into drums of compatible materials and then directed for EPA-acceptable disposal. This division serves schools, hospitals, labs, research firms, and other small-quantity generators. The household hazardous waste division provides communities with periodic collections for home owners to enable proper disposal of common household chemicals.

Clean Harbors Field Services Division provides planned site cleanups, transformer decommissioning, lagoon cleaning, ground water reclamation, and total services for underground storage tanks. The Clean Harbors Engineering Division works closely with Field Services to assess contaminated sites, consult on waste reduction for clients, and develop specialized treatment processes.

Because federal laws will ban most wastes from landfill waste sites by 1989, Clean Harbors has proposed to build a rotary kiln incinerator at its Brain-

Clean Harbors employs more than 850 dedicated professionals.

tree facility. Of the Massachusetts-generated waste that the firm handles, 62 percent has to be transported out of state. However, the Superfund Act of 1980 stipulates that each state must demonstrate capability for disposal of hazardous wastes by 1989 or lose cleanup grants. Currently considered to be the best available technology, the rotary kiln incinerator will provide capacity for disposal of 45,000 tons of waste, bringing to the state an important tool for maintaining its environmental quality. Clean Harbors Inc., is dedicated to providing the highest-quality environmental services to enable the protection and preservation of the environment.

SEARS, ROEBUCK AND CO.

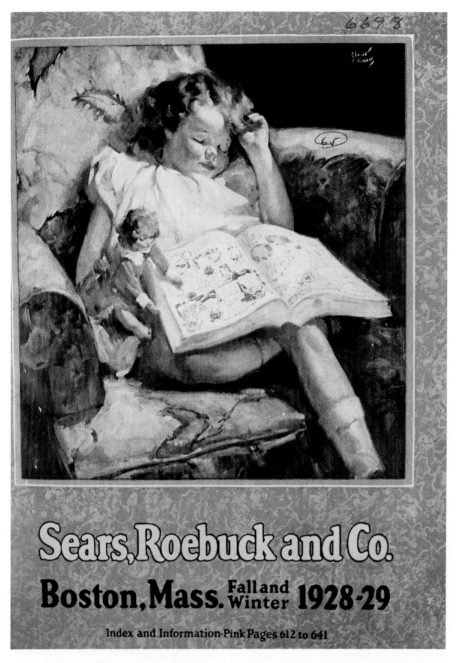

Sears, Roebuck and Co.
Boston, Mass. Fall and Winter 1928-29
Index and Information-Pink Pages 612 to 641

The year was 1928. One could buy a boy's suit with vest and golf knickers for $8.75, a Russian fox scarf for $35, and a Truphonic home phonograph for $75—all through the Sears, Roebuck and Co. catalog. Or, if living in Boston, one could take a short stroll from Fenway Park and buy the goods directly from the city's first Sears store on Brookline Avenue, which opened just in time for the Christmas rush that year.

"The opening of this big store is something to which the public of Boston has long looked forward because of the reputation which has preceded Sears, Roebuck and Co. in New England," a *Boston Herald* editorial proclaimed, "and there is no doubt that the public will be well pleased."

Although the store on Brookline closed in 1968, Sears continues to please its public in 12 retail stores in and around the city in towns such as Peabody, Saugus, Burlington, Dedham, and Braintree. Today Sears continues to open new stores in the area, and plans to open a host of paint and hardware stores in 1988.

Regional offices are located in the large Natick store. This office administers the more than 50 stores and offices throughout Massachusetts, Maine, New Hampshire, and Rhode Island. Sears Merchandise Group employs more than 9,000 people in the Boston area.

Sears continues to reach the local populace by distributing its famous catalog, first published in 1886. The original catalog spawned a family of 23 mail-order catalogs distributed annually.

Not only does Sears sell merchandise to Bostonians and the people of Massachusetts, but the retailer buys from them as well. More than 190 Massachusetts companies provide merchandise for Sears to sell nationwide.

Over the years Sears has become more than a chain of stores and a mail-order house. By branching out into insurance, real estate, and financial services, Sears, Roebuck and Co. has become one of America's largest corporations, with sales topping $48 billion in 1987.

All together Sears consists of Allstate Insurance Group, the Dean Witter Financial Services Group, and the Coldwell Banker Real Estate Group. Corporate headquarters are located in Chicago.

In 1987 these business groups employed more than 11,300 people throughout Massachusetts, operating more than 190 stores, offices, and other facilities. The Bay State is also home to nearly 17,000 Sears shareholders.

Formed by Sears in 1931, Allstate Insurance originally offered automobile insurance through the catalog and at desks in Sears stores. It is now the largest property-liability stock insurance company in the United States and one of the biggest life-health insurers.

Allstate offers a full range of insurance products for individuals and businesses, including auto insurance, home-owner insurance, renters' insur-

Middlesex County, as well as in the financial network centers that can be found in the larger Sears stores in the area. Dean Witter also markets and operates the Discover Card, a combination credit and financial services card introduced nationwide in late 1985.

Also in 1982 Sears acquired the Coldwell Banker Real Estate Group. Acting as a broker in residential and commercial real estate, the group invests in, develops, and manages commercial real estate and provides mortgages and other real estate-related services.

Since Sears acquired it, Coldwell Banker has significantly increased its activity in the residential market. The broker sells nearly one out of every 10 houses for resale in America, making it the nation's largest residential broker. In the Boston area, Coldwell Banker has 20 residential real estate offices. Representatives can also be found in in-store financial network centers. The commercial division maintains offices in downtown Boston and in the suburb of Wellesley.

ance, and a variety of personal and group life and health products. In 1987 Allstate handled claims totaling more than $150.3 million for Massachusetts individuals and businesses in all lines of insurance. In greater Boston, Allstate has sales and claims representatives in eight locations.

In 1982 Sears acquired the Dean Witter Financial Services Group. Currently Dean Witter is engaged in a wide range of activities, including securities and commodities brokerage; securities principal trading; investment management for mutual funds, pension funds, and others; investment banking, deposit taking, and lending; consumer credit; and mortgage banking to domestic and international retail and institutional clients.

In 1987 the group helped Massachu-

setts state and local governments raise funds for schools, hospitals, transportation, and other services by managing or co-managing more than $460.4 million worth of municipal bond issues. Locally Dean Witter services clients out of offices in Boston, Braintree, and

The Saugus store is one of many full-line Sears facilities in the Boston area. Photography by Howard J. Rosenfeld

THE SHERATON CORPORATION

Sheraton Mirage in Port Douglas, Queensland, Australia.

The global hospitality chain is continuously seeking ways to make business travel easier, more pleasant, and, ultimately, more productive.

Fortunately, the company had a few years of preparation for today's tremendous task. In 1937 two college friends from Harvard, Ernest Henderson and Robert Moore, acquired their first hotel—the Stonehaven in Springfield, Massachusetts. The brick building with 200 rooms was valued at $350,000—not pocket change back then.

The reality profits from the Stonehaven made possible the purchase of two more hotels within two years. One of these was a small Boston residential unit named the Sheraton Hotel. According to co-founder Henderson, the decision to adopt Sheraton as the name of the burgeoning chain was strictly a practical one: The cost of removing the building's electric rooftop "Sheraton" sign would have cost more than the hotel's purchase price.

In 1941 the firm purchased more than 50 percent of Boston's famed, but financially ailing, Copley Plaza. The acquisition of the Copley Plaza and its subsequent facelift propelled The Sheraton Corporation into the major leagues. By postwar 1946 the company had merged with United States Realty, selling off valuable properties gained through the merger and using the money to expand Sheraton's hotel holdings. Before long the company owned hotels large and small from Maine to Florida. By the end of its first decade The Sheraton Corporation had become the first hotel corporation to be listed on the New York Stock Exchange.

Before the close of the 1940s, Sheraton would become the first to install a Telex system for processing room reservations. It was a foreshadowing of Sheraton's Reservatron room-reservation network, the product of four generations of electronic technology. In 1949 Sheraton became the first American International chain by acquiring two Canadian hotel chains.

In the 1950s acquisitions took place at a furious rate. Between 1954 and 1956, for example, Sheraton bought 33

A hotel chain that hopes to cater to this country's business community is in for a lot of hard work. Every day corporations are years ahead in their planning of hundreds of meetings to be held in multitudes. When executives aren't in a meeting, they're preparing for the next. The incentive travel business, a good portion of which includes business travel, is said to be a $3-billion business, growing at a clip of 8 to 10 percent per year. A demanding group, traveling businessmen and -women expect to find comfortable and stylish rooms, top-quality service, great food, and state-of-the-art recreational facilities when they arrive.

The Sheraton Corporation embraces this busy, demanding business clientele. A vast and ambitious company in itself, this Boston-based chain circles the globe with nearly 500 hotels in 65 countries, making it the world's largest hotel chain in coverage. Thirteen of those 500 circle the world of Boston. The entire corporation is organized under six divisions. Four of these, the North America Division; the Europe, Africa, and Middle East Division; the Latin America and Caribbean Division; and the Franchise Division, operate from Boston. Once located on Atlantic Avenue, corporate headquarters are currently found in the Sheraton World Headquarters Building at 60 State Street. Two hundred and fifty employees work in this high rise with windows overlooking Faneuil Hall, the Customs Tower, and Boston Harbor.

Sheraton Hotels is staffed by approximately 123,000 employees and linked by a centralized worldwide reservations system and computer network.

Sheraton Grande Hotel lobby in Los Angeles.

hotels, initiated construction of two luxury hotels, broke ground for four "highway hotels," and opened the country's largest convention ballroom, in Washington, D.C., at the Sheraton-Park Hotel. World War II was over, and throughout North America the Sheraton name was becoming synonymous for the good life. Popular stars of the day, including dancer Ray Bolger and chanteuse Hildegarde, were featured in the supper rooms of some of the larger hotels. "The Honeymooners" television series was broadcast from the ballroom of the 1,500-room Park Sheraton Hotel in New York City.

At the end of its first 20 years The Sheraton Corporation had grown to a network of 53 hotels across the continent. In addition to its aggressive acquisition plans, the corporation designed and built its first new hotel, the 1,000-room Philadelphia Sheraton, completed in 1957. Henderson told

the Greater Boston Chamber of Commerce that a $100-million new-construction program was under way. In 1958 Sheraton unveiled Reservatron I, the first automatic electronic reservations system to serve the hospitality industry. Ten years later the computerized Reservatron II system would be able to confirm rooms and rates within seven seconds anywhere in Sheraton's world.

In the United States, Sheraton, a wholly owned subsidiary, established Sheraton Inns Inc. in 1962 to grant franchises for the development of hotels and inns. The overseas international expansion effort began to gear up. In 1961 Sheraton's first hotel in the Middle East opened, followed two years later by the first Sheraton in Latin

America, the Macuto Sheraton in Venezuela.

By 1968 the corporation operated 165 hotels and motor inns that served more than 12 million guests each year and employed nearly 20,000 people. Sheraton's geographic focus was principally domestic concentrated primarily in the United States.

Almost from the beginning the corporation had tied its future to the moves of the business community. Early Sheraton advertising featured a cigar-smoking, suited businessman being carried out of a hotel in an upholstered chair by bellhops, one of whom was fanning him with a palm branch. In 1960 another national campaign, featuring a businessman with a wind-up-key mechanism grafted onto his back, proclaimed: "Keyed Up Executives Unwind at Sheraton."

In 1968 the Sheraton Board of Directors and 19,000 shareholders voted to become a wholly owned subsidiary of the International Telephone and Telegraph Corporation (ITT). Following the acquisition, Sheraton's development strategy broadened considerably with the encouragement of its new parent. It was at this point that Sheraton would begin to look more seriously, as the rest of corporate America had, to those lands across both oceans. Recognizing the need for substantial international growth, the company embarked on an aggressive phase of a worldwide expansion and built deluxe and first-class hotels, many of which were financed with Sheraton and/or ITT capital.

And while venturing farther afield for customers, Sheraton was making it easier for customers to find them. The firm entered the 1970s with a free one-number reservation system. Sheraton pioneered the single 800 number concept that could be used from coast to coast in the United States for room reservations at any Sheraton hotel in the system.

Growth at this time was explosive. Between 1971 and 1973 The Sheraton Stockholm Hotel became the company's first new hotel project in Europe, and the Conquistador Sheraton Hotel in Guatemala City became its first franchise property outside North America. First-class and luxury hotels soon followed in Munich, Buenos Aires, Brussels, Lima, Vancouver, Perth, London, Paris, Hong Kong, and Rio de Janeiro. In eight years as an ITT subsidiary, the Sheraton imprint extended to 285 properties—nearly 98,000 guest rooms in 34 countries—including the 1,800-room Sheraton Waikiki Hotel, now the largest in the system. New hotels were also under construction in 14 other countries.

By the late 1970s changing commercial and leisure patterns and the 747 aircraft had reshaped the face of travel. The roster of countries to be seen, sampled, and traded with was growing quickly. A global advertising theme, "Taste Sheraton," promoted Sheraton's worldwide image of quality and invited guests to try its many destinations during the late 1970s and early

The Jefferson Sheraton Hotel in Richmond, Virginia.

1980s. And Sheraton expanded some more. In 1982 alone Sheraton opened large convention hotels in Texas, Montreal, Louisiana, and the state of Washington. It added hotels in Australia, Taiwan, Iraq, Benin, and Pakistan.

New resort properties in New Zealand, Hawaii, and Arizona joined the Sheraton chain, and in a unique twist, it added four Nile cruise boats as floating hotels cruising the Nile.

In 1985 Sheraton was the first international chain to enter the Republic of China and operate on a management contract under the chain name, The Great Wall Sheraton Hotel in Beijing.

Sheraton had become one of the

opened with a special 800 number specifically for North American travel agents. The national reservations office was moved from St. Louis to new state-of-the-art facilities in Austin, Texas, to ensure top-quality service for individual and corporate customers in the United States and Canada. With its new direction summed up by a new company credo, "One company, one system," Sheraton revamped and standardized the training programs of its employees. Gearing its efforts to the quality and attitudes of personal service, Sheraton developed and introduced the Sheraton Guest Satisfaction System℠ to ensure the quality, consistency, and sincerity of the service staff, along with a comprehensive consumer research-based program to measure actual service performance hotel by hotel.

Today the challenge for Sheraton is to combine the convenience of a huge chain with the personal service of a small organization. For its 50th anniversary in 1987 a new advertising theme debuted to stress just that "At Sheraton, Little Things Mean A Lot." Also for its 50th, Sheraton commissioned Forecasting International, Ltd., to do an analysis of future changes that will affect the hospitality industry. The study predicted that hotels will use robots for tailoring services and voice-activated computers for taking reservations. Large-bodied 1,000-passenger airplanes will further reduce the cost of travel. To attract increasing numbers of businesswomen and retirement-age travelers, the competitive hotels of the future might consider adding day-care/learning centers, beefed-up security systems, menus with lighter meals, and fitness/wellness centers.

The Sheraton Corporation will be looking to countries with growing populations that are being targeted by the international business community. In the next 50 years politically and socially stable countries that combine population growth and low-cost labor will see overseas business expansion and will become new hospitality destinations. And where business goes, Sheraton will follow.

most widely known and recognized brand names in the world, and it seemed that Sheraton had hotels in every corner of the planet. And it was then that the company took another direction, sparked by new chairman, president, and chief executive officer John Kapioltas' Blueprint for Change. From a bricks-and-mortar real estate company, Sheraton would evolve into a sophisticated management organization.

Sheraton's development focus shifted from that of a major real estate development organization to one of hotel management.

A renewed commitment to top-quality service and facilities in each property became the priority for the 1980s. From 1981 to 1986 more than $5 billion was invested in new and upgraded services and facilities. A Sheraton Travel Trade Reservations Center

FILENE'S

Great Hall, First Floor, Boston store.

No trip to Boston is complete without an excursion to Filene's in the heart of the city's business district. The fashion department store has plenty of vigorous competition these days, but a trip to the glittering Filene's downtown store and its legendary discount basement at Downtown Crossing is still mandatory for visitors, and a regular ritual for residents, some of whom admit to taking daily trips.

With 18 stores throughout New England and New York State, Filene's has grown and prospered beyond the most ambitious expectations of its founder, William Filene. A 21-year-old German immigrant and tailor by trade, Filene opened his first small shop on Hanover Street in Boston's North End in 1851. Although this first venture failed, he successfully opened and operated a number of thriving dry-goods stores in New England and a wholesale bargain business in New York. But the Stock Market Crash in 1868 left him in financial ruin. Undaunted, he started over again, opening new stores in Lynn and Boston, Massachusetts, and in Bath, Maine, between 1872 and 1887.

William Filene's legacy was to be fully realized through his two sons, Edward and Lincoln. The sons took managing control of Filene's in 1890 when William retired, and became owners of William Filene & Sons when their father died in 1901.

Accessories, First Floor, Boston store.

Edward and Lincoln made a good team. Together they charted an innovative merchandising direction for Filene's. Edward's skills lay in merchandising, while Lincoln excelled at people skills and developed an expertise in staff management and store administration. Both were committed to making Filene's into New England's premier specialty store for women by providing them with fashionable ready-to-wear apparel and accessories at af-

fordable prices. Filene's later diversified its merchandise to include men's and children's apparel and home furnishings.

A series of well-orchestrated business moves culminated in the acquisition of Filene's 65,000-square-foot Washington Street store in Boston, an area known today as Downtown Crossing. Originally five floors with a basement, an addition added three floors to the structure, which now occupies a full city block.

The original Filene's automatic-markdown bargain basement, begun by Edward in 1909, is today an institution in itself. A revolutionary concept for its time, Filene's bargain basement was created to make a home for the store's surplus stock and unwanted or irregular merchandise. It took 10 years for the basement to turn a profit, but its ultimate success was an unforeseen bonus to Edward's original marketing scheme. The basement has spawned imitators nationwide. Since 1984 Filene's basement store has operated independently of Filene's upstairs.

The Filene brothers pioneered other retail firsts. Edward Filene founded and supported the first Credit Union National Extension Bureau run by employees. In doing so, he sparked a national movement, mobilizing support to legalize credit unions across the United States. Under Lincoln Filene, a champion of employee rights, the store was one of the first to institute a minimum wage, sick pay, a paid-vacation benefits policy, and a retirement plan. Lincoln was also instrumental in making Filene's the first store in New England to adopt the five-day, 40-hour work week.

Filene's was also one of the first retailers to recognize the potential of suburban markets and shopping centers. The first branch store was opened in Wellesley, Massachusetts, in 1924. Filene's Chestnut Hill store was the first branch to appear in a shopping center; in 1950 it opened on Boylston Street

Fashion to suit her executive style at Filene's.

to name but a few.

Filene's remains a constant source of interest in Boston, due in no small part to its fashion promotions and special events. During the 1950s, for example, Filene's downtown French Shop caused a stir in fashion circles by serving tea from silver tea services to ladies gathered to view top European designs. In 1954 some 60,000 children visited the petting zoo—complete with lions, monkeys, and a baby elephant—that perched atop Filene's Boston store until it was leveled by the same hurricane that toppled Boston's Old North Church Steeple. In 1987 Filene's was the talk of the town when Elizabeth Taylor appeared to promote her new perfume, Passion.

Evolving, prospering, and planning future expansions, Filene's continues to serve the needs of its customers and communities with vitality, enthusiasm, and imagination in the finest tradition of its founding family.

Discover the names, the styles, the choices— all at Filene's.

in Chestnut Hill. Considered Filene's flagship store, the branch, now located in The Mall at Chestnut Hill, was completely renovated in 1987.

Edward and Lincoln left behind substantial reminders of their civic role in the Boston community. Edward willed the bulk of his estate to form the E.A. Filene Good Will Fund upon his death in 1937. It later went to fund WGBH-TV, Boston's public television station. As a founder and president of the Greater Boston Chamber of Commerce, Edward was involved with many community organizations during his lifetime and donated $5 million in securities to the Twentieth Century Fund for research and public education in economics. Boston's universities and colleges found Lincoln Filene to be one of their most ardent supporters, and the Harvard Graduate School of Business Administration honored him with a Lincoln Filene Professorship of Retailing. Filene's continues to make major gifts of money and resources to The Boston Symphony, the Institute of Contemporary Arts, The Boston Ballet, the Combined Jewish Philanthropies, the Dana Farber Cancer Institute, and the New England Medical Center,

OMNI PARKER HOUSE

Since 1855 weary travelers, workers, and shoppers have gravitated to the Parker House, where dark mahogany paneling, thick carpets, velvet-upholstered chairs, and twinkling chandeliers never fail to lift spirits and inspire thoughts of days gone by.

Nestled between several historic sites along the Freedom Trail—Kings Chapel and Burial Ground, Park Street Church, and the Granary Burial Ground—the Omni Parker House is always animated by a constant stream of natives and tourists alike looking for

The Omni Parker House, the oldest continuously operating hotel in the United States, welcomes visitors to bustling downtown Boston.

shelter and sustenance in the middle of busy downtown.

The sight of buses, inching their way around the corner of School and Tremont streets to deliver another load of guests to the hotel, is a common one to Bostonians. Three hundred and thirty-five modern rooms await tourists who've come to town to soak up more

than 200 years of American history.

For Bostonians, the Parker House also brings to mind its several dining and drinking establishments. Parker's restaurant and bar, and The Last Hurrah saloon are drinking and dining institutions in their own right.

In its earliest days Parker House was a five-story marble structure built by Harvey D. Parker to house this thriving restaurant. It was there that a German baker named Ward created the famous Parker House roll.

In an atmosphere of hospitality and elegant comfort, poets and philosophers gathered, and politicians and visiting performers mingled. Ralph Waldo Emerson, James Russell Lowell, Henry Wadsworth Longfellow, John Greenleaf Whittier, and Nathaniel Hawthorne gathered at Parker's, home of the literary Saturday Club of the 1860s and 1870s. Other well-known guests included generals Ulysses S. Grant, William Tecumseh Sherman, Winfield Scott Hancock, and James A. Garfield. Charles Dickens took up residence for a time in Suite 338. Entertainers Sarah Bernhardt and Edwin Booth also stayed at the Parker House.

The hotel prospered, continuing to host the city's most prestigious groups and enjoy the patronage of presidents and statesmen. For the next quarter-century, up until his death in 1884, Parker purchased and expanded his operation onto surrounding property.

In the 1890s the Joseph R. Whipple Corporation took over Parker's complex and leveled it in 1925 to construct a modern hotel of steel and granite, the structure that stands today. Fourteen stories high, the new building contained 800 rooms and a special rooftop ballroom—the only one in town to this day.

Hard times that followed the stock market crash of 1929 brought a mortgage foreclosure and transfer of ownership to Glenwood Sherrard, who operated the property until his death in 1958. Ten years later the Dunfey family acquired the hotel in a state of disrepair and pumped $12 million into its restoration.

Currently the hotel is managed by

Omni Hotels of Hampton, New Hampshire, which owns the operation jointly with Wharf Holdings Ltd. Omni owns 29 hotels nationwide and intends to expand its management and joint-ownership ventures. Nationally, Omni seeks to enhance its profile by franchising the Omni name to small, independent hotel operators seeking an edge over their competition.

The construction of several new luxury hotels in Boston over the past four years has led to the Omni management's decision to diversify its marketing efforts at the historic Omni Parker House as well. In addition to housing traveling business people and tourists in the 535 rooms, smaller rooms in the inner court serve as home to airline personnel.

The Omni Parker House has developed a niche within a business community forever seeking comfortable sites for important luncheon meetings. Small corporate meetings are held daily in the boardrooms of the mezzanine level.

Luncheons are also held in the green Kennedy Room or the china-blue Dickens Room, which contains the same marble fireplace recovered from Dickens' old room. A banquet kitchen on the same floor serves all the boardrooms under the watchful eye of Executive Chef Joe Ribas.

The rooftop lounge and ballroom are popular spots for larger banquets, parties, and weddings. In the wedding season, as many as four weddings may take place each weekend in the ballroom. Draperied windows on three walls offer stellar views of Boston Harbor, the Commons, and the Charles River.

Omni plans to protect this grand dame of Boston establishments, the oldest continuously operating hotel in the United States, with the regular infusion of capital that an old and valuable institution requires. Brass elevators, carved door frames, and loyal employees who have been a part of the Omni Parker House for 10 years and more—it all adds up to a setting that is difficult to reproduce at any modern price.

With its brass elevators, carved doors, and elegant chandeliers, a visit to the Omni Parker House is an exciting unequaled experience for a night of dining or dancing, a business meeting, or a stopover to tour the historic sites of Boston.

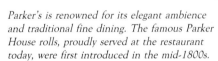

Parker's is renowned for its elegant ambience and traditional fine dining. The famous Parker House rolls, proudly served at the restaurant today, were first introduced in the mid-1800s.

BOSTON MARRIOTT LONG WHARF

Though the glorious days of the clipper ships are long gone, Boston's oldest wharf thrives, due in large part to the Marriott Long Wharf hotel. Opened in 1982 on what was once the Boston Pier, circa 1710, the Marriott building came about as part of the Boston Harbor area renovation. This hotel's most distinctive feature is its long, triangular-shape and half-moon windows. If viewed from one of its neighboring wharves, the brick structure resembles a ship with portholes that is "floating" out into the harbor.

With the construction of the Rowes Wharf complex, Marriott Long Wharf is no longer the only hotel at the harbor's edge, but it is still the easiest one to get to. A stone's throw under I-93 from Faneuil Hill and Quincy Market, the hotel is built atop the subway's Blue Line, only two stops from Logan International Airport. The hotel is also next door to the New England Aquarium and the loading dock for harbor sight-seeing ships. When the weather is warm, strolling crowds congregate at the sidewalk cafes that are spread along the north side of the hotel, facing Waterfront Park.

Though perfectly suited for tourists, a majority of the Marriott's guests are business travelers. The hotel is equipped to handle up to 800 people for meetings, but rooms can be tailored to meet a group's individual needs. The Grand Ballroom in the hotel's lower level can accommodate large receptions of 1,000 but can also be broken down into 12 sections to create various "salons" for smaller groups. Four conference rooms with harbor views on the first floor accommodate groups of 25 to 50.

In addition to its separate banquet kitchen and catering service, the Marriott Long Wharf has two dining fa-cilities, the Harbor Terrace Sea Grille and the Palm Garden Restaurant. Rachael's lounge, the most popular in Boston, entertains the pre- and post-dinner crowd.

Because of the hotel's architectural design, most of the 400 guest rooms have either a harbor or a skyline view. The Presidential and Long Wharf suites have outside decks overlooking the harbor. The hotel also has four parlors and 11 suites. A concierge level fea-

The Boston Marriott Long Wharf hotel, a brick structure resembling a ship floating in the harbor, is perfectly situated for tourists visiting Boston or travelers with business in the surrounding area.

tures an honor bar and a private lounge serving continental breakfast daily. A member of the concierge staff will arrange tours and arrange for concert or theater tickets upon request.

An indoor pool as well as a hydro-therapy pool are open year round for hotel guests. Marriott also runs a full-service health club featuring an exercise room with Universal gym, barbells, exercise bicycles, and men's and women's locker rooms with saunas.

Amenities, location, the Marriott name—all these factors help account for the high occupancy rate Marriott Long Wharf enjoys—a figure approaching 90 percent. Indeed, in 1987 readers of *Business News Travel* rated the Marriott chain their number-one choice, the third year in a row that the Washington, D.C.-based chain has been so honored. The successful Long Wharf has annual sales revenue of $30 million.

The Long Wharf is one of the Marriott international chain of 300 hotels, and like most of Marriott's hotels, the Long Wharf facility is managed by Marriott under contract. The building is owned by Boston Properties and managed by Marriott under a 30-year contract. There are seven other Marriotts in the Boston area, including the Copley Place Marriott, which, like the Long Wharf, is located within Boston's city proper. Marriott has had hotels in the Boston area for more than 20 years. The first Marriott hotel in Boston, the Newton Marriott, retains its strategic position at the junction of Route 128 and the Massachusetts Turnpike.

Blueprints of Long Wharf show there will be more renovation and development in Marriott's backyard. A future water-shuttle stop will be built at the end of an adjoining dock. A historic boat will be moored alongside a future Visitors' Center and Interpreting Center. The hotel itself is constantly redecorated and refurbished, say hotel officials who are keenly aware that Boston's recent hotel boom has more than doubled the number of available rooms in the past five years.

But not to worry. With the 1988 opening of the rebuilt John B. Hynes Veterans Memorial Convention Center, convention forecasters expect a 10-percent annual increase in delegate travelers for the next three or four years—all of whom want accommodations somewhere downtown. And then there's the growing number of foreign tourists in Boston, no doubt lured by the devalued dollar. All in all, it seems the hotel can "float" tranquilly as a third century dawns on Boston Marriott Long Wharf.

BOSTON CELTICS

Today the word "dynasty" is seldom used in professional sports, but if ever a team has dominated a sport over the years it is the Boston Celtics in basketball. Over a 42-year span the Celtics have won 16 National Basketball Association championships and many more conference titles. Their procession of eight consecutive world championships from 1959 through 1966 remains unmatched by any other team in a major professional sport.

The reasons for the team's success can be capsulized in one familiar expression, "Celtic tradition"—the persistent, unswerving dedication to winning.

The sculptor of Celtic tradition is Arnold J. "Red" Auerbach, who joined the organization in 1950 as head coach, later became general manager, and is currently president. As the backbone and driving force of the Celtics, Auerbach has given the tradition continuity and meaning over four decades.

Founded by Walter Brown in 1946, the Celtics were one of the original 11 franchises of the Basketball Association of America, predecessor of the NBA. When Auerbach came on board four years later, the team was struggling, both financially and on the court. Though his first half-dozen years were only moderately successful, these years

A tense moment in the Boston Garden captured for all time. Photo by Stanley Rowin

proved to be a mere prelude to the accomplishments that followed.

Auerbach made the first of many key personnel moves when he acquired the draft rights to center Bill Russell in 1956. Led by Russell—and supported by many other top stars, such as Bob Cousy, K.C. Jones, Sam Jones, Bill Sharman, and Tommy Heinsohn—the Celtics went on to win 11 championships in 13 years, a dominance unparalleled in the history of professional sports.

In the 1970s, led by John Havlicek, Jo Jo White, and Dave Cowens, the Celtics added two more championship banners to the Boston Garden rafters. And in the 1980s, the era of Larry Bird, Kevin McHale, and Robert Parish, the Green and White have brought home three more NBA crowns.

The 1980-1981 title, fueled by rookie sensation Larry Bird, who Auerbach had selected as a junior eligible in the 1979 NBA draft, was particu-

Boston fans turned out en masse to honor the World Champion Celtics in 1986. Photo by Steve Lipofsky

larly noteworthy. After the Celtics' dismal 61-103 record over the previous two years, the championship completed the most dramatic turnaround in the history of the NBA.

Though the Celtic name will always be associated with winning, the organization has also been a pioneer. In 1950 the Celtics drafted the league's first black player, Chuck Cooper. During the 1963-1964 season the Celtics became the first NBA team to put five blacks on the floor at the same time. In 1966 the Celtics made history by becoming the first major league team in any sport to name a black head coach, Bill Russell.

Today the Boston Celtics are the only major professional sports team to be traded publicly on the New York Stock Exchange. Under the front office leadership of chairman of the board Don F. Gaston, treasurer Alan N. Cohen, and secretary Paul R. Dupree, Jr., and, of course, president Auerbach, the Celtics expect to hang many more championship banners from the Garden rafters in the 1990s.

BOSTON HARBOR HOTEL

Even the most well-traveled, hardened to the much-ballyhooed perks of luxury hotels, will be bowled over by all that is the Boston Harbor Hotel. Located on lapping shores of the Boston Harbor, the opening of this 230-room hotel was awaited with the kind of anticipation few other Boston hotels have seen—and many new hotels have sprung up recently.

Much of the excitement comes from the unbelievable location on Rowes Wharf, unbelievable that such a large complex—the hotel, two restaurants, a bar, and neighboring condominiums and office suites—could perch so closely on the ocean, its many brick sidewalks and plazas precariously ending at water's edge. With unobstructed views of the harbor, the complex is unlike any approaching its size on the city's waterfront.

The rest of the excitement comes from the majestic look of the complex itself, particularly the great Italianate copper dome that divides the complex in half and preserves the view of the harbor for its downtown neighbors located on the other side of the central artery. Water shuttles arriving from the South Shore and from Logan International Airport dock behind the hotel on the southern half of the wharf complex.

The interior of the Boston Harbor Hotel matches the elegance of its exterior. Floral-print carpets, marble floors, overstuffed chairs, and priceless art adorn the lobby areas. The restaurant, with both formal and informal menus and seating, is regal as well. Plush royal-blue carpet and mahogany trim radiate under indirect lighting from red lamps in the formal dining area. An extensive kitchen that hosts both a pastry and

The interior of the hotel is a visual treat with its floral carpets, marble floors, and priceless art.

chocolate room makes everything served in the dining room, except the breads. Two private dining rooms and a ballroom can seat 20 to 120 people for special affairs. In addition, the hotel has six meeting rooms, one of which is specially designed for board meetings.

Guest rooms start on the eighth floor. All have either city or harbor views, some have both. Guests can slip down to the health club and spa, take a dip in the 60-foot lap pool, work out on state-of-the-art resistance equipment, and finish with a sauna, herbal wrap, and a smoothie by the pool.

The Boston Harbor Hotel is an independent property not affiliated with a hotel chain; it is owned and operated by the luxury division of Beacon Hotel Corporation. The firm currently owns 20 hotels and operates a division of Beacon Companies, developer of the entire Rowes Wharf complex. Under the direction of vice-president and managing director Dennis Mills, the hotel handles its own reservations, but it is also marketed through the Small Luxury Hotels of America Association, of which it is a member.

The Boston Harbor Hotel is not only a first-class home away from home for out-of-town guests, but also a vibrant after-work meeting place for Bostonians who want to slip away for dinner, drinks, or a workout and treat themselves to a bit of the high life.

Epilogue
A Look to the Future

BY GERALD PEARY

Read through the promotional material: every city in America routinely proclaims itself an all-American success story, undergoing a massive facelift or rejuvenation to proudly face the future. How to separate Boston from the pack? Well, here all the hurrahs, huzzahs, and hosannas are undeniably true. What the Mayor's Office, the Chamber of Commerce, and the everyday Bostonian say are exactly the same: the Hub is the grand centerpiece of the internationally proclaimed "Massachusetts Miracle."

Yes, there was a time a decade and a half ago when haughty Boston was decidedly slipping. Development in the downtown area had stopped dead, and what *was* there closed shop shortly after the dinner hour. The city government was a creaky, archaic patronage machine, and what Boston revealed on the six o'clock news were riots about busing. The citizenry fled the inner cities for far-away suburbs. The best and brightest dreamed of Making It the only conceivable way: by moving to New York City.

What a turnaround! Since the U.S. Bicentennial, when hundreds of thousands of Americans converged on the Cradle of Liberty, Boston has never stopped moving onward and upward. The downtown has been rebuilt and reborn, and the streets are alive with the ebullient sounds of music, moving bodies, motion pictures … and money—being made and being spent. The Boston area is, of course, high-tech heaven, and millions upon millions of software and hardware dollars have been pumped into the economy. There are fabulous new hotels everywhere, with four-star restaurants in them, and tourists from around the world.

The hotel occupancy rate? A very healthy 73.4 percent in 1987, and expected to rise. The Greater Boston Convention and Visitors Bureau estimates 500,000 foreign tourists in 1988, and predicts confidently even more visitors from abroad in the future. The newest influx? Groups from Japan: 114,000 Japanese in 1987 visited Quincy Market and Faneuil Hall and walked the Freedom Trail, taking photographs.

The economic impact? In 1987 about 8.5 million people, from the U.S. and abroad, came to Boston and spent $6 billion mighty dollars, enjoying the "chowdah" and the Celtics, the baked beans and the Boston Symphony Orchestra. Crowds in the millions continue to stop at the Park Street subway station asking how to transfer from the Green Line to the Red Line for a chance to see the city of Cambridge and Harvard University. And these millions sit down in restaurants at the end of a thrilling day of sightseeing and pop the invariable question about the local seafood: "Just what is scrod?"

However, the first priority for Boston must be the life-style and welfare of its native citizenry. Tourists come and go, happily, but it is essential that locals endorse the changed, upbeat, urban environment.

They do, and to prove it, the flight to the suburbs of the late 1970s has reversed completely. In the early 1980s, only 30 percent of downtown jobs were held by people who actually lived in Boston. By 1986 the figure had increased to 40 percent, and longtime Mayor Raymond Flynn has set a reachable goal of 50 percent residency for the near future. Richard D. Hill, ex-chairman of the board of the Bank of Boston, has explained it succinctly: "People now move into Boston instead of out. It has become a very populated city. This has been due to improvements in public facilities, parks, waterfronts—great improvements in transportation facilities."

Nobody will deny Hill's rave review for Boston's revitalized waterfront area, or that the Boston Common has been vastly improved by the addition of nineteenth-century gaslights and some delicate retouching and landscaping. Or that the much-traveled Orange Line of the Boston MBTA has become a pleasure ride because of the splendidly redesigned and new stations along the way. And everyone is awaiting the monumental new AMTRAK depot at South Station, which will greet travelers from New York, Connecticut, and Rhode Island in grand style.

But outsiders always wish to know: what is Boston's current racial climate? The tumultuous TV coverage of South Boston is not forgotten.

The outspokenly integrationist administration of Mayor Ray Flynn is credited through the 1980s by both white and black persons for encouraging a new era of racial tolerance. The mayor has made much-publicized visits of support to the homes of persons threatened because of the color of their skin or their foreign tongue. And the Boston Police Department has been quick to move in force to quell violent incidents with racial or ethnic overtones.

In 1986 Ray Flynn, an Irish Catholic from South Boston, was reelected mayor with overwhelming approval from Boston's minority neighborhoods. For the first time there are indications that some Boston blacks are beginning to find a piece of the Hub wealth: a February 1988 article in *Black Enterprise* was entitled, with guarded optimism, "Cashing in on the Beantown Boom."

Holiday lights lend festivity to this Boston cityscape. Photo © Paul Corkum

And in once-infamous South Boston? In the spring of 1988 several black families moved cautiously into previously all-white public housing. Though cynical local media predicted old-time trouble, the families instead found old-time Boston neighborliness. All of Boston sighed in collective relief.

The era of the insulated, isolated Boston neighborhood is hardly over. Still, the hostile pro-busing vs. anti-busing days seem bygone ones. Quietly, they have been replaced by a better time and by less provincial attitudes. In the last decade an unofficial Rainbow Coalition of American blacks, settled Chinese, and refugees from El Salvador, Haiti, Vietnam, and Cambodia have made Boston a more exciting ethnic melting pot than ever before in history.

Nowhere are the virtues of this new ethnic and racial Boston on better display than at Bunker Hill Community College on the edge of Charlestown, with its 40 percent minority enrollment among a total of 6,500. More than 500 refugees are among its student population, explains Harold Shively, proud Bunker Hill president: "These new people will become part of us. We may as well equip them to be productive. Education is a start."

And for Boston's already educated classes? Culture as never before, even for probably the most intellectually astute city in America. In 1987 Boston boasted 166 art facilities, and 362 organizations shared funding from the Arts Lottery, according to the Boston Arts Commission. The City of Boston's newest, most extravagant show space is the 2,000-square-foot gallery inside the downtown Transportation Building. These walls are reserved, appropriately, for the best of Boston painters.

And more delightful news: the Boston Redevelopment Authority has made public its gargantuan plan to transform the ancient, crumbling Theater District. Instead, look for a world-class Midtown Cultural District of galleries, theaters, and performance groups, with affordable space to let for local arts companies and non-profit organizations.

That's Boston's near future!

There are still major problems, of course: the polluted Boston Harbor, the dilapidated city zoos, traffic congestion, and lack of parking. There is a dire need for major federal funding to provide far more low- and middle-income housing (a Raymond Flynn top priority). Also, the public school system is still recovering from a stormy period of decline in the 1970s. Fortunately, given Bostonians' strong commitment to education and the unusual degree of cooperation between the city's academic and business communities, continued and even complete recovery appears possible.

Despite the problems, would a Bostonian live anywhere else? If ambitious Bostonians of a decade and a half ago planned to whiz off to New York City, all of that has changed. The culture is here and the business opportunity is here—without the Big Apple stress! It's still possible to bicycle to work, to talk to neighbors, to walk to Fenway Park. And to have an enormously healthy, prosperous life.

Governor Michael Dukakis summed it up best: "If we remember to respect each other, and love this city on a hill, we can leave our children a legacy of economic opportunity for each of Boston's many and diverse communities and a quality of life that continues to be the envy of America's cities."

Kenmore Square is readily identified by this landmark Citgo sign. Photo © Martha Everson

Patrons

The following individuals, companies, and organizations have made a valuable commitment to the quality of this publication. Windsor Publications and The Greater Boston Chamber of Commerce gratefully acknowledge their participation in *Boston: In A Class By Itself.*
Affiliated Publications, Inc.*
Alexander & Alexander*
Ames Safety Envelope Company*
Anchor Capital Advisors, Inc.
Anderson-Nicols & Company, Inc.
AT&T*
Babson College*
Bank of Boston*
Bank of New England*
Bay State-Spray Provincetown
    Steamship Inc.*
Bear, Stearns & Co. Inc.*
Bentley College*
Beth Israel Hospital*
Boston Athletic Association*
Boston Business Journal*
Boston Celtics*
The Boston Company*
Boston Edison*
Boston Harbor Hotel*
Boston Health and Swim Clubs
The Boston Herald*
Boston Marriott Long Wharf*
Boston Thermal Energy Corporation*
Brandeis University*
Briggs Associates Inc.
    Consulting Engineers*
Burns & Levinson*
Cablevision of Boston*
Harold Cabot & Company*
Cameron and Colby Co. Inc.
The Christian Science Publishing Society*
Clean Harbors, Inc.*
Commonwealth Land Title Insurance
    Company

Connell Limited Partnership*
Converse*
Cushman & Wakefield of Massachusetts,
    Inc.*
Day, Berry & Howard
Deloitte Haskins & Sells*
Digital Equipment Corporation*
Epsilon
Ernst & Whinney*
Exclusive Temporaries, Inc.*
Farragut Mortgage Company*
Fidelity Investments*
Filene's*
First International Life Insurance Company
The Flatley Company*
The Forum Corporation*
Gaston & Snow*
The Gillette Company
Hale and Dorr*
Frank B. Hall & Co. of Massachusetts*
Hill and Knowlton Advanced Technology
    Practice*
Honeywell Bull*
Houghton Mifflin Company*
Human Resources Policy Institute School of
    Management-Boston University
Hutchins & Wheeler*
International Business Machines*
Issues Management Inc.
Jaymont Properties, Incorporated*
Jewish Memorial Hospital*
Jung/Brannen Associates, Inc.*
Thomas A. Kershaw
Richard A. Kingsbury
Lahey Clinic Medical Center*
Laventhol & Horwath*
J.H. McNamara, Inc.
George B.H. Macomber Company*
Massachusetts Bay Transportation Authority*
Massachusetts Eye and Ear Infirmary*
Massachusetts Higher Education Assistance
    Corporation and The Education Resources
    Institute*
Massachusetts Port Authority*
MCI*
MerchantsBank of Boston*

Meredith & Grew, Incorporated*
New Balance Athletic Shoe, Inc.*
The New England*
New England Medical Center*
North American Security Life*
Olympia & York Developments Limited*
Olympic International Bank & Trust Co.*
Omni Parker House*
Paine Webber*
Palmer & Dodge*
Peabody Office Furniture Corporation*
Peat Marwick Main & Co.*
Phoenix Distributors, Inc.
Riemer & Braunstein, Esq.*
Ropes & Gray*
Rose Associates, Inc.*
Schneider, Reilly, Zabin & Costello*
Sears, Roebuck and Co.*
Shapiro, Israel & Weiner*
Shawmut Bank, N.A.*
The Sheraton Corporation*
Albert Sherman-Boston University
The Smith Companies
State Street Bank and Trust Company*
Mr. & Mrs. David B. Stith
Suffolk University*
Sullivan & Worcester*
Symmons Industries, Inc.*
Tofias, Fleishman, Shapiro & Co., P.C.*
Trammell Crow Company*
The University Hospital*
University of Massachusetts at Boston*
Vappi & Company, Inc.*
Wang Laboratories, Inc.*
WBZ-AM Boston*
Wellington Management Company/Thorn-
    dike, Doran, Paine & Lewis*
WMJX-FM/WMEX-AM*
WNEV-TV, Channel 7
Xenergy*
Zayre Corporation*

*Partners in Progress of *Boston: In A Class By Itself.* The histories of these companies and organizations appear throughout the book.

It's lunchtime at the Hood milk bottle snackstand. Photo © Lee C. Hauenstein

Selected Bibliography

BOOKS

Adams, Russell B. *The Boston Money Tree.* New York: Thomas Y. Crowell Co., 1977.

Amory, Cleveland, *The Proper Bostonians.* New York: E.P. Dutton, 1947.

Bailyn, Bernard. *The New England Merchants in the Seventeenth Century.* Cambridge, MA: Harvard University Press, 1955.

Berk, Susan and Jill Bloom. *Uncommon Boston.* Reading: Addison-Wesley Publishing Co., 1987.

Brooks, Van Wyck. *The Flowering of New England: 1815-1865.* Boston: Houghton Mifflin, 1981.

Chesler, Bernice. *In and Out of Boston, With (or Without) Children.* Chester, CT: Globe-Pequot Press, 1987.

Clark, Judith Freeman. *From Colony to Commonwealth: Massachusetts.* Northridge, CA: Windsor Publications, 1987.

Crawford, Mary Caroline. *St. Botolph's Town: An Account of Old Boston in Colonial Days.* Boston: L.C. Page and Co., 1908.

Handlin, Oscar. *Boston's Immigrants: A Study in Acculturation.* Cambridge: The Belknap Press of Harvard University Press, 1979.

Hardy, Stephen. *How Boston Played: Sport, Recreation and Community, 1865-1915.* Boston: Northeastern University Press, 1982.

Harris, John. *Historic Walks in Old Boston.* Chester, CT: Globe-Pequot Press, 1982.

Howe, M.A. DeWolfe. *Boston: The Place and the People.* New York and London: The Macmillan Co., 1903.

Howland, Llewellyn, ed. *A Book for Boston.* Boston: David R. Godine, Publisher, 1980.

Jones, Howard Mumford and Bessie Zaban Jones, eds. *The Many Voices of Boston: A Historical Anthology 1630-1975.* Boston: Little, Brown and Co., 1975.

Kay, Jan Holtz. *Lost Boston.* Boston: Houghton Mifflin, 1980.

Knowles, Asa S. *Shawmut: 150 Years of Banking.* Boston: Houghton Mifflin, 1986.

Lampe, David, ed. *The Massachusetts Miracle: High Technology and Economic Revitalization.* Cambridge, MA: The MIT Press, 1988.

Linscott, Robert N., ed. *State of Mind: A Boston Reader.* New York: Farrar, Straus and Co., 1948.

Lukas, J. Anthony. *Common Ground: A Turbulent Decade in the Lives of Three American Families.* New York: Alfred A. Knopf, 1985.

Mills, Nicolaus, ed. *Busing U.S.A.* New York: Teachers College Press, 1979.

Morison, Samuel Eliot. *Maritime History of Massachusetts.* Boston: Houghton Mifflin, 1969.

O'Connor, Thomas H. *Bibles, Brahmins, and Bosses: A Short History of Boston.* Boston: Trustees of the Public Library of the City of Boston, 1984.

Primack, Mark L. *Greater Boston Park and Recreation Guide.* Chester, CT: Globe-Pequot Press, 1983.

Russell, Francis. *The Great Interlude: Neglected Events and Persons from the First World War to the Depression.* New York: McGraw-Hill Book Co., 1964.

Seaburg, Carl. *Boston Observed.* Boston: Beacon Press, 1971.

Southworth, Susan and Michael Southworth. *The Boston Society of Architects' A.I.A. Guide to Boston.* Chester, CT: Globe-Pequot Press, 1987.

Thernstrom, Stephan. *The Other Bostonians: Poverty and Progress in the American Metropolis, 1880-1970.* Cambridge, MA: Harvard University Press, 1973.

W.P.A. Federal Writers' Project. *Boston Looks Seaward: The Story of the Port, 1630-1940.* Boston: Northeastern University Press, 1985.

Weiss, David I., John R. Boynton, and Marcia Guntzel, eds. *The Directory of Holistic Practitioners for the Greater Boston Area.* Boston: David I. Weiss Publishers, 1987.

Weston, George F., Jr. *Boston Ways: High, By, and Folk.* Boston: Beacon Press, 1957.

White, Gerald T. *A History of the Hospital Life Insurance Company.* Cambridge, MA: Harvard University Press, 1955.

Whitehill, Walter M., and Norman Kotker. *Massachusetts: A Pictorial History.* New York: Charles Scribner's Sons, 1976.

Williams, Ben Ames, Jr. *Bank of Boston 200: A History of New England's Leading Bank, 1784-1984.* Boston: Houghton Mifflin, 1984.

Winsor, Justin, ed. *The Memorial History of Boston, Including Suffolk County.* Boston: Ticknor and Co., 1880.

OTHER RESOURCES

Associated Industries of Massachusetts

The Boston Globe

Boston Redevelopment Authority

Chamber of Commerce of Greater Boston

Community Health Worker Program

Federal Reserve Bank of Boston

Harvard University

The Health Alliance

Massachusetts Executive Office of Economic Affairs

Massachusetts High Technology Council

Massachusetts Industrial Finance Agency

Massachusetts Office of Business Development

Massport

New England Business magazine

U.S. Bureau of Labor Statistics

The Old West Church is located at the corner of Lynde and Cambridge streets. Photo © Martha Everson

INDEX